Lisa Appignanesi was born in Poland and grew up in France and Canada. She is former Deputy Director of the Institute of Contemporary Arts in London, was President of English PEN and is Chair of the Freud Museum. She is General Editor of Profile Books' Big Ideas series.

A prize-winning novelist and writer, she co-authored *Freud's Women* and has written many bestselling novels. Her family memoir, *Losing the Dead* received critical acclaim and her book on the history of the Mind Doctors from 1800 to the present day, *Mad, Bad and Sad*, was shortlisted for four prizes, won the Medical Journalists' Association Open Medical Book Award and the 2009 British Medical Association Award for the Public Understanding of Science.

She has been made a Chevalier de l'Ordre des Arts et des Lettres in recognition of her contribution to literature. Lisa Appignanesi lives in London.

All About Love

Anatomy of an Unruly Emotion

Lisa Appignanesi

W. W. Norton & Company

New York • London

For information about permission to reproduce selections from this book,
write to Permissions, W. W. Norton & Company, Inc.,
500 Fifth Avenue, New York, NY 10110

For information about special discounts for bulk purchases, please contact
W. W. Norton Special Sales at specialsales@wwnorton.com or 800-233-4830

Manufacturing by Courier Westford
Production manager: Anna Oler

Library of Congress Cataloging-in-Publication Data

Appignanesi, Lisa.
All about love : anatomy of an unruly emotion /
Lisa Appignanesi. — 1st American ed.
p. cm.
Includes bibliographical references and index.
ISBN 978-0-393-06945-7 (hardcover)
1. Love. 2. Marriage. I. Title.
BF575.L8A67 2011
152.'41—dc22
2011006756

W. W. Norton & Company, Inc.
500 Fifth Avenue, New York, N.Y. 10110
www.wwnorton.com

W. W. Norton & Company Ltd.
Castle House, 75/76 Wells Street, London W1T 3QT

1 2 3 4 5 6 7 8 9 0

To my loved ones and those they love

Contents

PART THREE:
LOVE AND MARRIAGE

PART FOUR:
LOVE IN TRIANGLES

Acknowledgements

Over the years I have learned so much from so many on the subject of love that my acknowledgements could extend for the length of this book. I owe a debt to all the novelists, thinkers, commentators and individuals who appear in its pages, as well as to my family and friends. Many, in the course of its writing, have put up with indiscreet probing as well as with long conversations, or consented to more formal interviews. To name even some of them is not enough, but it is the best I can do here. So my thanks for all their help, their ideas, their encouragement extend to Devorah Baum, John Berger, David Borenstein, Judit Carrera, Marie-Noelle Craissati, Maria Duggan, Eva Hoffman, Derek Johns, Helena Kennedy, Hari Kunzru, Hanif Kureishi, Darian Leader, Suzette and Helder Macedo, Giovanni Menegalle, Maxine Molyneux, Jasmine Montgomery, Susie Orbach, Lianna Schwartz-Orbach, Renata Salecl, Gillian Slovo, Martha Spurrier, Deborah Thom, Marina Warner and Lisa Wood.

I owe special thanks to Adam Phillips for his ever stimulating thoughts and conversation. My children, Josh Appignanesi and Katrina Forrester, have been particularly scintillating informants on the ways and waverings of their generation: their subtlety and provocation are a constant inspiration. Since we are all in our own way experts on love, none of the above will necessarily agree with what I have made of my subject.

I am grateful to Monica Holmes, an early and sagacious reader, and to Jamie Martin who helped patiently with the details of footnotes and bibliography.

Lennie Goodings, as ever, proved an ideal editor, encouraging and perceptive. My great thanks go to her and to Clare Alexander, my talented agent, as well as to Angela von der Lippe, my New York editor, whose acuteness and discernment are a constant boon. I am also grateful to Elise Dillsworth at Virago and my copy-editor Sue Phillpott.

And finally, my partner John Forrester put up with my moans and groans about love over the course of the book's making. He has been both a stalwart companion and a meticulous reader, making good my lacks and dotting my real and metaphorical i's.

Lisa Appignanesi
London, November 2010

PART ONE

Overture: The Riddle of Love

Love is a canvas furnished by Nature and embroidered by imagination.

Voltaire

Where does one start in writing a book about love? It's an emotion or state that casts a bright light on all of life or shadows it by its lack. North, south, east, west, love is both essential and conflictual. It transforms and it destroys. It seems to matter because life matters. Yet seen from the outside, it's also plain silly or simply mad. Subject of countless myths, lyrics and stories, as well as philosophical and sociological interrogations, embedded in our ways of thinking and seeing the world, love's manifestations are not only as various as the individuals who experience them, but are different at different points in our lives. Intensely personal, unpredictable, love often seems allergic to generalizations, yet its continuities through history and its commonality also make these inevitable and ubiquitous. So the only place to begin in unravelling some of love's riddles seems to be with the self. And the only point in doing so may be to grow a little wiser in love's ways.

I don't know exactly how old I was when I first became aware of love. Aware enough so that it stirred an emotion sufficiently significant to become memorable, even though its meanings were confusing. Aware of it as a word that stood in for a host of feelings.

I was probably around seven and the memory is linked to a French song. French was my first clearly *spoken* language amidst all those others that floated through my parents' immigrant trajectory, which brought its own traditions of love in train. Like all immigrants they felt alternately ambivalent about these traditions and idealized them, subliminally communicating this to us. In the way of most songs heard or learned by

children, the lyrics were only half grasped, but the refrain of this one
stayed with me . . .

'Il y a longtemps que je t'aime. Jamais je ne t'oublierai.'

A translation might read:

'I've loved you for a long time. I'll never forget you.'

Maybe what imprinted the song within me was the mysterious arc of
the refrain: it moved from a past of love through the present and
abruptly into a future where, though love is lost, memory and longing
are for ever. Maybe it was also the collective embarrassment of raising
our children's voices into the palpably intimate, a region hovering on the
forbidden. I clearly recall musing over what it might all mean. Loving, it
seemed, stretched back into the mists of a time past and was so significant
it continued for ever, tumbling into a vague future of the imagination.

It must also have been the song's melody, replete with a tender
yearning, which fixed the refrain in my mind, alongside the jaunty,
oft-repeated ads for toothpaste, instant coffee and that oily tiger in
everyone's tank.

The rest of the song, entitled 'À la claire fontaine', tells a sentimental
tale of a man coming across a fountain during a walk. It's so enticing, he
is tempted to bathe. At first I thought it was the fountain he was in love
with, so important did the place itself seem to be. While he dries himself
off, he tells us he lost his mistress because he wouldn't give her the
bouquet of roses she desired. Now, oh how he wishes they were
together again! Love, it seemed, though so significant, was also evanes-
cent and prone to hazard.

Not exactly scintillating lyrics, one might say. Yet a half-century
later, the song still brings tears to my eyes. And its template of love as a
brief moment of presence between a paradise lost of bliss and a future of
yearning still carries descriptive, and, yes, emotive power.

In the many interviews I carried out while working on this book, most
people mentioned songs as introductions or spurs or accompaniments to
love – from Elvis to the Beatles to Dylan, Leonard Cohen, The Smiths,

Nick Cave, Amy Winehouse and a score of others. This is hardly surprising. Music wraps emotion into itself and plays on the body. If pop music has love in all its manifestations — from longing to joy to pain and regret — as its principal lyrical theme, so, too, does the classical literary canon. In Marcel Proust's formidable analysis of love, memory and society, *À la Recherche du Temps Perdu*, a little haunting phrase from his fictional composer Vinteuil's sonata becomes both triggering motif and transposed essence of the philandering aesthete Swann's love for Odette, the unsuitable object of all his desires whom fate finds him married to, but only once he has discovered he is no longer in love with her. Passion's disappearance may be no barrier to marriage.

The word 'love' wove itself into my childhood in other equally, or perhaps more, perplexing ways.

I grew up amidst several cultures. One was French and Catholic, adept in the language of the sins of the flesh, of confession, repentance and salvation. The other was English and Protestant, versed in Puritanism and unspoken guilts. Both had been transplanted into the newish world of Quebec, a province of Canada and also of its influential neighbour to the south, the United States of film, television and pop music. My family were immigrants of Jewish lineage from central Europe, which added a potent ingredient of world-weariness and oft-humorous pessimism to the cultural brew.

My brother was seven years older than me. He had a habit of assuming a severe paternal role. Often enough it came with shouts, raised hands and disciplinary threat from which I would flee, to cower in the bathroom behind the only locked door in the house and there await my working parents' return.

'But he loves you,' my mother would say when I wept my version of events to her. 'He really does.'

So love was also being locked in a lavatory, one's will brutally impeded by what felt very like a version of hate. Love brought a series of power relations in its train. The one time I remember my father taking off his belt and administering a number of thwacks across my bottom, it turned out that this punishment for a now forgotten crime was also carried out in the name of love.

My mother, like me, had an older brother, but her love for him had no fear in it and took an altogether different form. Her brother was a handsome uniformed picture: the man it represented had been lost, had vanished during the war. There were lots of dead relatives in my family and few living ones. Mostly they weren't spoken of. But this beloved and heroic brother was the subject of countless tales, lyrically recounted. My mother also saw him here, there and everywhere – though it never turned out to be him. So this storytelling and ghostly spotting was also love, fraternal love. My father, on the other hand, had a brother who had lived in New York ever since my father was a babe. He had eagerly gone off to see him twice or thrice during my Canadian childhood, and the brother had once visited us. Then, he too vanished, though there was no picture of him to be seen anywhere in the house. Nor was he ever spoken of again. It seemed the word 'brother' didn't have to be attached to love, after all.

Growing up into love, let alone understanding its contours, was hardly a straightforward business.

For instance, my mother and father presumably loved each other. We all somehow knew that love and marriage went together like a horse and carriage. The princesses in fairy-tales all got married and lived happily ever after. Yet my mother and father rowed regularly and vociferously.

Once, too, I caught my mother in the long hall of our house, clasped in embrace by a family friend I inevitably didn't like. I had only ever seen that kind of passionate clasp on the film posters of *Gone with the Wind*. I knew, in the way children always know by the sheer intensity that hiding brings into play, that what they were up to was forbidden and secret. I also knew that it was loathsome, as all adult sexuality is to children. For some reason, in those ever fluid associations that memory brings, that illicit moment is caught up for me with the lyrics of that 1950s American song 'I saw Mommy kissing Santa Claus'.

I hadn't actually seen *Gone with the Wind* yet. We Quebec children were rather deprived of cinema in the fifties and early sixties, officially because of a fire that had taken many lives back in 1927. The dominant reason, however, was that the then ever vigilant Catholic Church which ruled the morals of the province with a heavy hand didn't want us to see Rhett Butler and Scarlett O'Hara, or anyone else, clasped in embrace. When I asked my mother why, she said it was because they thought love stories were bad for children. Dangerous. The confusion over that was compounded by the fact that we were allowed to see special screenings of cartoons and Disney films. *Cinderella* and *Snow White* were two of my favourites, and here love and its shadow side, hate, featured large. Cinderella's struggle to escape the envious clutches of her wicked stepmother and sisters ended with a kiss and the promised bliss of marriage, while Snow White was woken from poisoned sleep by one and the same. So maybe it was animation that made kisses and love OK, their unreality somehow confounding the danger of the 'real'.

Other influences came to shape my growing and ever more mysterious picture of love. In the small Québécois town where I spent a part of my childhood, stories of who was in love with whom circulated freely. Love was gossip – a private, but publicly titillating, matter. I don't think I paid much heed. These were stories about adults, after all, who inhabited a different world. But stock characters remain in my memory, I imagine because of their repeated visits in these stories. Then, too, a mystery attended their roles, rife ground for childhood misunderstanding. There was the *coq du village* – a phrase my mother loved, which apparently designated the man–rooster who fancied he ruled over all the chicks in the village. I would watch these local Lotharios carefully when they appeared, in the hope that I might catch a glimpse of their chickens, before I realized they were meant to be women.

Another stock character was the ardent, swooning, ever desirous male who, in my beautiful and much desired mother's lore, figured as a plus or a pest, whatever his suffering. There was also a rather gaga version of this: the aged, besotted swain and his too young mistress, both figures of ridicule. A 'cheat' was part of the panoply, too. Usually this one figured as female, and came with a derogatory description of too much lipstick and too many flounces. Finally, there was the forlorn female, disappointed in love, who was always approached with a halting cheer admingled with awe and a slight fear, so it wasn't quite clear whether she was ill and contagious or on a plinth built out of suffering.

Sometimes these love stories hurdled across the child–parent divide and love acquired another adjectival usage to produce a love-child. The one that remains in my mind, perhaps because of the intensity of the whispered gossip, had to do with a customer in my parents' local store, where often enough I spent my after-school hours tucked, half hidden, behind the till counter doing homework or drawing. The customer was a blowsy teenager who transfixed me by coming in one day with no teeth, then the following week with a gleaming set. The transformation was almost as potent as Cinderella's: teeth and slippers, both in their different ways attached to the body, seemed to have magical properties somehow related to love. Anyway, rumour amongst the sales assistants had it that this young woman was bearing a love-child by — wide-eyed murmuring — one of the priests in the seminary, right next door to the convent school I attended.

So love was also something to do with the making of children, a secret activity it seemed; though children could hardly be secret since I knew lots of them.

I had no idea back then how children were, in fact, made. There were storks, of course. (Birds seem to flutter in to confuse the sexual picture in myths, fairy-tales, poetry and kitchen talk, forever displacing it into flight and the possibility of human transformation.) Storks dangled babes from their beaks in whiter-than-white bundles on the picture greeting-cards. But there were no storks in Canada — yet there were certainly babies. According to one tale, I had grown in my mother's tum because she had eaten a great many pears, which she continued to delight in though they now produced no little siblings. In other parental versions, babies came when a man and woman slept with one another. I grew terrified of sleeping in the same bed as my brother in case a swaddled shape materialized in the night between us.

The provenance of babies did finally figure in the sex education classes my — by then English-language, Montreal — school laid on when we were about twelve. But the process the projected diagrams illustrated on the school screen remained more than a little opaque. Nor was the word 'love' ever uttered. The atmosphere in which the teaching took place — girls segregated from boys presumably so we could talk about frightening blood and menstruation, the teacher wielding a punitive pointer, the use of clinical words I don't think I had ever heard – had more to do with warning and prohibition than anything good.

When, afterwards, the boys in the playground made a circle with thumb and forefinger and inserted the index finger of the other hand into it, I had no idea what the gesture meant, nor why it should be accompanied by sniggers and that other four-letter word, f**k, rarely heard when and where I grew up, and all the more potent as an expletive. I wasn't the only ignoramus. None of my girlfriends alto-gether understood, and I'm not even sure the boys did. If an atmosphere of sexuality and excitement accompanied it all, we were still largely ignorant of the facts – not that even those would have helped much without some tangible experience. Children may be sexual beings in the sense that their bodies can give them pleasure, but there is a deficit in the knowledge that comes from adult experience. In that sense they are innocents: they only glimpse, and often enough faultily, what their bodies may know. And biological facts remain opaque until lived reality arrives to join up the dots.

In a famous set of observations about the sexual enlightenment of children, Freud notes that a child's intellectual interest in the riddles of sex, his desire for sexual knowledge, leads to delightful hypotheses about the origins of babies. The Freudian child, long before puberty, is capable of all the psychical manifestations of love – tenderness, devo-tion, jealousy, which are often enough associated with physical sensations – so that he has a sense that the two may be related. If ques-tions lead only to misleading parental explanations or a prohibitive silencing, the child's curiosity is stymied and the result may be inhibi-tion of both a sexual and an intellectual kind accompanied by later difficulties. Differentiating between the anatomy of boys and girls, Freud also hypothesizes, may as one of its effects induce in boys a fear of cas-tration and in girls an envy of the visible phallus and, by metaphorical extension, of its powerful owners.

Penises were familiar enough to me from my utterly non-puritanical home where doors were often open and the occasional nudity hardly remarkable. I don't think the sight of my father's or brother's penis stimulated a sense of envy or of my own lack, though such matters or their symbolic afterlife rarely produced a conscious rumble. But when

penises erupted in strange places, they could be frightening. The perennial flasher might be giggled at when we girls were in a group, but took
on fearful moment if one was alone.

On one confusing occasion when I was made aware of a man's erect
penis, I made a scene, which is probably why the event can still be
recalled. I must have been about ten or eleven, that prepubescent Lolita
moment that so fascinated Vladimir Nabokov. It could only have been
a Sunday, since we were off into the Laurentian Mountains for a family
outing, this time accompanied by some friends of my parents. The car
was crowded and my place was on a pair of bony male knees. Let's call
him Bill kept hugging me to him, purportedly for safety's sake, and
occasionally rocking me as if I were a tiny tot who needed calming.
This did little to put me in a sunny mood. At some point during the
long drive, the rocking took on too regular a rhythm and something
that felt like a third bony knee wedged against my bottom. I don't know
what came over me, but I hollered that I was going to puke and
demanded that the car be stopped. I ran out and away alongside the
highway until my angry father caught up with me and forced me back.
But I just wouldn't take my place on those knees again. I think I must
have felt a sense of disgust – why else say I was on the point of being sick?
Nor was I to be consoled. I was finally persuaded back into the car only
when I was allowed to squeeze into the front seat next to my mother.

I couldn't tell my parents what had happened. I couldn't tell myself
either, since I didn't know. This was secret matter. Only much later
and with fuller knowledge did it take on a kind of sense. I didn't speak
to Bill for ages and was severely reprimanded for my lack of politeness.
Bill wasn't a bad man and I now imagine he must have been rather
shamefaced. Such things happen to most children in a more emphatic
or a lesser way, sometimes forgotten, sometimes recalled. They're just
part of growing up into love and its regular enough stalking partner,
sex. To the child, they're part of a puzzle in which the pieces only
slowly, if ever, fall into place.

My older brother presented a riddle, too. Having arrived at young manhood while I was still an innocent, he would often be entertaining
young women I wasn't allowed to meet in the basement of the family

home. This was also the place where I listened to my Elvis Presley records. Going all gooey when Elvis crooned 'Love me Tender' certainly had something to do with love, as far as I was concerned. I loved Elvis with all the passion that collectively shared idols awaken in the pubescent young, at that moment when the body puts cravings for one doesn't know quite what into motion and rampant fantasies focus on actor or pop star to provide a ready object.

It didn't need a great leap of the imagination to link that vague gooey Elvis-shaped longing with whatever it was my brother was up to on those occasions when the basement door was kept securely locked. Our dog, who served as his guardian, barked effusively if anyone tried to enter, or even knocked. The dog certainly knew more than I did. He might even have understood why it was that Elvis's voice could make me go soppy with love, while any approach from an embodied male of the local species made me gag with disgust. When at some point during his young virile manhood – he must have been about nineteen – my mother declared that my brother was in love, I knew it was obscurely linked to the locked basement door and its secrets. The word 'love' on this occasion was uttered in a dirge-like tone that evoked doom rather than promise.

My brother's chosen love was a slender brunette I had only glimpsed in passing. I knew, however, from the family rows that she was a French-speaking Québécoise, and therefore Catholic. My brother's refrain that she came from a Communist family, which meant she had no religion at all, just like us more or less, cut little ice. The arguments went on and on until the two sets of parents met. They were polite enough as far as I could tell from the eavesdropping position I took up in the kitchen until I was caught out. But after that meeting, the girl-friend disappeared and my desolate brother was whisked away on some summer jaunt.

I hadn't read *Romeo and Juliet* yet, though their names came up. Nor had I seen *West Side Story* with its evocation of star-crossed lovers trying to bridge a social divide. But the lyrics were everywhere and I had the LP. Ever after, this moment in my brother's life was caught up with the realization that love, far from being 'a many-splendored thing', was also an occasion for stiff-lipped parents from ill-matched or warring social groups to come together in judgement: love was a disturbing force which had to be battened down, so that its ill, certainly tumultuous, winds didn't wreck the good ship Family. I later realized that love was also that first trembling step we take into the wider world of the *polis*, the world of others who bear no relationship to us except that created by the bond of 'I' and 'you'. Without that bond, we would be poor creatures, forever mired in our limits.

By that time I had started to read books other than *Nancy Drew* and *Anne of Green Gables*. In fact, through these teenage years I was becoming a rather bookish sort and would read anything that came to hand from the school or small home library, from friends, or the local drug store's swivelling racks. So many of these books found a primary theme in love. Like those Australian children who know from books a great deal about English seasons, fauna and flora, though none of them exist in Australia, I learned a great deal about passion without ever having experienced it.

When I look back at that reading, it seems to fall largely into two basic templates, at least in so far as love is concerned. The first kind of love came out of English literature. Jane Austen was key, as were all her progeny in countless tales of girl meets boy (or nurse meets doctor), overcomes pitfalls, vaults hurdles of both inner blindness and outer difficulty to arrive at that glorious end-point, which is also a promise, where love and marriage meet.

The other strand came out of continental literature. Here love had little to do with marriage, which was always a backdrop of convenience or misery. Instead, it had everything to do with secret desire and the grand illicit passion of adultery. Enter Madame Bovary and Anna Karenina with their transgressive desires and suicidal fate. Meanwhile, heroes like Balzac's Rastignac and Stendhal's Julien Sorel climbed the social ladder through the scaling of each step by seductive acts of love, often with older women.

I never paused then to reflect on the contradictions embedded in these two models: the happily ever after of one and the miserably ever after of the other. After all, each in its own way played out the patterns that had already been laid down by the family stories and fairy-tales I'd been told or read earlier. Nor did it seem strange to me that at one and the same time I could be pining away for Darcy or his rather uncouth equivalent spied at school, and singing, with great clanging brio, 'I never will marry, I'll be no man's wife. I intend to live single, all the days of my life.'

In that flux of emotions and hormones which is adolescence, contradictions live side by side. It's only later that we think we have to settle for an either/or, and all the while wish wistfully that an 'and' were still possible. Meanwhile, all these stories, tragic or comic, had a common point. Love conferred meaning, filled life with significance. If it entailed suffering, had a dark side, it was also a school in sensibility: without it we would never know the sublime heights and perfidious lows of others – or ourselves.

If I anatomize all this as preamble, it is because love always carries an individual story, whatever its universal weight as an emotion or condition and whatever discourses of love our culture has conferred on us. The childhood instances I post here were unique to me and inflected the way in which I grew into an understanding of love. What is common to all children, however, is that the little four-letter word accrues so many contradictory meanings that it emerges as a consummate mystery, one trailing importance, yet hardly easy to decipher or live.

Well before I'd actually been to bed with a man or used the word about my emotions, well before I'd experienced that obsessive madness of passion that links the lover to the lunatic and the poet, I already carried within myself a host of oft-conflicting templates of love, habits of mind and body, wishes, expectations, fears, let alone those fluttering ghosts of those of my sibling and parents – all born out of a brew of family life, cultural and bodily forces. These were rekindled, tugged at and pulled into varying shapes, whenever I later 'fell in love' or simply loved. And each new accretion came into play the next time round.

Love shows little heed of physical age, much as we may try to constrain it into age-appropriate form. Which is why grown women may find themselves on occasion as needily dependent as a crying toddler, or a grandfather may be as obsessed as he was as a young man by a pretty young thing. In the film *Moonstruck* an ageing, philandering lecturer, rebuked by a mature woman with the words, 'You're too old for her', aptly replies: 'I'm too old for me.'

Now, as I grow older, I rarely think of love as divine or carnal rapture. Rather, I think of those ties that bind me to my children, somehow the most important people in the world, as idealizable and as irritating, each in turn, as the long-term partner with whom I share my days, my ups and downs and that necessary tedium in between. Or I think of my mother's distorted face staring at my father's dead body, a man she was prone to criticize, but whose life she had shared through thick and thin for over forty years. I think of the numerous couples I know, estranged by the turmoil of life, coming back together in times of extreme need or illness, to share pain and difficulties, the old enmities laid aside. All that, too, is love.

Why write about love? It's just a four-letter word, after all, one often casually used. It can feel empty and platitudinous or bring with it a queasy embarrassment or a contemptuous sneer of dismissal. Its yuck factor is high. Over the last decades, love has been scoffed at as senti-mental goo, derided as a myth to keep the masses enslaved, exposed as a mental malady and inveighed against as a power-monger in romantic garb bent on oppressing women in particular.

Yet love bears within it a world of promise, a blissful state removed from the disciplines of work, the struggle for survival and even the rule of law and custom. The promise coexists with the knowledge that love can bring with it agonizing pain, turmoil, hate and madness – and in its married state, confinement, boredom, repetition.

Indeed, love carries a freight of experience that takes us from cradle to grave. It frolics amongst the daffodils, dances to the secret tunes of perversity and transgression, drives some mad and others insanely happy. Its object can be long dead and exist only as a picture in a frame enlarged by imagination, or an all but naked man hanging on a wall, or a pop idol. It can be the subject of laughter or insufferable longing and often both at the same time. It can exist as an unbreachable attach-ment between couples of whatever sex, who seem on the surface to despise each other or engage in tortuous power games. It can play itself out intensely between fathers and daughters or mothers and sons –

sometimes with deadly outcomes, at others happily enough. It often comes accompanied with the intense pain of jealousy or rejection.

The Ancients split love apart into Eros and Agape, desire and affection, or benevolence. They tellingly gave Eros or Cupid, a sometime god, a physical embodiment: that playful, rambunctious, charming winged toddler who grows into a fetching nubile youth. In some versions Eros is passionate about other youths, but in his longest narrative he falls in love with the imaginative Psyche, or soul, she who can love in the dark, sparked by stories whispered into her ear. Son of the beautiful Aphrodite (Venus) and warring Mars, Cupid creates both havoc and pleasure. His arrows land in unexpected places, urban alleyways and romantic vales, and show little respect for gender or the status of their object.

Following Aristotle's lead, the great essayist Montaigne as well as the creator of Narnia, C.S. Lewis, designated four kinds of love: the natural, that is, affection, that ordinary bond of everyday life between familiars; the social, or those bonds, like friendship, formed through mutual projects and commonality; the hospitable, which in Christian terms becomes charity, the brotherly love offered to neighbours and outsiders; and finally and perhaps most problematically, the erotic, that sexually fuelled, driving or transforming power, both creative and destructive, that passion is. The last, some have thought, may also play a part in the others, acting as an energetic force that is then diffused or sublimated into other bonds.

In the following pages, I have compacted this voluminous subject into something of an arc of love through individual time — a life history of love, one might say. I begin with a phenomenology of our first forays into love and attempt to anatomize passion's constituent parts. I move on to marriage and more durable coupledom, its triangulation in adultery, love in the family and finally love and friendship. Throughout the book, smatterings of condensed history provide illuminating ways of seeing other than our own. Underlying it all is an attempt to understand the dynamics of the way we live desire and love today. Since our social moment impacts on the way we experience love and helps to shape our desires, some of the imbalances that our times have produced are also my subject.

Given the nature of the oft ungovernable emotion under consideration, the voyage this book takes us on inevitably bears the traces of
my own experience and observation. If I have structured it in part
along the trajectory of a life, it is because we live love differently –
though never altogether differently – as we grow up and older. I am
as interested in the Himalayas of voluptuous passion as in the plateaux
of what might be called ordinary, quotidian love. Appreciating the
latter, I have learned in the course of my days, is as much of an art
and perhaps, also, an ethics, as succumbing to the sublimities of the
first.

Love crops up in multifarious discourses – from soaps to statistics,
from cyberspace to science, from religion to fiction, philosophy, psychoanalysis and sociology, and many of those guidebook and self-help
points in between. It has long been part of an energetic cultural conversation, which loops from life to writings and images and back again,
each shaping and reshaping the other. Since a single book is no ency-
clopaedia, I have had to wend my way through sources, magpie-like,
and pick and choose. These choices reflect what I have learned about
love through partners, friends and children, from reading, observation
and gossip as well as from the more structured interviews I conducted
in the course of research (though, of course, for reasons of privacy, I
have anonymized these in the text). So I should say something about
my choices, limits and prejudices.

Humans live love as a narrative: we tell ourselves stories embedded in
the stories our culture and traditions have given us. Purported facts,
often contradictory, sometimes garnered from the labs of biologists,
cognitive psychologists and neuroscientists, as well as their theories,
feed into these and into our cultural definitions and expectations of
love. I have used all these but often focused on the narratives: they
simply reveal more about how love is lived. So the stories people tell
about themselves or others, whether in interviews or more artfully, in
fiction, form the bedrock of this book. Because some of the great psychoanalytic thinkers have made love their subject and illuminated its
vagaries, I find myself often enough drawing on Freud, Melanie Klein,
Donald Winnicott and Adam Phillips. Given that their observations are
garnered from years of listening to and observing those who came to see

them often because they were troubled by love's unruliness or failure or their own incapacity to love, this seems apposite. If, as my last book *Mad, Bad and Sad* showed, the profession isn't uniformly reliable, some of its best thinkers offer up intriguing perceptions on that mysterious and paradoxical creature that the human is.

One dominant and fashionable set of explanations about love comes from the thinking of evolutionary psychologists and biologists. The impetus of science is to reduce, in the best sense of that word, complexity to a generalizable hypothesis. But to assume that we are primarily, like animals or selfish genes, driven by a reproductive urge which can explain all the manifestations of either sex or love, adultery or jealousy, hetero- or homosexual, is a reduction too far. Of course, the analogy with animals can be drawn, and sometimes fruitfully, particularly when we take into account the huge diversity of the animal world. Yes, we want to survive and many of us want to have children and look after them as best we can and in security. But humans also have language: they make and tell stories about themselves, elaborate their urges, play out their fantasies through complicated technologies, construct hypotheses, and remember all of these. They bear little resemblance to single cells or the proverbial birds and bees, which themselves may bear little resemblance to each other. A great part of our lives, which includes love in its manifold forms, has little to do with being driven by evolutionary forces. We spend little enough of our time reproducing, and some never do, sometimes out of choice rather than failure. I'll believe in evolutionary psychology more, perhaps, when it's used less as an explanation for male philandering and female nesting. These natural men and women, after all, don't still shit in their back gardens.

Then, too, while it's exciting to think that neuroscientists have, according to press releases, found love or God spots in our hard-wiring, located chemical compounds in our brains which determine our love choices and their success or failure – and sometimes jump to grand conclusions, based on limited studies in laboratory conditions, about innate gender differences – this may tell us as little about the way we live love as a leap in a synapse in our prefrontal lobes tells us about Kant's *Critique of Pure Reason*. The best of them, whose work I am familiar with from earlier research, would concur. So there is only a little of these kinds of sciences in the love in this book.

In drawing limits somewhere, I have concentrated on the Western world, which is, of course, permeated by influences from the East and elsewhere. But the West is what I know best, so it seemed presumptuous to attempt to draw on traditions I could only know in the most cursory manner.

I have also rarely singled out homosexuality as an altogether specific form of love, or focused on the cultural practices which in various epochs have attended homosexuality. I apologize in advance for this lack and for too often erring on the side of 'he and she' rather than the doubling of one and the other – even if in the interviews that have informed this book there have been a variety of homosexuals and in the sources I cite there are many. I have a kind of rationale here, apart from the one of space.

Societies and religions have long constituted themselves by drawing a line between the permissible and the criminal. But desire, even of the ordinary enough 'he and she' kind, always seems to have been something of a loose cannon where rules are concerned. Rapture at bottom contains something of the asocial, the criminal, and desire may indeed be fuelled by the breaking of bounds, whether of clans, families or godly and social rules.

Through history, everything has been done, while various epochs have sanctioned things for one group of individuals, though perhaps not for another. Shepherds in mountain regions have buggered their sheep, people have pleasured themselves whatever their Church's edicts; in a gathering tide during the eighteenth and nineteenth centuries solitary sexual acts were turned into a medical condition to be disciplined and expunged. The ancient Greeks sanctioned particular kinds of homosexuality but not others, and practised what we would now call paedophilia: we have come a long way towards legitimating homosexual practices and gay marriage, but draw the line at paedophilia. What is clear is that most systems of law and most regimes want to disallow certain aspects of the polymorphously perverse creature that the human animal is – able to take his pleasure in so many ways and to suffer for so many others of them, including unrequited love. The nature of these desires, the love that fuels them or results from them, may in its living-out — when not socially ostracized — depend less on the gender of the couple than on the individuals in play.

Freud, who thought we were all bisexual — in other words, that we all contained the mental and psychological attributes of both sexes — once noted that the sex of our chosen object in love was not in any simple way related either to our physical sexual character or to our mental sexual character. Object choice was simply the *visible* indication of homosexuality or heterosexuality. So, I, a woman who ostensibly lives with a man, might in fact be living out a homosexual relationship with him, loving the mother or sister in him — and so on through countless permutations. Yet the fact that I may love the soft pleasing feminine creature who inhabits my otherwise ordinarily virile man and despise other more masculine bits of him, does not make me gay by any contemporary definition of identity.

Nor is gender itself, as we know from the transgender politics of our time, an altogether stable category. We make mistakes about the gender of others, emphatically so in early childhood. The little girl who came home from playing with another pretty curly-haired creature and announced to her mother that Andrea is a nice girl, but you know she has a willy, is not unusual. Others feel out of place in the gender to which they have been assigned and go to great lengths to change it — through hormones and surgery. But desire and gender identity through the length of a life may not always coincide. In one case, recounted to me by a friend, a father of two decided at the age of around thirty that he was in fact homosexual. He abandoned his family to pursue his now spoken desires. After a while, dissatisfied, he came to the conclusion that he was inhabiting the wrong gender and was in fact a woman. He went through surgery and became one. Soon enough, he determined that he was not a heterosexual woman, but a gay woman, and started living with another. When one night his-now-her partner thought it would be nice to experience penetration, he/she broke down ...

In what follows, I have on the whole steered clear of such matter, and of identity politics as a whole, and instead steered into the dynamics of love as they take us through life and time. Though I may talk of 'he and she' in couples, it could often enough as easily be 'she and she', while my use of the word 'marriage' for contemporary unions intended to last includes cohabitation as well as the kinds sanctioned by Church and law.

Nor have I focused on the more sensationalist reaches where Eros can lead — material I have culled in *Mad, Bad and Sad* and elsewhere. Extremes of sadomasochism, murderous abuse, bleak distortions of maiming love, dramatic perversions of power and fantasy: though all these are part of an extended picture of love and its stalking partner, hate, it seemed to me more important, in times when excess is so rampant in the media, to attempt a rebalancing and concentrate on what I call ordinary love, in itself already quite extraordinary enough.

My sources are various: literature of all kinds, from fiction to 'fact', to memoir or philosophy, and interview. We are all, in one way or another, experts on love while remaining puzzled by its vagaries. If I turn in some sections mostly to fiction, it is in part because truth and lies in this area of the passions and intimacy are so often mixed up in each other. Talking or writing about their own lives within a factual mode, people are hardly guaranteed to tell the whole truth or even part of it — even in so-called objective questionnaires. People lie about love and sex, or 'fictionalize', tell their story in one way or another, depending on when they tell it or when they are asked and by whom. So fiction, which observes life, including one's own, may be as reliable here as other kinds of truths.

It's interesting, parenthetically, to note that academic discourse has in this last decade moved some steps away from theorizing sexuality and gender and into love. This may be another indication that our culture feels a need to rebalance what has gone awry. The 'desiring machines' and performances of gender that characterized an intellectual moment of pleasure and plenty are being edged aside. This may, in part, have to do with the renewed prominence of religion in the public arena. In these pages I have not ventured into the love of God, that ultimate absent presence. That would take another book — though this doesn't mean that the impact of the Abrahamic religions on the way we love hasn't informed my thinking.

Nor have I dealt with the love of those significant others that pets can be, the love of nation and patriotism, the love of art or place, or that mainstay for many, the love of work – though all of these can evoke our energetic passions. I hope that neither the constraint I have had to prac- tise, nor my choices, are too delimiting.

Working on this book, I was often enough aware that writing about love was not unlike writing about life. My little four-letter word simply carried too many meanings and went charging off, like Cupid himself, or Freud's libido, into a host of unruly directions. Living does really seem to be 'all about love', which carries the best and the worst of us.

But onwards, to the starting point on our journey – the tumultuous seas of our first passions. What is it that constitutes them and drives their intensities, so that even if they don't last for ever they mark us ineradicably, making us the beings we are? What is this thing called rapturous love?

PART TWO

Configurations of Passion: First Love, Young Love

There are few things we should keenly desire if we really knew what we wanted.

La Rochefoucauld

It is yearning that makes the heart deep.

Saint Augustine

I had no first love. I began with the second.

Turgenev

Falling . . .

They were thirteen or thereabouts. He was a moody, beetle-browed boy; she, a radiant creature with honey-coloured skin, slender limbs, brown bobbed hair and a big bright mouth. His mother had died when he was three: her elder sister stepped in with a 'fatal rigidity' to look after him and his philandering, straight-talking, adored Dad. The girl's parents were conventional and as strict as the boy's aunt.

He lived on the French Riviera. Her family had rented a villa for the summer nearby. Clean sand, sea vistas, bright sun or clusters of pale stars attended their meetings. Already at the first, they had everything in common: tennis, a preoccupation with their own minds, infinity. Their thoughts floated into one another. The same dreams, they discovered, had long permeated their sleep. They were both moved by the softness and delicacy of baby animals.

And suddenly they were madly, frenziedly in love. Their agonizing desire for each other could only be assuaged by taking each other in, body and soul, assimilating every particle of the other. Prevented by youthful clumsiness and the perpetual presence of vigilant elders, they managed only half-hidden touches, a grazing of fingers, knees, salty lips. Then one night, they stole away to a mimosa grove to slake their passion with deeper kisses and more ardent caresses, no less ecstatic for being broken off by the interruption of parental voices. There was only one other tryst before she was taken away. Four months later, she was dead. He never forgot her.

*

Falling in love, as everyone knows, is intoxicating. It catches you unawares. It's magic. It's the light or the place. It's chemistry or the brush of an angel's wings. It's beyond reason. It's instinctual. It's unwitting.

And when you fall, you plunge into an ungovernable ocean. The first time in, the intensity is at its greatest.

Anything, large or small, can ignite the attraction. The toss or turn of a lock of hair, the arc of a nose, the quick stride, the lolloping run, the sudden upturned glance, the tickle of a laugh, the bashful smile, the pallor or glow of a cheekbone, the lulling timbre of a voice, the scent caught in the air, a thought solemnly declared, a shy or earnest aside, the brush of fingers on skin . . . The subject may be a passer-by, a face in a crowded room, an acquaintance, or someone you've long known. The 'who' of them is all that counts.

Once you've fallen, you discover that you're twinned. You're permeable, your thoughts 'float into one another'. You mirror each other. You have everything in common. It's ecstasy when you're together, agony when you're apart. When reality conspires, as it so often does, to put obstacles in your path, to prohibit, to make secrecy a need, passion is fuelled, excitement doubled. All your senses are newly alive. The universe accrues in significance. The smallest signs are meaningful. When your lover is absent, you long, you yearn, you adore the memory of him. When he's present, you're blissful, omnipotent.

Unrequited, spurned, love turns into hate. The very singularity of the desired one metamorphoses into a set of loathsome attributes. Overweening pride, gross indelicacy, cheap taste, meanness . . . the list is unending. Though once, there was only him or her.

If death or that death-in-life which is rupture intervenes, it is as if a knife had hacked out bits of yourself. As potent as love is its loss. Love tumbles into searing, enveloping hatred. Or mourning, a sense of utter destitution.

This arc of love with all its individual variations embosses itself within you, ever ready to mark or underpin subsequent experience.

These bare phenomena of early love seem to be universal, though not everyone experiences them. Or not the first time round.

My initial account of first love between the beetle-browed boy and the radiant girl is culled from the early pages of Vladimir Nabokov's *Lolita* —

that 'Confession of a White, Widowed Male'. Here the 'demented diarist', the notorious Humbert Humbert, having died in legal captivity and asked in his will for his memoirs to be published, recounts his adolescent passion for Annabel Leigh, the girl-child who is a precursor to Lolita, his later more outrageously illicit lover. Indeed, as Humbert Humbert underlines, without the time-stopped Annabel and the imprint she left on him, 'there might have been no Lolita at all'.

First love, as the poets, songwriters, filmmakers and chroniclers tell us again and again, can be the most intense of life's passions. The heightened perceptions, the tumultuous sensitivities of adolescence, the wakening sense that anything and everything is possible, play into its power. 'It is a commonplace,' Stendhal, the great French Romantic realist wrote in his book *On Love*, 'that sixteen is an age which thirsts for love'. The rub is that it's also an age that 'is not excessively particular about what beverage chance may provide.' As yet himself unformed, the teenager's love object can be equally fluid and shifting — like Proust's Marcel, enraptured by all the girls 'in a budding grove' who race by on their bicycles, conferring glamour as they go, yet seem hardly distinguishable from one another, until one in particular leaps to his attention. Biologically driven, suffused with desire which may have no immediate object, alive to nature and to sensation, filled with expectation and an inwardness through which the lyrics of pop songs, stories or poetry play, the dreamy adolescent is ripe for passion of turbulent proportions.

The narrator of Turgenev's novella, *First Love*, captures the febrile state with precision:

I knew a great deal of poetry by heart; my blood was in a ferment and my heart ached — so sweetly and absurdly; I was all hope and anticipation, was a little frightened of something, and full of wonder at everything, and was on the tiptoe of expectation; my imagination played continually fluttering rapidly about the same fancies, like martins about a bell-tower at dawn; I dreamed, was sad, even wept . . . At that time the image of woman, the vision of love, scarcely ever arose in definite shape in my brain; but in all I thought, in all I felt, lay hidden a half-conscious, shamefaced presentiment of something new, unutterably sweet, feminine . . .

When the slender, flirtatious and slightly cruel twenty-one-year-old Princess Zinaida comes to live nearby and shows him a little favour, Turgenev's sixteen-year-old hero, Voldemar, tumbles into the 'melting bliss of the first raptures of love'. In that chaos of emotions, that keen awareness through all the senses, which all lovers recognize, pleasure and pain walk hand in hand: 'I spent whole days thinking intensely about her . . . I pined when away . . . but in her presence I was no better off. I was jealous; I was conscious of my insignificance; I was stupidly sulky or stupidly abject, and, all the same, an invincible force drew me to her . . .' One day, obeying the incomprehensible and desired Zinaida's careless command, Voldemar jumps off a high wall. In his state of semi-consciousness he feels her covering his face with kisses, hears her say she loves him. His bliss is total.

If Turgenev's young lover sounds like a hopelessly old-fashioned romantic hero, here's an account from a seventeen-year-old contemporary Londoner: 'When I am with her . . . I get grabbed by a feeling and get thrown around,' he tells his therapist, evoking the roller-coaster of emotions that attend his first love. The girl is so perfect for him that they are one and he no longer knows where his own body ends and hers begins: 'When we are in her room nothing else matters. I forget about everything. Sometimes hours afterwards I notice that I was lying uncomfortably, like the edge of the bed has cut into my arm, but I don't even notice that. It's like magic. Is that normal?'

Whatever the verdict on 'normality', it's clear that the experience is hardly unusual.

Adolescence is a time of labile intensity. Giddy heights reached when the desired one acknowledges you, plunge as quickly into depths of rejection when he doesn't. Yearning is a predominant emotion and can be so painful as to shade into morbidity. Suicidal thoughts stalk the young lover. Death seems a warm, embracing oblivion, as attractive as the living 'other' who will shatter the discomfort and banality of the quotidian. A sense of cocooned isolation persists through these years, even within the floating groups of friends. Most teenagers, whatever they may seem from the outside, feel something in common with Morrissey's 'half a person', whether 'sixteen, clumsy and shy' or fifteen, clumsy and fat. Desperate to break out of the childhood self the family, however good or bad, keeps structurally imprisoned in just that self, they sense that love is the consummate escape artist. Only in the gaze or embrace of the 'other' can the butterfly inside them be recognized and take wing.

The psychoanalyst Adam Phillips observes that the potency of first love lies in the particularly intense way it brings both body and imagination into play. In adolescence, a set of physical cravings upon which our survival literally depends are elaborated into feelings, beliefs, thoughts – indeed, a whole series of stories and ideas which have the meeting of two people at their core. It's 'an imaginative elaboration of physical functions'. Carnal desire transports the lovers into a heightened world and everything in that world takes on powerful new meanings.

The shape of the stories the lovers tell themselves can be romantic, spiritual, marital or, in our ironic times, confined to a sexual or even a chemical and neural register. Narratives, images, the language of reflection we give to love are always already there in our culture and our history. Our desire may sing of beauty, of seduction and challenges overcome, a meeting of true minds or a laddish conquest, or the self-abnegating pain of terrible longing. We project all our wishes on to the desired one and make them the keepers of our happiness and our solace.

This passionate, sexually charged love is in no simple way a mere invention of the individualist West or the idealizations of romance. Lovers in all cultures attribute inordinate power to the beloved. Poetry extolling passion's raptures and ills has been found amongst Egyptian papyri and on vase fragments dating back to 1000 BC. Scholars agree that such poetry was part of an oral culture in Southeast Asia and India, and was shared through trade routes. 'The sight of her makes me well! ... Her speaking makes me strong,' hymns one Egyptian lover, underscoring the 'love as sickness' theme. And another, exulting that love gives him strength, chants

> My heart bounds in its place,
> Like the red fish in its pond.

O night, be mine for ever,
Now that my queen has come!

The Chinese legend of the 'Butterfly Lovers', adapted in traditional opera, dates back to the late Tang Dynasty (618–907). It tells the tale of a young woman, Zhu Yingtai, who takes on a male identity to pursue her studies in a distant city. Here she meets Liang Shanbo, a fellow student. They become inseparable friends. When a parental order comes for Zhu to return home, she begs Liang to visit her – so that he can meet her younger sister. He does and is overjoyed to discover her true identity. They vow eternal love, but Zhu has been betrothed by her wealthy family to another man. Forced apart, Liang pines away to die of a broken heart. Learning of his death on her wedding day, Zhu's wedding procession takes her to his grave. Her tears move heaven and earth. The ground cracks open and she leaps in to die beside him. But love conquers. The two are miraculously transformed into butterflies and flutter away together, never to be separated again.

Sanskrit literature abounds in tales of passionate, sensuous love, saturated in romantic longing. The cow-herding maiden, Radha, grows up with Krishna: the two play, fight, dance together and never want to be parted, but the world pulls them apart. He leaves to embark on great battles and adventures, as well as the search for virtue. He becomes lord of the universe. Radha waits. She waits for him through his marriage to two other women, through the raising of a family. But at last, in great bliss, the two lovers are reunited and marry in front of a vast cohort, which includes all the gods and goddesses of heaven.

The anthropologist Bronislaw Malinowski, listening to the spontaneous outpourings, gossip and tales of the Trobriand Islanders, observed: 'Love is a passion to the Melanesian as to the European and torments mind and body to a greater or lesser extent; it leads to many an impasse, scandal or tragedy; more rarely, it illuminates life and makes the heart expand and overflow with joy.'

Whatever the structuring narrative and its personal inflections, this passionate young love, both carnal and soulful, is an agent of change, while its violent intensity imprints the experience on mind and body alike.

Coup de Foudre

One of my informants, let's call her Clio, an attractive and successful woman of thirty-five, self-avowedly a romantic, was emphatically marked by her experience of first love. The daughter of American parents who worked in Southeast Asia, she was sent to an English boarding school at the age of fourteen in the early 1980s. She had almost no experience of sex, though, of course, she had some received knowledge. She had kissed before, yet despite her enthusiasm for the act in make-believe (she had, as a child, played with her Ken and Barbie dolls and left them in wild compromising positions about the house), the actual act had always filled her with disgust. She had always been taught by her mother to think of sex and love as a pair.

On the first day of school in the foreign — and one can only imagine lonely — country that England was for her, she saw a boy in the common room. Their eyes met. She remembers his gestures minutely, though she can't any longer picture his face: he had a trilby hat and he flung it and his coat on to a chair. Everything grew vibrant, as if a light had been switched on. She knew she was in love.

It is worth pausing over this description of the moment the French call the *coup de foudre*, the lightning bolt that signals falling in love. The 'look' of the loved one may be central, as all those Renaissance sonnets hymning the beloved's eyes and lips tell us; or Shakespeare's Friar Lawrence in *Romeo and Juliet* who opines, 'young men's love then lies/ Not truly in their hearts, but in their eyes'. Today's advertising industry similarly relies on manifest beauty to sell its products. It's backed up in this by psychological research which shows that individuals regularly rate as most attractive features that appear proportionate and symmetrical. In such experiments, the test subjects also regularly select out as desirable images that bear a relationship to parental features. Yet for all this, Clio, like so many others, cannot in retrospect picture the face of the beloved, not even in that crucial moment when the thunderbolt struck.

Proust, that acute and agonized observer of human foibles, remarks on this common enough phenomenon. His adolescent namesake hero is infatuated with Gilberte, whom he meets regularly in the tree-lined parklands of the Champs Élysées. Yet the actual face of his first love, while he is embroiled in passion, continually eludes him. Proust offers this explanation:

> The questing, anxious, exacting way that we have of looking at the person we love, our eagerness for the word which will give us or take from us the hope of an appointment for the morrow . . . our alternate if not simultaneous imaginings of joy and despair, all this makes our attention in the presence of the beloved too tremulous to be able to carry away a very clear impression of her. Perhaps, also, that activity of all the senses at once which yet endeavours to discover with the eyes alone what lies beyond them is over-indulgent to the myriad forms, to the different savours, to the movements of the living person whom as a rule, when we are not in love, we immobilise. Whereas the beloved model does not stay still; and our mental photographs of it are always blurred.

The 'activity of all the senses at once' — which Clio described in her falling-in-love moment as 'everything grew vibrant, as if a light had been switched on' — blurs sight. Love, it seems, is blind in more ways than the conventional one, that is, of choosing an object for our passions who may be far from socially convenient: it also blinds one to the very face our fantasies have singled out as the only possible object for our love. Even if we carry on thinking that the 'look' of the other is crucial to our love, it may be difficult to recapture the face of the beloved in memory. Here, too, one could speculate, is an echo from buried childhood perceptions of parental figures.

The simultaneous 'activity of all the senses', the vertigo of 'falling' in love, may also be what introduces the sensation of 'for ever' into such heady passion, whatever reason may simultaneously tell us. When the senses are all so keenly in play, the present is all, and it seems to stretch into infinity.

For a week, Clio and her boy teased and ribbed each other, listened to Billy Joel songs, stole outside to smoke secretly. Then inexplicably he 'dumped' her, didn't speak to her for a month or more. When they finally met up again at a party, he invited her outside and kissed her. That was it.

Misunderstandings and hurdles in the path of love – a common trope in fictional treatments as in life – like prohibitions, can increase the desirability of union. Breaking the boundaries of the self is a difficult and sometimes frightening business. Fear walks hand in hand with a sense of adventure. Sensitivities are high, vulnerabilities in play, the slightest rejections are magnified. Fantasies and anticipation inevitably collide with a 'real,' who has through the very process of imaginative elaboration been idealized. The other may feel intimately familiar and yet is a stranger. Excitement, a sense of risk and hope are inevitably tinged with anxiety and blundering steps. Then, too, in the obsessiveness that love releases, family and often friends are cast aside, sometimes with fractious effect. So the path to love is rarely altogether easy.

For Clio and her boyfriend, the coming together after the period of estrangement was sheer joy. A group of friends had congregated at one of their houses for a week: they told the other parents, mostly abroad, that term was finishing a week later. Sex was 'steamy' and 'wonderful' from the start. For a whole year, they were blissful together, utterly wrapped up in one another.

Then the school authorities discovered them in flagrante. They were both summarily expelled, sent down like a teenage Adam and Eve from the garden of their delights. The term 'falling in love' seems already to hold a 'fall' in itself: a fall away from the quotidian, reasonable self, and a falling out, during which that mundane self is slowly and at least partially restored. For Clio, the vertigo of the falling out, the dislocation it entailed, was terrible. Her parents had recently moved to North Africa and didn't yet have an address. The school kept her in quarantine, as if she were diseased, until they could be reached. On top of the ostracization came the headmistress's threat of 'virginity tests' and warnings that she would contract cervical cancer. In the eighties, and indeed even today, the age-old mantra that sex is a dirty business, polluting girls in particular, is still in play side by side with a more permissive culture. When at last Clio's mother was contacted, she grasped the situation instantly. But the terror of confronting her father remained: white lies, reasons and excuses had to be fabulated. In the midst of all this worry and displacement, Clio completely lost touch with her boyfriend.

She didn't see him again until fifteen years later. Through the interim period, despite a series of other encounters and affairs, the experience of this first love stayed with her, never to be equalled in either intensity or 'rightness'.

The pain of sudden separation inevitably played a part in the powerful hold of this first passion — a word which in its Christian resonances already entails suffering. Indeed, this kind of heightened love wraps pain into itself. As Simone de Beauvoir has so saliently noted: 'pain is normally a part of the erotic frenzy: bodies that delight to be bodies for the joy they give each other, seek to find each other, to unite, to confront each other in every possible manner. There is in erotic love a tearing away from the self, transport, ecstasy; suffering also tears through the limits of the ego, it is transcendence, a paroxysm … the exquisite and the painful intermesh.'

Clio traced her first love again when she was working in Southeast Asia. Now a successful executive in her early thirties, adept at Web searches, she recognized him from a review he had posted, despite the fact that thousands bore the same name as his. She sent him an email: he didn't respond until three months later. She was then on the point of returning to England for a Christmas holiday. They met in a north London park: after fifteen minutes they were kissing and madly in love again, as if 'time had folded in on itself'. Suddenly everything made sense for her; everything 'fitted'. She thought, 'This was it. This was happiness.' It would never go away. She felt he was a part of her, no matter who or what he might have become.

He told her he had broken up with his wife just at the time that she had emailed him. (The little miracles of timing attend all accounts of romantic love, as do many other kinds of magical thinking that in the cold light of day, like horoscopes, are labelled 'superstitious'.) He told her that she would meet his children: everything in their conversation was to do with a future in which they would be together. In that 'for ever' which heightened senses make of the present, she felt secure. They saw each other every day and when she had to return to her post abroad, she gave him an airline ticket to come and visit her in his Easter holiday. Meanwhile, they spoke daily across the distance and wrote passionate letters.

Then, three days before he was intended to fly, he rang to say he wouldn't be coming. She was utterly devastated. She continued for years to gnaw away at explanations for his behaviour, for the split. Nor has she ever altogether recovered from the powerful emotions of this first love or found another to equal it.

What does Clio's story tell us?

The very force of the emotions and sexual cravings attending first love, the risks it runs, the meanings it gathers into itself and finds in the world, mark it out as a unique experience amongst the many that life will offer. Its inevitable attendant anguish deepens our sense of inwardness and enriches our experience, in the process making us more aware of others and their fragility. Filled with 'deep devotion' and the 'heavenly touch' of an embrace that sings of 'only you' and 'for ever', it sweeps time past and future away, rolls up the world 'into one ball', and sites its centre in the here and now of rapturous embrace. 'Many-splendored thing' that it is, it even overwhelms our ironies. Yvaine, that heavenly emanation in that most romantic of modern tales, the film made from writer Neil Gaiman's graphic novel *Stardust*, puts it admirably as she addresses her sleeping earthly beloved, Tristan:

> I know a lot about love. I've seen it, centuries and centuries of it, and it was the only thing that made watching your world bearable. All those wars. Pain, lies, hate … it made me want to turn away and never look down again. But when I see the way mankind loves … you could search the furthest reaches of the universe and never find anything more beautiful. So yes, I know that love is unconditional. But I also know it can be unpredictable, unexpected, uncontrollable, unbearable and strangely easy to mistake for loathing, and … what I'm trying to say, Tristan, is, I think I love you … My heart … it feels like my chest can barely contain it. Like it's trying to escape because it doesn't belong to me anymore. It belongs to you.

The sense of young lovers being destined eternally for one another walks arm in arm with a generalized knowledge that the word 'first'

inevitably marks the first of a series. Statistics, never altogether accurate
in this area, suggest that at the very most, 25 per cent of people actually
marry their first loves – though other statistics suggest it is only 3 per
cent. The lower figure may, indeed, be a good: experience teaches us to
temper our hopes and desires of the other, to live with inevitable frustration and still love. But it also means that passion and loss are
powerfully bound up with one another. The very power of first love,
imprinted in us, can serve as a template for later loves. The lover may
seek a new incarnation of the first beloved or a replay of that first intensity. An attempt to repair what went awry may also feed the search for
later editions. So, too, may an obsessional need to repeat the precise
experience, which reality, ever obstinate and in flux, impedes.

Lost or dead loves, enshrined in an aura of imaginary perfection,
seem to hover over all our loves. This may be why yearning, that longing forwards as well as backwards, is such a potent emotion and
shadows our lives, as well as enlarging them. Sometimes that yearning
can be stronger than lived love itself: humans are nothing if not perverse creatures, ever alert to the lacks of their present – compelled to
look back, like Orpheus on Eurydice, even if it brings down the gates of
hell and those sufferings propelled by absence.

Many feel the anguish of anticipated loss with each parting. Indeed,
absence in love often looms as potently as presence. This may be
because it is absence that in part ignites the capacity for worship: we
worship our dead, our distant gods, our ancestors, our lost loves,
sometimes, by a romantic slippage, even our present ones. Within the
imagination, they take on a magical and healing power. We idealize
their attributes, make them the bearers of all our good and wholeness,
the healers of our wounds. Sometimes we reinvest these emotions in
our children, making them the vehicles of our hopes, our aspirations,
all our losses and failings, the carriers of both our dented narcissism
and our ego ideals, our transcendent dreams. Buried in our passionate
love is a redemptive structure borrowed from Christian theology (or
perhaps it was the other way round): love, anguish and salvation are
bound into one. 'Love makes your soul crawl out from its hiding
place,' as the Harlem Renaissance writer Zora Neale Hurston once
put it.

In Love Again . . .

Why is it that passionate love and loss seem to be so bound up with one another?

Psychoanalysts, our contemporary experts on the inner life alongside novelists, poets and the occasional philosopher or priest, might tell us that first love is never altogether first. It is but the first and conscious reawakening of earlier forgotten loves: that utterly dependent yet omnipotent love, blissful in its plenitude, of the avid child at mother's breast, an early symbiosis which, willy-nilly, must end, leaving in its trail a bodily sense of lack for an enchanting object ever after slightly out of reach. The sheer intensity of the infant's initial encounter with a world that isn't yet conceived as 'other' may have not a little to do with the fact that the babe inhabits a preverbal and pre-narrative state, in which a thinking being, an 'I' who defines and delimits, hasn't yet been constituted. Freud's famous 'oceanic feeling' – 'a sensation of eternity, a feeling as of something limitless, unbounded' – springs from this early state and is re-enacted in love, as it can be in faith. Here the boundaries between I and you, self and world, inner time and clock time melt away. We enter that other dimension to which some have given the name, 'spiritual'.

But earthly time moves us on. The babe hurtles onward from that first symbiotic love. Rupture is built into our raptures. The pain of loss, torments of grief are already written into our passions. Learning to love seems also to be about learning how to accommodate the passage away from that brief, excited, blissful glimpse of plenitude.

The incestuous bundle of contradictory feelings the child has for its godlike parents or carers, and indeed its siblings, as it grows, also powerfully finds its way into first love outside the family. These early experiences mark first love with a particular sense of transgression and extremes of both attraction and vulnerability. All the psychological positions that love takes on find their crucible in our childhood relations. Gender is no necessary determinant. Male or female can be devoted, serving, self-abnegating, worshipping or possessively all-consuming, like a possible mother. Either can also be distant, unapproachable, a height to be scaled, or calling out for rescue . . . and so on in countless permutations.

Through these early moments, a barely grasped, some would say unconscious, narrative of love is shaped within us. It takes on accretions from the stories that circulate in our culture – romantic tales of trans-figuration, worldly tales of pleasure, conflict-laden tales of power and submission, spiritual tales of ecstasy and self-abnegation. We reinvent these and they're reignited as we move through life. If shades of the past may be put to rest, they also recur in unexpected moments. Each time we fall in love, even when we're old, the experience feels new, freshly transfigurative. It both is and isn't. There can be an uncanny familiarity in our love choices. They feel like soulmates, twins, as if we've known them all our lives. The structure of our relational story is there, too, within us. And our initial loves, like revenants, continue to lend their contours to later ones, while later ones take up the tune composed by earlier ones – and fill in all the necessary notes in our repertoire.

Edmund White in *A Boy's Own Story* puts it like this: 'People say young love or love of the moment isn't real, but I think the only love is the first. Later we hear its fleeting recapitulations throughout our lives, brief echoes of the original theme in a work that increasingly becomes all development.'

Casting this reflection in a more worldly idiom for his middle-aged hero, Swann, Proust observes how we elaborate on our loves to make them fit an original template:

> At this time of life one has already been wounded more than once by the darts of love; it no longer evolves by itself, obeying its own incompre-hensible and fatal laws, before our passive and astonished hearts. We come to its aid, we falsify it by memory and by suggestion. Recognising one of its symptoms, we remember and recreate the rest. Since we know its song, which is engraved on our hearts in its entirety, there is no need for a woman to repeat the opening strains . . . for us to remember what follows. And if she begins in the middle – where hearts are joined and where it sings of our existing, henceforward, for one another only – we are well enough attuned to that music to be able to take it up and follow our partner without hesitation at the appropriate passage.

Turgenev's *First Love* begins not with Voldemar's first passion for Zinaida but with a telling conversation between older men who are challenged by their host to narrate the story of their first loves. This sets the frame within which the main story of the novella, the youth's and his father's love for the same woman, is told. But the first respondent, plump, light-complexioned Sergei Nikolaevitch, declares:

> 'I had no first love . . . I began with the second.'
> 'How was that?'
> 'It's very simple. I was eighteen when I had my first flirtation with a charming young lady, but I courted her just as though it were nothing new to me; just as I courted others later on. To speak accurately, the first and last time I was in love was with my nurse when I was six years old; but that's in the remote past. The details of our relations have slipped out of my memory, and even if I remembered them, whom could they interest?'

This dialogue seems startlingly Freudian, until we remember that Freud learned from novelists and poets. The simple fact that we grow up means that early shaping attachments, remembered or shrouded, are always ruptured and lost. Yet, since the inner child never altogether vanishes, the yearning, the repeated desire, the sense of lack which often enough attends our lives harks back to these earliest loves, as irretrievably dead and gone as those years themselves, yet with the power still to haunt and to trigger how and where and with whom we fall in love.

John Updike reflects on it with his usual brilliance. 'What is nostalgia,' he asks, 'but love for that part of ourselves which is in Heaven, forever removed from change and corruption?' A loved woman, he suggests, 'eases the pain of time by localizing nostalgia: the vague and irrecoverable objects of nostalgic longing are assimilated, under the pressure of libidinous desire, into the details of her person.' Inanimate details and images, hoarded from the past, also lie in wait to come together in the object of our desire: 'a certain slant of sunshine . . . a kind of rasping tune that is reborn in her voice; they are nameless, these elusive glints of original goodness that a man's memory stores towards an erotic commitment. Perhaps it is to the degree that the beloved crystallizes the lover's past that she presents herself to him, alpha and omega, as his Fate.'

So our deepest and earliest sensations and experiences shape the patterns of our love lives, and the figure fuzzily buried in their depths wears the aura of mother.

It is hardly surprising that the ever wisely wry Nabokov in introducing his Humbert Humbert gives him a mother who died in a freak accident when he was only three. He remembers her as 'a pocket of warmth in the darkest path', as a furry, animal warmth which he likens to a 'haze' of golden midges above a hedge in bloom at the end of a summer's day. Though Humbert apologizes for his overblown prose, it serves to heighten the sensuous atmosphere that mother is, a warm blur in distant memory — as much a place as a separate being. Place, too, recurs and plays its part in the arousal both of his first conscious love with Annabel and of his second with Lolita. The warm summer days, the sea and the greenery of the Annabel days become the pool of sun in the garden where Lolita is first seen, the 'haze' that is also her family name.

Both of Humbert's first loves are dead and for a long time it is as if he has died with them. The end of love is indeed like death, a wrenching away from the coupled self that was, which catapults the lover into that half-life of melancholy. When Humbert is woken, like Sleeping Beauty or a character from the tales of Edgar Allan Poe, it is by Annabel's reincarnation, Lolita.

Poe himself offers an early punning double for Annabel Leigh in his poem 'Annabel Lee', which intertwines love and death. Poe, like Humbert Humbert, was the child of a mother who died when he was very young. And he was also the lover of a girl-child. In that play of allusiveness that *Lolita* provides, it is fitting that Nabokov's ironic romance with America and obsessive romantic love should refer back to the early master of American gothic.

> It was many and many a year ago,
> In a kingdom by the sea,
> That a maiden there lived whom you may know

> By the name of ANNABEL LEE;
> And this maiden she lived with no other thought
> Than to love and be loved by me.

Envied by the heavens for its perfection, this lovers' union of body and soul can only end in death:

> The angels, not half so happy in heaven,
> Went envying her and me —
> Yes! — that was the reason (as all men know,
> In this kingdom by the sea)
> That the wind came out of the cloud by night,
> Chilling and killing my Annabel Lee.

Like the paradises lost of childhood, lost first loves populate literature and life. But then all love, it seems, takes on some of its force from being a return: a return to a primal sense of oneness where lover and beloved merge, like mother and child — or brother and sister — and there is no demarcation between inside and outside. We are recognized, known by, and know the other. Everything is shared. In the loving gaze of the other, we also love ourselves: our best self comes into being, one filled with new potential. Existential fractures are healed. That abiding loneliness, that emptiness that human beings are prone to, recedes, at least momentarily. A sense of pastoral at-homeness reigns. If and when the rupture comes, whether through death or abandonment, the suffering can be as searing, as transcendent as the initial rapture.

Part of the popular force of a film like *Slumdog Millionaire* hinges on the way its embedded love narrative, despite early loss, allows a happy, redemptive end. No sooner does the child hero Jamal's mother die, murdered in an anti-Muslim riot, than the girl, Latika, appears in a mist of rain, to take her emotional place. Separated from Latika by the callous rivalry of his older brother, agonized, lonely Jamal spends much of the film trying to find her, then win her once more — an act which entails killing off his rivals and jumping the hurdles of the quiz show that makes him an adult millionaire. In the film's final scene, when the two meet again, a sequence of images from the past, showing his veiled mother and the child Latika forlorn in the rain, coalesce into an image of the adult Latika waiting for him on a railway platform. They embrace and kiss: loss and loneliness are made good in this double return.

Twin Souls

In the elaborations we give to our cravings at whatever age, certain templates and themes recur.

However much our social and cultural mores change, however acutely we may know – emphatically so in our times – that in humdrum reality, sentimental happy ends are rare or at least rarely outlast the euphoria of a time-stopped moment, the sense of love as a meeting with the long-sought lost half of ourselves persists. Individuals are fragments seeking to be made whole. 'Love,' Coleridge wrote, 'is a desire of the whole being to be united to some thing, or some being, felt necessary to its completeness.' People may find that sense of completeness in God, in a political party, in a nation or place. Many will find it, certainly dream of it, first of all in another.

The idea of twin souls comes to us wrapped in a romantic idiom. We may read it as propelled by sexual desire, but it is also more than that, reaches beyond it to a sense of visionary identification. As Catherine Earnshaw says in *Wuthering Heights*, 'I *am* Heathcliff . . . He's more myself than I am.' She tries to explain this sense of being repeated in another to Nelly Dean: 'What were the use of my creation, if I were contained here?' she asks. 'My great miseries in this world have been Heathcliff's miseries, and I watched and felt each from the beginning: my great thought in living is himself . . . He's always, always in my mind, not as a pleasure, any more than I am always a pleasure to myself, but as my own being.' Brought up as brother and sister, this transcendental love has an incestuous core. It is based on sameness and proximity, not on the difference and distance which more usually fuel desire for the young as they wrench themselves away from their families. Soulmates are not always and ever sexmates. For Catherine, her love for Heathcliff, forged in childhood, is not the love of men and women, which is 'like the foliage in the woods: time will change it'. Rather, her love for Heathcliff resembles 'the eternal rocks beneath'.

In her *Memoirs of a Dutiful Daughter*, published when she was fifty and hardly a young romantic, Simone de Beauvoir evokes her twenty-one-year-old self and her encounter with Jean-Paul Sartre in terms of twin souls destined for each other: 'Sartre corresponded exactly to the dream-companion I had longed for since I was fifteen: he was the double in whom I found all my burning aspiration raised to the pitch of incandescence. I should always be able to share everything with him . . . I knew that he would never go out of my life again.'

Love as twinning or doubling is as old as Western culture, already there in Plato's myth of the origin of love. In *The Symposium* Aristophanes, his emphasis in part satirical, tells us that humans were originally rounded creatures of three sexes – some of them double males, some double females, some one of each and androgynous. They had four hands and feet and a single head with two faces, and were so strong and 'the thoughts of their hearts' were so great that they attempted to scale the realm of the gods and assault them. To prevent this, Zeus cut them in two. As a result, human life is fuelled by a yearning to make good our fractured, lonely incompleteness, to find the 'lost' half of whichever gender, with whom we can fuse. The desire and pursuit of that other who will make us whole, restore us to our original nature and make us happy and blessed, is one aspect of what *The Symposium* calls love.

Sex, in Aristophanes' speech, comes into being because Zeus, taking pity on his poor, fractured Humpty Dumpties, adroitly repositioned their organs and made them capable of congress. Not that all sex acts result in a transcendental sense of unity, or heal our narcissistic wounds or knit together the ruptures of a fragmented world. But love can, and the all-embracing love that poets and pop lyricists sing does, echoing the ancient notion that lover and beloved are one soul in two bodies.

That Romantic Feeling

Romance may be only one imaginative elaboration of physical cravings, but it has been with us as long as stories have been told. And far from being the women-only terrain contemporary gender discourses assign it to, it has long also been male: from Sir Galahad to *The Great Gatsby*, men have wooed and pined, made over their lives, tempted death, to win a Guinevere or a radiant Daisy, designated as the missing half that will make them whole. What we think of as the self is goaded into being by love, which also promises the self's realization.

One day during the Great War a young woman who has happened on a job as a librarian in Carstairs, a small Canadian town, receives a letter from a man she doesn't know, but who identifies himself as Jack Agnew. He is a soldier at the Front. He tells her what books he read in her library, what a change for the better her arrival made to the place and how grateful he was to her. She can't put a face to him, but she answers his letter. She is lonely.

In his next letter, he remembers how one day, having been caught in the rain, she took the pins out of her hair and brushed it out. She hadn't seen him there, but when she did, they exchanged a smile.

The correspondence continues. She sends him a photograph of herself. Her interest in the war and her surroundings mounts. The world takes on a new depth. He asks her if she has a sweetheart. She hasn't. He tells her he doesn't think they will ever meet again, but he loves her. He thinks of her up on a stool in the library reaching to put a book away and he comes to lift her down. She turns in his arms, and it is as if they have agreed on everything.

There is no further letter. When the war ends, she scans the papers daily to see if he appears on a list of the dead, and finally sees his name on a list of those coming home. In a frenzy and despite the raging flu of 1918, she keeps the library open, she searches for him, is ill herself and still waits. Then one day, she reads a wedding announcement in the paper. Jack has indeed come back, but he has married someone else, a girl he was engaged to before he went overseas. She learns this from a scrappy note he leaves for her in the library. She has still never seen him. She gives herself to a passing salesman.

Time passes. Jack is sensationally mown down, decapitated, like some latter-day John the Baptist, in an industrial accident in the town's main factory. Arthur, its owner, who has had to deal with the head, the blood and the human fall-out, brings Jack's surreptitiously borrowed books back to the library. He takes to coming to the library. He sits there, a site of respite. When one autumn evening, as rain clouds gather and burst, the librarian with controlled, but visible, excitement asks him more about Jack's accident and tells him the way he dealt with it was remarkable, to his own surprise the factory owner, a restrained man of dark-suited dignity, finds himself proposing to her. The feelings love stirs can be contagious.

More time passes, together with another war. Arthur, with whom the librarian has led a good life, is dead and she now has a son at university. She has come to a distant town to see a heart specialist. She hasn't been well, but the doctor makes light of her ills. She wanders through town and comes across a rally in honour of the Tolpuddle Martyrs: at the doctor's an announcement, bearing the words 'local martyrs honoured', had already sent her pulse racing. Now sitting in the park, waiting for the ceremony in which a certain Jack Agnew is to speak, she feels a sickening agitation. She leaves. She wanders in a disoriented way searching for the station where a bus will take her home. She is hot, disturbed. She finds refuge in a squalid café, sips a Coke, and when she opens her eyes Jack Agnew, the man she never met, but instantly knows, the man who met a lurid end, is before her. He is older, but authoritative, attractive, something of a working-class hero. 'Love never dies,' he says to her, and though she protests inwardly, she is giddy with an amorous flare-up of the cells, a surge of old intentions.

'Carried Away' is one of Alice Munro's remarkable stories. With deft strokes, it distils the essence of a lifetime, which here is the quintessence of romantic love. Wooed by letters and language, those forms which seem to leap directly to women's hearts – even today, when they may take the form of texting – Munro's small-town heroine falls in love with a man she has never seen, but who fires her imagination. Jack's revelation of his watchful attentiveness and the specialness she has acquired in his mind – both sensuous and idealized by her association with the books he loves – give a new significance to her life. The first also has an immediate carnal effect. Though Louisa has her own share of contemporary scepticism, though 'she would have said love was all hocus-pocus, a deception, and she believed that', at the prospect she still feels 'a hush, a flutter along the nerves, a bowing down of sense, a flagrant prostration'.

Munro's astute depiction of her heroine's 'flagrant prostration' evokes the traditional psychosexual posture of women in relation to love. It is incited from without, provoked by the attention of another. It excites an initial submission.

Women's age-old susceptibility to talkative seducers, to the forceful rakes and Casanovas of story, may in part be due to the way women's desire is only consciously stirred through the desire of another. Until that imaginative process is set in train, she remains secret, even to herself. If to some this may reek of male mumbo-jumbo, it's interesting to note that women researchers studying female sexual arousal in laboratory conditions have also found a distinct split between women's conscious or reported desire and their bodily state of arousal, a split not found in men. As one of the researchers, Meredith Chivers, stated, 'I've often thought that there is something really powerful for women's sexuality about being desired. That receptivity element.'

In Munro's story, it is the desire the letters from Jack set in motion, the intimate link they establish, compounded with the proximity of death which turns this ordinary man into a hero, that seals a transforming tie. Life, for Louisa, is raised beyond its daily banality. Even though, or perhaps because, Jack disappoints her and she suffers, the bond is not broken. It lasts beyond his sensational death, sparks her marriage, and at her own end, is reignited in her imagination. Her love adds a singular, one might say, a civilizing dimension to a life that might otherwise feel petty and banal.

The goods passion can foster are laid out early, if rarely, in Western history. In *Phaedrus* Plato engages in a discussion of passionate love, quite unlike that described in *The Symposium*. In the latter the aspiring intellect alone is drawn, through the pursuit of beauty, to the higher philosophical plane that Diotima, his 'instructress in the art of love', defines as love's goal. In *Phaedrus,* Eros is in full unruly play amongst humans – those souls who have lost their wings. Yet the sensual receptivity passion provokes results in a complex aspiration that leads to the good life.

When one who is fresh from the mystery ... beholds a godlike face or bodily form that truly expresses beauty, first there comes upon him a shuddering and a measure of that awe which the vision inspired, and then reverence as at the sight of a god; and but for being deemed a very madman he would offer sacrifice to his beloved, as to a holy image of deity. Next, with the passing of the shudder, a strange sweating and fever seizes him: for by reason of the stream of beauty entering in through his eyes there comes a warmth, whereby the soul's plumage is fostered; and with that warmth the roots could grow.

Wonder and passion allow the soul to take wing and be moved through devotion to greater understanding. Enmeshed in emotions of tenderness and awe, the person in love is inspired. He recognizes from the other's approval that certain acts are good. Our once higher state may be a distant memory, Plato seems to be saying, but passionate love for one who bears in beauty, wisdom and goodness a likeness to that original perfection allows us to grow closer to our once winged state.

In our sophisticated times, we tend to maintain an ironic distance from both this Platonic version of love and its romantic successor which bound passion, pain and loss into one. Munro's own irony in 'Carried Away' is gentle. If her Madame Bovary of Carstairs is in some sense a martyr to her epistolary love for a man she has never met in the flesh, it nonetheless permits her to lead a full life and one which gains an added dimension from his existence. Through this love her inner life grows deeper, her powers of imagination more acute.

Crazy about You

Propelling us out of our ordinary everydayness, falling in love at whatever age shares not a little with a falling into madness. Passion is a fevered state, a divine delirium, as Plato called it, and it can mimic pathology. It acts upon the body engendering bliss or pain. Reason, which splits and divides, cannot capture its transports: nor, ultimately, can language, itself a commentary on experience – which may be why we resort to (or shun) the simple enunciative force of 'I love you', those words which link inside and outside, I with you, in a performance of love.

Passion makes us oblivious to the world and to responsibility. We are out of control. Our thoughts and our pulse race. Our consciousness is altered. All that matters is our desire and the other who is its object. Opposites are collapsed. Abjectly vulnerable to the other, we are also exalted – omnipotent. We take risks. We transgress. The sense of danger is part of the very charge of the erotic. Judgement vanishes. In its place comes a skewed sense not only of the configuration of the real, but also of the real of the other who floods our imagination. We idealize madly: all the best in the world rests in the object of our love. 'You're the top!' Cole Porter's lyrics sing – the Coliseum, the Louvre Museum, the tower of Pisa, the smile on the *Mona Lisa* – in short, everything that's best.

And with the slightest twist, all the worst rests with him or her, too. Love metamorphoses into hate at the flicker of suspicion.

Our love fills our thoughts: they scurry round in obsessive circles – Will she? Won't he? How? When? In the same way as for people suffering from paranoia, the lover's world is charged with new meaning, magical: there are signs of our love everywhere, in the stars, in the weather, in the smile or scowl of a random passer-by. Everything signals ecstasy or rejection. If we try to focus on anything outside our love, random day-dreams, hopes or fears invade. Blissful dreams of oneness run into terrors of rejection. Thoughts are uncontrollable, just as that initial act of falling was involuntary.

So there is good reason that the 'lunatic, the lover and the poet', as Shakespeare put it in the last act of *A Midsummer Night's Dream*, are so often linked. The three are of 'imagination all compact', judicious Theseus tells us at the moment when the night of love's unruly dream, lived out in the wildness of the forest and under the aegis of sprites and fairies, has given way to the daytime of reason and socially sanctioned nuptials.

> Lovers and madmen have such seething brains,
> Such shaping fantasies, that apprehend
> More than cool reason ever comprehends.

Under the sway of Eros – which, given its unreasonableness, might as well be kindled by Puck's potion, so magical is its suddenness and force –

queens fall in love with asses, see regal beauty in brutes and cede their once dearest wards. We are literally enchanted. Long-held attractions give way in the blink of an eye to others. Couples realign. Suffering is heedlessly engendered. Others wonder whether our 'sanity' is utterly gone.

In its choice of object, love seems to know little rhyme or reason: Cupid, son of Venus and Mars, wears a blindfold, after all, as he shoots his troublesome arrows. In the words of Carson McCullers in *The Ballad of the Sad Café*:

> The most outlandish people can be the stimulus for love. A man may be a doddering great-grandfather and still love only a strange girl he saw in the streets of Cheehaw one afternoon two decades past. The preacher may love a fallen woman. The beloved may be treacherous, greasy-headed, and given to evil habits. Yes, and the lover may see this as clearly as anyone else — but that does not affect the evolution of his love one whit. A most mediocre person can be the object of a love which is wild, extravagant, and beautiful as the poison lilies of the swamp. A good man may be the stimulus for a love both violent and debased, or a jabbering madman may bring about in the soul of someone a tender and simple idyll.

From the outside, the choice of beloved may appear utterly crazy and indeed be so — like that snail in the *New Yorker* cartoon, who while gazing at a curvaceous snail-shaped tape dispenser declares to another snail, 'I don't care if she is a tape dispenser. I love her.' For the lover, the beloved speaks to some intimate part of himself, has perhaps awakened some long-held need. The reel of that inner story is then projected on to the screen the beloved becomes. She may fill a deep unconscious lack in the lover. She may in the way she moves her head or in the wave of a hand evoke a preverbal childhood memory of a long-buried, excessive love. He may envy something she has or represents, or alternatively need to be rescued. She may feed some hungry part of himself. The scenarios are infinite and to others, even to himself, invisible.

Imagination nurtures the process. In love, we are all poets, for good or ill. We are also akin to psychotics. Psychosis is, after all, that aberrant condition of the mind or psyche in which contact with reality is lost and a delusional state prevails. Taken literally rather than metaphorically, John Donne's poem 'The Sun Rising' aptly describes the lover's delusional state:

> Love, all alike, no season knows nor clime,
> Nor hours, days, months, which are the rags of time . . .

> She's all states, and all princes I;
> Nothing else is.

Torn or separated from her beloved, the lover may, like a person in the grip of psychosis, hallucinate his presence, his words, his actions, for good or ill. Or the lover, in the grip of jealousy, love's nether twin, may persecute the beloved, imagine betrayals, punish the real or hallucinated slight to his power with violence. Driven jealously mad, his reason unseated, Othello murders his beloved Desdemona, attempting to extinguish his jealousy and her being in one fell act. Or the lover may grow addicted to her jealousy and pain, and over and over seek others who will feed a core masochism, inflict humiliation and loss.

In *The Act of Love*, Howard Jacobson's unflinching account of a character who becomes pain's slave, the narrator, at the age of fifteen, suffers his first self-shattering betrayal. He reflects:

> If you wanted to be in love – and I wanted nothing else – then you had to welcome into your soul love's symptoms and concomitants: fear of betrayal which was no less potent than the fear of death, jealousy which ate into the very marrow of your bones, a feverish anticipation of loss which no amount of trust would ever assuage. Loss – loss waited upon gain as sure as day followed night . . . You loved to lose and the more you loved the more you lost. Fear and jealousy were not incidental to love, they *were* love.

The pain of lost love is as total, as self-obliterating an emotion as the initial ecstasy. In our own time, when we vest so much in the durability of love, see it as a path to self-realization, abandonment can engender a dissolution of the once merged self. Some passionately re-enact the loss over and over again, its low an emotion more intense than the initial high. Indeed, contemporary love lyrics – Bob Dylan's, Leonard Cohen's, Nick Cave's – more often sing of sorrow and loss than of joy.

The influential French psychoanalyst Jacques Lacan postulated that loss and the continuous inner sense of lack it sets up in us originate in the moments when the infant's early state of symbiotic plenitude with mother and world – his primary narcissism – is ruptured by the intervention of the father, the symbolic law-giver, and in that sense the keeper of language itself, which makes us social beings. This is the moment when the infant's own separate 'I am' is constituted. In other words, the speaking subject comes into being with the loss of unity. To say 'I am' is already to say 'I have lost.' In successive loves, ever haunted by a sense of lack, the arrival of any third party reignites the first triadic structure, its threat and pain. Only death permits the final healing of that first split which is already in ourselves. So the romantic agony, the pendulum swing between longing and mourning, may be embedded in our very nature as speaking humans. Incapable of relocating that originary plenitude, we may seek it or its attendant loss, over and over again. Ecstatic love and loss may, it seems, be a fundamental couple, thrusting us into a bodily confusion which words alone cannot assuage. Thin-skinned, as vulnerable as babes, we're prone to fall apart when we part.

Neil Gaiman's Rose Walker in *The Sandman* says it all:

Have you ever been in love? Horrible isn't it? It makes you so vulnerable. It opens your chest and it opens up your heart and it means that someone can get inside you and mess you up. You build up all these defenses, you build up a whole suit of armor, so that nothing can hurt you, then one stupid person, no different from any other stupid person, wanders into your stupid life . . . You give them a piece of you. They didn't ask for it. They did something dumb one day, like kiss you or smile at you, and then your life isn't your own anymore. Love takes hostages. It gets inside you. It eats you out and leaves you crying in the darkness, so simple a phrase like 'maybe we should be just friends' turns into a glass splinter working its way into your heart. It hurts. Not just in the imagination.

Not just in the mind. It's a soul-hurt, a real gets-inside-you-and-rips-
you-apart pain. I hate love.

Within the annals of madness, love has long played its disreputable part.
The first register of precipitating causes of lunacy in London's great
public asylum, Bethlem, ranks love high on its list. Love gone awry,
hopes crushed in rejection by parental prohibition or by the appearance
of a successful rival, can tumble the lover into a state of delirium or
depression akin to mourning. A beloved has effectively died, but won't
die in us. In this state, suicide or its attempt is not infrequent. Back in the
1790s, the young Charles Lamb checked himself into a madhouse after an
early love went awry. Arguably, his sister Mary was precipitated into
madness when Charles's affections left her. Goethe's Werther commits
suicide when it is clear that his beloved, Charlotte, can't return his passion. A Europe-wide bestseller, based on an early unrequited passion of its
author's, *The Sorrows of Young Werther* precipitated copycat suicides in significant number. Even the courageous and redoubtable Mary
Wollstonecraft attempted suicide when it became clear that her lover
Gilbert Imlay, father of her first child, had rejected her.

It is interesting to note that the tumultuous passions championed by
the Romantic movement and its *Sturm und Drang* German precursor —
passions arguably amplified in France by the Revolutionary decade —
more or less coincided with the origins of psychiatry, or 'alienism'. The
French physician Jean-Étienne Esquirol ranked passion both as cause
and symptom of madness. His distinguishing diagnosis of monomania
mimics the obsessiveness of passionate love: a fixed unshakeable idea
dominates the sufferer.

Freud's patients, too, fell ill of love, internalizing slights, glances, real
or imagined seductions, and playing out conflicts spurred by love in
neuroses or bodily symptoms — those coughs, loss of voice, limps, even
paralyses, which went under the name of hysteria. The early-twentieth-
century psychiatrist Gaëtan Gatian de Clérambault gave his name to a
syndrome of love gone awry: the journey of erotomania, a parody of
love lived out in a shadowy fantasy world of delirium. His patients grew
obsessed with strangers, usually grander than themselves, projected
their own sexually charged desires for love or recognition on to them,

tracked and stalked them jealously and obsessively, knew by distant signs that their love was returned, suffered from persecutory delusions – everyone, it seemed, was against the culmination of their love – and in a sudden vulnerability or moment of omnipotence hit out violently at the forces that they imagined impeded their love.

The British analyst Peter Fonagy, using current professional terminology, draws parallels between the passionate lover's experience of 'impaired affect regulation', compounded with 'the lack of a sense of boundariedness', 'the wish to control and manipulate' and 'identity diffusion', and the clinical picture of a patient suffering from borderline personality disorder. Indeed, psychiatrists have suggested that the so-called personality disorders are on the rise in part because parents, loving or negligent, find themselves unable to say no to their young and to establish necessary limits. Inside and outside, one's own desires and the desires of others grow confused, sometimes irredeemably.

If we grow sick of love, if part of its journey parallels morbidity, it is because love also loosens our established boundaries, the very limits of our self-definition. In love, we are no longer our known, delimited selves, but suddenly permeable. As vulnerable as a newborn. This very permeability, the new fragility of our once bounded state, can now only be bound once more in the presence of the other. It matters little if the beloved is a creature largely made of our imaginings, those phantasms that spring from body, heart and mind. 'When the lover encounters the other,' Roland Barthes writes in his brilliant *A Lover's Discourse*, 'there is an immediate affirmation (psychologically: dazzlement, enthusiasm, exaltation, mad projection of a fulfilled future: I am devoured by desire, the impulse to be happy): I say *yes* to everything (blinding myself).'

In that state of permeability to the other, transformation can take place. 'Crazy about you', 'all shook up', I can also become somebody else in a world newly rich in meanings and signs. Recognized by the loved other, in her potent gaze, another version of myself comes into being. Frogs turn into princes, kitchen maids into princesses, disabled war veterans into avatars. But this business of moulding a newly edited self in the image of another is painful. It needs the act of attention, of recognition. Absence becomes an agony of waiting replete with hallucination. The doorbell is ever about to ring, announcing his arrival.

The next face in the crowd will be his. The next text on the screen will signal he's thinking of me.

Absent, the beloved awakens in the lover a time of utter dependence when he was a mere vulnerable babe at mother's breast. Taking his cue from the psychoanalyst D.W. Winnicott, Barthes notes that as with the mother's breast for the infant, '"I create and re-create it over and over, starting from my capacity to love, starting from my need for it": the other comes here where I am waiting, here where I have already created him/her. And if the other does not come, I hallucinate the other: waiting is a delirium.' Rejected, unrequited, abandoned, the lover becomes unbound, a frail skein subject to destruction. That new self, recognized only by the other, taking its shape from the other, is now subject to catastrophe – a disintegration akin to madness.

Proust's young Marcel spins an entire template of love out of the nightly ritual of awaiting his mother's kiss, the only act that will offer him the peace that allows sleep. The kiss is at once benediction and confirmation of an identity secure enough to be broken up, tossed and turned in the fracturing world of dreams. But his mother's kiss is so quick, so fleeting, so soon gone, that he would rather put off the assuagement of his wish as long as possible, since it already announces the subsequent pain of her absence. Worst of all, if there are guests present, his mother may not offer the kiss of fleeting solace. Jealousy spirals.

Inherent in the Proustian understanding of love is the pendulum swing between anticipation and suffering. If he could, the Proustian child would be a cannibal, incorporating the beloved other on which his being is so dependent – eat her up like the big, bad wolf tries to eat Little Red Riding-Hood. But the other is free to come and go, can't be eaten or controlled. There lies the maddening rub of love: the very separateness of the other who incites it, who keeps it alive, is what we want to make our own, merge with, possess, and in the process annihilate, thereby annihilating the desire that keeps love going.

Freud's grandchild, evoked in *Beyond the Pleasure Principle* (1920), shares an affinity with little Marcel in his need somehow to come to terms with the presence and uncontrollable absence of his beloved mother. Like so many children, he does so by inventing and engaging in a game. He has a wooden reel on a piece of string. He thrusts this away from him, while uttering an infant version of the word '*fort*' (gone), and then pulls it back to him with a gleeful '*da!*' (here). Through the obsessive repetition of a game in which the toy stands in for the mother who is no sooner present than once more absent, he learns to master an absence which is also potentially the feared permanent loss of the loved one.

If the obsessiveness that characterizes lovers bears a close kinship with its morbid enactments, it also has something in common with the process by which Freud's grandson masters his situation. As the analyst Ethel Spector Person notes,

> obsessiveness is no mere appendage to love, it is the very heart of love; it is that which permits love to act as an agent of change. The working and reworking of the same ideational content is similar to the 'working through' that occurs in psychoanalytic therapies. The lover is written in, as it were, into every conceivable experience and dream. Such 'obsessions' are signs that a major psychic shift is occurring, with changes in allegiances, values, perceptions, goals, and the sense of self.

Orhan Pamuk's *The Museum of Innocence* recounts the story of just such an obsessive love. Kemal, the book's hero, on the point of announcing his engagement to Sibel, a woman of his own class, falls in love with his distant and poorer cousin, Füsun, who for a few brief moments which feel like for ever on the afternoon of 26 May 1975 casts him into a luminous state of perfect happiness, suffusing him with the deepest peace. Of course, he realizes it only when she has vanished. Obsessed with her, he spends a year tracking her through Istanbul. Finding her married, he convinces himself that he can win her back, if only he abjects himself sufficiently. For nine years he becomes a pitiable appendage to her family. During that time, he begins to pilfer objects connected to Füsun – underwear, bits of jewellery, cigarette butts – which he hoards in his growing Museum of Innocence. His self-abasement is punctuated by moments of morbid ecstasy as he licks and sucks his treasures, in them recreating the gesture or look of his beloved that each piece has been selected to memorialize.

Pathological morbidity here rises to the heights of lyricism; but its obsessiveness is only overcome after years.

Love as divine rapture or intoxication is our socially sanctioned form of madness. We may judge it severely when we're not entrapped in its ways. But it carries on merrily, or painfully, whether we approve or not. Which is why our many attempts to control it, by averting risk, by filling in dating agencies' questionnaires with our lists of preferred qualities, will rarely propel us into the 'falling' that passion entails. When the daylight of 'reason' returns and the socially confirmed nuptials can take place, they usually augur a falling-away of passion, if not of love in its other, more tender and affectionate guises.

While cynics and realists may denounce this mad version of love, it is clear that our lives would be poorer without it, our imagination depleted and our ability to live in a world of others much reduced. As Stendhal, at once a realist and prone to bouts of ever unrequited passion, noted: 'Half— the most beautiful half— of life is hidden from him who has not loved passionately.' Or, as André Malraux wrote almost a century later in Man's Fate (1933), his novel set in China during the failed Shanghai insurrection: 'It is very rare for a man to be able to endure ... his condition, his fate as a man ... There is always a need for intoxication ... Perhaps love is above all the means which the Occidental uses to free himself from man's fate.'

The Lure of the Forbidden

The intensity of passionate love, its transformative potential, gains much from prohibition, which, before the more liberal regime of the Western present, was often a generalized prohibition against sex itself— certainly, for women, sex before marriage. Shakespeare's 'star-crossed lovers' Romeo and Juliet live out a 'death-marked love', doomed by the warring families from which they stem. Their passion feeds on defiance. So too does Humbert Humbert's for Annabel, lived as it is against parental vigilance. His later love for her reincarnation, Lolita, gathers its obsessive power from the very fact that it is a transgressive passion, lived out in the breach of taboos.

Outside the bounds of fiction, first love follows suit. The ever protean young must rebel, break away from parents and indeed their circle of friends, in order to forge a new bond.

Why do prohibition and the consequent need for secrecy, sometimes self-imposed, augment passion? Freud links this, first of all, to the incest taboo and the way we re-experience early moments when our sexual and affective instincts had an unobtainable incestuous object. Whatever weight we attach to his arguments, it is clear that the forbidden often doubles attraction, and that rebellion against prohibition is part and parcel of first love, and indeed in many cases, later loves, too. Sex, after all, is in the first instance about overcoming difference and distance.

For the young, this may be linked to a growing and insistent sense that separating oneself off from parents who can only designate one as 'child' is a dangerous and often messy business and needs radical enactment to be successful. Only with the impetus of a parental 'no', spoken or already understood and internalized, can a push away from Mum and Dad be strong enough to propel one into the distance of separateness and adulthood – and into a sexuality which is more and other than imaginings. Lurking, too, in the recesses of the mind is that fluttery sense that all fully desired ones are somehow forbidden, caught up in an incestuous family romance where Mummy and Daddy are coupled and close the doors on the child's omnivorous wishes. So passionate love is always already an experience that in fantasy exists within the realm of transgression. This may be why people so often find themselves so forcefully attracted to love objects of different ethnicities, class, or simply met on distant holidays – their unfamiliars.

After the advent of the pill in the sixties, when sex even for young women became generally permissible and a cohort of parents arrived who prohibited less systematically, it didn't take long for new self-generated prohibitions and rules to slot into place, particularly in the US. Fleetingly 'liberated' by the women's movement of the 1970s and the pill, momentarily free from the later plague of STDs, female desire was quickly enough again shackled by fear: men were not only exposed as power-mongers and oppressors, but increasingly subsumed under the category 'rapists'. Sexuality, briefly and freely 'fun', a site of open exploration, once more became dangerous. The sexuality of gays was no sooner out in the open than it was tragically shadowed by Aids. Regimes of 'safe sex' came into play and were often enough rebelled against: again, sex seemed to lose some of its lure without the impetus of transgression. Increasingly through the eighties and nineties, dating and love rules made their way on to American campuses in a flurry of political correctness: desire, love and sex were re-bound within a set of strictures that demarcated the limits of the permissible or the socially acceptable.

Outside the campuses, particularly in America, religion returned with a vocal evangelicism, again wrapping sex and love into the safe bundle of marriage. Where more liberal regimes were in operation, say in Britain or France, dating rules began to prescribe a kind of strict serial monogamy which forbade the casual infidelities of the brief moment of liberation.

In other quarters today, particularly amongst the urban very young, commodified, off-the-shelf, almost anonymized sex has become de rigueur, and the taboo is against linking it with any form of intimacy or love, any sense of commitment or continuity. Women as well as men are in play here. In a reversal of older romantic codes, to be 'cool' is to fuck, to perform sex in any position except the one that engenders feeling or sometimes even talk. This contemporary libertinage, seemingly transgressive, is itself as rule-bound as the older one that made virginity or purity the boundary which needed to be broken through for love to flourish.

Overcoming barriers in the self, catapulting inner defences and inhibitions, can be as potent as external prohibitions when it comes to falling in love. Traditionally, a father's forbidding 'no', internalized as a rule, could act as a stimulus. Today, it may be the equally forbidding 'no' to engaging fully with another human being as more than a body, a mere breathing version of a porn-site image, habitually revisited.

To love entails breaking through the secure, established, fixed boundaries of the known self. For some, particularly young women, this can mean conquering the disgust which the carnal — with its link to generation, to the dying human animal — can elicit. In one of their guises, this was the purpose of those old arts of seduction: the older man charmed the innocent maid into taking the bodily leap. For others, particularly boys, it can mean having to engage in aggression, where one might wish to be tender; tangling with power, where one might rationally prefer being equal. Love, in short, means violating inner defences: even that ideological defence which so-called sexual empowerment and its tally of casual sexual partners can today supply. A young woman who has had any number of sexual partners may well find herself 'in love' with the one man who won't sleep with her.

A breaking-away from the old, encased self into a new one forged through the link with another is what falling in love is all about. Risk is involved. So, too, is the adventure of finding oneself newly vulnerable, and despite this, hurtling towards the unknown who is the other. Without obstacles, without difficulties in the path to sexual satisfaction, Freud once wryly noted, 'love becomes worthless and life-empty'. In our permissive age, we grapple with new obstacles to re-infuse life and love with meaning.

The appeal of Stephenie Meyer's hugely popular young teen *Twilight* series and its accompanying films owes something to the way in which fantasy prohibitions stand in when society fails to provide real ones. Child of divorcees, no sooner has the heroine, Bella, been shipped away to the paternal home from the maternal one (while her mother holidays with her new husband) than she falls into romance with moody teen vampire, Edward. Now vampires really are more dangerous than the boy next door (who in this case anyway happens to be a werewolf). Thus there are substantial prohibitions for Bella to overcome so that the course of love may run deep and true – even if Edward's family has substituted a diet of animal blood for the traditional human one. The 'True Love Waits' pro-abstinence movement of its author has far fewer attractions in its prescriptiveness than the seductive danger of falling in love with a vampire – the daunting prohibition of supernatural exogamy. And when Bella in the last book of the series finally marries her vampire, she really does undergo that transformation that true love promises. She becomes an immortal. Heaven, it seems, comes with fangs, though Edward's have been whittled down and his teeth merely glow pearly white.

Orwell's *Nineteen Eighty-Four* provides a more radically textured instance of forbidden love's dangerously metamorphic potential. In this totalitarian dystopia where all life and thought outside the reach of the state are forbidden by the omnipresent surveillance of the Party, Orwell's hero Winston Smith acquires an inner existence, a sense of vital individuality which also means the ability to think for himself, through his secret and rebelliously risky love affair with Julia. 'If a right to a secret is not maintained, then we are in a totalitarian space,' the philosopher Jacques Derrida has written. Winston Smith's dawning secret and inner life, sparked by love, constitutes a revolt against the totalitarianism of Big Brother. The grave hazards he and Julia run in their love affair not only reshape them, but define a resistance to the state. Love is the ultimate challenge to an annihilating conformity which would stamp out the heart of individual life and the very language in which it thinks.

Indeed, the ultimate challenge for Orwell's imagined state is to repress and eliminate love and sex, including that rich, old English language which feeds and enshrines it. Love, of its very nature, Orwell underlines, breeds unorthodoxy. It's a loose cannon on the social scene. The imposed daily hate sessions which ritualize the sublimation of sexual energy are vehicles for turning all private love into a love and devotion directed only at Big Brother. The state's horrifying triumph at the book's end is marked by the fact that Winston, subjected to an exquisitely mental torture which requires him to betray his love, has subjugated his inner life. He now, at last, loves only Big Brother, the omniscient deity of the post-religious surveillance state, where privacy is outlawed.

In our far more ordinary lives, too, risk, rebellion and danger strengthen the love bond, and provide our inner lives with a range of deeper textures and hues. The combination of danger and sexuality is most potent during the years between puberty and the early twenties. As neuroscientists underline, the adolescent brain is still incompletely formed in its reasoning and planning centres. Charged with disturbing hormonal surges, it is also highly malleable. Just as in earliest childhood, impressions and sensations received during adolescence run deep. This is arguably what makes first love so powerful and memorable that it trails us for life, for good or ill. Some social scientists have even suggested, one would hope ironically, that it might be better somehow to skip its excitements, so as not to damage future, more stable, attachments. 'In an ideal world you would wake up already in your second relationship. If you had a passionate first relationship and allow that feeling to become your benchmark, it becomes inevitable that future, more adult partnerships will seem boring and a disappointment.'

Happily, we rarely allow social scientists altogether to rule our desires and dreams. Measures to promote our well-being, happiness quantifications, rarely alter the attraction we seem to feel for the torments of love and the anguish of displeasure. We are not in any simple way rational beings, nor do we always know where our satisfactions lie. Counter to rational expectations and despite the weight of a feminist critique of romance, the general belief amongst the young in transformative love remains, whatever the anguish quotient. It persists alongside ironical grumblings and cynical expressions of disbelief, and despite the flux of partners.

The New Religion

In *The Normal Chaos of Love*, sociologists Ulrich Beck and Elisabeth Beck-Gernsheim indeed argue that love has far too emphatically taken on a central role in shaping how we think of and live our lives. Love – unlike its nearest kin, the religion it displaced – gives us the illusion of being free agents who make intentional decisions. In an increasingly atomized late-capitalist world, where families are dispersed through financial imperatives, where society has become a matter of virtual networks and where politics has been devalued, love has become the prime measure of individuality and authenticity. It has become our god of privacy, meaning, romance, and all the highs of experience. We expect self-realization through our intimacies. When love is absent, we feel its lack strongly and set out to seek the raptures it may provide.

An overvaluation of passionate love may well bring disappointment in its train, particularly, as the authors argue, in times when parity between partners is seen as crucial. But so too does the kind of pragmatism that shuns any possible intensity and settles for mere convenience in relations.

Despite and alongside our preferred ironic mode, everywhere there are signals of renewed cultural hope in love. The extraordinary worldwide success of *Mamma Mia!*, the highest-grossing film musical of all time, is one such. A romantic fairy-tale dreamed by baby-boomers, it also acts as a mild corrective to the gender and generational relationships they put in place.

The film's heroine, Donna, played by Meryl Streep, is a feisty single mother who looks no more than forty. The blurring of time frames is part of the dream: we know she's sixty and the ABBA music dates from 1976. Donna has lived out her adult life on a paradisial Greek island where she has raised her daughter, Sophie, and built her slightly ramshackle home-hotel. On the verge of marriage, Sophie feels driven to find out who her father is: she can't make the leap into matrimony, break away from her mother and her childhood, without acquiring the stamp of paternal legitimacy. Indeed, there is a sense that her project of marriage, whatever love may be involved, is also the enactment of her wish to give her mother a responsible husband. Fathers are crucial, even if only symbolically, for the journey into adulthood, however fully the independent woman may have loved and provided for her child.

Enter three possible candidates, three icons of modern fairy-tale paternity, secretly invited to the wedding by Sophie: the architect, Sam, who drew the design of Donna's hotel on a sheet of paper; the roving über-male writer-adventurer, Bill; and the shy gay banker, Harry, for whom Donna marked his sole sexual encounter with a woman. Each of these anymen could be the perfect fairy-tale father. Having lived out her generation's 'hippy' and sexy adolescence, Donna has no idea which potential father is the actual one. But it is Sam who is her first and great love and, at the altar, it is he who steps in to be wed to Donna. Having supplied a husband for her mother, Sophie is now free to leave home and travel the world with her boyfriend, without needing to care for her parent, who was not quite complete in her single form. And Donna is free to live out the ultimate romantic fairy-tale, a return to that first transformative love, now publicly legitimized in marriage.

Ironically, the newest of technologies of both dream and information, the Internet, is abetting the traditional power of first love. Social sites such as Friends Reunited and Facebook make it easy to trace 'friends' long lost. Life may have ruptured that passionate first love because its partners were simply too young for 'commitment', or had disparate universities or jobs to go to. They may, in the intervening years, have married, had children and divorced. Now, through the Internet, they can rekindle that first passion. In an American survey of randomly selected adults, one-third said they would reunite with their first loves if they could. According to anecdotal lore, it's not altogether unusual for couples to rediscover each other and take up again, if not quite where they left off. Everyone seems to know one such happily-before-and-ever-after couple.

After the upheavals and disillusionments that life brings, it seems that first love can retain its old power and also bring new advantages. The old lover now feels almost familial, easy to be with. The new-old partners are returned to a more carefree youth. Each sees something in the other beyond the accretion of wrinkles. Love, Adam Phillips has noted, is, amongst much else, a recognition or mirroring, a making available through the other of aspects of oneself that have hitherto been occluded. So the return of first love may be a version of Blake's notion of wise innocence, the ultimate redemptive step after that innocence lost through the journey of experience. In the process, it may well be that our capacity for loving has also grown more generous, less rapacious. If first love is the breaking-out of revolutionary passion, its return, after the disappointments of life, is a form of re-pairing. The best of reparations, it brings youth and age together.

The Question of Sex

> Love is the answer, but while you're waiting for the answer, sex raises some good questions.
>
> Woody Allen

Voluptuous pleasure. All the senses in play – sight, sound, smell, touch. The body rampant, deliciously, supremely alive.

That will do. Sexual pleasure and words aren't natural bedfellows. If sex scenes have proliferated in contemporary literature, it's simply because sex for humans, even when performed alone, is rarely simply sex. The physical act with its soaring excitements, its pleasures and pains, usually comes accompanied by a host of often obscure desires, fantasies, needs, aspirations, familial and cultural attitudes – whatever our episodic wishes for a Lawrentian animal spontaneity. Trying to explain to himself the character of G., his revolutionary Don Juan of a protagonist, the writer John Berger reflects:

> When analyzed, sexual desire has components which are violently nostalgic and lead us as far back as the experience of birth itself: other components are the result of an ineradicable appetite for the unknown, the furthest away, the ultimate of life – which can only be found in its negation – death. At the moment of orgasm these two points in time, our beginning and our end, may seem to fuse into one. When this happens everything that lies between them, that is to say our whole life, becomes instantaneous.

The creation of erotic excitement is rarely a mere matter of the rubbing together of two epidermises. It can be, the psychoanalyst Robert Stoller writes, 'every bit as subtle, complex, inspired, profound, tidal, fascinating, awesome, problematic, unconscious-stalked, and genius-haunted as the creation of dreams or art'. Brain-imaging studies concur: orgasm is a subtle mixture of psychological and bodily impulses; it also requires 'a release of inhibitions, engineered by the brain's centre of vigilance'. In clinical trials of people who complain of low libido, placebo effects work as well (or as badly) as hormonal patches.

So sex begins well before penetration and its aftermath colours future acts. It may in many cases not include penetration at all, which is why President Clinton's assertion that his doings with Monica Lewinsky were not 'sex' raised such consternation. Why, too, technical sex education classes raise sniggers from the young and rarely hit the mark. Even in adolescence, when, particularly for boys, the body's urges feel paramount, the physical act brings much else in train – guilt, hatred, status, a sense of power, accomplishment or disappointment, perhaps even love.

A mere kiss, let alone penetration, transports you inside another's body: the liberation of breaking your own boundedness can be exalting.

Someone else is sharing you. Acknowledging the bits you hated or may have been ashamed of. You've emptied yourself of problems.

It can also be terrifying. You might be swallowed up, sucked into an abyss, disappear. Or you might feel invaded, poisoned, no longer an intact self.

Indeed, sex calls up the most intense, the most difficult feelings we have. The act is intrinsically bound up with who we are or may want to be. And even when there is no animal act in question, even when we're abstinent, we carry on having a relationship to desire or its lack.

When I was an undergraduate in the sixties, before the pill had come in and the women's movement had taken hold, virginity was still a freighted fact, far more substantial than the hymen which distinguished it. Losing one's virginity carried all the significance of a rite of passage from childhood to adulthood. There was a distinct before and a mysterious after. An aura of danger attended the act. The risk of pregnancy, the tales of torrents of blood, were real enough. But there was less tangible matter, too. If something was to be lost – what did that loss entail? Purity and chastity were symbolically loaded words. Yet what meaning could they hold after all those excited fumblings on sofas and back seats of cars? God had little place in my family, and my Dad, his only representative, much as he might scowl at some of the boys who entered the family house, had little time for such decidedly female matters. Mothers, and not only my own, were clear enough: what potential husband would want used, let alone soiled, goods?

None of my circle of female friends paid much heed. We were rebellious. We were certainly not going to become suburban wives and mothers. Though we were still some years away from Alex Comfort's *Joy of Sex* (1972), we all knew that in sex lay a treasure trove of experience. We read D.H. Lawrence, after all, and Lawrence Durrell's *Alexandria Quartet* was making the rounds. Though his sly character Pursewarden may have written a postcard upbraiding Lawrence for his 'habit of building a Taj Mahal around anything as simple as a good f—k', we somehow wanted both the sacred Taj Mahal and the excited seriality of Durrell's 'simple' sex. All that stood in the way of both was virginity. But that tiny membrane was resistant and sometimes felt as big as Sisyphus's boulder. You'd get to a certain point and something would stop you. Boys, too, were a little in awe, even when they had managed to lose their own less burdensome virginity with one or t'other of the more 'forward' girls at school.

Much has changed since my youth, when sex and pregnancy came in one dangerously glittering package. Now first sex, if not necessarily first love, comes for most young people at the age of about sixteen and a half in the US, Canada and Britain, far younger for some. The rest of Europe has followed suit. First sex often long predates marriage or cohabitation, which comes for the majority as they move towards thirty. Most women, like most men, will have sex in their teens and may well have a series of partners before engaging in a long-term relationship. Young women who grow up in immigrant families from more traditional cultures are caught in painful contradictory tugs between what their families ordain and what their peers enact. The increasing number of young Muslim women in Britain who have donned the hijab or the burkha, in the process perhaps rebelling against the more moderate customs of their parents, are engaging in a rebellion against both their parents and the culture's permissiveness.

For women first sex may still invoke or provoke first love. But the experience that once united them is now widely separated. In clubs or on campuses in Britain and America, the young hook up for a night or three or more, with no strings or even names attached. Intimacy, not to mention social or emotional continuity, is not an issue. Alternatively, in another standard arrangement, 'friends with benefits' provide sex for each other without any acknowledgement that the act has taken place, until one or other of them may grow attached, and then it's time to 'move on'. The package of love and sex has been dismantled – or so the blithe, socially accepted, hypothesis would have it.

Though disciplinary voices decry our sexually permissive times and idealize earlier supposedly more moral epochs, these, for certain sections of the male population, had equally casual sexual arrangements. More stringent codes brought their own burden of ills, and not only for those sectors of Western society who sought to conform to the rules of 'respectability' that the nineteenth century enshrined and which were reinvigorated for some fifteen years after the Second World War. In his novella *On Chesil Beach* Ian McEwan minutely describes the excruciating wedding night of a 'young, educated' couple whose lives are blighted because their union took place at a time just before the sexual revolution, 'when a conversation about sexual difficulties was plainly impossible'. His hero Edward's sudden and premature ejaculation, which sends his heroine Florence into a panic of revulsion, precipitates the end of their marriage before it has quite begun. This despite their genuine love for one another: Edward never meets anyone, he reflects in his sixties, 'he had loved as much'.

Freud was only one of many reformers to analyse the human damage repressive sexual mores can precipitate. Before the Great War when middle-class men married late and women were kept shrouded in sexual ignorance, the toll in middle-class neuroses was high. It was more than equalled by the social cost of rampant prostitution and the often destructive, cavalier relations between the bourgeois male and any number of shop or servant girls, sexual stand-ins for 'respectable' women imprisoned as objects of idealized love, even when their own desires might eventually dictate otherwise.

It's useful to remember here that people have always coupled once their bodies permitted it and often enough before, whatever the prevailing moral regime and attendant public discourse. Agrarian workers, servants, the industrial working class, the hordes of child prostitutes who populated Victorian cities engaged in what we now call teenage and unmarried sex, even when the Church railed against it and the moral climate was one that sought to keep the middle classes pure and sexual activity repressed. Though illegitimacy rates through history are hard to come by with any accuracy, they do indicate that in country and city alike 'illicit' sex was engaged in and babies born at rates that bear comparison with our own, though whether our high rates of contraception equal previous epochs' unreported rates of illegitimacy is something that can only be guessed at. Suffice it to say that as the nineteenth century turned into the twentieth, in Munich, one-third of *all* children were born out of wedlock. The growth of foundling hospitals suggests a similar story for an earlier period; while the ravages of syphilis throughout the nineteenth century until a cure was found in 1910 indicate that human beings engaged in the 'animal act' outside marriage whatever the dictates of Church and state.

Indeed, as that greatest of Renaissance sages, Michel de Montaigne, wrote towards the end of his life and centuries before Freud or Lawrence or our permissive West had launched its sexual revolution: 'The whole movement of the world tends and leads towards copulation. It is a substance infused through everything, it is the centre towards which all things turn.' Nor did Montaigne, who lived in times when chastity for women was prized and enforced, here differentiate between the sexes: both women and men are subject to Venus's 'frenzy', he tells us, citing a host of classical texts from Plato to Virgil to bolster his case – and, good modern that he is, propping it up further with ethnographic examples.

Our own sexual revolution has come in tandem with a social revolution. We no longer quite so emphatically have differing 'rules' for the rich and for the poor, for men and for women. The double standards of past centuries no longer prevail. Gone are the epochs that saw one law for the male, permitted sexual congress from a young age, albeit sometimes under the cloak of hypocrisy, and another for the young woman exhorted to keep her virginity intact until what might well be a late marriage. Yet the traces of such attitudes linger within us and without, even when they no longer carry the weight of general consensus. In our globalized and multicultural world, we are ever and always aware of places elsewhere and in our own midst where they are also intact. The vying forces of puritan religions – for instance, the Catholic stance against contraception, Evangelical edicts against premarital sex, Muslim injunctions on female modesty and against homosexuality – and commercialized sexual permissiveness are internalized as contradictions and rumble uncomfortably through individual lives.

We may want sex and hate our bodies or feel little pleasure in what they get up to; or engage in sex, while feeling alienated from or disavowing what we do. We may perform sex with the rampant exhibitionism or increasing brutality of porn stars. In a West where neural and chemical explanations are becoming so dominant, we instrumentalize sex and translate it into a matter of healthy highs – less intercourse, a conversation between two bodies and the people inhabiting them, than a solitary performance enacted for our own seeming good.

Pleasure can remain elusive, or become as addictive as a drug, its compulsively sought highs never quite satisfying enough in repetition. Alternatively, as one suspects from the confessional detailing of the sex stars of the blogosphere, such as Abby Lee aka Zoe Margolis, the pleasure may come as much from the anonymous telling, sharing and writing of it as from the assiduous repetition of performance. Teenagers today may get far more satisfaction from detailing their conquests to friends than from the act itself, sometimes forgotten in a mist of accompanying drugs or drink. We are narrative creatures, and the stories we tell friends and ourselves occupy our consciousness for longer than the acts we engage in.

Excess and Its Discontents

In contemporary Western societies, the radical transformation of woman's condition has probably been the most important factor in leading to a shift in attitudes to love and sex. Girls brought up in the eighties and nineties largely believe they can do anything that boys can do, whether it is a question of career, working life or having a multiplicity of sexual partners and 'behaving badly'. Manifestations of girl power are everywhere, most notably in school achievement and university attendance. Equality is hardly total, as the statistics on glass ceilings and women's pay make clear. However, since the sixties, a proliferation of women has moved out of the private world of home into the public sphere. Politicians, journalists, newspaper editors, broadcasters, business leaders, academics, even scientists can be and are female. So, too, is a panoply of celebrities, some of whom have risen on little more than a display of surgically enhanced body parts.

Change, of course, is never simple and brings backlash from certain quarters as well as a host of paradoxes in its wake. Women no sooner win certain equalities in the workplace than studies with a scientific imprimatur come along to naturalize an array of characteristics which clearly contain a large cultural component – from their supposed shortcomings in the field of scientific abstraction to their supposed relational proclivities. Men are no sooner applauded for bringing their 'sensitivities', their 'new man' sides, into play than evolutionary biologists remind

them that they can't help their genetically propelled selfish rapacious-
ness. With the boost of a twenty-four-hour and omnipresent media,
ever hungry for stories and simplifications, such 'science' feeds into the
creation of urban legends and cultural myths and engenders contagious looping effects, self-fulfilling prophecies: as with horoscopes, we
tend to find in ourselves and others the very properties we are told we
have and name them 'essential'.

So, too, within our personal lives, there are no clean breaks where sex
and love come into play. Embedded in the structures of family life and
in the cultural sphere, their traditions haunt us through the generations and shape what are often enough unconscious habits and
expectations. We may not always want what we think we want. Nor do
we want it all the time. We may want exhilarating sexual freedom, yet
tire of its enactment. Women may want what men have always seemed
to have. They certainly want equality and no longer go along with male
primacy and sexual dominance, or they may want to mimic the supposed dislocation between sex and emotion that men seem to find so
easy – one of the plot lines for *Sex and the City*.

Yet women may still in intimate relations also want men who are or
can be idealized as superior to them – stronger, more powerful, more
intelligent, more like that Daddy who stood so tall and powerful in
their infancy, before he went off to satisfy his lusts and left Mummy
crying in the bathroom. Or they may love the Mummy in their men,
since that was where they learned to love, yet that tenderness may bear
little relation to the penetrative act. They may laugh at the trappings of
romance, yet simultaneously yearn for it, with either a gay or a heterosexual partner. They may want to engage in 'easy' sexual relations –
with men or women – while continuing to believe in and wanting 'the
one and only'. They may want babies, though they may not necessarily
want them with the men with whom they have sex. These inner contradictions breed dissatisfaction: when unacknowledged, they can lead
to a succession of partners blamed for the lacks that reside in the self's
own murky conflicts.

Driven by the damaging, hypersexualized images in our media,
women certainly internalize too young an injunction to look attractive
and be brazenly 'sexy', enact a Barbie-like aesthetic or mimic glamour

models or play at *Sex and the City*. But at the same time, they want to be considered for more and other than their looks. Or they may confuse 'empowerment' with the freedom to behave like porn stars, to 'behave badly', learning too late that when the men they want to entice behave badly, it often brings violence in its train.

There is nothing unusual in any of this. The muddle exists and is all too human. It can only grow in our image-rich world where young women's bodies, air-brushed into the year's iconic perfection, are still used to convey the desirability of any number of products, while women themselves are urged to tone, exercise, massage, diet, and undergo surgical interventions to attain that perfected youthful desirability. All this brings along with it the heavy goods train of rampant anxiety.

When things change for women, they change for men, too: women's sexual liberation has liberated male sexuality. It has also created equivalent muddles and ambivalences for men. Even if young men, before the advent of the pill, had easier access to sex than women, they would certainly, if middle-class, have had to scale a class or age divide to find lovers. Their peers were forbidden sexual territory: here respect, courtesy, an extended courtship ritual was demanded of them. This is far less necessary if women do the chasing or the asking or have already engaged in sex with numerous partners.

But while, rationally, a young man may have bought into the 'sexual equality' culture, he may nonetheless feel ill at ease with it, threatened by a woman's sexual experience, let alone her dominance. This can somehow 'unman' him. Boys, young women say – and it is largely to women that they speak their fears – worry about their comparative experience, prowess and size. Often, too, they can have a residual sense that a woman who has had a string of partners is somehow unclean, something of a slut, and can be no sooner had than abandoned. Though they say they want a partner who is sexually, intellectually and economically their equal, they are also uneasy about it and complain that 'women have lost their capacity for kindness', that 'they don't know how to compromise'.

The challenge to men to rewrite traditional sexual scripts has come hand in hand with a growth in pornography and reported violence against women. A 2009 report by the British children's charity, the NSPCC, revealed that a third of teenage girls suffered from unwanted sexual acts; one in four, some as young as thirteen, had been hit by their boyfriends, 'one in nine had been beaten up, hit by objects or strangled', while a million women a year were victims of domestic violence.

Immersed in film and visual violence, sometimes alongside a history of violence at home, trapped in a sense of inadequacy, young men lash out, exhibiting strength where it doesn't otherwise reside. The increasing sexualization of ever younger women's bodies abets the process, making it difficult for a 'no' to sex to be respected. So, too, does porn, so pervasive now amongst all age groups, even children, that it is radically altering our experience of human bodies and sexuality, distorting our expectations of the human. A stimulus to solitary sex, porn provides none of the challenges of an embodied other, who can come and go, talk back and laugh or evoke a need that can't be answered. Instead it offers an array of sexual objects who stimulate, without demanding emotion or intimacy. The gaze is in charge, the two-dimensional image complicit in returning to the man absolute phallic power. The rise of violence against women and the rise and rise of porn, the total and addictive power of the click that can delete and make manifest in rapid succession, are perhaps in part a destructive response to the waning of female complicity in assuring men of their dominance. For the young, particularly girls, porn, like all visual culture, educates them in aspiring to a 'look' that asks to be mimicked, since this is what men seem to want. So on with those five-inch heels that damage backs, and a variety of sexual acts that may garner applause for performance, but little more. Gay culture is enmeshed in the same dynamic.

Our cultural emphasis on sex as 'casual' – that body, mind, sexuality and psyche somehow walk separate paths – can mask the fact that all sexual relations carry some intimate meaning, however short-lived or hidden. Defending against that meaning, disavowing it, can store up difficulties for those occasions when it needs to come into play. Witness the slide into so-called commitment-phobia that plagues the agony columns of our day. Even when the young may feel a need for 'commitment', it is all too easy to fall prey to the unending search for the perfect partner, blind to the fact that no being, let alone oneself, is perfect.

Our desire, Adam Phillips has noted, is always in excess of the object's capacity to satisfy it. Humans regularly want more than they can have or can in fact live with. We all know stories of children (or adults), like Freud's daughter Anna, who dream of more and more 'stwaberries' or chocolate cake, yet the gorging results in stomach ache. Our sexual fantasies, whether spurred by romance or porn, can as easily disguise or displace our wants as express them: the satisfactions they promise can lie in the promise alone. Though we may pursue them, they are rarely an utterly realistic indication of our wants.

One way of understanding the Don Giovanni character ever in pursuit of a new conquest is to grasp that he is as much or more interested in keeping the tally of his *mille tre* – one thousand and three – with his servant, Leporello, than in the conquest of the actual women he rapes or seduces. The satisfaction of the mounting list seems to be greater than that of the activity engaged in. Indeed, fantasies may well keep at bay a sense of hopelessness, but their realization, like the wishes fulfilled in a fairy-tale, often end in unhappiness.

So, too, the restless pursuit of ever more women may disguise or displace inner difficulties and inhibitions: the man may not want a 'better' or 'more suitable' woman at all, but to be recognized by his peers, or by his mother or father. This is complicated by the fact that men seem to have a particular talent for separation: early in childhood they give up their first love object – the mother who, at best, offered unconditional love – in order to become males, like their fathers. A casual sexual environment makes the repeated leaving of relationships far simpler for them than it is for women – even though it may leave neither particularly satisfied. Or the man may need to hide, especially from himself, an unconscious dependency on a powerful mother: fearing her replication in a girlfriend, fearing a trap or engulfment, his manhood is proved by abandoning her. Indeed, men's age-long misogyny, amongst much else, masks a panic about helplessness, a fear of the overpowering mother of infancy.

Added to all this, men's bodies too have now become objects of consumer desire, eased, certainly in the media, by an acceptance of gay culture. Gone are the days when men were valued largely for their actions or status. Beautiful muscled hunks adorn hoardings and strut through ads. Well defined shoulders, the six-pack abdomen, preoccupy youths in gyms and – sometimes guiltily – outside them. Just as women now bear the challenge of competing in the workplace, so men now feel they need to compete in the body-beautiful stakes. Eating disorders amongst young men are on the rise.

The relative ease and acceptability of homosexual encounters, while a definite plus for men and women who are certain they are gay, has created other kinds of difficulties. If you make love with someone of your own sex, as a proportion of the young do and have long done, does that mean you have to enter a domain of fixed biological or cultural identity? There may be pressures to do with 'coming out' or even deciding on a permanent 'identity' for yourself, gay or straight, at a period of love and life when experimentation is rife and all identities relatively fluid. Then, too, while it can be exhilarating to have a greater option of gendered and age relationships, too much choice can be hard to bear. Its very proliferation can create deep anxieties, or indeed that paralysis of the will which has now become medicalized into depression. A choice means giving something up, and we have lived through a long cultural moment in which a greedy more and more, rather than an austere less, has been vaunted.

The public climate has altered radically since my youth in another way, too. Lady Chatterley no longer has to be read covertly under the bedsheets in order to gain a sense of what sex might be: images of love and sex proliferate. Advice is everywhere on hand: 'Tips for Mind-blowing Foreplay', '40 Ways to Have the Best Sex of Your Life', '100 Sex Positions You've Never Tried' – such articles fill magazines for young and middle-aged alike, even increasingly for the old. Film, television, magazines, newspapers, books and the Internet explicitly not only portray sexual acts but also make available an attendant language of emotion and relationship. Millions of columns and websites offer know-how on everything from how to get and keep your mate to how to behave in bed to maximize an assortment of pleasures. Details of intimate lives, real or fictional, circulate freely. Sex sells, as does sex advice. Yet its commodification brings us little pleasure and less fulfilment, though it brings its purveyors a great deal of dosh.

Throughout the nineties and the beginning of this century, 'to have sex' — as if it were a thing rather than an act which brought some interiority of self and other into play — has become something of an injunction in the West. Sex is ubiquitous. Millions of billboards, films, adverts, television programmes and porn sites have turned sexiness into a desirable commodity, one that brings glamour, cool and happiness. Yet this visual sex that turns us all into voyeurs bears little relationship to the reality and variety of living bodies, their feel, their touch and smell, their imperfections and precise delights — not to mention the reality of the people who inhabit them.

Meanwhile, self-help and how-to books tell us how to perform sex well and often, while achieving the necessary orgiastic bliss for both partners and on every occasion. Polls count the too-much or the too-little of it that people have or want, and simultaneously count the discrepancies in truth-telling between the sexes: men, it seems, exaggerate upwards and women downwards. (Memory is as selective in this area as in others; we'd rather forget what doesn't accord with our self-image.) Divorced from love or any idea of an enduring relationship or, often enough, the marker of 'health' in an ongoing one, frequent, varied and orgasmic sex, perhaps accompanied by one or other of a proliferation of toys and aids, has become the measure of a good life. Even grandparents feel they have to have 'it'.

Whereas the Freudian superego, that part of the self which, like a conscience, takes in and acts on behalf of the parental and public order, turned sex into something prohibited, dirty and a drain on vital inner resources, today's superego could be said to issue a command to rampant, calisthenically perfected sexuality. Sex has become hard work. The goals and targets issued by an equally rampant advice industry defy the pleasurableness of pleasure. To cap it all, sexual performance has also become a crucial marker on that touted gauge of 'self-esteem' we are all urged to live by — as if self-esteem could always be rationally elicited. Girls of thirteen in Philadelphia suburbs feel impelled to give boys blow jobs on school buses. Other young women, prey to the culture that makes advertised images more potent than lived experience,

post mobile-phone pictures of themselves 'doing it' to boyfriends, only
to find them generally available on the Web once the relationship is
over. Pensioners on singles holidays boast of their exploits, often fuelled
by Viagra. Families are torn asunder because wife or husband isn't providing that seemingly most vital of commodities, according to the
performance targets or rates laid down by the latest magazine or expert.
Young, middle-aged and newly young old inwardly flagellate themselves because they're not living up to the supposedly universal
standard of sexual fulfilment now enshrined as a right – as well as a
marker of good physical and mental health.

Few seem satisfied, or satisfied for long, under this new aegis. It is as
if a public disciplinarian authority has stepped in to encourage and
monitor activity in a private park where pleasure lies in the very fact of
secret intimacy, unexpectedness and at least an aura of transgression.
Therapeutic or medicalized 'normality' may have displaced Victorian
morality, but anxiety about performance targets or pleasure levels
seems to be no easier to bear than guilt. A balance here has been tipped,
and things are awry. We have grown more concerned about this
fetishized thing called sex than about those with whom we engage in it.

What does it mean to live in a society where excess is seen as a desirable
good – enshrined in the lives of our stars, whose insatiable greed often
extends beyond multiple partners to drugs, wealth, even an accumula-
tion of babies; or alternatively, into an excess of purity, of the kind that
we see in anorexia or religious fundamentalisms? The excess of others,
as Adam Phillips has pointed out, can fill us, sometimes simultaneously, with both fascination and amazement as well as envy, disgust
and a wish to be punitive. So what is this excess about? Phillips cites
examples of so-called commitment-phobes, men who come to the consulting room because 'they are either more promiscuous than they
want to be or more celibate than they want to be'. He also cites the case
of Kafka's Hunger Artist, a man who performs fasting for a living.
'Asked why he devoted himself to starving himself in public,' the
Hunger Artist answers he couldn't help doing it '"because I couldn't
find the food I liked. If I had found it, believe me, I should have made no
fuss and stuffed myself like you and everyone else."'

So excesses of appetite can be ways by which we conceal from ourselves what we actually hunger for. We grow greedy because what we are getting is not what we want, and believe that more might meet the need and satisfy. We grow greedy, too, out of envy, that most insidious of emotions, 'that pain caused by the good fortune of others', as Aristotle put it: in our times of relative plenty, trumpeted through the image global-sphere, others' sexual plenty is always there to entice and propel more want and more hate.

Excess may also be a way of avoiding making choices, since choosing entails giving up some pleasures for others. Excess, Phillips states, is always linked to some kind of core deprivation and is a noisy statement about that hidden lack. Excess may be a shout of despair or a sign of frustration or an underlying fear of scarcity. The excess of others, reminding us as it does of our own lacks and putting envy into motion, also leads us to want to punish them for what we perceive them to have.

Evangelical groups in the US and religious authorities everywhere have for several decades been fulminating against our 'permissive' society and its loose sexual mores. They have made attempts to keep the young pure until marriage vows are exchanged by promoting the 'blessings' of abstinence through movements such as the 'Silver Ring Thing'. But now, even amongst the urban young brought up on *Sex and the City*, there are voiced indications of discontent with excesses of casual sex and its decoupling from love. The young want change. Several of my informants in their early twenties, who had had a string of sexual relations in their teens, told me there were moves afoot towards a new 'celibacy'. Although they profess themselves too wise for any 'thunderbolt' view of love, they have a wish to 'resacralize' love and confirm its privileged status. Sex, casually or drunkenly engaged in, has lost its meaning and its moorings. Celibacy has taken on some of its transformative potential: no sexual behaviour has become more transgressive than the defiant avoidance of sex itself.

In her book *Chastened: No More Sex in the City*, Hephzibah Anderson, a London journalist in her thirties, charts the year of celibacy she decided to undertake because 'the kind of sex I was supposed to be cool with as a post-feminist, twenty-first-century woman — a casual sort of intimacy without intimacy – was not working for me'. Sex and its pursuit, she notes, had become such 'blood sports, their rules so confusing and their standards so exacting', that she had begun to wonder whether it was worth engaging in another round of 'bedroom tennis'. The decision to spend a celibate year is sparked by a coincidental sighting of her first love in New York, the great passion of her university years, the only man who had said 'I love you' to her. The love didn't survive the move into careers. Though single life at first beckoned with all the glamour of a giddy succession of liaisons, the sighting of her first love buying a ring for someone else precipitated a sense that her chosen life had lost its meaning. A steamy affair in which she felt utterly 'twinned' with her lover followed, only to end with him returning to the absent partner he had never lied about having. In the comedown that followed, she decided that she'd 'had enough sex without love. Maybe it was time to look for love without sex.'

Some of the young, it seems, are rebelling against our oversexualized culture that robs sex of meaning and replaces it with the anxiety of goals and pursuit. More does not necessarily mean better. 'Others' are not commodities conferring glamour. The supermarket of sexual dreams may have reached its sell-by date. A rebalancing towards austerity may offer greater satisfactions. It may also provide greater passion.

Finding Mr Right

After the intense and shaping passions of first youth, after the pleasures and pains of serial sexual encounters, most of us, straight or gay, wish for more settled loving unions. But how – in a world of glossy, throwaway consumables and few repair services, a world where women are economically independent and men have been loosened from the traditional masculine bond of protecting and providing for wife and family – are we to establish relations of love that will last beyond the next temptation to instant gratification or the next shopping expedition? And how do we identify Mr or Ms Right while simultaneously 'falling' into love?

In 1995 a self-help book appeared on the American market which spoke to our anxieties about the whole process of locating the right mate and also pointed to its underlying contradictions. *The Rules: Time-Tested Secrets for Capturing the Heart of Mr Right*, by Ellen Fein and Sherrie Schneider, quickly became a *New York Times* bestseller and made its way across the world – from Japan and Korea to Romania and Iceland and twenty-six languages in between. The book not only sold millions of copies but found its message reproduced in thousands of column inches, websites and television programmes. It had tapped into a malaise at the core of millennial culture.

Part of the book's success may simply have had to do with the fact that it satisfied a subliminal wish for rules per se at a moment when too few existed, and freedom, let alone its slippery linkage with the pursuit of happiness, was proving hard to handle. But the 'time-tested' rules the book offered for capturing hearts also spoke to independent women who woke up in their early thirties to find that marriage, despite the satisfactions of work and a string of affairs, might be as elusive as it was desirable. Indeed, the popularity of *The Rules* betrays a continuing contemporary bewilderment, a deep anxiety about appropriate modern codes for a mating game which will somehow lead to that ancient, and still desirable, state of marriage or enduring cohabitation.

Immersed as we are in a market turnover culture, most especially so in America, it would seem that we have unconsciously allowed its consumerist diktats to segue into the way we form sentimental attachments, chucking them aside as soon as they lose their gloss. We urgently make use of those 'mating' opportunities that parties, singles nights and holidays supply. Thousands of Internet sites display warehouse quantities of potential partners, each more glittering in their attributes than the last, and reduce human connection to a spree in a hypermarket. Speed-dating and 'eye-gazing parties' – two minutes per gaze, fifteen gazes – diminish that potential special someone to an object, no sooner found than disposable.

There's more. Mobile, often cast adrift from family and that major social space, the workplace – from which flirtation, 'eye-gazing' and certainly sexual contact has in theory, if not in practice, been banished by another set of rules – the contemporary individual is often hooked on virtual networks of friends and fantasy life. Yet this free market in fantasy, with its aura of infinite possibilities, its underlying injunction to get the best and most out of our lives and loves, clashes with what we understand as love. The Mr or Ms Right who ticks all the boxes of our rationalized desires on dating websites only rarely ticks quite enough of them when we meet.

Falling in love has long been an unpredictable and risky business, dauntingly allergic to management codes of risk assessment and risk aversity, never mind health and safety, that we seem to have imported to the task. Romance and instrumentalism, loving and using the other as a means to an end, just won't sit happily side by side. Though, of course, if we take love out of the marriage equation, instrumentalism has long been the name of the marital game. Women have traded their compliance and sexual favours for security and a step up the financial ladder; while men have found either a domestic servant or a cultural or monetary asset in a wife, all the while securing the family line.

In fact, dating agencies bear some relationship to old-fashioned matchmakers. They act as higher authorities taking on the onus of choice for the individual in question. We may consciously spurn 'arranged marriages', and yet we turn to the contemporary virtual arrangers. Arranged marriages, from all the evidence even within Western minority cultures, can work, but the kind of love in play is rarely that tumultuous racing of all the senses that we associate with the 'falling' of falling in love. Security and the unpredictability that governs passion are ever at odds.

The philosopher, Jacques Derrida provides us with a clue here. When we say we love someone, do we mean that we love him for his absolute singularity or do we love something in him, a set of qualities? People often confuse the 'who' and the 'what'. When we fall in love, we seem to focus on the who, the singularity of the other. Yet, when we fall out of love, we usually name a set of characteristics that irritate. When we search for love through dating agencies, we list qualities, yet the singularity of the person, when met, doesn't match up: we just don't fall. This underlying division in love between the who and the what confounds affairs of the heart.

In our cultural emphasis on choice, another obstacle lurks. A single choice of mate, once made, locks out other possibilities. Our time's pervasive wish for more and future better can cast a pall of dissatisfaction over the here and now. Propelled to carry on the chase of choice, anxiety sets in, a whiff of desperation, particularly for women who have the added worry of the ticking away of the biological clock.

Trapped as we are in this predicament, it is perhaps not surprising that a 'time-tested' solution to the mating game might appeal. Perhaps grandmother's rules were right. She got her man, after all. And the way to get him, the rule book tells us, is to resist. To play hard to get. To play the romantic game. Those feminist fulminations against romance for imprisoning women in a masquerade of femininity deserve a backlash.

'*The Rules* isn't just a book. It's a movement, honey,' Oprah declared, evoking an AA for troubled women daters. More rules speedily followed — *The Rules 2: More Rules to Live and Love By*, *The Rules for On-line Dating* and *The Rules for Marriage*. *The Rules* website, which offers telephone consultations with the authors, courses, success stories, support groups, also offers the top ten rules for capturing Mr Right. The first exhorts the reader to 'Be a creature unlike any other':

> Being a creature unlike any other is really an attitude, a sense of confidence and radiance that permeates your being from head to toe. It's the way you smile (you light up the room), pause in between sentences (you don't babble on out of nervousness), listen (attentively), look (demurely, never stare), breathe (slowly), stand (straight) and walk (briskly, with your shoulders back). When a relationship doesn't work out, you brush away a tear so that it doesn't smudge your makeup and you move on!

The Rules goes on to offer the kind of advice my mother, born early in the last century, was prone to: success in the dating game depends on playing hard to get, letting the man chase you until you catch him, never being too forward, listening, and making the poor male (who of course never has an inkling that you're game-playing) feel superior.

Here are some of those rules.

1 Don't talk to a man first (and don't ask him to dance).

2 Don't meet him halfway or go Dutch with him on a date.

3 Don't call him and rarely return his phone calls.

4 Always end phone calls first.

5 Don't accept a Saturday night date after Wednesday.

6 Always end the date first.

7 Stop dating him if he doesn't buy you a romantic gift for your
   birthday or Valentine's day.

8 Don't see him more than once or twice a week.

9 No more than casual kissing on the first date.

10 Don't tell him what to do.

11 Don't expect a man to change or try to change him.

12 Don't open up too fast.

13 Don't date a married man.

14 Be easy to live with.

15 Don't stare at men or talk too much.

16 Don't live with a man (or leave your things in his apartment).

Some of this advice adds up to what our grandmothers would have
taken as the givens of womanly self-respect, accompanied by the need
to 'charm'. Pleasing those in power has always been the strategy of
those who have less. Given centuries of economic dependence, women
had long internalized the value of it, learning its ways in the Oedipal
hothouse of the family where Daddy's attention was a good competi-
tively to be sought. Independent working lives brought other
characteristics to the fore and threw the ever uneasy balance between
the public and the private askew for both sexes. Yet if past witnesses to
our inner lives are anything to go by, negotiating intimacy has rarely
been simple, whether one is Stendhal, that expert analyst of the process
of love whose own most ardent desires were never requited, or
Elizabeth Barrett Browning, whose miraculous love affair with Robert

Browning lifted her from her sickbed only at the late age of thirty-nine and because, as a poet, she had already accomplished much.

The Rules may mark a wish for dating to revert to a delicate romantic game between a wooing man and a courted woman. Yet the basis of its programmatic exhortations is decidedly modern. These dos and don'ts of male manipulation assume that a show of that feature basic to most modish self-help manuals, 'confident self-esteem', will stand in for those characteristics that might genuinely elicit it. Attitude, it seems, is all for material girls made in Madonna's image, whether it's a self-invention of supposedly empowered sexiness or traditional submissiveness. The right mix of makeup, clothes and a coy manner will turn everywoman into Cinderella. But if posing as the person you're not is the way to catch Mr Right, this hardly bodes well for the subsequent marriage.

Comforting as it may be to have time-tested rules to live by, the injunctions for capturing the heart of Mr Right contain a number of decidedly odd underlying assumptions at which our grandmothers would have baulked. They take it as given that there is a single, unique Mr Right, and that he belongs to a wild male tribe, so contemptible as far as intelligence is concerned that he can be captured by a manipulative performance of femininity as 'bait'.

The linked assumption is that men don't want to be 'tamed' – or to change the discourse, that men are in fact the evolutionary psychologists' fundamental male: a hoary hunter only and ever in search of reproduction, for whom the female of the species is a mere receptacle for sperm. Both presumptions contain a large element of fantasy and an admixture of observed truth. In traditional societies, and before the pill, men of course had the power to roam freely, to seduce and abandon. In our more equal and permissive times, men (but women, too) may indeed change partners more readily than our grandparents would have approved. Like women, all too many have bought into the metaphor of the 'selfish gene' and expanded it into a template for serial relationships. However, men marry or live in partnerships as often as women do – more often, if one calculates the current tendency for late divorce and men's greater access to younger generations. (That, indeed, may be the rub!) Nor are many men the rakish Don Juans women seem both obsessed by and – in fantasy, at least – so attracted to.

Even that arch-seducer Valmont, at the end of his *liaisons dangereuses*, finds himself in love with the virtuous Madame de Tourvel, the woman he had set out merely to seduce. Men are, indeed, as complicated as women – and since we serve as their mothers, we would hope they are as capable of loving.

The year following the publication of *The Rules* a different kind of dating book appeared, this time in Britain. *Bridget Jones's Diary*, a sparkling satire of everyday singleton life, also rose into worldwide bestsellerdom, spawned a sequel and a series of films. Plump, boozy, chain-smoking, foul-mouthed and accident-prone, Bridget Jones is an endearing working woman in her early thirties. Though she loathes the 'smug marrieds' in her entourage, she longs for a romantic attachment that will transport her into the married state: after all, she doesn't want to die alone, her remains to be eaten by some mangy dog. Meanwhile, her diary chronicles her obsessions, her love life, her countless ever broken resolutions to transform herself into the svelte, non-smoking, perfected self who will win Mr Right. There are two men in her sights: her publishing boss, Daniel Cleaver, the deceitful seducer whose charms are impossible to resist despite his 'fuckwittage', the emotional tumult his doings cast Bridget into; and Mark Darcy, the upright and uptight human rights lawyer, at first infinitely resistible.

Bridget Jones's Diary as everyone knows is a contemporary take on Jane Austen's *Pride and Prejudice*, that other surprise hit of the turn of the century, made into an oft-repeated television series first screened in 1995, and a film in 2005. In 2008 came *Lost in Austen*, another popular television series which has a contemporary young woman, mad about *Pride and Prejudice*, travelling back in time to the original site of 'courteous' love. Post-feminists, it appears, yearn for the weddings Jane Austen provides to culminate a span of courtship, itself replete with pitfalls and hurdles. Americans, *Time Magazine* noted in 2007, spend $50 billion a year on weddings. An Irish bridal gown website went so far as to use Simone de Beauvoir's famous adage about the cultural conditioning that made girls into subordinate creatures – 'One is not born, but rather becomes a woman' – as advertising copy. The topsy-turvy suggestion here is that a deliciously cream-puff-white wedding is all any girl needs so as to become that now desirable entity, woman – and married, to boot.

Comparing Jane Austen's comedy of manners to *Bridget Jones's Diary* and *The Rules* tells us something about the road love and marriage have travelled. Published in 1813, though begun before the turn of the century under the title 'First Impressions', the novel coincides with the period when the sentimental marriage, a union based on love, was effectively consolidated as a cultural wish, if not quite a reality: the book still bears many of the traces of marriage's older aristocratic form in which property and family alliance took precedence over any sentimental attachment, let alone those spurred by sex. Part of its contemporary drama arises precisely in the tug between these forms of union.

Marriage, indeed, is the book's subject: it is as much a social and economic imperative as it may be a sentimental one. The famous opening line makes this clear: 'It is a truth universally acknowledged, that a single man in possession of a good fortune, must be in want of a wife.' The corollary of this is that women, particularly if not in possession of a good fortune, which is the five Bennet daughters' case, must be in want of a husband.

If the search for the 'right' partner is a modern gloss on the book's theme, Austen emphasizes that success in the endeavour entails inward adjustments and a recognition of one's own failings: it is not only a matter of behavioural ploys. Both her male and female characters undertake what we would now call the 'emotional work' of relationship, something the film versions inevitably make less clear. Both sexes, too, are in search of partners. Austen gives us various possible kinds of marriage, together with an ironical gloss on what 'rightness' may mean. Her principal heroine, Elizabeth Bennet, like Bridget Jones with Daniel Cleaver, is initially greatly taken by the charming Mr Wickham. But her 'first impressions' prove faulty here, as they do in her assessment of her eventual Mr Right, Fitzwilliam Darcy, considered for a good half of the book to be a disapproving prig, overblown with pride in his superior status.

Austen imbues Lizzy with wit, intelligence and independence of mind: she is hardly a submissive, simpering puppet obsessed only by the chase that will allow her to be caught. In that sense, she is something of a protofeminist. Despite the real possibility of future insecurity, she refuses her first offer of marriage from the sententious and fawning Mr Collins. When Darcy initially proposes to her, stating that he does so against his will, she adamantly refuses him: passion is not enough to justify union with a man who manifests so much simultaneous contempt for those she values. Only when he has recognized his own lacks as Lizzy has hers, only when she garners an insight into his character as composed of more than pride, does she begin to fall in love with him. Judgement, good sense and some of those traditional virtues – generosity, just action, helpfulness, devotion – rather than an excess of 'sensibility' are always core values for Austen. The choice between one partner and another is not a matter of romance, but of argument and discussion, of shared values and hopes of the world.

If attraction at first sight can be said to play its part in the eventual union of Lizzy's sister Jane to the affable Mr Bingley, it hardly makes the path towards it smooth. Jane may not have read *The Rules*, which advise women 'not to open up too fast', but her temperament is such that she conceals her special affection for Bingley. As a result 'he cannot trust it', while his interventionist friend Darcy can't see it at all and shepherds him quickly away from what he understands as a less than perfect match, one in which a rise in social status alongside financial advantage would be all on Jane's side. Lizzy's friend Charlotte, an unmarried twenty-seven-year-old, who is the wise pragmatist in the novel, says to her:

> There is so much of gratitude or vanity in almost every attachment, that it is not safe to leave any to itself. We can all begin freely – a slight preference is natural enough; but there are very few of us who have heart enough to be really in love without encouragement. In nine cases out of ten, a woman had better show more affection than she feels. Bingley likes your sister undoubtedly; but he may never do more than like her, if she does not help him on.

Charlotte herself accepts a marriage proposal from Mr Collins after the briefest acquaintance, even though she considers him 'neither sensible nor agreeable' and thinks highly neither of men nor of matrimony.

Nonetheless, it is the only honourable provision for 'well-educated young women of small fortune'. Indeed, Charlotte's views on marriage counterbalance the high hopes Lizzy and Jane have of it: 'Happiness in marriage is entirely a matter of chance,' Charlotte states. 'If the dispositions of the parties are ever so well known to each other or ever so similar beforehand, it does not advance their felicity in the least. They always continue to grow sufficiently unlike afterwards to have their share of vexation.' Lizzy's silly and effervescent sister Lydia, who elopes (at the dizzy age of sixteen) with the ever charming Wickham, soon to be strong-armed into marriage with her, will be proof of that, Austen suggests at the end of the book. Nor is there much 'felicity' in the central marriage we are shown: that of the intelligent, diffident, passive Mr Bennet and his coarse, controlling, histrionic wife, a union propelled by lust and lived in estrangement. Bridget Jones's parents live out its modern parallel, which includes an affair on the mother's part, yet the author, Helen Fielding, seems intent on having them come together in happiness at the end.

Despite easy access to divorce and the knowledge that half of marriages will end in one, despite women's greater economic freedom, despite an abundance of youthful sex and cohabitation figures which in Britain estimate that some two million people are living together, we seem to want marriages based on love to work 'till death do us part' even more than Austen did. A YouGov poll commissioned by the *Sunday Times* in 2008, based on interviews with cohabiting, married and once divorced men and women in almost equal numbers, found that 66 per cent of people who were cohabiting and 77 per cent of those in their first marriage thought that marriages should entail a commitment for life. Broken down into age groups, 80 per cent of the under-forties believed in lifelong marriages, as did 76 per cent of the over-forties.

Though in 2010 actual marriage figures in England and Wales had fallen for four consecutive years and cohabitation figures had risen, 60 per cent of those cohabiting believed in marriage, and simply wanted to be sure. Some, of course, like Hugh Grant in the perennially popular *Four Weddings and a Funeral* (1994), may be sceptical about the formal trappings of weddings and humorously contemptuous of conventional marriage. But what they seek in cohabitation is a marriage in all but name. In America, cohabitation figures increased by 88 per cent between 1980 and 2007, while about 55 per cent planned to marry their partners.

The young men and women I interviewed talked of marriage as a wish or a lack, even if their parents had divorced. Like gay men and women, they spoke of it as a public and symbolic act: an important ritual – of which we now have so few – in which a community witnessed their vows. As the Flemish writer Erwin Mortier said to me about his marriage after twenty years of 'sinful cohabitation': 'It's a triumph of endurance over hope.' So even if we marry late, often having cohabited first, marriage maintains its aura as a good ignited and inhabited by love.

Can it be that marriage is simply the best way human beings have found to live together even though it may also sometimes be the worst? And what kinds of love precipitate and inhabit it? Are we talking about the romantic swoon of the courting lover, the anguished heights and obsessional lows of passion, a contract between admired master and submissive or pampered servant, a companionship based on attraction, affinities and mutual projects, a shelter against loneliness and the terrors of mortality, or a union that mingles several of these?

Inventing Love

Western ideas of love have their source in fiction as much as in lived history. Like fairy-tale, the fictions carry an element of wish, rather more than they may reflect any immediate and widespread reality. But shaping aspirations and daydreams as they do, as well as delineating appropriate behaviour, fictions help to form the psychological bedrock of the way we live love. As that mordant seventeenth-century French aphorist La Rochefoucauld observed, 'People would never fall in love if they had not heard talk of love.' Indeed, fictions are society's way of carrying on a conversation with itself about what it values and what it detests, about what may invoke happiness or produce despair, and what we mean by both.

Notions of romance and courtship find one starting-place in the select atmosphere of the Provençal courts of the eleventh to thirteenth centuries. The very word 'courtship', which has now taken on its more specific sense of anyman wooing anywoman, derives from the courtesy, the good manners and behaviour expected of a courtier in the presence of queenly beings more elevated than himself. Love and seduction here are part of a civilizing enterprise exacted by high-ranking women of lower-born men. These codes of civility spread through the Renaissance courts. They played an important part in the entourage of Louis XIV, and were very gradually disseminated through the rising middle classes of Europe. Here they eventually – and always unevenly – found themselves bound into the union of love and marriage.

In the love poetry of the Provençal troubadours, the mistress is inaccessible. Like Lancelot's Guinevere, she is married. Courtship is secret. She is wooed through brave deeds and through verse which sings her beauty and ineffable charms, as well as the lovesickness of the poet-lover. The sickness or madness is central: romantic love, often unrequited, is tantamount to a mental or imaginative imbalance, an anguish which catapults the lover into an obsessive concentration on the beloved. His idealization of her makes him blind to all faults and other concerns.

The secrecy is important, too. It heightens the meanings the twosome takes on. Gradually, in the eighteenth century, one aspect of this secrecy was transmuted into an idea of individual privacy: matters of love and sentiment became emphatically personal, something to be enacted far from the prying eyes of other family members and ever-present servants. It was then that the new family houses of aristocrats and bourgeoisie sprouted separate bedrooms and boudoirs with closed doors, as well as halls to reach them by: sex became a private matter.

The arts of seduction spelled out in courtly poetry were formalized by Andreas Capellanus sometime between 1174 and 1190 in *The Art of Courtly Love* – perhaps at the behest of King Philip II of France, or, as earlier scholars assumed, of Marie de Troyes, the daughter of Queen Eleanor of Aquitaine. The social and amatory forms the book describes were those of Queen Eleanor's 'Court of Love', the most sophisticated court of its period. Here love of the highest courtly kind was believed to ennoble both lover and beloved. Capellanus used Ovid's notorious *Ars Amatoria* as his source text, an earlier rule book where seduction consists of a series of cunning ploys with a distinct sexual end in view. This was not an altogether compatible source if, as scholars agree, the Provençal poets had a rather more spiritual process in mind, one in which Platonic influences, transported and revivified through early Arabic mystical writings and the Cordoban philosopher Ibn Hazm's *The Ring of the Dove*, played their part. In these, the mistress's earthly beauty is an intimation of heavenly beauty and angelic wisdom. These inspire the lover to great deeds. Love's labours are a quest, here, for a transcendental truth, an ideal Platonic form, more akin to the Christian saint's love of God than to Ovid's altogether carnal seductions.

Capellanus' *De Amore* takes the form of a letter addressed to a friend who is being initiated into the civilizing art of love. It proceeds through various dialogues between men and women of different classes. Capellanus embraces the more spiritual form of courtly love due to the most highly placed of ladies, as well as the more mundane variety which includes lust and a tumble in the hay with peasant girls. There is an assumption that affection, even if immoderate, between man and wife is in no way akin to 'true' love's highest calling, which has no place in marriage. Capellanus' famous 'rules' of love grow out of these dialogues. They include the following:

A true lover does not desire to embrace in love anyone except his beloved.

When made public, love rarely endures.

The easy attainment of love makes it of little value: difficulty of attainment makes it prized.

Every lover regularly turns pale in the presence of his beloved.

When a lover suddenly catches sight of his beloved his heart palpitates.

Good character alone makes any man worthy of love.

He whom the thought of love vexes eats and sleeps very little.

Every act of a lover ends in the thought of his beloved.

A true lover considers nothing good except what he thinks will please his beloved.

Though Capellanus includes the rule that 'It is not proper to love a woman whom one would be ashamed to seek to marry', marriage is not the aim of courtly love. It is assumed that whatever the strength of the passion or the suffering it entails, both lover and beloved can be displaced by others. Yet for the length of time it lasts, 'true love' is based on faithful devotion.

Beatrice, the guiding spirit who finally leads Dante out of Purgatory and into the Paradiso of *The Divine Comedy*, is an instance of the idealized beloved of the courtly love poets. So, too, is Petrarch's Laura, immortalized in the famous sonnets of the *Canzoniere* (Song Books). In both cases, the real women served as inspiration for poetry, but had little lived contact with the poets who translated them into the iconic mistresses of their work. Dante first met Beatrice when she was eight and he nine – a 'first love', one might say, which stayed with him for life, though both of them married others. Petrarch only glimpsed Laura in a church in Avignon, yet this fugitive beauty ignited a passion.

During the seventy-two-year reign of France's Sun King, Louis XIV (1638–1715), those early bluestockings, the *précieuses*, took on the subject of courtly love. They debated and refined it in their *salons* to give love both a new psychological depth and a woman's perspective of estimable values. In *La Carte de Tendre*, that map of an Arcadia of love which forms the frontispiece to her ten-volume novel *Clélie* (1654–60), Madeleine de Scudéry set out the correct and gallant path to winning a woman's heart, as well as the dangers on the way. After the moment of 'new friendship', what count on the journey along the river of inclination towards love – apart from gallantry, little trinkets and *billets doux* – are characteristics such as sincerity, integrity, sensibility, respect and generosity. Persistence, too, is key. Amongst the pitfalls in this country of love, the Lake of Indifference and the Sea of Hostility loom, plus negative attributes such as indiscretion, pride, treachery and, interestingly, inequality. Women's place in courtly love is at least equal – if not superior.

Madame de Lafayette's hugely successful *La Princesse de Clèves* (1678) plays itself out, with new psychological intricacy, on this terrain of love. Set amidst an astutely observed court filled with envy and intrigues, the novel charts her introspective heroine's trajectory from the age of fifteen when she is married off to the older Prince de Clèves. Soon, the

Princess develops a closely analysed passion for the dashing Duc de Nemours. But their love, though she sees how it alters her relationship with her husband, is not one that can be fulfilled. Torn, like one of Racine's classic heroines, between love and duty, even after her jealous husband dies, the Princess ends her days in a convent. Love here bows before the time's aristocratic demands of form and honour.

It could be said that courtly love separated out to shape two different, though not always utterly distinguishable, trajectories: the profane focused on carnal passion; the sacred emphasized the romantic, the soulful, the transformative heights and depths of passion. The first tradition is a libertine one. Casanova and Byron or the fictional Valmont and Don Giovanni are its male exemplars, rakish and gallant by turn but ever concentrated on the seduction and pursuit of women, who are their prey, however willing or complicit. The chase, here, is as important and arguably more satisfying than any ultimate consummation, whatever its pleasures. As for the prey, unless they are already married and protected by class, they suffer the anguish of abandonment, and the wrecked lives that illegitimate pregnancy entailed. Amongst the female libertines are all those coquettes and courtesans of yore and the sirens of today, more often in search of fortune than fornication, who use their wiles to play the amoral mating game. Love here is mental and carnal, but rarely strays, except unwittingly, into the emotions.

In its playful, flirtatious French version, seduction can indeed be an art. Embedded in a tradition which understands passion as pleasure, it makes of love a titillating game, one that inhabits so special a place in life that even when it bursts out of the rules of the game to engage ungovernable emotions, laws as well as social forms are bent to give it room: a crime of passion is not an everyday crime. Passion is understood to have its own logic, which is in a certain measure beyond the law. Women in this tradition have a heightened, often civilizing, importance: they are, indeed, the mistresses of love, most particularly once they are already married.

Translated into contemporary manuals of behaviour, the arts of seduction gain a deadly earnestness which robs them of much of their allure and any of their potential link to love. They become utterly instrumental, as well as hard toil. In his racy *The Art of Seduction* (2001),

Robert Greene, author of *The 48 Laws of Power* (1998), demonstrates seduction tactics for both sexes: 'how to cast a spell, break down resistance, and . . . compel a target to surrender, all in the twenty-four maneuvers and strategies of the Seductive Process'. Manipulation, though it involves pretence, is never altogether art, and seduction here can look more like stalking than an engagement with pleasure. In a world where women are equal and sex casual, the attentiveness of a seducer, if unwanted, is less titillation than bullying.

When the tropes of courtly love left the royal courts of France to move across the English Channel and, in time, down the social ladder, they were very gradually naturalized into an idea of romance that often found its happy end in marriage. In the most summary fashion, one could say that chivalric heroism, the pursuit of wedded and unattainable queens – products of feudal societies who were regularly at war with near-neighbours – gave way by the sixteenth century to a literature which reflected both the lives and the aspirations of a new, more settled gentry and a rising middle class. Here, in the English language at least, the civilizing features of romance find a licit end. In *As You Like It*, Shakespeare combines old romance with new. Orlando is a noble, courtly lover – ever pinning verses declaiming his love of Rosalind to the trees. His verse is hardly of the highest calibre and Rosalind mocks it gently. Yet this love at first sight, proved by bravery and good character, finds its romantic end in marriage. Shakespeare provides a template replayed in fiction down the ages, from its more textured examples in Jane Austen or Charlotte Brontë to the popular romances.

When marriage doesn't mark the triumphant climax of love, death comes in its place. In Goethe's *The Sorrows of Young Werther* (1774), written when he was just twenty-four, the young artist-hero's romantic lovesickness for an unattainable Charlotte moves from intense idealization into an abject melancholy and eventual suicide. The book attained a celebrity akin to that of a pop hit today. A wave of copycat suicides across Europe followed, while Napoleon himself was inspired into verse and carried *Werther* with him on his Egyptian campaign.

The long eighteenth century saw the first great growth in the fiction-reading public in England. Richardson's mid-century epistolary classics of sentimental psychology, in part conceived as manuals of good conduct, *Pamela or Virtue Rewarded* (1741) and the tragic *Clarissa* (1748), became the bestsellers of the day, read in towns and villages alike. They spawned both parodies and imitations. The rise and rise of popular romantic fictions and verse followed.

Popular romances emphatically twinned romantic love with marriage, making the first a sufficient motive for the second. The new circulating libraries extended the reach of these novels. In 1772, the *Universal Magazine* observed: 'Of all the arrows which Cupid has shot at youthful hearts, [the modern novel] is the keenest. There is no resisting it. It is the literary opium that lulls every sense into delicious rapture.' Both Samuel Johnson and Mary Wollstonecraft criticized these addictive fictions, reflecting that the romantic love they described was no more than a male cover for lust. But their readership grew and the form proliferated, eventually to be condemned by Victorian clerics and mind doctors alike, who found them inimical to the health of young girls. By imbuing women with impossible fantasies of love which had all the redemptive features of a secular religion, they threatened to displace the godly one. 'He who burns a romance purifies the human mind,' wrote Richard Carlile, the radical nineteenth-century publisher, capturing the visceral tone of puritan revulsion that romance would elicit in the public sphere in the Victorian era. His disapproval may have been strengthened by the fact that, in that sexual division of labour which at the time placed emotion and the intimate life in the feminine camp and public life in the male, such popular romances were increasingly written by women.

The strength of the Victorian attacks on romance betrays a double fear. It is as if the reading of romance has begun in some mysterious way to stand in for sexuality itself. The pleasure women readers take in these stories of courting males and passionate or resisting heroines is illicit. Reading wives, daughters and servants will be led forever astray, rebel against parental or husbandly wishes, once their imaginations have been fired by the likes of Ouida's audacious cross-dressing heroine, Cigarette, in *Under Two Flags*, or indeed, by Madame Bovary, whom Flaubert in part makes a victim of that same romantic impulse.

Not all men have been quite so vitriolic about a literary form read largely by women – one which offered both escape from drudgery and dreams that somewhere love and marriage (if not only love and death) could be combined. Earlier, at the height of literature's Romantic period, the venerable Sir Walter Scott, whose own fictions charted the heights and depths of grand passion, had criticized Jane Austen for not being romantic enough. Cupid, he complained in a review of *Emma*, was unfairly left out of popular novels. Romance can render young men's characters 'honourable, dignified and disinterested'. For Scott, it seems, the reading of romance could provide a sentimental education for men, as much as for the women usually assumed to be its regular readers.

If romantic fiction in part charts the changing mores of relations between the sexes and ideas about love and marriage, it nonetheless has a fairly permanent psychological core. It is assumed that the business of love – of locating, wooing, getting to know and coming together with the other – is an elevating or civilizing vocation that *matters*, whether it ends in tragedy or in the domesticity of marriage. Despite our sophisticated and openly sexualized times, simple, happily-ever-after romances still sell in their millions around the world, in Mills & Boon and Harlequin novels as well as in a fertile swell of other popular fictions.

The principal characteristics of these stories were laid down early by Jane Austen and then with greater romantic and moral aplomb for the Victorian reading public by the Brontës. Stripped down, only a little unfairly, to its essential narrative line, Charlotte Brontë's *Jane Eyre*, a bestseller then as now, provides the template. A young outsider, with inner rather than flagrant beauty, meets a wild and reprobate, landed Byronic male, Mr Rochester. After a variety of misadventures and mis-understandings, he is tamed by fire and blindness as well as by Jane's educational and spiritual ministrations into the domestic bliss of a marriage which unites body and soul. Near the end of the novel, after Jane has memorably declaimed, 'Reader, I married him', she spells out the lineaments of this ideal marriage:

> I have now been married ten years. I know what it is to live entirely for
> and with what I love best on earth. I hold myself supremely blest – blest

beyond what language can express: because I am my husband's life as fully as he is mine. No woman was ever nearer to her mate than I am: ever more absolutely bone of his bone and flesh of his flesh . . . We talk, I believe, all day long: to talk to each other is but a more animated and an audible thinking. All my confidence is bestowed on him, all his confidence is devoted to me; we are precisely suited in character – perfect concord is the result.

Scores of lesser romantic fictions followed the Jane Eyre model. Boots, the English chemist, which ran popular lending libraries from 1898 to 1966, itemized the essential features of the form in their first literary course for librarians. These consisted of an essentially strong and silent hero from a good family who, owing to some misunderstanding, has cut himself off from society to brood about it in the outposts of Empire. The heroine is well bred, with a distant ethereal beauty, and needs to find someone to lean on. These two opposing poles meet: at first she is repulsed by the brute, but gradually her delicate charm, like Beauty's with the Beast, brings forth a softer side to his nature and the story ends in a fervent embrace. The man is transformed, that is, educated in the value of an intimate life, and tamed, while the woman recognizes where her true desires lie – and, indeed, that she has desire – which can be fulfilled by the man in question through marriage.

Contemporary 'chick lit' is not fundamentally different. Of course, empires – except for business ones – are gone; and sexuality, rather than being expressed in lightning storms or sublimated into purple prose, is lived out. Heroines are now independent working women and have some sexual experience. In many of these novels, they have been through a bad first marriage: their 'delicacy' lies in their hurt, which can sometimes be the earlier hurt of an abused childhood. The hero is still inarticulate and his actions are thereby rendered incomprehensible to the heroine. His rescuing her from whatever plight she may find herself in is simultaneously her rescuing or 'taming' of him, whether he is a real or an imagined rake, so that he can become the better man it is in him to be. Both, in the gaze of the other, recognize parts of themselves to which they had previously been blind. One might say that in the other's loving attention – and what else is courting and the pursuit? – they become aware of a new value in themselves and in life.

In *Rosie Meadows Regrets* (1998) by the bestselling Catherine Alliott, the heroine is freed from a miserable marriage by the sudden death of her odious first husband, a man she weds because she has a less than high opinion of herself. The sculptor hero, at first seemingly cold and contemptuous, also has a dead wife, plus a bitchy new one, too hastily married. After various false starts and tribulations of his own, the hero saves the heroine from a sorry end, but not before she has made some strides in refashioning herself and becoming the woman it has always been in her to be.

Elizabeth Gilbert's hugely popular and wittily exuberant *Eat, Pray, Love*, though cast in the memoir mould our century has convinced itself is somehow truer to life than fiction, has many of the same tropes. An attractive and successful journalist, Gilbert's marriage has failed, as has the affair engaged in on the rebound. Depression ensues. Needing to find a better version of herself, she sets forth on a healing journey, one which will enable her to explore the arts of life: pleasure in Italy, spirituality in India; and in Indonesia, the balance between the two. All this achieved, the last part of her journey catapults her into a dashingly romantic love affair with an older man, who in the next book also becomes her husband. Gilbert acknowledges that her story has a 'ludicrously fairy-tale ending', while protesting that 'I was not rescued by a prince; I was the administrator of my own rescue.' So, one might say, was Cinderella – with a little help from her benefactors, who provided the wherewithal if not to go to Bali, at least to go to what felt like an equally distant ball.

Indeed, many of such women's romantic fictions bear a distinct relationship to the Cinderella story – and not only because of the magical transformations that love and its happy end in marriage can bring. One way of thinking about why romantic fictions continue to hold a popular appeal, and are read and watched by young and old despite the changing status of women, their key players, is that they are in a sense all stories about the mysteries of growing up and acquiring some kind of more adult – or better – self. How does one move out of the constellation of the first family and that first familial romance in which the child finds itself — amidst Mum and Dad, absent or present, and siblings — and shapes its first attachments into a place where adult desire and desiring are possible and somehow bring out the best of oneself, or make one into the best possible adult version of oneself? These are never-ending stories and ones that can be repeated, with innovations, throughout life, even after a failed first marriage which didn't do the trick.

The powerful, mysterious, incomprehensible hero in popular romance, one who too often transgresses, bears a decided resemblance to Daddy seen from the little girl's perspective. How to capture and tame that powerful figure's ever wandering attention? The answer must in part be to grow up and become like mother, that sexualized being he desired (at least once). Then she'll be rescued from the plights of dependent childhood. But that's not so easy. Mother's in the way, the adult woman the girl must somehow become and also separate herself from. If the mother is dead and hasn't been replaced, then there is the danger that Daddy will want to keep or imprison the girl at home, far from sexualized rivals.

In life, mothers are both good and bad, often in turn, sometimes at the same time. In Cinderella stories, they're often enough split into two. Good mothers come as fairy godmothers — sometimes displacements, as in *Cinderella* itself, of the good mother who is dead. (In the Brothers Grimm pre-Disney version of the story, the dead mother has told Cinderella she will look after her from above, and it is the animals around her grave that Cinderella assiduously tends who take on the magical helping function.) Good/Godmothers abet the process of growing up. They find familiar objects around the child — pumpkins, mice, her own sense of herself and her desires — which will help transform her into a princess.

Wicked stepmothers hinder the process, recognizing that Cinderella or Sleeping Beauty is a rival for paternal attention. They enslave the girl in a nether, dependent position, or send her into oblivion. In Alliott's *Rosie Meadows Regrets*, both the heroine's mother and her accomplished elder sister, as well as her best friend, urge on her diminished self-estimation as an ugly duckling. In *Pride and Prejudice* Mrs Bennet largely contributes to Lizzy's humiliation, making her undesirable to Prince

Darcy, while her aunt paves the way towards the happy end, providing a fairy godmother she can identify with as a woman, as well as a coach trip to Pemberley.

Within the family it is clear that jealousy and envy are abroad, and the fear of stimulating them chains the heroine to subservient duties and guilts, as do the envious actions of other women: in *Pride and Prejudice* the manoeuvres of the envious Miss Bingley serve the purpose. The bullying, or often enough the too passive presence of fathers, tied in the first instance to their wives, offers no help. Cinderella's father, like Lizzy's, fails his daughter. In finding or being found by Prince Charming, the heroine has first to locate her own desires, her own ball-gown glamour: Daddy is not for her and he can't be her rescuer. This done, she can become a beautiful stranger to her own father. (Cinderella's doesn't recognize her at the ball; Mr Bennet doesn't recognize in Darcy's letter the Lizzy he knows.) Only then can she answer the persuasive Prince's desire, fit her foot into the lost slipper and 'fall' away from the duties and restraints the family has tied her to. For women, this can often enough be compounded by an unwillingness to give up the Daddy who is implicated with Mummy, and who in countless Victorian instances enslaves his willing spinster daughter at his side to look after him.

In fairy-tales with male heroes, or the masculine romance of the *Boy's Own* stories, the journey into adulthood is different. Boys leave home to go off on adventures without a backward glance, often sent away by their fathers, who see a rival in their sons and won't countenance displacement by youth. The task of separation from the family is easier, or at least quicker, for boys: like girls, they have performed an early childhood version of this during weaning, but unlike girls, they don't have to engage in the complicated process, often surrounded by ambivalence, of then identifying with mother in order to become female. In tales such as Freud's chosen Oedipal template, boys are often given an early kick-start by father abetted by the highest authority of prophecy – though, in the contemporary real versions and in other older ones, when fathers stray (or die) they may stay home to look after Mum.

In Grimm's tale 'The King's Son Who Feared Nothing', the youth is bored with home and, like any good adolescent testing his manhood, leaves it to wander. He stumbles upon a giant's estate – a big Daddy, you might say – and challenges him: 'O you blockhead! You think only you have strong arms. I can do everything I want to.' The giant responds with a dare: 'If you are one of that kind, go and bring me an apple of the tree of life. I have a betrothed bride who wishes for it.'

The tree is not only distant – involving a foray into a kind of 'empire' – but guarded by lions. To get at the apple of life, the youth must breach the ring that protects it – a task that takes 'luck'. Symbol hunters might easily find a sexual reading here in the ring that guards the apple of life, and they wouldn't be altogether wrong, for no sooner does the youth put his arm through the ring than he feels 'a prodigious strength flowing through his veins'. When he returns with the plucked apple, the castrating big Daddy giant immediately blinds him and tries to throw him off the top of a cliff. But the lucky, plucky youth is helped not only by the giant's (maternal) betrothed, but by a lion who has become his loyal familiar – and, by God, the biggest of Daddies. Water from a stream returns his sight and he sets out on his next adventure, the one that will finally turn him into a man.

This leads him into an enchanted terrain where a young woman – always that final test in the transition into manhood – has had an evil spell cast over her which has turned her quite black (a hint of Cinder's ashes here, which similarly blacken or hide a natural beauty that the princely hero is nonetheless attuned to). In order to release her from the spell, the youth must spend three nights in the great hall of the enchanted castle without uttering a peep, even though a pack of gambling devils bludgeon him and try to pull him asunder. Part of this feat of endurance, part of the self-sacrifice that will enable rescue, has all the overtones of a sexual struggle: to release the princess, to conquer her desire, the youth must remain pure and loyal despite lacerating temptation. After each night, the heroine brings the water of life to him to heal his wounds, and on the last morning, when he comes to, he sees that he has released her and the castle from the evil spell. 'Love' transforms the beloved as well as the lover. The girl is a great king's daughter. And regal nuptials are celebrated with much rejoicing.

As the reading public expanded through the nineteenth and twentieth centuries, romance became specifically gendered female, frivolous, morally suspect and secondary; and adventure stories, male. This splitting mirrored the division of labour in society as a whole, which placed the emotions and domestic life into the woman's camp and the public world of action into the man's. However, as Victorian values and their attendant sexual division of labour gave way in fits and starts – and never seamlessly – to a rebellious modern moment, the whole edifice of love and its psychological weight was reassessed.

In a 1914 review of a popular women's romance, that subtle modernist Henry James, positioning himself against the tide, noted that there had been quite enough fiction describing man's relationship to 'the pistol, the pirate, the police, the wild and tame beast'. It was time, he said, to turn to the ladies, since 'It is the ladies, in a word, who have lately done most to remind us of man's relations with himself, that is, with woman.' For James, born into an America where women tended to do all the work of 'civilization' while men went about getting and spending, the whole matter of love was an education in the complexities of the inner life, as well as in a subtler morality. In the consummate artifice of his fiction, the way his characters love, or fail to, defines their lives – indeed, their 'character': in either case, it is the attention paid to loving which deepens being and refines those 'free spirits' who act as his primary moral registers.

Milly Theale, his 'heiress of all the ages' in *The Wings of the Dove*, dies when she is betrayed in love: only the tug of that intimate relation which is far more than sex, James suggests, could have kept her alive. Isabel Archer, the fieriest of his young American women, fearful of passion, makes the wrong choice in marriage. The seeming Mr Right is Mr Wrong. The union with the effete, decadent Osmond results in a dead child and her imprisonment in a world of empty forms, not unlike the marriage of Dorothea Brooke to Casaubon, that jealous dried-up old stick of a scholar in *Middlemarch*. Strether, the mature hero of *The Ambassadors*, released to the teeming life of Europe from puritan America, counsels the young artist Bingham to 'live, live all you can', by which, of course, he means, love, love all you can – even though it may transgress social conventions. In James, love takes on the high seriousness with which it was treated by the Provençal court poets and, indeed, by George Eliot, the greatest of what seemed to him the 'old-fashioned', far too sprawling, too loose and baggy English novelists, from whom he hoped to distinguish himself by focusing on form, on 'balanced composition'. Yet James remains oddly true to Eliot: only by plunging into the sphere of love, the trajectory of feeling, can the Jamesian hero access a spiritual maturity.

For Eliot, steeped in both religion and philosophy, the heart rather than the head emerges as the organ of epistemology. Love enables knowledge and is itself a kind of knowledge garnered through the stumblings of experience. In *Middlemarch*, her seventh novel, written when she was fifty and at last settled in a vibrant, if at first socially ostracized, 'marriage of true minds' with George Henry Lewes, she gives us the benefit of her own accrued understanding. Virginia Woolf called the book 'one of the few English novels written for grown-up people'. Martin Amis has called it the greatest novel in the English language, a view upheld in many contemporary popularity rankings.

Three trajectories of love weave their way through the novel. In their own way, each of Eliot's central characters is shaped and reshaped in life's ways through their experience of love: their transformed perspectives on the world at once illuminate and constitute knowledge which is as powerful as that gained from any philosophical inquiry.

Lydgate, her idealistic man of science, contemptuous of the matter-of-factness of provincial life, nonetheless conventionally believes that a pretty, doting young thing is just what a man needs. Through the travails of daily domesticity he realizes that he has mistakenly bound himself to a selfish, materialistic, manipulative airhead who can share none of his reforming zeal. Life, and not science, brings him a measure of wisdom.

No idealist, Fred Vincy is the most ordinary of pleasure-loving young men. He is in love with Mary Garth, 'the best girl I know', but his own wayward actions, the debts he haplessly incurs – as he recognizes in his humiliation – prevent her from finding him worthy of love. For her and through her, because she demands the best of him and because she does, despite herself, love him, his imagination stretches to feel the harm he has done to others, and he takes on heft, grows in good.

Dorothea, Eliot's latter-day St Theresa, is something of a satirical self-portrait of her own youthful, idealistic self. Determinedly serious,

Dorothea at first demarcates love as a puritanical school in intellect's service. Like so many young, intellectual women, fascinated by and susceptible to the sway of theory (or dogma) in authoritative male guise, she ties herself to a man whom she would wish a Milton, but who is in fact a stifling pedant, a narrow, impotent bully. Disappointment, suffering, self-recognition, as well as attraction, lead her to understand the values her second love, Will Ladislaw, describes: 'To be a poet is to have a soul so quick to discern, that no shade of quality escapes it, and so quick to feel, that discernment is but a hand playing with finely ordered variety on the chords of emotion – a soul in which knowledge passes instantaneously into feeling, and feeling flashes back as a new organ of knowledge.' Dorothea learns through the pitfalls of experience to feel with her head and learn through the heart.

In central Europe, another major writer was contemplating the force and nature of love. In 1907 Sigmund Freud, who had already immersed himself in woman's terrain – small-talk, superstition, dreams, gossip, and tittle-tattle about love and marriage – to give birth to a revolutionary theory about the wayward workings of the human mind and the primary place of the 'sexual drive' in shaping behaviour and imagination, turned his attention to a popular romantic novelette, *Gradiva: A Pompeiian Fancy*, by a German contemporary, Wilhelm Jensen. Freud's reading of the novelette became his longest sustained interpretation: *Delusions and Dreams in Jensen's Gradiva*. It was here that Freud launched his idea of the 'cure through love' in which the psychoanalyst takes his cue from the intelligent lover to facilitate a treatment that is in fact better enacted by the psychosexual process of love itself. Freud's cure is more epistemological than redemptive: love (like his view of the psychoanalytic project) prompts knowledge of the self and of the other. But then, the Bible, taking its cue from Hebraic usage, had already elided the verb 'to know' with carnal knowledge, a slippage which is also there in the word 'intercourse', whose larger senses include all kinds of conversation.

Norbert Hanold is a young archaeologist who is mesmerized by a bas-relief of a Grecian girl with a striking gait. He falls in love with her and baptizes her 'Gradiva' – the woman who walks. Gradiva invades his dreams. In a nightmare, he sees her die in Pompeii, buried under the volcanic ash of an erupting Vesuvius. From that moment on, in his delusionary beliefs Gradiva is both buried and alive, past and present. He travels to Pompeii, thinking himself in AD 79, the moment of the eruption, and here he encounters Gradiva in the flesh.

Not a spectre, this Gradiva is in fact Norbert's old hometown playmate, Zoë Bertgang, another woman whose name bears a 'walking' in it. Alert to his state, she sympathetically elicits the entire arc of his delusion and plays along with it. In other words, she shares his fantasies, just as, notes Freud, a real psychoanalytic cure must 'begin by taking up the same ground as the delusional structure and then investigating it as completely as possible'. A clever young woman, Zoë realizes that Norbert's hidden love for her is the 'motive force behind the delusion'. In the unfolding of the story, it becomes clear that she too is trapped at a point in childhood. She is dedicated to her father, who, like Norbert, has time only for his intellectual work. A zoologist, he is obsessed by his specimens, named in the dead languages of Latin and Greek, from which Zoë gets her name. To make good the 'life' the name promises, she has to escape the attachment to her father and win Norbert back to life and love. Indeed, her courting or 'therapeutic' activity follows from her perception that Norbert's delusions are distorted expressions of his love for her. 'It was only this knowledge,' Freud writes, 'which could decide her to devote herself to the treatment; it was only the certainty of being loved by him that could induce her to admit her love to him.'

When Norbert touches her hand in order to shoo away a fly, she bursts out, 'There's no doubt you're out of your mind, Norbert Hanold!' Hearing his name spoken, Norbert is roused from his dream state and at last recognizes his old friend. Zoë now exposes for him how his revivification of buried Pompeii and his infatuation with Gradiva have been spurred by his childhood affection for her. His entire turning to the dead world of archaeology is uncovered step by step, stratum by stratum, and disclosed to have been impelled by a turning away from a dangerous living attraction. It is now up to Norbert to take a step into life: he embraces his own Gradiva, 'the childhood friend who had been dug out of the ruins'.

Freud applauds this happy ending. He takes his cue, he says, from female readers rather than rationalist critics who might see it as an arbitrary appendage. For Freud, the women are right: love can release inner blockages: Norbert really has undergone cure through love, because of a woman's unsceptical faith in its powers. And the psychoanalyst takes his cue from Zoë, who has provoked a return of the repressed, washing away Norbert's earlier struggles 'by a fresh high tide of the same passions'. Every psychoanalytic treatment, Freud writes,

> is an attempt at liberating repressed love which has found a meagre outlet in the compromise of a symptom. Indeed, the agreement between such treatments and the process of cure described by the author of *Gradiva* reaches its climax in the further fact that in analytic psychotherapy too the re-awakened passion, whether it is love or hate, invariably chooses as its object the figure of the doctor.

Zoë/Gradiva, Freud notes, is, unfortunately, better placed than the practitioners of psychoanalysis to effect a cure. Like the doctors, she has made the repressed conscious. Through her, explanation and cure coincide more nearly than they can in the consulting room, since Zoë can return Hanold's love as it makes its way from the unconscious into consciousness: 'The doctor has been a stranger, and must endeavour to become a stranger once more after the cure; he is often at a loss what advice to give the patients he has cured as to how in real life they can use their recovered capacity to love.'

So the lover, through intelligence and passion, can reanimate the beloved, while the psychotherapist who stands in for the lover and calls his own 'affect into play' must needs stand back and merely point the way for the patient. Many analysts since Freud have used the analogy of the therapeutic encounter as a cure through love. In the analytic encounter, we re-enact all our affective relations, loves as well as hates, and those sticking points on which we've become so fixed that we repeat them over and over, without being able to budge. Through the process, we may become a little wiser about our own frailties and lacks, as well as learning how to love a little better.

But if we are to understand that the lover – in Freud's estimate – has this high calling and that love itself is a transformative experience, which releases and reorganizes the components of the beloved's (as well as the lover's) inner experience, is this enough to sustain a happily-ever-after in that institution called marriage, even if Mr Right has met his Ms Right? If there were a simple yes to this question, the growth of the talking cures, with their large clientele amongst the married, might never have been quite so spectacular. If the answer is a simple no, why do we go on believing, or certainly hoping, that the answer is yes? Perhaps it's simply that the love-and-marriage bundle, a little like Churchill's estimation of democracy, is clearly far from perfect, but it's the best we've come up with.

Freud himself, after an ardent courtship of Martha Bernays, 'his dear, sweet girl', entered on a lifelong marriage. He had met Martha at a family dinner in April 1882. She was twenty-one, he twenty-six, an ambitious but penniless researcher at Brücke's physiological laboratory in Vienna. A little over a month later, they had their first walk alone together: by June they were secretly and unofficially engaged. The distinction and warmth of her family may have played a part in his choice of her, as he later confided, but that very factor made him fear the family would refuse the engagement on the grounds of his poverty and lack of prospects. The engagement, eventually made public, lasted over four years and several thousand letters: the length of these protracted and one assumes chaste betrothals, the later Freud notes, is a factor in precipitating neurosis.

The voluminous correspondence between Sigmund and Martha, of which only Freud's side is available, shows him as a jealous and tyrannical suitor, one often tipped into despair and who demands unconditional love from his fiancée, as well as utter veracity about all her relations with others. Even her family relations constitute grounds for jealousy: 'no matter how much they love you I will not leave you to anyone, and no one deserves you; no one else's love compares with mine'. Martha meets his demands with tact, but with a spirited resistance too. Her rights and independence are crucial to her. He doesn't always respond with equanimity, yet he writes, 'it would be a ghastly loss for us both if I were compelled to decide to love you as a dear girl, yet not as an equal, someone from whom I would have to hide my thoughts and opinions – in short, the truth'.

Undoubtedly, love shifted Freud's sense of himself. His conquista-dorial ambitions were tempered and displaced by a domestic sentimental idyll, a 'little world of happiness' which he and Martha would share, 'filled with beds, mirrors, a clock, an armchair, linen tied with pretty ribbons, hats with artificial flowers'. Over a year into their engagement, he writes:

> we are certain to achieve what we are striving for — a little home into which sorrow may find its way, but never privation, a being-together throughout all the vicissitudes of life, a quiet contentment that will prevent us from ever having to ask what is the point of living. I know after all how sweet you are, how you can turn a house into a paradise, how you will share in my interests, how gay and painstaking you will be.

Sigmund and Martha were finally wed in late September 1886. Their marriage lasted the length of their lives, over fifty years, despite having produced six of those dangerous rivals Freud had foreseen: 'once one is married . . . one lives rather with each other for some third thing, and for the husband dangerous rivals soon appear: household and nursery'.

These dangerous rivals, many long thought, were the underlying purpose of marriage, whether sentimental and love-based in its inception or not. Indeed, the now sanctioned notion of an emotional and sexual link between Mr and Miss Right, the idea of a happily-ever-after in a freely chosen marriage, seedbed for the full flowering of each party's individual potential, are late arrivals on the historical scene.

PART THREE

Love and Marriage

Two of the fundamental human properties that human societies have been most anxious to limit are the capacity to relate oneself to the world by knowledge and the capacity to relate oneself to others by marriage.

Stanley Cavell

Love is an ideal thing, marriage a real thing; a confusion of the real with the ideal never goes unpunished.

Goethe

Marriage has many pains, but celibacy has no pleasures.

Dr Johnson

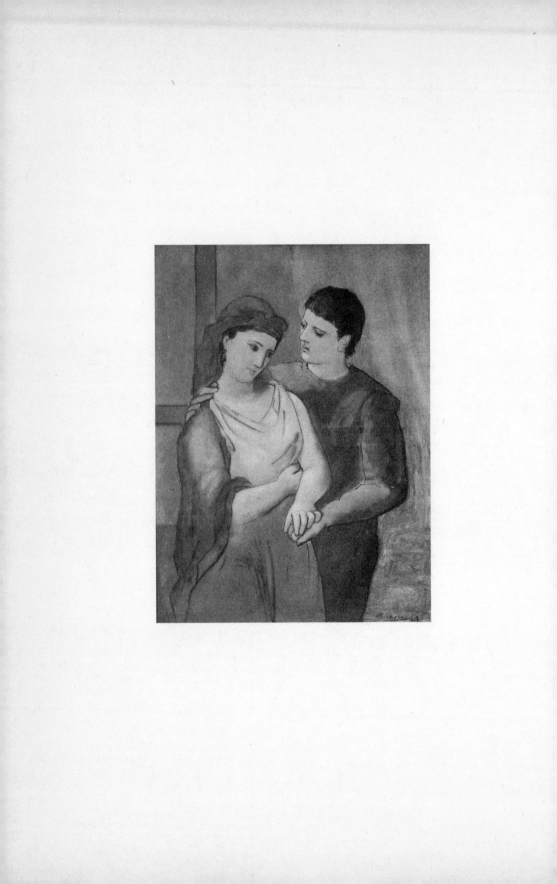

Love and marriage — the words trip off the tongue as if they were themselves an established couple. Yet love is deeply private and particularly in its passionate form oft-ungovernable, while marriage is an institution, championed by regulatory states in the name of an ordered society. The contradiction between the two can produce a deep malaise — from which long-term and public cohabitation, that intermediate arrangement, is hardly free. Yet despite the economic independence of women in our time, despite the high turnover rate of unions, despite the far greater cultural acceptance of singletons, despite the loss of innocence that our sex-strewn media and lives engender, we continue to harbour a profound fantasy of the enduring couple. We hunger and search for the 'right' match that will allow us to establish coupledom — that point where love meets the world in hopes of a happily-ever-after. We carry on, indomitably, but with growing anxiety, even after failed attempts.

In the mid-1950s, Frank Sinatra jauntily sang that love and marriage went together like a horse and carriage. The horse may have bolted, the carriage been replaced by a car, but the inseparable duo of love and marriage still contains a wished-for life, though we may need to re-imagine the contours of our pleasures and satisfactions if we're to attain it.

So it's worth pausing to highlight some of the social forms, laws and ideas, often informed by religion, which have fed into our understanding of settled love, as well as the various guises marriage has worn in its long history. Against that background, the nature of our pursuits and what makes contemporary unions so unsettled grows clearer.

*

Rarely in its history has marriage been the idealized institution the
Victorians prescribed and often failed to live; or that 1950s America
rolled out as a suburban union sparked by passionate love which went
on for ever and delivered all the goods of life. Indeed love, though it
may have emerged in the course of a marriage, has only relatively
recently been understood as a major inciting factor.

> A good marriage (if there be such a thing) [Montaigne, that father of
> modern scepticism, writes early in the French Renaissance] rejects the
> company of Cupid: it strives to reproduce those of loving-friendship. It
> is a pleasant fellowship for life, full of constancy, trust and an infinity of
> solid useful services and mutual duties. No wife who has ever savoured
> its taste – would ever wish to be the beloved mistress of her husband. If
> she is lodged in his affection as a wife then her lodging is far more hon-
> ourable and secure.

We may no longer agree with Montaigne, but it is clear that greater or
lesser elements of pragmatism have generally played into marriage's
making. Marriage, as the adage goes, is too important a matter to be left
to those getting married.

History in this area is tricky. Marriage is a social, institutional and
legal form. As for love, it falls into that area of subjectivity where, even
when diaries or letters exist, we cannot be certain that our readings are
weighted in the way of their authors'. After all, we find the emotions
even of near and dear ones opaque, never mind our own. So unearthing
the value they may have held in past times is inevitably a contested
matter. Then, too, no one template fits all classes or even proximate
geographical locations in any given period.

Fictional sources are sometimes our best guides, although, as already
seen, they carry an element of wish, and shape daydreams as much as
reflecting the real and invoking temporal paradigms of right conduct.
Such fictions, together with religious and philosophical ideas, pedagogical texts and prescriptions for living, percolate through society,
often moving downwards from a dominant group and being re-
inflected in the process. With the growth of schooling and literacy,
they have circulated more widely through education, as well as in

guidebooks and love and marriage manuals. In our own times of mass media and instant communication, these ruling ideas can also instil untenable notions of perfection: standards of 'rightness' that induce anxiety and make reality ever harder to bear. So the briefest dip into some of the different forms of love and marriage that history has given us may prove salutary.

In primitive societies marriage takes many shapes, few of them the intimate pair-bonding of modern conjugality. Different rules of sexual exclusiveness and propriety as well as responsibility for children pertain, while complex kinship systems govern who one may or may not marry. Amongst the upper-caste East Indian Nayar studied by Kathleen Gough, for instance, matrilineal descent prevails. Once a girl is ritually betrothed by the tying of a gold ornament, the 'tali', to a boy of her kin's chosen group, she is free at puberty to take on sexual relationships with others. Any resulting children are raised by the matrilineal household. Her main obligation to her 'husband' is to perform appropriate burial rites.

The work of anthropologists makes it clear that marriage is a political and institutional form, one forged by group alliances, rather than by the individuals involved. Marriage codes, in turn, shape the structure of the society and its arrangements for domestic life. That said, marriage itself seems to be universal. Amongst the Trobriand Islanders, Malinowski writes, there were no unmarried men of mature age, except undeniable idiots, incurable invalids, widowers and albinos. In societies where labour is shared, a union is necessary, the closer to puberty the better; a bachelor is only half a human being. Working children are necessary to the welfare of the kinship group. Love here is hardly the question.

From Antiquity to the Reformation

Greek literature and myth supply us with an assortment of marriages and grand passions which embody the extremes of emotion that play through ordinary mortals. Hera and Zeus, the leading Olympian couple, are ever at war and ever united in a marriage from which he strays wildly and she exacts the occasional jealous vengeance. Wily Odysseus wanders for nineteen years before returning to ever courted and ever faithful Penelope, who tests his identity by referring to their marriage bed, which only he would know was immovably constructed around a tree. They lie in it companionably and recount the events of the years. Dazzling Helen, abducted from her husband Menelaus by Paris, launches the Trojan Wars, while adulterous Clytemnestra murders Agamemnon on his return from battle, in part because he has sacrificed their daughter Iphigenia to obtain favourable winds for his ships. She, in turn, will be murdered by her own son. When Jason abandons Medea for a new wife, she kills their children.

All this gives us a sense of the fierce loves and hates which may form the emotional substratum of marriage, but have little immediate bearing on the place of the institution in Greek life.

Though there may have been instances when citizen marriages were sparked by passion – and indeed Greek literature here and there expresses a wish for love in marriage – scholars largely agree that 'the purpose of marriage was to engender and rear legitimate children ... rather than to gratify the emotional needs of either husband or wife'. Athens was 'a society which denied the validity of love as the basis for a happily married life'. As the orator Apollodorus (c. 180–120 BC) is often quoted as saying, the citizen Athenian had recourse to three types of women: a wife for producing children and looking after his household; a concubine for catering to his daily needs; and hetaerae, or prostitutes, for pleasure. Yet the state encouraged contractual marriage and enforced monogamy. In Athens under Pericles, single men were excluded from taking on certain major public positions, while the legislator Solon considered making marriage compulsory. For the Stoics, marrying and having children was a moral duty for any man who respected the divine will. Homosexuality was sanctioned, may indeed have often been the site of passionate love, was certainly sung of by the philosophers as the place of, or path to, an idealized love, yet childless men were derided. A man married in his thirties, his bride was usually in her teens, and would have been chosen by his father.

Under the Roman Empire, men and women had near-equal legal and property rights in marriage. These were arranged by parents, were

monogamous, and were entered into during the late teens: either without a ceremony, the couple having lived together for a year; with a
more formal ceremony in front of witnesses; or, for the rich, with an
elaborate wedding in front of a priest and ten witnesses. Divorce was by
mutual agreement and easy to arrange: equivalent ceremonies were
held. Concubinage was common and homosexuality acceptable, while
sexuality in marriage, many agree, was targeted at procreation rather
than pleasure. St Jerome quotes a lost text by the philosopher Seneca,
tutor to Nero, as saying: 'Nothing is more impure than to love one's
wife as if she were a mistress . . . men should appear before their wife not
as lovers, but as husbands.'

For the Hebrews, if the Bible is to be believed, marriage, the union of
man and wife, is a primary duty. No sooner does Eve's creation take
place than we are told: 'Therefore shall a man leave his father and his
mother, and shall cleave unto his wife, and they shall be one flesh'
(Genesis 2: 24). A nomadic people for whom children not only constitute the continuation of the family line but also provide labour, the
Hebrews were bound by the imperative to 'go forth and multiply'. They
were also bound by an injunction to obedience, first to God and then to
his representative on earth, the father. This is a patriarchal culture.

But while the father's command may trump all others in importance,
the Bible in its very first pages also presents a model for disobedience: parents, it seems, must needs be left, injunctions challenged, laws broken,
knowledge – which is also knowledge of 'the other' and sexual knowledge – sought. Tempted to eat from the forbidden tree of knowledge, Eve
transgresses, soon to be followed by Adam. This sets in train that inevitable
move away from the first parent in which husband and wife 'cleave' to one
another through the travails of life outside a paradise forever lost and forever pursued. Precarious site of disobedience, marriage, for the Hebrews,
is nonetheless both benefit and blessing: 'Whoso findeth a wife, findeth a
good thing, and obtaineth favour of the Lord' (Proverbs 18: 22).

Love and attraction also had a place in ancient Hebrew unions, even
if fathers usually did the choosing of mates and obedience to their will
was enjoined. Nor did love's path run smooth. Paternal law governs the
institution of marriage. Love, as Auden noted, 'we can't compel or fly'.
Law and love have thus ever been at odds. Abraham's grandson Jacob –

he who masqueraded as a 'hairy' man like Esau, his elder brother, in order to dupe his blind father Isaac into blessing him – is the first person in the Bible to be described as a lover. (Desiring is already present in its pages: Abraham's wife, Sarah, unable to conceive for long years, 'desires' a son.) When Jacob is ready to find a wife, he is sent east to Syria by his mother Rebecca, who recognizes the present danger of fraternal retribution from Esau. Her brother, Laban, has an estate there. Laban has two daughters: Leah, the elder, and Rachel, her younger sister. 'Leah was tender-eyed; but Rachel was beautiful and well-favoured. And Jacob loved Rachel' (Genesis 29: 17–18).

Jacob works for Laban for seven years to win Rachel – though, since he loves her, they seem 'but a few days'. This labour constitutes a bride price, which marks a legal betrothal. But Laban cheats Jacob, in a mirroring of the way in which Jacob cheated his own father, Isaac. In the darkness of the wedding night, it is Leah Jacob beds with. Laban has substituted one daughter for another. In law and custom, Laban points out, the elder daughter must be the first to wed. Jacob has to labour for another seven years to win his beloved Rachel, while poor Leah pines. If labouring, overcoming odds, is the lover's task, labouring to produce children is the beloved's. Leah and Rachel compete with each other in conceiving the desired sons, to Rachel's detriment and everyone's unhappiness. In an early version of assisted reproduction, Rachel enjoins her servant's help in the task of procreation: Bilhah acts as her surrogate in Jacob's bed, and gives birth to two sons, before Rachel at last produces Joseph.

Like all desert peoples, the Hebrews sanctioned polygamy, though monogamy gradually became the favoured marital form. Islamic law continues to permit a husband to have up to four wives at a time, if he can distribute time and money equally amongst them. Though the early Hebrews frowned upon divorce, it was permissible – though for the woman, only if the husband agreed. Amongst Islamic peoples, divorce can be initiated by either party: according to scholars, divorce rates during the medieval Islamic world and in the Ottoman Empire were far higher than they are in the Middle East today.

Christianity introduced a radical new note into the Western history of marriage. Love was elevated into an ideal, an emotion targeted, in its highest form, at God and his only begotten son. Christ also 'loved' his followers, who found salvation both in loving him and in being loved. This redemptive form of love has no earthly parallels in the Gospels in the love between man and woman, though its tropes have long affected earthly unions. Sacred love gradually migrated into the sanctified union of couples in marriage: all other love was marked as profane.

The early Christians valued celibacy above all states. Women, as Eve's inheritors, become the unclean agents of original sin, their flesh a temptation to be denied. The primary marriage between Mary and Joseph is not consummated until after the miraculous birth of Jesus, who himself remains the exemplar of chastity. Mary, as the incarnation of motherhood, exhibits the wifely virtues of sweetness and obedience, and an iconic purity – despite the oft-forgotten fact that she bore Joseph some six children. As Paul states, 'It is good for a man not to touch a woman', but to avoid the sin of fornication 'let every man have his own wife . . . for it is better to marry than to burn' (I Corinthians 7: 1, 2, 9).

Since not everyone could equal St Paul in asceticism, sexuality was tolerated by the early Church hierarchy, but for the purposes of procreation only. Adultery as well as divorce and remarriage were prohibited. The highest ideal remained chastity: 'He that is unmarried careth for the things that belong to the Lord, how he may please the Lord: But he that is married careth for the things that are of the world, how he may please his wife' (I Corinthians 7: 33–4). In the same vein, virginity was valued above the marital state. Paul does give marriage a spiritual value by comparing it to the union of Christ with his Church, thereby leaving the way open for later more positive interpretations of the married state. But Christianity had to move a long way from the early Church Fathers to arrive at a statement like Samuel Johnson's to his biographer, Boswell, in an increasingly secular eighteenth century: 'Marriage is the best state for a man in general; and every man is a worse man, in proportion as he is unfit for the married state.'

How much impact ascetic Christian ideals had on everyday mores varied, of course, during the Church's long history and across geographical locations and social strata. Up until the Reformation in northern Europe and a little longer in the Catholic countries, nunneries, monasteries and the priesthood had not only a moral, but also a

practical social agenda. They provided the landed classes with voca-
tional establishments for 'excess' sons and daughters whom family
wealth couldn't sustain. In countries where primogeniture didn't hold,
younger sons' entry into the priesthood also allowed property to move
undivided from generation to generation.

If Christian love was often tough love, its underlying forms of adoration and abjection, along with the difficulties put in the path to
salvation, achieved or requited only through the magic of grace, were
nonetheless mimicked and internalized in secular patterns of courtship.
Indeed, the patterns of courtly and romantic love were deeply influenced by the redemptive Christian paradigm, as was the value placed on
women's chastity and virginity. Women's purity and obedience are paramount because they ensure the legitimacy of the paternal line. In
traditional societies, women's purity also takes on symbolic weight and
stands in for her husband's and brothers', a doubling still evident today
in instances of so-called honour killings.

Chaucer's *Canterbury Tales*, written between 1387 and 1392, offers a
revealing picture of the sexual and marital habits of everyday life.
These hardly always conform to the normative aspirations of Church
dogma. The Wife of Bath has had five marriages all at the church door,
the first at the age of twelve, rather than the single marriage prescribed
by the Church. Weren't human beings made both for duty and procreation? she asks in self-defence, all the while singing the beauty of
sexual parts and telling us that marriage is an economic and sexual
union, whose secret to happiness lies in the wife's dominion over her
husband. The Wife of Bath may or may not have been altogether typ-
ical, but her tale does indicate that everyday practice was far more
unruly than the religious prescriptions laid down. Then, too, the
status of 'widow' brought many more benefits than that of 'wife', since
widows had both legal and financial rights which wives, as their husband's dependants, did not.

Marriage only very gradually came under the Church's full legal
aegis. Lawrence Stone, the great historian of marriage and divorce in
England, points out that until the eighteenth century marriage was an
engagement that 'could be undertaken in a bewildering variety of ways'.
Polygamy was widely practised, divorce a matter of consent, remarriage

frequent, and cohabiting, or concubinage, widespread. Marriage was a private contract concerning property: it gave the woman some protection in case of the husband's death or divorce. For those without property, the community acted as a monitor of the wedding contract and would instil in the partners a sense of what was largely approved or disapproved. Church ceremonies were for the rich.

If practices continued various, by the thirteenth century the Church had established itself fully enough to take over at least the *rules* governing marriage – 'to assert the principle of monogamous indissoluble marriage, to define and prohibit incest, to punish fornication and adultery, and to get bastards legally excluded from property inheritance'. Divorce was now prohibited, but annulments on a range of grounds were possible, though largely only available to the rich. The process of marrying could entail several stages. If propertied, the parents of the bride and groom would first enter into a contracted financial arrangement. A formal spousal – a kind of promissory note or engagement – took place before witnesses in which the couple made their vows to each other. This was considered to be a binding 'marriage' if the couple then consummated their relations, even if no church ceremony followed. If it did, banns were proclaimed three times, or a marriage licence obtained. Finally, the wedding was blessed in church and the mutual consent of both parties orally verified. Not until 1439 did the wedding ceremony itself become a sacrament in England – that is, a rite in which God was active and conferred his blessing or grace on the wedded couple. Only after the Reformation did the Catholic Church insist on the presence of a priest for a marriage to be made valid.

Needless to say, not all marriages followed these various steps. Given Christianity's focus on the individual, all that was fundamentally necessary for marriage was the free consent of bride and bridegroom – as long as the two were of sound mind and of age, which was twelve for a woman and fourteen for a man. This had the effect of liberating the young from parental authority: so-called secret marriages entered into without parental consent and purely by verbal contract in front of a witnessing priest or by licence abounded, since verbal consent by the parties alone was binding. Willing priests, for a fee, were not difficult to find: Shakespeare's Romeo managed to find one easily enough; and despite the tightening of the Church regime in 1604 (which made banns essential and raised the age of consent to twenty-one), they continued to be. The great metaphysical poet of love and later Dean of St Paul's, John Donne, in 1601 secretly married his beloved, Ann More, against the wishes of both her father and her uncle, Donne's own patron. The marriage cost him (and the attending priest and witness) a stay in the Fleet Prison, as well as his post as chief secretary to the Lord Keeper of the Great Seal, Sir Thomas Egerton. It was not until eight years – and almost as many children – later that Ann's father recognized the marriage and offered up her dowry.

The incidence of runaway couples who defied their parents to find an obliging parson rose through the late seventeenth and into the early eighteenth century: if Restoration comedy bears any relationship to the real, parsons could be as obliging as the proverbial French hotel receptionist. In George Farquhar's *The Stage Coach*, Captain Basil talks of a parson who 'first gave us his blessing, then lent us his bed'. 'Common law' marriages – a partnership by mutual agreement and for which no ceremony was necessary – were also plentiful: in America, certain states still recognized these until the 1970s, and some eleven still do so today. In England, common law unions were prohibited only by the Marriage Act of 1753, when the Church of England was put in charge of marriage.

The splits in Christianity that came with the Reformation greatly affected regimes of marriage. Luther championed marriage as a state 'divinely ordained': man and woman were 'created to multiply', and only very few of them made for a chaste spiritual calling. His own marriage to Katarina von Bora in 1525, a nun he had helped after her escape with eleven others from a convent, set the seal on clerical marriage. Katarina bore him six children, and his marriage to this feisty, enterprising and hardworking woman was as influential an affair as Henry VIII's divorce.

By abandoning the concept of original sin and emphasizing the significance of individual conscience as well as private communion with God, Protestantism gave weight both to personal autonomy and to that inner life where love plays so major a part. In England and America, where Puritanism had such a strong hold in the sixteenth to seventeenth centuries, conflicting trends emerged. On the one hand the Puritans, taking their cue from the Bible, insisted on patriarchal authority, that respect and obedience due to the father as head of the family: this underscored paternal power in the choice of a marriage partner and obedience to the husband from both wife and children. On the other hand, the Puritans rebelled against the Catholic ideal of chastity, not only for the priestly classes but as a virtue for all Christians. In his 'wedding sermon' or 'direction for married persons' of 1619, *A Bride-Bush*, the preacher William Whately encourages 'mutual dalliances for pleasure's sake'. Not only is marital sex condoned by the Puritans for the sake of generation, but it is intended for the equal satisfaction of both husband and wife. In the bedchamber, the wife is 'both a servant and mistress, a servant to yield her body, a mistress to have the power of his'.

Amongst many others, the leading Elizabethan Puritan clergyman William Perkins declared marriage 'a state in itself far more excellent than the condition of a single life'. Marriage was now sanctified into 'holy matrimony', a union which not only permitted fornication to be avoided and legitimate children to come into the world, but which according to the Prayer Book of 1549 was conducive to a better life, enabling 'mutual society, help and comfort, that the one ought to have of the other, both in prosperity and in adversity'. These words are an early version of those still used by the Anglican Church today in wedding ceremonies. They are evidence of a general Protestant endorsement of the need for mutual affection in marriage.

Milton, in that great defence of marriage embedded in his *Doctrine and Discipline of Divorce*, takes us one step closer to modernity. He argues that God's intention in creating a 'helpmeet' for Adam was based on the understanding that 'It is not good that man should be alone.' The only conclusion to be drawn from this, Milton goes on to write, is that 'a meet and happy conversation is the chiefest and noblest end of marriage, for we find no expression so necessarily implying carnal knowledge as this prevention of loneliness to the mind and spirit of man'. It is worth noting, in thinking about marriage, how often conversation, another version of that many-faceted word 'intercourse', recurs as one of the underpinnings to its happy state.

The horrors of the Civil War, which had split families apart, often leaving women to fend for themselves and their children, had empowered

women as 'helpmeets' in a new way. Some, like the Leveller women, had
even engaged in direct political action. It could be argued that in England
the ideal of a companionate marriage came early because of the shift not
only in political but in sexual power instigated by civil war.

The Companionate Marriage

Following the trauma of the Civil War, and the brief excesses for the
privileged few of the Restoration, the Glorious Revolution initiated an
epoch of growing secularism alongside economic and political liberal-
ism in England. The end of absolute monarchy brought a diminution of
paternal power in its wake. Self-interest, the pursuit of individual happiness, which John Locke had defined in his *Two Treatises on Government*
(1690) as the basis of liberty, was now understood as something which
extended to the good of the community as a whole. As Alexander Pope
put it in his *Essay on Man* (1733): 'That reason, passion, answer one great
aim/ That true self-love and social are the same.' Individual gratification
was edging away filial duty in the hierarchy of values.

In America, Locke's idea of the 'pursuit of happiness' would find its
way into the Declaration of Independence of 1776. Abigail Adams, wife
of John Adams, who was to become the second president of the United
States, urged him during the process of drafting the legislation to
'remember the ladies' and the state of marriage. He dismissed her
request, even though their own union had been based on a loving
courtship, while respect, mutual care and friendship characterized their
long lives together. But this highly intelligent woman's description of
the balance of power in an affectionate marriage, her use of the term
'happiness', point to the new understanding that had grown up
through the century: 'Do not put such unlimited power into the hands
of the Husbands,' Abigail writes. 'Remember all Men would be tyrants
if they could ... give up the harsh title of Master for the more tender
and endearing one of friend ... [R]egard us then as Beings placed by
providence under your protection and in imitation of the Supreme
Being make use of that power only for our happiness.'

It is clear from fiction and drama from the late medieval period on, that love had long played its part in the making of marriages, despite familial opposition: families ever ranked property, financial gain and enhanced status above the mere matter of love. But, as Lawrence Stone has argued, from the late seventeenth century on in Britain there was a far more general trend towards 'affective individualism' and the 'companionate family'. Love, gradually even romantic love, now took on a central role in the making of marriage. Affection between partners, which includes sexual affection, became widely understood as a good. The statesman and essayist Sir William Temple, whom Jonathan Swift served as secretary during the 1690s, was one prominent voice to put the case for love, decrying materialistic marriage as a 'popular discontent': 'our marriages are made just like other common Bargains and Sales, by the mere consideration of Interest and Gain, without any Love or Esteem, of Birth or of Beauty itself, which ought to be the true Ingredients of all Happy Compositions of this kind, and of all generous Productions'.

Four vying arrangements exist in the making of marital matches. The choice of a mate can rest entirely with parents and kin: this is the order of the day in patriarchal societies amongst the property-owning classes. A second option has parents making the choice, but with a right of veto by the child. There is an underlying assumption here that compatibility is necessary for a good marriage and that a child's antipathy to the parental choice will prevent a reasonable outcome. The next option is that the choice is made by the child, but now the parents have the right to veto a mate made unacceptable by reason of either financial or social place. This is the version of match-making that gains preeminence, though is hardly universal, during the eighteenth century in England and some other parts of Europe, as well as in North America. The final option, in which children make their own choice and then inform their parents, is the one which largely reigns today in the West, except in enclaves where arranged marriages are still the rule.

Marriage based on individual choice and love was on the ascendant during the Enlightenment. But the trend did not go unopposed, in the first instance by parents of the propertied classes themselves. The heated public debates which led to the controversial English Marriage Act of 1753 paint a various and conflicted picture of everyday marital mores, which the Act sets out to tidy in the best interests of the governing class. They indicate, as do the growing number of diaries and autobiographies in this period of increasing individualism, that the course of true love was decidedly bumpy, with steep precipices on both sides.

Subtitled 'An Act for the Better Preventing of Clandestine Marriage', the legislation set out to outlaw bigamy and make it impossible for those under twenty-one to marry without parental permission. The period had seen a boom in clandestine marriages, popular with the poor from 1660 onwards. Elopements by under twenty-ones under the influence of 'love' were numerous: a rash of cartoons show girls climbing out of the windows of boarding schools into waiting carriages. The clandestine activity was abetted by the fact that marriages could be cheaply bought in London marriage shops and in the precincts of the Fleet Prison. There, too, partners for pregnant women could be found for a fee, and unions backdated to legitimize illegitimate children.

Equally troubling to the rising numbers of the bourgeoisie and the landed classes was the laxity of a marriage regime that permitted adventurers and courtesans – 'sharpers', 'bawds' and 'strumpets', as the 1753 parliamentary debate had it – to marry the under-age children of the propertied classes. Men, but also women, on the make seduced the impressionable young of greater wealth and status into marriages rich families could not approve. A bigamist, having seduced a young woman in one part of the country and often got her with child, could move elsewhere and enter into a second marriage, with no one the wiser. Parish records could not instantly be tapped, while poor priests could easily enough be induced into falsifying them. Action had to be taken, as Attorney General Sir Dudley Ryder put it, 'for guarding against the many artful contrivances set on foot to seduce young gentlemen and ladies of fortune, and to draw them into improper, perhaps infamous, marriages'.

The Act brought a law into being that legalized solely marriages performed in a public ceremony according to the Book of Common Prayer, in a local church where the parties would be known, and before witnesses. (Exceptions were made only for Jews, Quakers and the Royal Family.) Marriages had to be registered in a document signed by the parties, witnesses and a priest. For minors under twenty-one, paternal consent had to be given. The Act made all clandestine marriages null and void. Appeal to ecclesiastical courts – as had often been made by women promised marriage, seduced and then abandoned – was prohibited. 'Young innocent girls' under the age of consent led astray by 'rakish young lords and squires' could no longer sue for breach of promise. This was a law made for the privileged. Elite parents needed the state, it seems, to help them keep control of children who might contract 'a scandalous or an infamous marriage'. It also prevented children from prior 'secret' marriages suing for inheritance. Property was paramount.

The Act's opponents, as David Lemmings has argued, were hardly all the champions of love, of individual choice or of defenceless girls and the poor, despite their persuasive speeches. They may have decried 'paternal authority' as being 'whimsical and selfish', and indeed, often enough 'abused by parents'. They may have criticized the Act for attempting to control 'all the emotions of love and genuine affection in youth by the frigid maxims of avarice and ambition imbibed by age'. But amongst the Act's most vocal opponents were instances of men behaving badly that would make today's excesses pale by comparison. Robert Nugent, for instance, spoke in the House of that 'tender and elegant passion we call love' and pleaded the case for the 'fair sex' for whom the Bill would 'prove a snare for entrapping many of them to their ruin . . . A young woman is but too apt by nature to trust to the honour of the man she loves, and to admit him to her bed upon a solemn promise to marry her.' Yet this was a man who twenty years earlier had abandoned his cousin in Ireland, leaving her with a son he refused to recognize, and who had then married ever richer heiresses and a string of affluent widows, all the while 'whoring' elsewhere. Robert Walpole was inspired to coin the word 'Nugentize' to characterize such doings.

Marriages based on that troublesome entity, love, may have been both cultural wish and sometime practice in an eighteenth century that prioritized a degree of individual freedom. This is the period, after all, when for the first time men have their portraits painted with their wives – witness Gainsborough's famous Mr and Mrs Andrews gazing out at their estate and Jacques-Louis David's Lavoisier looking up at his wife with admiration. Yet little was put in place, either legally or through custom, to make women the loving, equal companions Daniel Defoe had in mind when he observed: 'Love knows no superior or inferior, no imperious command on the one hand, no reluctant subjection on the other.'

Though greater and greater numbers of women, stretching to the daughters of artisans and shopkeepers, were taught in the course of the century to read and could take in the breadth of a magazine like Addison and Steele's *Spectator*, alongside a burgeoning variety of novels and journals aimed specifically at women, their schooling was still largely a matter of learning ladylike 'accomplishments'. Grace or deportment, a little piano, some French, and above all needlework and embroidery were skills calculated to allow them to please their husbands and at best run a household. Such an education was often less than sufficient to permit women to establish that 'conjugal happiness' for which it was essential 'that the husband have such an opinion of his wife's understanding, principles and integrity of heart as would induce him to exalt her to the rank of his first and dearest friend'. Though there was a marked improvement in women's education by the end of the century, its aim was limited to turning girls into genteel ladies of leisure, at best mothers able to provide their toddlers with the rudimentary principles of good behaviour. In *The Subjection of Women* (1869) John Stuart Mill could still observe that women's whole education had as its object to please men, their masters, who in the course of the nineteenth century added to the restrictions on women the presumption of an inferior 'mental capacity'.

Crucially, women once married had no status in law. As the jurist Sir William Blackstone put it in his *Commentaries on the Laws of England* (1765–9), 'the husband and wife are one, and the husband is that one'. A wife gave up her entire legal person to her spouse, a fact Daniel Defoe bemoans in *Roxana* (1724): 'the very nature of the marriage contract was . . . nothing but giving up liberty, estate, authority and everything to a man and the woman was indeed a mere woman ever after – that is to say a slave'. Little of substance had changed when Mill came to write 145 years later. Property, children, the wife's very body belonged to her husband, the first two even after his death, unless he bequeathed otherwise. If she left him, he could compel her to return. Any earnings or gifts she might

receive were his. Beatings were no crime. During the nineteenth century there were some slight improvements, but these pertained only to
wealthy women who could afford legal interventions. The marriage
contract could include a clause about a regular sum of pin money being
put at the wife's disposal. Formal separations in which the wife was
granted a financial settlement and possibly allowed to take one of the
children with her became slightly more common amongst the upper
classes. But husbands, unless they were otherwise inclined, had absolute
authority over their wives.

Yet, despite these long-lasting legal and social inequities, the eighteenth-
century ideal of a companionate marriage, one that was sparked by love
and went on to include friendship, mutual respect, sexual pleasure and the
possibility of 'happiness', wore a decidedly modern loving face.

So much so that, seen from Catholic Europe, this marriage based on
love seemed a decidedly odd beast. It could be said that Catholicism, by
allowing sin to be easily absolved through the simple recourse to a confessional, had an easier relationship to individual conscience and
transgressions of the flesh and helped to excuse adultery. As Oscar Wilde
quipped, the Roman Catholic Church is 'for saints and sinners alone –
for respectable people, the Anglican Church will do'. In Catholic Europe,
marriage long maintained its primary relationship to family, progeny
and property, while love resided elsewhere. The Duc de la
Rochefoucauld-Liancourt, travelling through England in 1785, observed
with great surprise that here 'husband and wife are always together and
share the same society', something that would be ridiculous in France.
'Three marriages out of four are based on affection.' Couples had an
'appearance of perfect harmony' and the 'wife in particular has an air of
contentment'. Comparing mores, he reflected: 'To have a wife who is not
agreeable to you must, in England, make life a misery.' In France, as long
as her wealth was intact, it presumably made little difference.

France: From Old Regimes to New

Montaigne, that supreme analyst of his own and the human condition, who bridges the classical past with modernity, was no great

believer in conjugal love. In his famous essay '*De l'amitié*', 'On Affectionate Relationships', he ranks marriage lower than friendship on the scale of affection, though allows that it could be otherwise, if conditions were different.

> As for marriage, apart from being a bargain where only the entrance is free (its duration being fettered and constrained, depending on things outside our will), it is a bargain struck for other purposes; within it you soon have to unsnarl hundreds of extraneous tangled ends, which are enough to break the thread of a living passion and to trouble its course, whereas in friendship there is no traffic or commerce but with itself. In addition, women are in truth not normally capable of responding to such familiarity and mutual confidence as sustain that old bond of friendship, nor do their souls seem firm enough to withstand the clasp of a knot so lasting and so tightly drawn. And indeed if it were not for that, if it were possible to fashion such a relationship, willing and free, in which not only the souls had this full enjoyment but in which the bodies too shared in the union – where the whole human being was involved – it is certain that the loving-friendship would be more full and more abundant.

Under France's *ancien régime*, marriages of whatever class were largely made for the economic convenience of parents and had little to do with the personal feelings or wishes of offspring. Young girls – those subordinate beings, in the eyes of both religious authority and natural philosophy – could be wed to men three times their age, gave over their dowries and all property to the husband's management, and had no separate legal power, aside from what inheritance rights might have been formalized in a prior marriage contract. By a *lettre de cachet*, a secret indictment, the husband could have his wife committed to a nunnery for life.

Ardent critics of a status quo that imprisoned children in parental choices based on status and property, Enlightenment thinkers attacked marriage as a tyrannical sacrament: *indissoluble*, it was an insupportable form of bondage foisted on society by a corrupt and superstitious Church. But the impetus of the *philosophes* was an anticlerical one.

Condorcet apart, who was married to the brilliant *salon* hostess Sophie de Grouchy, they were hardly proponents of marriages based on love.

Rousseau may have thrown the thousands across Europe who read *La Nouvelle Héloïse* (1761), in one of its seventy editions before 1800, into ecstasies and torments. He may have taught them the new romantic language of the emotions and shown them in *Émile* (1762), his treatise on education, that in adolescence the troubled boy turns into that 'loving and feeling being' who becomes a man only by learning 'sentiment'. But Rousseau's lovers, who in *La Nouvelle Héloïse* recast the great twelfth-century love of Abelard and Héloïse, were never permitted marriage. Rousseau's heroine Julie, rather than marry her beloved tutor Saint-Preux, engages in a paternally sanctioned union. She grows 'virtuous' — that word that had migrated from the ancients into the different register of Christianity, to return in this period and take on republican notions of heroism once more — through motherhood and devotion to duty, before dying as the result of trying to save her child from drowning. Meanwhile her heart-broken lover weds her best friend. Old marital conventions remain intact in Rousseau. Like many of the Enlighteners, he kept marriage and romantic love or passion decidedly separate.

The atmosphere of the *salons* the *philosophes* attended in some ways paralleled the old courts of love. Here dazzling, intellectual and married women were at the helm. Madame d'Épinay's *salon* was attended by Rousseau, Diderot, Holbach, d'Alembert and Baron von Grimm. Her intimate, Madame de Necker, entertained both the *philosophes* and writers such as Bernardin de Saint-Pierre. Madame de Condorcet, reputedly the most brilliant of all, entertained amongst many other notables Benjamin Franklin, Adam Smith, whom she translated, and the feminist Olympe de Gouges who early in the Revolution was to write the *Declaration of the Rights of Women and the Female Citizen*. These women were courted and paid heed to. Affairs, even long-lasting ones, were engaged in: Voltaire's with the formidable Marquise du Châtelet, translator of Newton, and his companion in scientific and philosophic pursuits, spanned more than a decade. But the *philosophes*' sense of the appropriate role for the huge mass of women within marriage was one that enshrined virtue, piety and obedience to their husbands.

Double standards were emphatically in place. Even the notorious Madame de Staël – three times exiled by her fierce, tyrannical opponent Napoleon; a woman known to all the intellectuals of the continent and a mass of readers; a woman whose many passions were open and vociferous and included Benjamin Constant, and who, as she turned fifty, married a handsome young hussar (though, as she herself said, her father was her greatest love and the man she would have married) – could do little to change that hard fact.

There was only one brief moment before the twentieth century when French law fully overrode property considerations and sanctioned affectionate marriage above and beyond any familial wishes. In 1792, in the midst of a Revolution whose leaders were intent on wresting power from the Church and promoting liberty and happiness, marriage became a matter of free choice between consenting adults over twenty-one. No longer a sacrament, weddings were now conducted by local mayors in a civil ceremony. Patriarchal power was further reduced by the implementation of laws governing the family. Daughters and sons were granted equal inheritance rights. Before the courts, married women were given the same rights as fathers regarding the welfare of their children. Illegitimate children were treated on a par with legitimate ones. Crucially, divorce was permitted by mutual consent and the grounds were broad: incompatibility of temperament, matrimonial fault – for instance, insanity, cruelty, dissolute behaviour – desertion for a minimum of two years, emigration or absence without news for five years. In distinct contravention of earlier Church rules, the divorced were free to remarry a partner of their choice.

The state of marriage under the *ancien régime* can be judged by the sudden overwhelming surge in divorce figures, particularly in the cities. Between 1792 and 1803 some thirty thousand divorces were granted. Women of the lower and upper bourgeoisie, suddenly empowered in this domain at least, were quick to cite matrimonial fault as their reason for seeking divorce: violence was evidently widespread. Given the upheavals of Revolutionary times, desertion also figures large in the divorce records.

But this decidedly revolutionary marriage regime was short-lived. Napoleon reversed the tide, partly, historians speculate, because of his personal experience. His passion for Joséphine de Beauharnais, a high-ranking, widowed Creole sophisticate — member of the elite, racy circle known as the *merveilleuses* — had resulted in a love marriage on 9 March 1796, just days before he embarked on his Italian campaign. Joséphine, the name Napoleon gave her to replace her own of Rose, was six years older than his twenty-six. After her husband and the father of her two children was guillotined, she had had several influential lovers, including Napoleon's own political patron.

Napoleon's love was real enough, though inevitably in the circumstances propelled by ambitious rivalry. In February 1797 in one of many ardent letters, he addressed her as: 'You to whom nature has given spirit, sweetness, and beauty, you who alone can move and rule my heart, you who know all too well the absolute empire you exercise over it!' But during his absence, Josephine quickly engaged in an affair with a young hussar. When Napoleon learned of it, he took on a mistress. Their relations were rarely less than tumultuous, and were further strained by her inability to produce an heir. Yet the empress of his heart, when he acceded to the title of Emperor in December 1804, did join him on the throne. Divorce would follow only six years later. This had the further effect of testing the Concordat with the Pope that Napoleon had signed in 1801 and which had officially returned Catholicism to France. Strategically, Napoleon then married Marie-Louise of Austria, a wedding the cardinals of France refused to attend.

Often misogynistic in his pronouncements, Napoleon is said to have remarked that this time he had married 'a womb'. He would legislate for just this in his laws on marriage. Marie-Louise dutifully produced an heir, though Napoleon II reigned for only two weeks, in 1814, and died at the age of twenty-one; it was Joséphine's heirs by her earlier marriage who would eventually gain the succession. Meanwhile, Napoleon's dying words have a wonderfully free-associative quality and give the trump card of his chronicle to Joséphine: 'France, army, head of the army, Joséphine.'

Under the Code Napoléon of 1804, married women were once more, like children, returned to the full control of their husbands, who exercised both marital and paternal authority. The new bourgeois marriage followed the old aristocratic codes: property and legitimate progeny were paramount. Women's inferiority in the union was spelled out: they owed submission to 'the man who is to become the arbiter of their fate'. Affection took second place to reinforcing the traditional family. Wives needed their husband's agreement in seeking employment. He took charge of any earnings and looked after their joint assets. Though she might have some rights by prior marriage contract over any property she had brought into the marriage, he remained the final arbiter of her goods and property and could have recourse to violence – though not such that caused public disorder – if she rebelled against his authority. Under the Divorce Law of 1803 husbands were allowed to divorce their wives on grounds of adultery, but women could only sue if the adultery had taken place in the family home. The Code shored up what became the conventional marriage in post-Revolutionary France. This was one in which the wife was honoured for her purity, her maternal abilities, the numerous children the French state (with its constant worries, throughout the century and beyond, over equalling Germany's birth-rate) expected of her, and her rectitude, leaving the husband free to pursue affairs of the loins and heart elsewhere.

Apart from the rather more open acquiescence to a double standard, a different code of 'respectability', bourgeois marriage in nineteenth-century France was in its quotidian aspects not poles apart from what it was in Victorian England. Men were the principal, though in the working and artisan classes hardly the sole, breadwinners. Presumed to be of lesser intelligence, kept far from education, wives softened the trials of the public and industrial spheres for their husbands and had ornamental, perhaps even spiritual value, in their role as 'poets of the hearth', as Madame Romieu put it in her mid-nineteenth-century guidebook for girls – or as 'angel of the house', as Coventry Patmore wrote in his 1854 poem idealizing domesticity. In Republican France and America, to the wife's role was added that of being an educator in civic virtues – the subject of many of the guidebooks of the time, which taught women how to instil their children with piety and patriotism. The hearth now also kindled the minds of the dutiful citizens of the future.

In France, as in much of the rest of continental Europe, marriage for the bourgeoisie long continued acceptably and largely to be a *mariage de convenance*. If love came into marriage's making, it was as a secondary benefit. Fiction both reflected the real and showed the way. Stendhal's and Balzac's heroes and heroines are largely enmeshed in loveless unions of convenience, while grand passions are lived outside their bonds and bounds.

Victorian Marriage

For the Victorians and the North Americans, love-inspired marriages remained the ideal: heart, soul and body – though the last not until the wedding night – were all to be bound into one within an institution that was also the foundation stone of society. Chaste, faithful wives became the keepers of morality, whatever its double standard. Towards the latter part of the century, this labour was more than symbolic. Women campaigned for moral reform and social purity against the commercialized sex of prostitution – the very sex their husbands often bought. Not surprisingly, marriage sometimes foundered under the weight.

Queen Victoria herself set the standard for an ideal union, the very one the romantic fiction available in her youth had evoked. She met her cousin, Prince Albert – who had been delivered three months after her and by the same midwife – when she was just sixteen, and then again at nineteen, by which time she was already Queen. Like all royal marriages of its time, this one was arranged. But her utterances make it clear it was also a love match – though to begin with the carnal attraction seems to have been far more on her side. Albert was, she noted, 'excessively handsome, such beautiful eyes ... my heart is quite going!' 'He is so sensible, so kind, and so good, and so amiable too. He has besides, the most pleasing and delightful exterior and appearance you can possibly see.'

As the wedding approached, Victoria suffered qualms: a queen, she would now, nonetheless, like all women of her time, have to obey another. In his biography of her, Lytton Strachey captures the young Queen's state with impeccable flourish:

she was suddenly prostrated by alarm, regret, and doubt. For two years she had been her own mistress – the two happiest years, by far, of her life. And now it was all to end! She was to come under an alien domination – she would have to promise that she would honour and obey . . . someone, who might, after all, thwart her, oppose her – and how dreadful that would be! Why had she embarked on this hazardous experiment? . . . No doubt, she loved Albert; but she loved power too. At any rate, one thing was certain: she might be Albert's wife, but she would always be Queen of England. He reappeared, in an exquisite uniform, and her hesitations melted in his presence like mist before the sun. On February 10, 1840, the marriage took place.

And if biography and her own letters are to be believed, the two did indeed – despite some early irritation and nine rapid pregnancies which the Queen did not altogether enjoy – live happily ever after. Albert overcame the discomforts of foreignness and the difficulties of being a consort. He established himself in the foreign clime, reorganized the large household, and gradually took over the duties of private secretary, so that Victoria came to depend on his political judgement. The bond between them grew. She prayed most fervently that the Prince of Wales would grow up to 'resemble his angelic dearest Father in EVERY, EVERY respect, both in body and mind'. Three years into the marriage, she writes rapturously to King Leopold of Belgium, 'Oh! my dearest uncle, I am sure if you knew HOW happy, how blessed I feel, and how PROUD I feel in possessing SUCH a perfect being as my husband . . .'

The huge popular and financial success of the Great Exhibition of 1851, devised and planned by Albert, saw her joyous. The event publicly consolidated their coupledom. Her letter to her prime minister just after the Exhibition had closed, on the very anniversary of her betrothal to the Prince – a 'curious coincidence' – expressed her deep satisfaction that her beloved husband's name was now universally recognized by the country and for ever immortalized. She was grateful that providence 'permitted her to be united to so great, so noble, so excellent a Prince'.

When Albert died suddenly, perhaps of typhoid, ten years later, Victoria went into deep mourning. She never abandoned her widow's black.

The romance of domesticity that was Victoria and Albert's union writ large could of course hardly be replicated by her subjects. But it set the tone and aspirations for the nation. Victoria had met and married her handsome prince, the union had been blessed with happiness and produced an ample brood: even a queen, it seemed, could be an obedient and dutiful wife.

Yet love, as desirable as it might be, was not as pre-eminent a driving force in the shaping of unions in Victorian England as it had been in the second part of the eighteenth century. Partly as a result of revolutionary upheavals and war throughout Europe, partly because of the rise of a large urban working class whose presence seemed to the ruling classes to demand more authoritarian social structures, attitudes in nineteenth-century England grew more conservative and the family more disciplinarian. Duty trumped individual inclination and was a primary obligation. The support of a family conferred the stamp of respectable masculinity on the male; while for the woman, the smooth running of a household and the duty of maternity were the marks of successful femininity. Within the family, the father's will was pre-eminent. Even though only the highest echelons of the aristocracy actually arranged marriages, parental agreement, largely tied to questions of class and finance, was essential. Paternal vetoes were not uncommon: letters and diaries of the period describe desperate young women taking to their beds and seeking consolation in long-lasting illness after beloved suitors were pronounced unsuitable or unwanted ones imposed.

In a society where economic independence for middle-class women was all but impossible and work outside of the home frowned upon, marriage, even loveless marriage, was the destiny of choice. The entire education of girls was a preparation for family and the separate sphere. The motherhood it brought was a fundamental obligation: only that conferred status. Families under Victoria grew large: six children or more was not unusual. Though parish records show that most marriages took place when women were aged between twenty-five and twenty-seven, the fear of spinsterhood put pressure on women from adolescence onwards.

Spinsterhood made a woman redundant, 'an excrescence on the surface of society', as Mill put it in criticizing the prevailing attitude. The spinster was not only relegated to the humiliating status of poor relation. She also bore the brunt of a medical and scientific discourse that naturalized maternity as woman's only destiny. Failing in that was to bear a stigma of mental and physiological malfunction. Beatrice Potter, the youngest of eight daughters and later to become the formidable Fabian intellectual Beatrice Webb, summed up the prevailing ideology in 1883 at the age of twenty-five, pointing to dutiful daughterhood as the only possible form of redemption from the stigmatized single state: 'It is almost necessary to the health of a woman, physical and mental, to have definite home duties to fulfil: details of practical management, and above all things, someone dependent on her love and tender care. So long as Father lives and his home is the centre for young lives, I have mission enough as a *woman.*' In contrast to eighteenth-century self-interest, self-sacrifice was the Victorian social ideal.

Competition amongst women in the marriage market was fierce, and exacerbated by various factors. Since economic independence for middle-class men was a necessity before they could engage in supporting a wife and children at the expected social level, from the 1840s on marriage was often postponed at least until the age of thirty. Equality of social status marked another constraint: convention decreed that one had to marry within one's social class. Marriageable women outnumbered men: indeed, there was an imbalance in the entire male-to-female population, which grew with the century. In 1851 there were 100 men to every 104.2 women; in 1881 this had risen to 105.5 and in 1911 to 106.8. Boys died in the first year of life in greater numbers than girls, though the skew in figures was also caused by the large number of middle-class men who worked abroad, either in the colonial service or in the armed forces. For every three men who emigrated, only one woman did.

The numerical availability of women did not, however, necessarily make things easier for the man, if a love match was in question. The onus was on the male to make all the first moves, a process complicated by the need for parental consent to courtship, not to mention the ultimate approval to marry. Neither was necessarily easy to come by.

Records proliferate of unrequited suitors. Parents wanted the certainty of financial security for their daughters. Fathers seem often to have been reluctant to release a prized daughter who provided household management, alongside affection. Disparities in age could also prove difficult to overcome, since convention — rather than example — had it that too great a difference would sow the seeds of later problems: a 'lovesick' suitor of forty might easily find himself rebuffed both by parents and by the far younger woman in question. Prime Minister William Gladstone's son, Stephen, at the age of thirty-seven suffered a rebuff from nineteen-year-old Constance West, as his own father had twice in his youth from women he admired. If the older male was a widower with children, often enough the case at a time when women still all too frequently died in childbirth, there was the added duty to a slew of stepchildren. The physical and mental health of partners also preoccupied Victorian parents as they pondered consent.

Should Mr Right or Miss Right be found, the Victoria and Albert romance had to be lived out according to the edicts of a growing number of marriage handbooks, each of them enjoining the wife to better home management and greater dutifulness to a husband who was permitted a morally and scientifically sanctioned tyranny for the price of 'protecting' wife and family. The conjugal balance had moved away from the previous century's ideal of pleasure for each within a friendly union. 'A true wife,' John Ruskin stated, bringing together the disparate tugs of love and power, 'in her husband's house, is his servant; it is in his heart that she is Queen.'

Sexuality, as recent historians have argued, was not in fact so much repressed by the Victorian middle class as kept away from any sphere of display or everyday discussion. For the young, public and parental silence induced ignorance and acted as a form of coercion: it helped, particularly for women, to keep that chastity in place which would ensure the purity of the eventual family line. Illegitimacy remained a blight for child and mother well into the 1950s, and often beyond. Within the private walls of marriage, sex was sanctified. Here chaste — that is, marital — sex and reproduction were tied into one happy or unhappy bundle. Sex found its way into the public sphere only in discourses of self-control, of vice squads battling against working-class immorality or the sins of prostitution. The public medical discourse functioned within the prevailing moral ethos and strengthened it: it tried to curtail either an unruly instinct, gendered male, which brought both syphilis and venereal disease in its wake, or that sapping of energies purportedly caused by solitary sex. An insistence on women's sexual innocence meant that doctors rarely disclosed a husband's syphilis to his wife: women were protected from knowledge, but not from the horrors of the disease itself. Medico-surgical interventions – such as clitorodec-tomy – also set out to 'normalize' women's desire, when it strayed from its sanctioned legitimately reproductive ends.

In the United States, where social and geographical mobility as well as the diversity of immigrants and races were far greater than in England, public morality was both less stringent and more emphatically linked to self-control – the mark of the middle class. The young were permitted far more freedom: Henry James's American girls in his transatlantic novels always fall foul of European conventions, though his American matrons are far more burdened by propriety than their European counterparts. Public education in co-ed elementary schools spread during the 1830s and 1840s; by 1890 twice as many girls as boys graduated from high school, while college education was available to those who could afford it. As ever, women's education had an impact on birth-rates. American family size fell as the century grew older, par-ticularly in urban centres, though not amongst new immigrants, or in the South or West. Interestingly, literature about contraception prolif-erated in a variety of marriage guides and circulars, as well as in newspaper ads. Public lectures on contraception were frequent, detail-ing the use of withdrawal methods, condoms and pessaries. The 1875 Comstock Act, which prevented such information circulating through the post, was a response to fears about a declining birth-rate as much as a moral crusade. But informal networks of female friends kept contra-ceptive knowledge in circulation. As in Britain, the exchange of information about contraception gradually helped to create a climate where sex and reproduction were uncoupled, and sex, for women as well, became a site of pleasure for its own sake, one not specifically linked to marital duty.

Queen Victoria, mother of nine herself, it is clear from her letters, had a rather unVictorian notion of the link between happiness in marriage and woman's burden of reproduction. Writing to her seventeen-year-old and recently married eldest daughter on 14 April 1858, she expresses a wish that she should enjoy her recent marriage for a while before embarking on pregnancy. 'All who love you hope you will be spared this trial for a year yet ... If I had had a year of happy enjoyment with dear Papa to myself how happy I would have been!' Again on 21 April, she writes: 'What made me so miserable was – to have the two first years of my married life utterly spoilt by this occupation! I could enjoy nothing – not travel about or go about with dear Papa ...'

Victoria's more general views on love and marriage were equally unVictorian. In 1858, she notes: 'I think people really marry far too much; it is such a lottery after all, and for a poor woman a very doubtful happiness.' The theme is reiterated on 16 May 1860, the year before Albert's death: 'All marriage is such a lottery – the happiness is always an exchange – though it may be a very happy one – still the poor woman is bodily and morally the husband's slave. That always sticks in my throat. When I think of a merry, happy, and free young girl – and look at the ailing aching state a young wife is generally doomed to – which you can't deny is the penalty of marriage.'

The ills and discontents of the bedchamber – whether occasioned by the trials of frequent pregnancy, ignorance or the moral double standard – would eventually find their way into the Freudian consulting room as hysterias, neuroses or phobias, or into the numerous clinics and spas of the period as neurasthenias or attacks of the vapours. In the public sphere, for years to come, sexuality's presence remained generally a negative one: linked to prohibition or illness, in total contrast to our own prevailing norms, where pleasure and desire are celebrated – so much so that they arguably produce their own discontents.

As the century moved on, love within the idealized Victorian marriage came under increasing strain. The proliferation of marriage guidebooks instilling the division of sexual labour, with the male as lord and protector and 'the poor woman ... bodily and morally the husband's slave,' itself suggests that imposing the conjugal ideal was proving difficult. Perhaps this was the case even for the Queen herself, who, after the death of Albert, rumour would have it, engaged in an affair, certainly a close relationship, with John Brown. Victoria, however, was hardly a champion of the rights of her female subjects. Having read a report of an 1870 suffrage meeting, she flew into a rage:

> The Queen is most anxious to enlist everyone who can speak or write to join in checking this mad, wicked folly of 'Woman's Rights', with all its attendant horrors, on which her poor feeble sex is bent, forgetting every sense of womanly feeling and propriety. Lady —— ought to get a GOOD WHIPPING. It is a subject which makes the Queen so furious that she cannot contain herself. God created men and women different – then let them remain each in their own position ... Woman would become the most hateful, heartless, and disgusting of human beings were she allowed to unsex herself; and where would be the protection which man was intended to give the weaker sex?

Yet agitation by and on behalf of women went on, and led to marked shifts within Victoria's reign: women, it seemed, and in the first instance, wives, needed protection from men, as much as their protection. If they were to be more than property, they needed to be able to control their own. The 1870 Married Women's Property Act, which allowed wives control of their personal property and income, marked the first substantive legal change in women's status. Much of the credit for the Act belongs to John Stuart Mill, elected to Parliament five years earlier, and his wife Harriet Taylor Mill, his long-time interlocutor and, as some have claimed, his occasional co-author, most notably in *The Subjection of Women*. The passage of the Act was seen by conservatives as a step towards the Americanization of English institutions: various American states had recently passed such measures. By separating man and wife into separate legal entities, the Act seemed to some to be a licence to equality and, hence, immorality. As the conservative MP Harry Raikes heatedly argued, the Act undermined the entire institution of respectable marriage: in a marital quarrel, any wife would be free to say, 'I have my own property, and if you don't like me, I can go and live with somebody who does.'

Despite resistance by both sexes and after much lobbying, the Act was extended in 1882 to give women full separate legal identities: the right to enter into contracts and dispose of property by sale, gift or will. For a woman subject to violence from her husband, the Act allowed for applications to be made for an order to protect her earnings and property and not to be visited by her abusive husband without consent. A mother's legal custody of her children up to the age of ten, and maintenance, were further provisions.

Such legal changes were crucial steps in the slow and always uneven road towards altering the everyday inequalities at least of middle-class Victorian marriage and the morality that underpinned it. Alongside these came a host of other forces for change. One was the growth in democracy itself.

Republican Marriage

The progressive policy-makers of the Third Republic in France provide a clear, modern indication of the way the institution of marriage is conceived by the state as a form both of regulation and of control of a wayward populace. Our contemporary debates about gay marriage or about marriage-inducing taxation can be read as recent equivalents of a parallel problematic.

Guided by a reformist agenda, the Third Republic introduced a new Constitution in 1875. This established universal male suffrage. All men were now autonomous citizens with political rights. But how to make men into *responsible* voting citizens? After what for the French was the traumatic defeat by Germany in the Franco-Prussian War of 1870, followed immediately by the violent upheavals of the Commune, masculinity itself seemed unstable. A national loss of confidence ensued, together with a worry about what some considered had been 'deviant' male excess. How to temper the male into a citizen?

Part of the answer, for the political elite, seemed to lie in propagating a particular vision of marriage. A loving and sexualized marriage, they argued, was a character-forming terrain in which the male, ever prone to wildness and crises during adolescence, instability and potentially irresponsible sexuality, could be contained and turned towards sociable ends. Through loving marriage, he would both learn responsibility and find satisfaction with an equal who was also other. Thus conjugal love, that union of body, mind and soul between two different yet complementary people who would engender more, emerged as a route to citizenship. A selfless, altruistic union which was also pleasurable would provide an important foundation for the shaping of responsible male citizens and sociability itself, the very glue of society. Marriage, for the Third Republic's reformers, thus became both model and modelling ground for a good life.

Within this marital settlement the political class conceived of woman as 'other', in both her vulnerability and her sensitivity. Not constituted for citizenly independence (and not granted suffrage in France until 1944), woman required care. Conjugal love provided that necessary protection and in turn allowed women to protect those other vulnerable entities, children. Odd as it may now seem, this was imagined as a progressive and anti-patriarchal union. Thinkers such as Henri Marion considered women 'morally' equal. Their 'vital solidarity' in union had to be won. Brutality was seen as odious in marriage, as was paternal repression.

Loving, sexual marriage thus both shaped citizens and engendered pleasure. It regulated male extremes and provided satisfaction as well as protection for women. So the reformers of the Third Republic promoted the ideal of conjugal love above marriage based on property or patriarchal wish and enshrined it in their new secular education programme, where women teachers with their capacity for affection rather than patriarchal authority also played a substantial part. Ever contested by more conservative patriarchal forces, though, this ideal republican model of the good citizenly and sexual marriage could be neither quickly nor evenly instituted. It became part of the Third Republic's ongoing cultural conversation and only gradually won ascendance. Progressive as it undoubtedly was in certain respects, it nonetheless left out of its thinking an essential and increasingly noisy force: women's independence.

Decline of an Institution

Ibsen's *A Doll's House* premiered to a scandalized public in Copenhagen in December 1879. The play dramatized what would become known over the final decades of the century as 'the woman question' – the canker at the core of respectable marriage. Brought up to be her 'Papa's doll-child' only to become her husband Torvald's ever pleasing 'doll-wife', its heroine, Nora, has never become a human being. In the third act of the play, after recognizing the growing estrangement between her husband and herself, she breaks free. To Torvald's statement that 'before everything else, you're a wife and a mother' Nora replies, 'I don't believe that any longer. I believe that before everything else I'm a human being – just as you are . . . Or at any rate I shall try to become one.' She needs to leave the doll's house before she can become an individual, become fully human – a full partner in that ongoing conversation that makes and shapes conjugal life. Her slamming of the door on marriage and children marks the play's end.

A Doll's House didn't have a British or American production until ten years later, but Nora's slamming door resonated in pamphlets and on platforms, her cause taken up by liberal males as well as by campaigning women. Interrogated, the sanctified institution of Victorian marriage with its well delineated separate spheres began to crumble under the weight of its own self-sacrifices.

In 1888, the Scottish feminist novelist and essayist, Mona Caird wrote an article entitled 'Marriage' for the *Westminster Review*. She pronounced the institution a failure because it made the wife a piece of property, wholly subservient to her husband, and initiated a bond in which her virtues and honour, or dishonour, became his. The *Daily Telegraph* invited readers to respond. Over the next two months twenty-seven thousand replies came in from women as well as men, even a few from the working class, detailing the tragedies and successes of marriage. They included portraits of drunken, abusive husbands, plaints of growing incompatibilities, stories of desertion and pleas for simpler means of separation. They also included portraits of marriages made happy by the patience of wives, the joy in children and grandchildren, and a reiteration of the willing subjection and frailties of woman – backed up by God and science – which necessitated her protection by the paternal male. Today's blogosphere could not have done better.

The increasing championing of education and rights for women; the insistence that women were not inferior beings ever best served by pleasing and by obedience to a superior masculine will and intelligence; the agitation of highly placed women in the public sphere, as philanthropists, suffragettes or campaigners for moral and social reform; the growing ranks of both single and married women demanding greater access to the professions and economic independence – all played a crucial part in the slow shift towards a different vision of marriage. So, too, did the very presence of an increasingly vocal and visible working and underclass who presented patterns of love, sex and marriage radically different from the ideal. Women constrained by the need to work and by poverty could hardly, whatever their aspirations, be pleasing reproductive household angels, buoyed by the labour of servants. Nor could the wages allotted to their husbands alone sustain a family.

Growing agitation by workers and by women fed into the anxiety about degeneration and the decline of the race that plagued the last years of the century. Men, it seemed, were cracking under the burden of duty – to work, to business, to nation, to God – alongside family obligations. Household violence, recourse to drink and illicit sex spread, and not only through the labouring classes. The clenched lips and fists of respectability and empire-building were taking their toll on the male psyche.

The prolific writer and philosopher Herbert Spencer, who had coined the phrase 'survival of the fittest', too often wrongly attributed to Darwin, is a case in point. Spencer, whom George Eliot had once wanted to marry, served as the model for the petty, dictatorial Casaubon in *Middlemarch*, forever in search of a complete system of knowledge. He was a vocal opponent of John Stuart Mill. In Spencer's vision, the patriarchal family was the model favoured by nature. Women were designed for domesticity. Their submissiveness, intuition and skills in deception, he wrote, were specialized functions, arming them for the business of rearing healthy offspring. Any deviation from that course, any move on their part towards education or intellectual aspiration, would inevitably lead to nervous ills and to the decline of the species. But that very 'nature' which underpinned the Victorian domestic arrangements Spencer championed didn't seem to extend to his own. He never married or fathered children. He also suffered from numerous breakdowns, those unspecific neurasthenias so characteristic of the time.

*

In the last two decades of the nineteenth century and the first two of the twentieth, birth-rates fell sharply in Western Europe and America. Eros and reproduction were becoming unbound. Ideals of sexual purity for middle-class women played their part in this, shadowed, as they were, by the growth of prostitution. In the US in the 1890s almost half of women with husbands in the professions or in business had two or fewer children. By 1910, almost two-thirds of families had no more than two. In France, the government instituted pro-natalist pro- grammes to reward mothers.

The sense of cultural decline which plagued the period was palpable across Europe. Thomas Mann's great saga of German life, *Buddenbrooks* (1900), breathes its very essence. Charting four generations of a Lübeck merchant family which rises with great competitive aplomb to the summit of wealth and prestige only to succumb to a mysterious failure of vitality, almost a love affair with its own dissolution, *Buddenbrooks* has as its central character Thomas, the scion of the third generation. Rigidly conscientious, cultivated, Thomas leads the family to its great- est successes. Yet he cannot shed the sense that he is only wearing a mask of duty, while the energy of maintaining it in place saps his core. His activity is meaningless, his doll-like musical wife an eccentric extrav- agance who prefers another man, his only son overly sensitive and sickly. His sister Tony, the princess of the family, is urged, against her instincts, into a marriage with a rich suitor that goes wrong, only to engage in another which similarly ends in divorce. At the age of thirty- four, she pronounces her life a waste. Thomas, too, succumbs to failure and weakness; his heir, too frail for life, dies. Migraines, bad teeth, blue shadows beneath the eyes, sickly pallor, nervous exhaustion, suffuse the novel. A once vibrant, meaningful world, bolstered by what the great sociologist Max Weber called 'the spirit of capitalism and the Protestant ethic', has come to its end. The dynamism that characterized an epoch has been drained from within: society has grown sick under the weight of its own mores.

In the early 1900s Sigmund Freud drew on his experience of the con- sulting room to pen his analysis of what ailed bourgeois civilization from within. In 'Civilized Sexual Morality and Modern Nervous Illness' (1909) he declared that the marital and sexual mores of the bourgeoisie were exacting a toll on Western health. Underpinning his analysis was the then radical notion that 'In man the sexual instinct does not originally serve the purposes of reproduction at all, but has as its aim the gaining of particular kinds of pleasure.' As Freud would more particularly state elsewhere, the objects of that sexual aim were diverse, both hetero- and homosexual.

The majority, Freud claimed, were constitutionally unfit to face the task of abstinence that was demanded of them before entering on a late marriage, or indeed throughout life if marriage didn't occur. 'Experience teaches us that for most people there is a limit beyond which their constitution cannot comply with the demands of civilization. All who wish to be more noble-minded than their constitution allows fall victims to neurosis; they would have been more healthy if it could have been possible for them to be less good . . .' Sublimation, that deflecting of the sexual instincts to higher cultural aims, was open only to a minority – that intermittently, and least easily 'during the period of ardent and vigorous youth'.

Then, too, the promises of love that marriage held out, after the celibacy of long engagements, were regularly disappointed. Often entered on with too little knowledge of the other sex, shrouded in worries about repeated conception, entailing methods of contraception that hampered satisfactory ends, marital happiness foundered:

> Fear of the consequences of sexual intercourse first brings the married couple's physical affection to an end; and then, as a remoter result, it usually puts a stop as well to the mental sympathy between them, which should have been the successor to their original passionate love. The spiritual disillusionment and bodily deprivation to which most marriages are thus doomed put both partners back in the state they were in before their marriage, except for being the poorer by the loss of an illusion, and they must once more have recourse to their fortitude in mastering and deflecting their sexual instinct.

Pioneering sex surveys backed up Freud's analysis. In the United States Katherine B. Davis, over a period of almost ten years, explored the sexual and marital lives of 2200 women through lengthy questionnaires.

Her wide-ranging sample came from women who had reached marriageable age before the First World War, two-thirds of them born before 1890. The results, published in 1929 in a thick volume entitled *Factors in the Sex Lives of Twenty-Two Hundred Women*, showed amongst other things, that a quarter of her sample were 'repelled' by their initial sexual experience. Little instruction about sex before marriage had been received, and Davis found a high correlation between this, a distaste for sex and unhappiness in marriage.

After five or so years of marriage, Freud pointed out, men often resorted to the sexual freedom that a 'double sexual morality' allowed them. Doubling carried a burden of lies, deceit and self-deception. It was 'the plainest admission that society itself does not believe in the possibility of enforcing the precepts which it itself has laid down'. For women, the effects of 'civilized' sexual morality were even more severe: 'women, when they are subjected to the disillusionments of marriage, fall ill of severe neuroses which permanently darken their lives'. Marriage had ceased to be a panacea for their nervous troubles. Indeed, Freud elaborated:

> the cure for nervous illness arising from marriage would be marital unfaithfulness. But the more strictly a woman has been brought up and the more sternly she has submitted to the demands of civilization, the more she is afraid of taking this way out; and in the conflict between her desires and her sense of duty, she once more seeks refuge in a neurosis. Nothing protects her virtue as securely as an illness.

Bourgeois society had been made sick by its sexual and marital arrangements.

The readiness with which Freud's ideas were taken up immediately before and increasingly after the First World War points to an underlying dissatisfaction with the 'sacrifices' demanded by the late nineteenth century's prevailing codes of love and marriage. It also indicates that a general erosion of patriarchal power and of the demands of 'civilized' double standards had been taking place – sometimes quietly and from within, sometimes more noisily in activism. Women were hardly alone: the bourgeois marriage had been under scrutiny and attack by socialists as well. Engels in *The Origin of the Family, Private Property and the State* (1880) had argued that with capitalism had come 'the world historical defeat of the female sex. The man took command in the home also, the woman was degraded and reduced to servitude; she became the slave of his lust and a mere instrument for breeding children.' For progressives, woman's rightful place had become the new standard of civilization.

All this was attended and abetted by a growth in secularism. The Church's aegis was under attack during the Third Republic in France, when republicans attempted to secularize education and wean wives away from the dominance of priests, bearers of a paternalism that the Republic's reformers understood as antithetical to constituting a responsible citizenry. Revolutionary and socialist movements throughout Europe questioned the Church's reactionary power. Darwinism and the ascendancy of science challenged first principles. 'God is Dead,' Nietzsche proclaimed in *The Gay Science* and again in *Thus Spoke Zarathustra*, pointing to the death of received wisdom and with it any absolute values.

Increasingly the individual, rather than any paternally dominated family group, had become the measure of both happiness and despair. That individual had also acquired a new and complicated depth in which sexuality played a prominent part. Conjugal settlements were poised for reinvention.

Unconventional Arrangements

The Victorian marriage could never encompass the entire variety of conjugal arrangements that people lived. Writers, artists, actors, revolutionaries, those members of what the French had in the 1840s begun to call Bohemia, had always strained against convention in searching to satisfy the needs of love and individual happiness. Even the redoubtable George Eliot, now seen as a bastion of the more capacious Victorian values, had, as Marian Evans, engaged in a radical marital configuration. In 1854 she had bravely and openly started to live with her lover, the writer George Henry Lewes. A radical, he had an 'open' marriage with his wife, with whom he had fathered three children, and took on the care of the three others she had with other men. Needless to say, the Eliot–Lewes intimacy was hardly looked on with favour. Social accept-ance was a long, slow process. Thirty-three years on, when Eliot's work had earned her fame, the couple was finally recognized by 'society', in the form of a meeting with Queen Victoria's daughter Princess Louise who was an admirer of Eliot's fiction.

But as the century moved towards its end and the new, more unbuckled Edwardian era dawned, a flurry of unconventional intimate relations began to be *openly* lived. Most of those that have been recorded are still in artistic, literary and progressive circles, but they do signal a gradual undermining of older codes of love and marriage. Torn between tradition and innovation, love had begun to take on an experimental edge. The balance between being faithful to one's feelings and desires and faithful to one's spouse and social convention tips in the direction of the first, as if the greater morality lay there.

In court during his notorious trial in 1895, Oscar Wilde delineated the classical delights of the 'love that dare not speak its name': all the while his wife, Constance, hovered in the background and never altogether ceased to support him. She didn't sue for divorce, though she did con-strain him, while he was in prison, to give up his rights over their two children. Among its many after-effects, Wilde's trial brought to public awareness the existence of an illicit homosexual subculture that had largely been invisible to the outside world. The exposure had the per-verse consequence of forcing homosexuals to rein in their activities, fearful as they now were of being 'recognized' in the glare of limelight.

Few did more in Britain than the writer and social reformer Edward Carpenter to attempt to normalize homosexual arrangements. Despite the 1885 Criminal Law Amendment Act outlawing sexual relations between men, Carpenter in the 1890s began to live openly with his lover, George Merrill, a working-class man from the slums of Sheffield. The relationship was a lifelong one. In his book *The Intermediate Sex* (1908), Carpenter noted: 'Eros is a great leveller. Perhaps the true Democracy rests, more firmly than anywhere else, on a sentiment which easily passes the bounds of class and caste, and unites in the closest affection the most estranged ranks of society.' Both D.H. Lawrence and E.M. Forster were deeply influenced by Carpenter. Lawrence translated

Carpenter and Merrill's relationship into a heterosexual register (merging it with Lady Ottoline Morrell's affair with a mason on her estate) in *Lady Chatterley's Lover*; while Forster was inspired by it to write his early novel *Maurice*, not published until 1971, after his death, by which time homosexuality had at last been legalized in Britain.

In *Howards End* (1910) E.M. Forster gave his heroine the phrase which summed up the new ethos: 'Only connect.' The understanding of the good life had shifted. The personal, the relational, the passionate – which also permitted congress across class and even gender lines – now weighed more heavily in the human balance than tradition and social convention. Given that in the division of labour which was the Victorian marriage, the emotions had long fallen predominantly into the woman's sphere, it is perhaps unsurprising that the growing forces for change in woman's condition should run concomitantly with a cultural shift which prioritized feeling – and also, on occasion, allowed women to pursue their own desires.

D.H. Lawrence met the redoubtable Frieda (von Richthofen) Weekley in Nottingham in 1912. From the ranks of the German aristocracy, she was certainly 'estranged' from Lawrence by 'class and caste'. She was also married and a mother of three. Soon after their first encounter, Lawrence and Frieda eloped to Germany, leaving her children behind. Divorce from Ernest Weekley, an academic at Nottingham University who also taught the evening classes that young Lawrence had attended, soon followed. In Germany, Frieda's sister Elsa, another free spirit, one of the first women there to do a doctorate in economics, was part of a circle which included Max Weber, with whom she had an affair. The circle also extended to the radical psychoanalyst Otto Gross, with whom Frieda had a brief affair. Gross, a proponent of free love, was involved in various of the pre-war quasi-anarchist, neo-pagan communities in Switzerland – lifestyle laboratories where love threw off the shackles of bourgeois convention.

In France during the *belle époque*, amongst a Bohemia that mingled with the upper class, a looser sexual morality prevailed than in England. Sidonie-Gabrielle Colette's largely autobiographical writings, spanning the first half of the twentieth century, provide an insight into the kind of adventurous intimacies that could be lived. They also chart a course which led Colette through all the permutations of a woman's life, taking us from provincial Burgundy into the inner precincts of the exclusive and all-male Académie Française. An early marriage with the gallivanting literary and theatrical entrepreneur Willy, a *papa-mari* twenty-four years older than her, had Colette chained in sexual-emotional bondage and living power relations that are echoed in many unions between older, experienced men and younger women – though undoubtedly hers have their own particular *belle époque* flavour. Colette depicts all this clearly in the *Claudine* novels which Willy forced her to write, then shamelessly signed himself. They became hugely popular bestsellers, re-enacted on the stage.

In the course of writing the *Claudine* books Colette engages in her first lesbian affairs, which are shared with Willy. She describes both her pleasures and her jealousy. Scandalous material, perhaps, though Zola had already described the lesbian *demi-monde*: nor did *belle époque* husbands bother to rank lesbian loves as adultery. When Colette left Willy, to take up life as a music-hall performer, she created a furore by kissing her then lover, the Marquise de Belbeuf, on stage.

There was a host of affairs with men, too, and a second marriage to a leading political journalist. In *La Vagabonde*, published in France in 1911 when she was thirty-eight, Colette calls love 'that hairshirt which sticks to the skin where love is born and tightens its grip as it grows'. The greatest obstacle to her escape from its torture, 'a hundred times more dangerous than the greedy beast [of lust,] is the abandoned child who trembles inside of me, weak, nervous, ready to stretch out her arms and beg: *"Don't leave me alone!"'* Throughout her life, her biographer Judith Thurman writes, Colette yearned to love and to believe in love. The two rarely coincided, though she engaged in many of the possible permutations. She had her first child in 1913 at the age of forty, went off to report from the front line during the Great War; and at forty-seven engaged in a passionate affair with her stepson before embarking on another marriage with a man seventeen years younger than her, the most peaceful of her long, bold and ardent life.

In Britain, differently inflected experiments in loving similarly engaged the young in the pre- and immediately post-war period. Within the intellectual elite that was the extended Bloomsbury circle, love's preferred form was the serially lived triangle, both homo- and hetero-erotic. As the journalist Kingsley Martin quipped, 'In Bloomsbury all the couples are triangles and live in squares.' To take just one of many examples, Lytton Strachey had a variety of homosexual lovers, briefly proposed to Virginia Woolf, took up in 1917 with the painter Dora Carrington, who was pursued by the artist Mark Gertler but was passionately in love with Lytton. Dora and Lytton lived together until his death some seventeen years later. In the meantime Ralph Partridge, with whom Lytton was in love, wooed Dora, whom he married, though she carried on living with Lytton, who remained homosexual.

All this is known from multifarious books and films documenting Bloomsbury lives. What is clear is that although Bloomsbury forms of coupling were not widespread, their influence, given the prominence of Bloomsbury ideas in the media, on the loosening of conventions in Britain in the aftermath of that vast shaking-up of hierarchies that the First World War produced, was hardly minimal. The new emphasis on 'feeling', on a desire for self-fulfilment, crucially by women as well as men, abutted against older strictures and gradually dismantled the rigid edifice of dutiful marriage, though its idealized ghost remained, ever to be reinvoked by politicians intent on 'family values'.

Already in 1909 H.G. Wells's novel *Ann Veronica*, his portrait of the new emancipated woman, had created a stir by breaching old moral taboos. Denounced as a 'sex-problem' novel, targeted by the *Spectator* in a campaign against 'poisonous literature' and banned from the circulating libraries which ensured a writer's income, the novel was prescient. Based on Wells's own affairs, the fiction lived out a future in which 'feeling' came first. Wells's vivid heroine tapped into the changing times and gave her name to countless other Ann Veronicas, satirized and censured in the press for their independent aspirations and their attempts to define a new kind of love and marriage.

Lively, pretty, intelligent, Ann Veronica is the daughter of an old-fashioned Victorian father who thinks that women are either angels or fallen (if secretly desirable) creatures. He would palpably prefer to keep his daughter by his side. Ann Veronica is both told that love and marriage are the paths open to her and made to feel that it is immoral to show too much interest in them.

> During her school days, especially her earlier school days, the world had been very explicit with her, telling her what to do, what not to do, giving her lessons to learn and games to play and interests of the most suitable and various kinds. Presently she woke up to the fact that there was a considerable group of interests called being in love and getting married, with certain attractive and amusing subsidiary developments, such as flirtation and 'being interested' in people of the opposite sex. She approached this field with her usual liveliness of apprehension. But here she met with a check. These interests her world promptly, through the agency of schoolmistresses, older school-mates, her aunt, and a number of other responsible and authoritative people, assured her she must on no account think about ... It was, in fact, a group of interests quite unlike any other group, peculiar and special, and one to be thoroughly ashamed of.

When Ann Veronica determines to further her education instead, her father makes it clear that studious pursuits 'unsex' a woman; and that befriending art students and going to fancy-dress parties is something he will not tolerate. 'The world, she discovered, with these matters barred had no particular place for her at all, nothing for her to do, except a functionless existence varied by calls, tennis, selected novels, walks, and dusting in her father's house.'

The headstrong, studious and rebellious Ann refuses the advances of a suitor, the older and conventional civil servant, Mr Manning. She runs away from home determined to make her own way in the world. But, despite attempts to find a job in London, no work that will support her is open to her. Through the friendship of Miss Miniver, a suffragette and follower of the socialists and Fabians, she attends lectures and discussion groups. She is both enticed by and sceptical of what she hears, which runs along the lines of 'While we were minding the children they stole our rights and liberties. The children made us slaves, and the men took advantage of it.'

When she sees the idolizing and romantic Mr Manning again, he tells her he too is a socialist but in the manner of Mr Ruskin: he would make the country a 'collective monarchy' and all women 'Queens'. In fact, since he has two votes, he is also happy to vote for her. Ann Veronica rejects his marriage proposal: given the example of her elder sisters, she thinks of the married as 'insects who have lost their wings'. Her brother Roddy, in colloquial idiom, tries to convince her to follow the straight and narrow for pragmatic reasons: 'Providence, I mean – HAS arranged it so that men will keep you, more or less. He made the universe on those lines. You've got to take what you can get . . . Babies and females have got to keep hold of somebody or go under – anyhow, for the next few generations. You go home and wait a century, Vee, and then try again. Then you may have a bit of a chance.'

Ann Veronica resists, but she is getting desperate. Her money is running out. Enter a neighbour of her father's, Mr Ramage, a broad-minded businessman who is enticed by her and loans her £40. Ann has no idea that the loan carries a sexual IOU. She is altogether intent on paying back the funds. Then, too, she likes Mr Ramage, likes talking to him over delectable dinners. With the new funds, she pursues her interest in science and enrols at Imperial College. Here she gradually and without quite realizing it falls in love with one of her teachers, Capes, who pays her little special attention. She learns on the rumour circuit that he is married, though estranged from his wife.

Perversely, it is Ramage who makes her realize that 'the problem of a woman's life is love'. One night he takes her to the opera. In the midst of the swooning music of Wagner's *Tristan und Isolde*, he declares his passion for her. The following night in a private and locked restaurant room, he makes a more aggressive pass. As the 'dozen shynesses and intellectual barriers' that have been built up in her dissipate, she recognizes his loan for what it is. She resists him and flees. In despair, she realizes she can't pay him back. Agonized by her state, she joins the suffragettes and in an action on Parliament is arrested. She spends two months in jail, during which she has ample time to think. She has been cruel to her father and aunt, she realizes. Selfishness has guided all her behaviour. She will change.

The change takes her home to her father and into an engagement with the adoring Mr Manning. He is happy for her to continue her

studies. But her feelings for Capes grow: she can talk to him about anything. He makes her feel alive. With Manning, she reflects, as the
engagement progresses, it is just the reverse.

> She was never able to trace the changes her attitude had undergone,
> from the time when she believed herself to be the pampered Queen of
> Fortune, the crown of a good man's love (and secretly, but nobly, wor-
> shipping someone else), to the time when she realized she was in fact
> just a mannequin for her lover's imagination, and that he cared no
> more for the realities of her being, for the things she felt and desired, for
> the passions and dreams that might move her, than a child cares for the
> sawdust in its doll. She was the actress his whim had chosen to play a
> passive part.

Ann Veronica's sentimental education thrusts her into the love idiom of
modernity. Capes, unlike Manning, sees her not as an abstraction of idealized femininity but as herself, sees her in the particular: 'Capes looked
at one and not over one, spoke to one, treated one as a visible concrete
fact. Capes saw her, felt for her, cared for her greatly, even if he did not
love her. Anyhow, he did not sentimentalize her.'

But Capes does love her. He has simply been trying to protect her
from the kind of scandal a relationship with him would unleash. He
cannot marry her in his present legal state, yet he desires her in a way
good girls flee. Ann Veronica is not afraid. A new sexual frankness is the
order of post-Victorian times. The two go off to Switzerland together
and on their return set up house. Roll on the years to the last scene of
the book, and we see them at home and finally married. Veronica is
pregnant.

Wells's idiom of love and eventual marriage includes desire from
both sexes as well as equality, that important element of talk, and sexual
honesty: it gives a primary place to individual fulfilment. If Ann
Veronica – like Lawrence's heroines – finds in herself a new talent for
submission once passion comes into the love equation, this, too, is part
of the dawning century's understanding. Unlike their Victorian sisters,
women now share in desire and can express it, though it may make
them dependent: the male's new power includes awakening that desire

and giving sexual satisfaction. The language of duty and protection has been displaced. If this is still largely the case only for the social vanguard, it will soon enough percolate through society as a whole.

Whether the new model of love and marriage brought the satisfactions it seemed to promise remains open to question: each subsequent generation has questioned the values of the parental ethos. But what is clear is that the patriarchal marriage of the Victorians with its distinct roles for male and female and a power balance largely in favour of the first has rarely since held with no questions asked, even amongst immigrants to the West from more traditional communities.

Wells in his own life marked the shift, never unproblematic, from the Victorian to a version of the 'modern' marriage. The youngest son of a struggling shopkeeper and a mother who returned to domestic service after her husband's early death, Wells was at first unhappily apprenticed to a draper, then a chemist, then another draper. His mother harboured lower-middle-class ambitions for her sons. He battled against her to return to school. His intellectual abilities won him a place in a national science teachers' training scheme at what was to become Imperial College. Here, under the Darwinian T.H. Huxley, he at first excelled, then grew bored and devoted himself to student politics and journalism. He taught at various schools and in 1891, his first major article on the marvels of the natural world having been published in the *Fortnightly Review*, he married his cousin Isabel.

A year later, now twenty-seven, Wells fell in love with one of his students, Amy Catherine Robbins, whom he dubbed 'Jane', 'a fine and valiant little being' who was also intelligent, educated and beautiful. The illicit couple lived together in a modest flat, where the bedroom was separated from the rest of the living space by folding doors. Like Ann Veronica and Capes, neither of them was particularly eager to engage in the institution of marriage. However, in 1895, when Wells's divorce came through, they wed, largely to escape the perpetual annoyance of prurient neighbours and landladies. Jane remained Wells's wife all her life, acting as secretary, business manager, hostess to an increasing array of friends as his books began to win him fame and fortune, and importantly, a still, secure, ever understanding centre of unconditional love.

The only problem was sex. In Wells's words, his 'delicate' Jane 'regarded my sexual imaginativeness as a sort of constitutional disease; she stood by me patiently waiting for it to subside'. Wells engaged in a series of passionate affairs with extraordinary women, the writers Elizabeth von Arnim and, famously, the feminist Rebecca West amongst them. What marked his and Jane's marriage out as different from the Victorian model was that a regime of frankness prevailed. They were allies, he later noted in his *Experiment in Autobiography*, rather than lovers. He told her of his affairs, which she referred to as 'passades' – the assumption being that he would always, and in fact always did, return to her.

This honesty at home, whatever the attendant unhappiness, was linked with the emphatically modern sense that not to act on passionate interests was itself a moral betrayal, an ethical imperative he shared with Rebecca West. In a 1911 article in the *Fortnightly Review*, penned after attacks on *Ann Veronica*, Wells wrote: 'We are going to write of wasted opportunities and latent beauties until a thousand new ways of living open to men and women.' Sex was now part of a new terrain, to be explored in writing as well as through a lived visionary politics. In a society which was still largely conventional, a host of problems attended both the project of an open marriage and open passionate affairs, but, like Sartre and Simone de Beauvoir some twenty years later, Wells and his various partners were convinced that only revolutionary experiments in living could shift prevailing double standards.

Yet the tangles of Victorian values in the sphere of love and marriage were too deeply internalized to shed easily. Indeed, they would enmesh several successive generations, making one wonder whether they are so engrained in family patterns that they hover like vengeful ghosts through all our couplings.

In her subtle portrait of Wells and Jane's marriage in *Uncommon Arrangements*, Katie Roiphe shows how Jane, despite her grace and surface unflappability, despite her apparent understanding that Wells needed the unconstrained embrace of purportedly more passionate women, suffered through his affairs and worried with each subsequent one whether this was the one that would rupture the marriage. Well before Virginia Woolf wrote *A Room of One's Own*, Jane kept one in Bloomsbury, a space never visited by Wells and a signal of her independent need for something other than the domesticity to which her marriage, at once shrine and prison, had confined her. More revealingly, Jane's own stories describe a woman rather different from the one Wells had idealized into his own pure Jane, who so beautifully kept his children and Easton Glebe, the idyllic home and garden his own parents could never attain. Rosalind, the vivacious heroine of Jane's 'Walled Garden', shares many of the attributes and circumstances of her creator. The wedding night she has so eagerly awaited with her beloved Bray brings little of the anticipated fulfilment: 'Bray made love to her delicately and reverently, and Rosalind, after the interval of puzzled discovery, settled down to her married life with a feeling of faint disappointment which she could hardly justify.' If this is any indication of the prevailing condition of Jane's marriage to Wells, it suggests a woman who, far from finding Wells's sexuality rampant and 'waiting for it to subside', had passionate cravings of her own which he, in his need to assume her delicate purity, was unable to meet.

This picture of the Wellses' marriage, for all its unconventional honesties and openness, thrusts one forcefully back to Freud's 'Contributions to the Psychology of Love' (1910, 1912). Here Freud unravelled what he understood as our civilization's universal tendency to split love into the sacred and the profane. Whether his 'universal' extends beyond his historical and geographical moment to our own is, of course, open to question, but it is worth keeping in mind, as are so many of the templates of love which seem to bracket a lived experience at least in part impervious to historical forces.

'Psychical impotence', Freud notes, is the most widespread complaint met in the consulting room. It affects men of 'strongly libidinous natures' who find themselves unable to make love when they wish to with women they may love. Some feature of the sexual object seems to give rise to an inhibition of their potency. The man may have 'the feeling of an obstacle inside him, the sensation of a counter will which successfully interferes with his conscious intention'. Freud argues that a split between 'the affectionate and the sensual current' has occurred here. The two have failed to combine, usually as a result of the young man's sensuality being unconsciously tied to incestuous objects – in other words, mother and sisters. Though initially desired, the child gradually realizes, mothers are for affection, for pure love. Forced to avoid the 'affectionate current', that is, women who in some subliminal way remind him of the mother – or whom in time he makes into 'mother' and thus can only avoid – the man seeks out for sexual satisfaction women whom he can in some way despise, or debase in order to despise. Only here can his sexuality be fully expressed.

'Psychical impotence' haunts not only those who make their way into the analytic chamber. Most, after all, have a childhood shaped by the incest barrier and are in some measure fixated on their first love object, the mother or mother surrogate, and undergo some sexual frustration in the years after puberty. Thus in various gradations, psychical impotence affects everyone who manages to perform the sexual act but takes little pleasure from it.

> They seek objects which they do not need to love, in order to keep their sensuality away from the objects they love; and in accordance with the laws . . . of the return of the repressed, the strange failure shown in psychical impotence makes its appearance whenever an object which has been chosen with the aim of avoiding incest recalls the prohibited object through some feature, often an inconspicuous one.

Hence, Freud drily notes, the unhappy condition of modern men: 'Where they love they do not desire and where they desire they cannot love.'

Women are hardly immune from this psychical impotence. It can manifest itself as frigidity, often present only with their 'lawful' spouses, though absent in secret or forbidden encounters. Prohibition plays the role for women that debasement does for men. Since women, in Freud's day at least, tended to stay pure until marriage, which came long after sexual awakening, their sensuality lingered far longer in secret phantasy. Thus, for women, forbiddenness itself becomes sexualized: only in secret or dangerous encounters do their passions find freedom. The need for secrecy may indeed also in certain respects underpin the need for 'a room of one's own'.

Freud puts his hopes with the sexual reformers – though, with his usual wry pessimism, he notes that his research 'cannot predict whether other institutions may not result in other, and perhaps graver, sacrifices'. For instance, he argues, if sexual freedom is unrestricted from the outset, that does not result in full satisfaction either, since 'an obstacle is required in order to heighten libido'. Where there have been few natural resistances to satisfaction, as during the decline of the ancient civilizations, love became worthless and life empty; so, Freud concludes, men have ever erected barriers of convention so as to be able to enjoy love.

For all of Wells's and other reformers' conscious intentions when engaging in sexual revolution, the unconscious return of that dividing line between the 'sensual and the affective currents' haunts their relationships. Jane Wells remains forever pure and perfect in Wells's imaginings, while the women who 'fulfil' his sexual needs are, certainly in his fantasy, either wild and disreputable like Rebecca West, married like Elizabeth von Arnim (and thus defiled by the very fact of adultery), or in some other way excessive or unstable, like the poor Hedwig Verena Gatternigg, the translator who pursued him to the point of attempting suicide.

As for Jane Wells, if she didn't quite escape the role of angel in the house, to which Wells, whatever his fictional derision of it, had confined her, she made the best she could both of the house and her enshrined status. Easton Glebe, with its gardens, grounds and tennis court, graciously welcomed a host of writers, politicians and glitterati. It had an aura of perfection. Meanwhile, the heroines of the stories she wrote in that Bloomsbury room that was her own suffer from frustrations and a sense of anxiety and abandonment that might well also have been hers.

If marital and sexual happiness for both partners was not within the early sexual reformers' reach – or indeed, of many since – it nevertheless insistently became the ideal for what heterosexual love should be. The Victorians had kept sex wrapped in veils of silence; and bodies, as well as any reminiscent parts, cloaked in ample swathes of textile, velvet and brocade. The post-war period lifted the veils and the cloaks. A new age of permissiveness and sexual candour dawned. That twosome of love and marriage was partially uncoupled. Where it held, it now openly included at least the desire for sexual satisfaction for both husband and wife.

Post-War

Permissiveness came hand in hand with a new self-styled, increasingly noisy and important social category: youth. Across Europe and America, the young, since the turn of the century, had become rebellious and vocal. They defied the rules and the authority of the fathers, who were no longer called upon to sanction love and marriage. They advocated change, political, social; and sexual reform or revolution. In Germany, the youth movement, the *Wandervögel* sang the values of nature – and sometimes free love – while deriding the materialism that industrialization and a coercive centralized government had brought in their train. *Jugend* – youth – gave its name to a magazine and an artistic style. In France, research questionnaires using the language of generation showed how distant the young had become from their rationalist and relativist teachers and parents. In Russia, revolutionaries like Alexandra Kollontai attacked the traditional marriage and family for an oppressive legacy intimately linked to property rights. They called for free love, that is, love untyrannized by the link to material values: sexuality was proclaimed a human instinct as natural as hunger or thirst. In Italy, *la giovinezza* – youth – became a rallying cry: Giovanni Papini in 1913 summed up the feverish feelings of his cohort, amongst whom were the Futurists, when he wrote of the need to cast aside 'the cloaks of religion, the cassocks of philosophy, the shirts of prejudice, the ties of ideals, the shoes of logic, and the underwear of morality' in order to become nude like Adam before the Fall.

Though it was the 'fathers' who had entered into that long agony which was the Great War, the zest with which the young threw themselves into the patriotic fray spoke of their desire for radical change. It came at a heavy cost. The toll of four years of war and an approximate total of 5.7 million dead for the Allies and four million for the Central Powers, alongside many more wounded, most of them young, finally unseated the old morality and the old hypocrisies. The brute proximity of death, of maimed male bodies an everyday sight for young female nurses, had loosened the hold of old conventions. Couplings, courtships, marriages had all been speeded up during the war years, and patriarchal authority was at an ebb: in the shadow of death, the young wanted to live, and live fully.

In the war's aftermath, frankness was in the air. All fixed values were under interrogation, and along with them the very constituents of masculinity and femininity. The new looseness of dress and behaviour echoed gender and psychic instability. Near memories of the dying and the visible presence of the crippled and wounded induced a counter-stress on the pleasurable uses to which bodies could be put. Frenzied activity was everywhere: dancing, cycling, motoring, sport, and sex itself, were the order of the day. In France, the poet and novelist Pierre Drieu La Rochelle returned from a war he had found transformative – a war that made the young the bearers of 'a revelation and a revolution' – to evoke a 'complex of desires, inevitabilities and miseries' which drove alienation, frantic activity and debauchery. 'They experimented with pederasty, and slept with one another's women out of boredom and in obedience to the law of novelty.' The German poet and novelist Erich Kästner evoked the heady and often desperate sexual permissiveness of Weimar Berlin's night-life in the new all-dancing and polymorphous epoch.

> Here specialists can hardly say who's who
> Or tell the kidney from the heart.
> Here women are an all-male crew.
> Here all men play the woman's part.
> Here young lads dance the latest hits
> At ease in gowns and rubber tits,
> While in falsetto they descant.
> Here women in tuxedos groan
> With Santa Claus-like baritone
> While lighting up – Havana brand.

A rhythmic music imported from the New World gave its name to the age: jazz. Flappers decked the dance floors of ballrooms and cabarets from Berlin to New York. Dancers, cyclists, sports figures and motorcars found their way into the new art of the period. Women, too, were now up and raring to go, their young, lean, racy, short-skirted movement informing ideas of beauty. The ample matron, as an image of desirable womanhood, retreated. So too did her double, the suited, rotund patriarch, rendered powerful by wealth or achievement. Male icons of the day were sensitive, daring youths, who Rudolph Valentino-like wore their hearts and nerves on their faces. Or they were golf and tennis players, motorcyclists whose dashing smiles adorned the new advertisements. The rise of film, news and magazine photography helped to invent and spread the new visual ideals. Celebrities were often photogenic twosomes, like glamorous Scott and Zelda Fitzgerald, who lived fast and drank hard and had an edge of palpable sexiness about them.

Women of all classes had taken up work during the war. After it, they could not and would not easily give up some of the pleasures of independence. Even though the numbers of returning soldiers needing jobs often meant women lost their wartime work, the taste for accomplishment and independence lingered, making them less 'dutiful' to both fathers and husbands. If marriage was still a general desire, if the stigma of 'spinsterhood' and redundancy still fell on single women, the moral burden of singleness lessened a little. The death of so many men in the trenches had created a significant gender imbalance in the population. Single working women and widows were more prominent than they had been and a widening range of permissible forms of work was open to them, from the professions to stenography to the growing entertainment industry.

In England, the young war widow Mollie Stack founded the Women's League of Health and Beauty. In 1923, Mrs Hilton Philipson — 'pretty and attractive', according to *Time* — once a Gaiety Girl, Mabel Russell, became the third woman to be elected to the House of Commons. A few years later, in a very modern version of the Cinderella story, the American press sang the romance of paper tycoon Archibald Robertson Graustein who fell in love with and married the Roseland hostess and dancer Claire Patton, a small-town divorcee, who took courses at Columbia University while working at the famous Manhattan dance club.

Not only had class divides grown a little more permeable, but so too had higher education for women. To some, the latter seemed a huge impediment to a good marriage. At a 1923 meeting to support the endowment of four women's colleges at Oxford, male voices deplored the fact that only 657 of the 12,607 women who had 'passed through' the university had married, a certain sign that they were 'hardhearted'. The principal of Newnham College, Cambridge, denied the charge, while a representative of the Women's Freedom League stated that there was little in marriage to attract highly educated women. Apparently, a Dr Joshish Oldfield agreed, pointing out 'that brainless women make the best wives'.

Throughout the twenties, debates about love and marriage – and whether they could survive women's work and education – were open and fierce. The so-called war between the sexes, which had been under way in its contemporary version ever since Ibsen's Nora had slammed the door on her 'doll's house' and Strindberg had drawn out its infernal lineaments in his *Dance of Death*, was now writ large in everyday life. Fear of the new emancipated woman sometimes expressed itself in the old nineteenth-century degenerationist idiom, into which a smattering of the more recent sexologists' language found its way. Sometimes the fear took on apocalyptic dimensions, which read like harbingers of our own time. Removed from her natural destiny as wife and mother, Anthony M. Ludovici declared in his *Lysistrata, or Woman's Future and Future Woman* (1927), woman became 'unsexed'. This marked a step towards the end of the species as we know it. Soon the triumphant feminists would be calling for 'extra-corporeal gestation . . . a means will be discovered by which the fertilized ovum will be matured outside the female body'. Men would become utterly superfluous. The idea of artificial gestation outside the womb had first appeared in the geneticist J.B.S. Haldane's *Daedalus, or Science and the Future* (1923/4). It was taken up by his wife-to-be, Charlotte Haldane, in her futuristic novel *Man's World* (1926), where female reproduction is controlled within a rigid caste system ruled by the masculine figure of the scientist. So the fears about power over reproduction in this era of changing gender roles already cut both ways.

The Earl of Birkenhead, Secretary of State for India, had a rather more nuanced and pragmatic, albeit conservative, view of women's independence and its impact on marriage. By 1928, working women, necessary in wartime when men were at the Front, had work only because they were cheaper to employ than men; furthermore, their employment kept men out of work. The impact on that desirable institution of marriage and on general happiness was great:

> Every woman in industry who by underselling her labor deprives a man of his post is making more difficult the setting up of a home by that man. This prevents some other woman from becoming mistress of his home and exercising the rights and privileges inseparable from that position ... Any skilled dramatist could simplify the problem, after the custom of his craft, by presenting to us a study of a man and woman about to marry and applying, each without the other's knowledge, for the same post. If he secures it, the play ends happily. If she secures it, the social loss is clear. This is what actually is taking place on a large scale — all over the world.

Birkenhead's measured polemic had already played itself out in popular fiction like the American Charles G. Norris's *Bread* (1923). No great novel, Norris's detailed narrative yet pointed to the difficulties confronting working women: their very independence, it seemed, made any enduring satisfaction in love and marriage problematic. From an impoverished family, Norris's heroine Jeanette finds work and rises through the ranks of business to become private secretary to the head of the firm. The man she is in love with, Roy, works alongside her, and though marriage is on the cards, she decides against it: it would lead to restricted means and living in a tawdry little house. She 'gives' Roy to her sister and they proceed to have children. When devilish Martin comes along, however, career woman Jeanette is swept off her feet. But the marriage is doomed: he's a spendthrift and she misses her work, so after four years they split up and Jeanette returns to her post. Fifteen years later, not only has she hit the proverbial glass ceiling, but the pleasure of work has run out. Jeanette finds herself lonely and ageing, with only maiden-aunthood for comfort. Her unambitious, maternal sister is better off. Norris's moral for women is distinctly: 'Home is best'; yet on the way this long novel raises problems of what is now called the

'life–work balance' that continue to perplex. Does independence unsuit
women for the traditional status of wife – the satisfactions and excitements of work being, at least in the first instance, potentially greater
than that of marriage, certainly once love has fled?

Polemicists, the popular press and eventually, with the Depression,
the economy urged women back into marriage and motherhood as
primary aims, willing them to give up notions of independence – financial, intellectual or indeed, sexual. The last proved the most recalcitrant.
Let out of Pandora's box, female desire was reluctant to be again
repressed, any more than the male's. The angelic, spiritualized wife was
now also publicly and sometimes self-avowedly a sexual wife, whether
too much so or not enough. Passionate love had publicly moved into
the marital bedroom. Here, too, the wife might need to be controlled.
But that control for many was hard to come by: pleasure was not necessarily within either man's or woman's conscious reach. Even
Mussolini, in that early Fascist discourse which hadn't yet turned
women into the state's idealized reproductive machines – symbolically
as wedded to the Duce as the old Catholic nuns had been to Christ –
presents an ambivalent message. 'Love is the prime pastime of
mankind,' he declares. 'Modern woman cannot get away from love.' In
something of a non sequitur, he draws on the primitivism then in
vogue, which designates the elemental and passionate as somehow
ancient, to conclude, as D.H. Lawrence might have: 'She is no new
woman . . . Crushed and yet conquering . . . she is just what man wills
her to be . . . Man is in full possession of woman's liberties, and measures
them out to her.'

Whatever the countervailing tides of moral panic, the public hunger
for debate and knowledge about the nature of love and sexual fulfilment in or out of marriage grew throughout the post-war period. Marie
Stopes's *Married Love* (1918) may have had a struggle to find a publisher,
but it sold an astonishing two thousand copies in a fortnight, made
Stopes famous, and was followed in the same year by a second volume,
Wise Parenthood. Banned in the United States because of its explicit advice
on and advocacy of the importance of sex in marriage, *Married Love* had
come out of Stopes's own marriage to a man she long hadn't recognized
as impotent. Her aim was explicitly to educate in an area where

'instinct' didn't suffice in dealing with the complex creatures that man and woman are. It was also to normalize the centrality of sex in marriage: 'In the following pages I speak to those – and in spite of all our neurotic literature and plays, they are in the great majority – who are normal, and who are married or about to be married, and hope, but do not know how, to make their marriages happy and successful.' With Stopes, as with Freud (though the idiom is different), sexuality, in part freed from reproduction, becomes its own category, intermediate between body, psyche and society. It continues to be a powerful player – key as it now is to happiness, love and marriage – throughout the century and into our own. Guidebooks and advice columns on sex and love begin to proliferate, as do the medical and state interventions that prescribe the shifting lines of normality and deviance.

The Mid-twentieth-century Marriage

Married Love earned Stopes the condemnation of the Church and the medical establishment in 1918, but by the thirties ordinary marriage guidebooks were offering up a mixture of her advice, plus a popularized version of Freud, as universally acknowledged truths. Here, from London in that decade, is *Every Woman's Book of Love and Marriage and Family Life*:

> ... we are still, unfortunately, suffering from the repression of the Victorian age which regarded all sex matters as unmentionable. Yet those who are best qualified to judge – ministers of religion, social workers, doctors, and all psychologists, agree that without proper sex education, there can be no upholding of the high standard of married relationships on which we have always prided ourselves as a nation.

The book's anonymous author even quotes the Archbishop of Canterbury as saying: 'I would rather have all the risks which come from a free discussion of sex than the great risks we run by a conspiracy of silence ... We want to liberate the sex impulse from the impression that it is always to be surrounded by negative warnings and restraints, and to place it in its rightful place among the great creative and form-ative things.'

Happy, healthy sex was now, it seems, part of the Church's (at least, the Church of England's) mission, within marriage of course, where it was important for all incumbents to know that the sexuality and sexual needs of men and women were different. For woman, presumed to be inexperienced, slow to be roused and slower to be satisfied, it was imper-ative to banish 'any fears and any holding-back of her true nature. Only if her mind and her spirit are in real sympathy with the physical expe-rience will she know the complete satisfaction which can come from it.' As for the man, 'as a rule [he] regards the sex act more naturally. As his satisfaction is more easily attained, he must teach himself to be patient.' The newly married maid must learn to let go, while the presumably more experienced man must, at the beginning of marriage, act as a teacher and initiator. 'Lack of response on one side or lack of consider-ation on the other can lead to frayed nerves, bitterness, and even a parting of the ways.' Worse still, the thwarting of this natural instinct of sex 'almost invariably leads to a certain lack of mental balance. It may be very slight – perhaps a gradual inability in fixing the attention, a poor memory, a slight hesitation in speech or manner or action, but it may lead to some breakdown of a much more serious nature.' So 'orgasm' is recommended – its lack may even affect the vitality of offspring.

The language of 1930s guidebooks is inescapably admonitory, even when dealing with pleasure. What is interesting here is that sexual sat-isfaction for both parties is urgently seen as fundamental to a good marriage. The openness about sexuality, the acknowledgement of it as an important element in marriage, found an interesting confirmation in the Kinsey Reports of 1948 and 1953, the first on the sexual behaviour of the human male, the second on the female. Kinsey linked the greater incidence of orgasm in marriage for those who had married in the 1920s to its 'sexual revolution', the more open attitudes and sexual frankness it had created.

The basic conjugal arrangement that the *Book of Love and Marriage* describes remains the old one – the man at work, the woman at home, managing the house and the children. There is nonetheless a new pre-sumed equality between the partners, and also a new tone to accompany this modern marital settlement. The wife is addressed as a rational being who needs to be persuaded, indeed cajoled, into giving up work during marriage – though a little part-time work is not amiss. The book's voice assumes both that she will understand that her husband's masculinity is at stake if she works as much as he does, and that she wants (for her own good) to keep that malehood undaunted:

> One of the most undesirable effects of both partners going out to work is the effect it has on their characters. For instance, the husband can scarcely adopt the right attitude of the male if his wife does the wage earning, too! It gives him an inferiority complex, whether he realises it or not – and she becomes dissatisfied, and may well wonder why she married at all, because all she seems to have gained is added responsibility. It is easy to say 'But that wouldn't happen with us; we understand each other.' Probably the people it does happen to understand each other all right – but all the same they find that they cannot account for sudden changes, for little dissatisfactions and quarrels, for this, that, and the other – and it all boils down to the fact that their natural reactions have been upset by the fact that they are both trying to do the man's part.

However, once this 'natural' division of labour is accepted, the woman is urged by the guidebook not to behave like a 'doormat', to have ideas of her own, to earn her husband's intellectual respect. The new wife is accepted as an intelligent woman, an equal partner in marriage, a joint decision-maker, though give and take here is underlined as important. A 'quick-change artist' who needs to be nurse, companion, housekeeper, cook, valet, comforter, sweetheart, counsellor, helpmate and entertainer, she is also occasionally enjoined as a complicit superior, equal to the guidebook's authorial voice. Men, the book clearly states, are susceptible to flattery. Particularly when he reaches a certain age, say his thirties or 'middle age', it is not uncommon for the man 'to imagine that he is in love with a little slip of a girl old enough to be his daughter'. The wife is counselled not to stand on her pride but to woo this now infantilized, adulterous male, who has succumbed to a little 'illness', and win him back with a new hairdo, dress, attentiveness and flattery. After all, she holds the trump cards: he loves her, she is the mother of his children. He'll soon realise 'what a fool he has been'. Men, too, are advised to look squarely at their own lacks and failings: if they see their wife's attention wandering, it may be for good reason. They are also advised to pay attention and set a good example through their behaviour to their children, and particularly to step in to provide their sons with sex education.

The new conjugal arrangement that *Every Woman's Book of Love and Marriage* sets out is one that largely prevailed as the ideal until around 1970. Inspired by love, underpinned by sexual satisfaction, frank, companionate and equal within its own boundaries, sustained where finances made possible by a largely stay-at-home wife who looked after the desired children and by a responsible, providing husband, this was the model that characterized what has become known as 'the golden age of marriage' in Britain, and with different emphases in non-Fascist Europe and America. As ever, there were differences in how the institution was lived, based on local community, class, religious or educational emphases, and generation. But during this period, people married at ever younger ages and in greater number. In Britain, for instance, between 1931 and 1935, the first-marriage rate per 1000 women over fifteen was 57.3, and for men 62.6. By 1966 to 1970 it had risen to 94.2 for women and 82.1 for men, while the mean age of first marriage had gone down from 27.3 for men and 25.4 for women in 1931 to 25.4 and 22.6 respectively in 1971. By 1981–5, however, the marriage rate had dropped to 59.9 for women and 48.1 for men and first age of marriage had risen again. Given increased life expectancy, the mid-century years are also those when marriages last longer than at any other time in history.

The thirties model of marriage shifted somewhat during the Second World War when women moved in large numbers into the workplace. It returned with the demobbed soldiers, who once again displaced them. In part as a reaction to the laxity and excess which the looser mores of war permitted – as ever, a time when teenage pregnancy and extra-marital sex increased, across class and national lines as well – the post-war marriage took on a more austere and less open sexual cast. The late forties and fifties saw a return to sexual puritanism within a general atmosphere of conservatism and conformity. But if there was less frank and public talk of sex in these years, the underlying marital principles remained the same. This 'golden age of marriage' championed its mutual and relational benefits, alongside individualist claims.

This was the great era of 'family life'. After wartime hardship and austerity, which in Britain lasted until 1954 when rationing finally came to an end, a new, more affluent world dawned under the aegis of welfare states throughout Western Europe. Health and the education of children were prioritized. Housing stock was improved to include indoor lavatories; more homes were built stretching out into the green suburbs. Heating systems changed: the Clean Air Act of 1956 in Britain marked a conversion to smokeless fuels, thereby putting an end to the smogs that had choked urban populations. The growing number of private cars fostered mobility and those seaside holidays and expeditions into the country which have played so central a role in the retro literature of the century's end.

Crucially, television brought entertainment into the private, familial sphere. British cinema was still too often tied to the exploits of wartime. The small screen, however, brought viewers young and old, seated in the comfort of their armchairs, everything from the homey thrills of *Dixon of Dock Green* and the laughs of *Hancock's Half Hour* to *Crackerjack*, *Andy Pandy* and *Blue Peter* — as well as, in 1966, the World Cup. There were quiz shows, the more demanding delights of *Quatermass*, *1984*, the *Armchair Theatre* series and the arts programme *Monitor*. Through these years, a host of Westerns and American cop shows gradually arrived to augment the schedules. Television had become one of the glues of common culture.

Companionate marriage, freely entered into on grounds of love and hopes of sexual satisfaction, as well as of children, was emphatically part of that commonality: the desired goal of men as well as women. Shared family life, an ideal of domesticity, 'a home of one's own', were understood as keys to happiness: self-actualization, the fulfilling of individual potential, through this mid-century moment, was wrapped up in marriage and family for both sexes. Using the criterion of durability, as Lawrence Stone points out, 'marriages in the mid-twentieth century were more stable than at almost any other time in history, despite the high divorce rate. In the United States in 1955, the average marriage lasted thirty-one years.'

The British anthropologist Geoffrey Gorer carried out two major surveys on marriage, one in 1951, the second in 1969. Based on responses to questionnaires from over ten thousand newspaper readers, the second survey shows how expectations of marriage had grown. The earlier period's sense of marriage, though based on love, described a rather more pragmatic relationship – a familial sphere of affection and responsibility divided along traditional gender lines. Over the intervening years the emphasis began to shift. Respondents to the second survey stressed the value of comradeship, companionship and communication, alongside love, a good sex life and emotional and sexual exclusivity.

The demands that marriage now had to meet were very exacting indeed. All the goods of earthly paradise had become bound up in a single social institution predicated on fulfilling unruly sexual and romantic dreams as well as the high callings of friendship and self-realization. All this for both parties, and through the birth and rearing of those dangerous rivals children, and their children – and all this faithfully and for ever. Disappointment and worse was inevitably at hand.

Unmaking Marriage

Many factors played into the rupturing of the mid-century conjugal ideal – though always unevenly and never absolutely, since it continues in our own time to haunt many public discussions, private conflicts and hopes about the lineaments of marriage. The list is largely familiar. The growth of university education for women and their access not only to work but to professions and a variety of employment opportunities understood as 'careers' – a sequence of posts which afforded advancement – ended the old economic balance which enshrined the husband as the principal breadwinner. The arrival and subsequent dissemination of the contraceptive pill in the sixties liberated women to engage in sex with various partners, without danger of pregnancy – and thus of the children who had always been central to the marital state. Reproduction within marriage too could be controlled, resulting in smaller families and, given increased longevity, potentially an ever longer period in which the couple had no children at home.

The women's movement of the 1970s, in part a response to inequality and the unhappiness of educated women in marriages that chained them to the home, freed women from their secondary and financially dependent status and made marriage a choice rather than a necessity. In doing this, it also inadvertently liberated men from the burden of responsibility to family life: marriage emerged as a choice that might implicate them in the loss of too many others.

The women's movement also involved a rebellion against an insidious ideology, particularly prevalent in fifties America and rolled out from the psychiatric professions. Based in part on a misunderstanding of Freud's work, though found in that of his disciple Helene Deutsch, this assumed women to be fundamentally 'passive', indeed 'masochistic', and saw their ultimate fulfilment, the resolution of all their problems, as lying in motherhood. Any straying from this assumed natural path was seen as a denaturing and marked the woman as a suitable case for treatment. In the same way, the psychiatric professions stigmatized homosexuality as an illness. Questioning such assumptions about femininity, repositioning gender, inevitably had an impact on marriage, the roles its players took on and the hopes it was expected to meet.

But the breakdown of the model of marriage that had persisted from the thirties into the early seventies was not only linked to women's changing condition and economic self-sufficiency or the rise of the gay movement. Many other and disparate factors came into play. One was the shift from urban to suburban living, particularly in the United States, which had made the 'home of one's own' a reality for ever greater numbers. This had a less than salutary side-effect. It displaced stay-at-home mothers into a distant, often solitary, sphere far removed from other family members and one-time friends. Meanwhile, 'hubby' worked hard to attain promotion in the city rat-race and provide the ever greater quantity of goods needed to maintain an affluent family life in an era marked by rising consumerism. Given that half of all American women in the fifties had tied the knot by the age of twenty (a significant proportion dropping out of university to do so or marrying immediately after), the child-centred isolation of suburban existence with its average of three children (2.2 in the UK), and surprisingly more amongst university graduates, led to a lifestyle replete with the tensions that gradually undermined the stability of this kind of marriage.

Suburban living, with its simultaneous and contradictory emphasis on competition and conformity, seemed to bring few psychic benefits to either partner in the marriage, though perhaps cleaner air, gardens and comfortable houses had some salutary impact on those baby-boomers who would eventually make up the rebellious cohort that brought into being the social changes of the late sixties. For women, suburban life had the perverse effect of escalating the household work-load, necessitating the ferrying of offspring to and from school, friends' houses, and activities. Wives in the US were putting in from fifty-one to fifty-six household working hours a week, while those who had to go out to work for a living (or to acquire the required goods for the desired lifestyle) were clocking up thirty-four hours of housework in addition to their paid employment. For men, caught in the corporate rat-race, it could mean increasing estrangement from the idealized lives they were helping to support.

Fifties affluence arrived earlier in America than in war-exhausted Europe. It came hand in hand with commercial media that fuelled demand for products, while enshrining an image of the perfectly groomed housewife, kittenishly sexy, surrounded by a panoply of labour-saving appliances, waiting for her darling husband to return home to a perfectly cooked dinner with their well scrubbed children. Doris Day and Debbie Reynolds were the period's film icons, replacing feisty, fast-talking and glamorous Katharine Hepburn and Rosalind Russell, who had portrayed married journalists and lawyers, though rarely maternal heroines. In the earlier period's comedies of remar-riage, in which the latter starred, courtship was a conversation underpinned by attraction: through it, man and woman changed, and achieved new perspectives on themselves as well as on the earlier, col-lapsed, union.

By the fifties, such popular big-screen films as *His Girl Friday* or *The Philadelphia Story* had given way to television series such as *Father Knows Best*. The programme had begun its media life on radio in 1949, when a terminal question mark was part of the title. It then ran on various networks from 1954 to 1960 and went into repeats until 1964, spanning the whole of the period's ideal marriage. Robert Young played Jim Anderson, a mid-West, middle-class insurance salesman, married to Jane Wyatt's Margaret, everyone's hard-pressed mom. Their three children present the sitcom issues that the couple need to deal with. The occasionally irascible father doesn't always know better than his level-headed wife, but between them the family allows the illusion to be good-humouredly maintained. If Dad is infantilized in more than one episode, this good-enough family permitted America both to laugh at itself and learn the values that underpinned the epoch.

Yet the fifties media ideal of marriage was often hard to achieve. The pressure on husbands to attain promotion at work and earn enough to maintain their families in required style was high. The pressure on wives to achieve familial perfection alongside personal and sexual satisfaction, equally so. This was the era of 'mother's little helper', those 'happy pills', Miltown and later Valium. To help them get through, mothers, if they could afford it, resorted to a shrink or to sedation, which induced a state not all that different from its satirized image in the 1974 film *The Stepford Wives*, in which perfect wifehood is achieved through robotic implants. Needless to say, men too took the pills or the drink that kept the sufferings of reality at a sufficient distance to allow the dream of happiness to roll on, at least for a few more years.

The television series *Mad Men* wittily portrays, with full period detail, the lifestyle of those 'hidden persuaders' of affluent America, the ad men who purveyed the happiness and glamour that could purportedly be bought into by the purchase of any and all commodities. It is 1960 in the all-drinking, all-smoking offices of Stirling Cooper, the fictional ad agency of the series. Sexism is as rife as it can get. Secretaries, preferably pretty, big-bosomed and ever-helpful, are rampantly pursued by a mostly married male cohort of ambitious creatives, whose come-ons are as crude as their rivalry. Meanwhile, the principal wish of the secretaries is to marry, leave work and take up the superior position of wives. Only Peggy hovers on the cusp of the old and the new, and rises to the position of copywriter.

Our hero Don Draper, rather more subtle and troubled than his mates and all the more seductive for it, tells an attractive client and potential conquest, who owns a Fifth Avenue department store in need of a make-over, that 'romantic love was invented by people like me'. While he pursues an affair with a Greenwich Village bohemian, his university graduate wife Betty, mother of two, has been languishing in the suburbs and suffering from growing isolation in her superficially ideal life. She develops nervous tremors with no organic cause. Don finally agrees that she can see a psychiatrist – though shrinks, he underlines, are supposed to be only for the unhappy. In this male world, the psychiatrist dutifully reports back to Don the content of his sessions with Betty. And while Betty lies on the analyst's couch, Don, not much happier than she, lies on his mistress's and ponders Freud's hoary question, 'What Do Women Want?' The answer, it seems, is 'any excuse to get closer' – not so mad as all that, given that Don barely manages to engage in any sort of conversation with his wife. But the insight is, of course, in the first instance only a copy-line for the firm's latest product, a male deodorant in that handy new invention, the aerosol can.

Richard Yates's fine novel *Revolutionary Road*, made into a film in 2008 but originally published in 1961, speaks of the time's malaise from within it. Yates subtly illuminates the cancer eating away at the suburban family dream. Ambitious, self-regarding Frank Wheeler, husband of April, father of two darling blond children and with an unwanted third secretly on the way, can fulfil neither his own once hoped-for potential nor his increasingly bored and fraying wife. Nor can the couple escape to their dreamlife of Paris, with tragic consequences for April.

By the mid-sixties the perfect fifties mom had grown into the sexually voracious, alcohol-fuelled, terminally bored Mrs Robinson (Anne Bancroft), who in the film *The Graduate* (1967) seduces a young Benjamin (Dustin Hoffman), struck by anomie after returning home from East Coast academe. Suburbia has become a land where grimacing adults can only offer the word 'plastics' to convey a vision of the future the young refuse. Husbands are disappointed and hard-drinking, or dull providers of material comfort. Everything is swathed in swimming-pool torpor and numbness of habit: 'People talk without speaking', as the Paul Simon song which sets the tone of the film has it. Even a conversation with one's mistress is an insurmountable feat. The sprightly fast-paced talk of forties comedies, which held up sexual and verbal exchange as a way of negotiating past and future, is several Grand Canyons away. Grim eater of young men and of her own blossoming daughter, self-avowedly 'neurotic', Mrs Robinson, like all those around her, is ripe for feminism and a different vision of marriage or at least of coupledom.

Urged to date the Robinsons' daughter Elaine by her own guileless father and his parents, Benjamin at first refuses, only eventually to fall in love with the one common spirit she provides. But when Elaine learns of his 'rape' of her mother, she storms off back to Berkeley. Soon she is engaged to be married. Learning of this, Benjamin sets off to stop her. He arrives at the church at the very moment the couple are about to consolidate their vows in a kiss. Perched Christ-like in a gallery on high, he screams her name and offers salvation from a frozen version of adult marriage and affluent suburban life. 'It's too late,' Mrs Robinson says to her daughter. 'Not for me,' Elaine lashes back, racing towards Benjamin. In the film's last scene, the two young people are pictured on an ordinary bus as they flee into an unknown future of undefined coupledom.

The continuing interrogation of gender roles by the women's and gay movements and an increasingly more permissive cultural consensus, which by the seventies had also introduced no-fault divorce in most Western countries, undermined the mid-century marital settlement. As women increasingly entered the labour market and became independent consumers, the centuries-old conjugal economy, dividing work in and out of the home along sexual lines, crumbled for the middle classes. The shift, perhaps suggesting long-pent-up problems internal to that earlier marriage settlement, saw an exceptionally high number of divorces during the late sixties and seventies, particularly in the US where the divorce rate doubled.

Despite the impression sometimes given by the press and by conservative politicians engaged in shouting the breakdown of marriage over the last thirty years, the number of divorces per thousand people in fact peaked in 1981, falling from that high point of 22.8 divorces per 1000 married couples to 16.7 per 1000 in 2005 in the US, and to 11.5 in the UK. (Interestingly, throughout the nineteenth and twentieth centuries in

the US, it is women who filed for just over two-thirds of all divorces.)
The conventional hearsay, however, that one out of every two marriages ends in divorce, holds: 48 per cent of marriages entered into in the
1970s did dissolve within twenty-five years. For first marriages entered
into in the eighties and even more so in the nineties, however, the proportion dissolved by each anniversary has been consistently lower.
Scholars sifting the statistics contend, perhaps surprisingly, that it was
the fifties and early sixties which bucked an earlier trend in length of
marriage, to which we have now returned. Only in couples over fifty
have divorces of late increased. These late divorces tell a many-layered
tale. The one-time old now stay young, and certainly have an aspiration
to stay young longer. If sixty is the new forty, then there's time for a
second or even third partnered life, particularly for men, whose ability
to start new families usually stays intact. In this the contemporary male
is not so different from his Victorian equivalent, though then the wife's
death in childbirth, rather than divorce, occasioned the new union.

But divorce statistics tell only part of the story. One of the main features of the more liberal consensus in the West has been the rise and rise
of cohabitation, particularly in Europe, since the 1970s. The end of
cohabitation doesn't register in the tally of divorce rates, of course, and
such unions can arguably be as stable or unstable as legally sanctioned
marriages. Americans today, however, still value marriage itself – far
more so than Europeans. They engage in it earlier and re-engage in it
after divorce, even after several divorces. Perhaps because of greater
geographical and job mobility, perhaps because of what Alexis de
Tocqueville called the country's 'restless temperament', Americans
have the highest divorce, romantic break-up and remarriage rates in the
world: 10 per cent of American women – a far greater proportion than
their European sisters – will have lived with three or more husbands or
domestic partners by the age of thirty-five. But now, it seems, cohabitation is on the rise in the US too, in part as a result of divorce rulings
and custody settlements which favour women.

In February 2010, the latest figures for England and Wales noted that
marriage had dropped to its lowest point since records began in 1862. A
similar fall is visible in the rest of affluent Europe. Yet researchers tell us
that marriage makes men, though not always women, live longer and

more happily, as well as both parties richer and their children more successful. A 2002 study by Warwick University showed that in material
terms 'a happy marriage was equivalent to an annual income of
£70,000', and its impact on health was equivalent to giving up smoking.
For women, who paradoxically wish for marriage more than men, the
marriage benefits are not so great: compared to single or divorced
women bolstered by friends, divorced men seem to suffer more from
depression and their careers are less successful.

Those who do make the choice of engaging in marriage as a public
ritual, researchers also say, are more committed to staying together
than those who cohabit. Recent research conducted by the University
of York shows that couples who cohabit are two and a half times more
likely to split up than the married: what keeps the married together is
not the certificate, but their understanding of their commitment and
their fundamental attitude to the union.

And if in much of Europe official marriage is on the decrease, royal
weddings continue to excite our fantasy. Meanwhile Americans still
seem to love matrimony itself – with or without that useful tool of a
prenuptial agreement. The National Marriage Project at Rutgers in New
Jersey has also pointed out: 'More than 90% of women have married
eventually in every generation for which records exist, going back to the
mid-1800s. Even the most extreme predictions for the current generation of women say that at least 4 in 5 will marry.'

Today's Unsettled Unions

While it would seem that we want marriage, long-term unions and
now civil partnerships as much as we ever did, and that we value them
as an ideal and as public rituals, we find it more difficult to make up our
minds to settle or stay in them. This is the case for women as well as
men. Interestingly, in the cities of the newly flourishing nations such as
China and India, the age of first marriage for women has risen sharply
in the last years and is now around thirty, matching the West. Women's
education and financial independence simply mean later marriage,
whatever the culture.

In the West, the desire for security and the desire for desire seem particularly embattled in our uncertain and overtly sexualized times. Against the background of our speedy, mobile, impatient yet risk-averse consumerist culture of equality, where everyone bears an entitlement to peaks of happiness, the decision to marry requires financial guarantees, a determination to fidelity on the part of both partners and a sense of certainty that life and love can rarely provide. The decision to stay together despite the inevitable harassments of everyday life, meanwhile, needs a devotion to the original wish and a realistic confrontation of the downs that any life brings.

If conjugality marks the union of the sexual with the social under the banner of love, it also entails the moment when we move from being children into being adults. Adults in our world have a less than good reputation. As parents they may have behaved erratically or irresponsibly, put a cachet on self-interest, and hardly hidden that behaviour from their children. These last decades have emphasized the value of youth, its freedoms, passions and excesses, far above any more measured maturity. Our icons could not be further removed from the serenely hatted middle-aged men and matronly women of the fifties. Our old, too, aspire to the lifestyle of youth, as ageing rock-stars tripping the boards have recently exemplified. So it is hardly surprising that the step into 'adult' versions of love should be delayed by the children of the long baby-boomer generation who made a virtue of behaving badly or rebelliously. Too much, it might seem, needs to be given up, particularly since marriage, and even long-term cohabitation, now once more carry a decided onus of monogamy. The sixties parental generation was more relaxed about the vow of fidelity.

The French art critic and writer, Catherine Millet, in her autobiographical *The Sexual Life of Catherine M* pinpoints a rather extreme instance of this casual relationship to fidelity. A sixties self-styled 'suffragette for the libertine life', she engages in adventurous and plentiful sexual exploits. It comes as something of a surprise in the midst of her cool, precise narrative to find that throughout she has also lived a conjugal life – in her twenties with one man and since her thirties with another, to whom she is married. The sheer number of her extra-marital partners may outstrip most, but what is common is that the generation of the so-called sexual revolution had a rather more ambivalent and differently weighted sense of the very *value* of faithful monogamy from their children. This was evidently in part because they rebelled against the freighted *époque* of the conventional fifties of their parents. In turn, their children, too, have rebelled, if in complicated ways.

For many of the young today, a stream of love and sex relations is common. The sex itself may feel more like a duty one is driven to perform for 'health' and self-image reasons, than a desirable transgression. Sex, after all, no longer has an altogether positive mystique surrounding it, tainted as it is by ideas of abuse, infection and inequality. Then, suddenly, when a 'serious' relationship is on the cards, fidelity and monogamy become crucial to the twosome (whether heterosexual or gay), as do equal and sometimes opposing rights to satisfaction.

One of my interviewees, an attractive film-maker in his thirties, provided a vivid insight into the relational morality of the young. He remarked that the parental generation had been in many respects much freer than his. Having come of age under the shadow of Aids, when sex might mean death for both if either partner strayed, fidelity was a given for his generation. No 'serious' union could be engaged in without that commitment to faithfulness being in play. And since that commitment came hand in hand with the decision to have children, it was difficult for both partners, not only the male, to undertake. Everyone knew that once children came on the scene, sex went out of the window and life became a matter of acquiring cribs and prams, the right house or flat, the right school – a consumerist progression that didn't stop for twenty years, at least. Bye-bye pleasure. Even if you wanted children, as he had in his last 'serious' twosome, the woman might not be ready. She, too, had a career to consider and had to make choices. Now, since he wasn't yet ready to engage again, when he met a woman in her thirties to whom he was attracted, he checked to see that she wasn't after a 'serious' relationship. It wouldn't be fair not to, since she might feel her biological clock was ticking away.

Given our culture's stress on rational decision-making, even in an area where reason is rarely at the forefront, little wonder that so-called commitment phobia is rife. Though the term is most vocally applied by women to criticize men, women, too, have their apprehensions about the symbolic rite of passage that marriage is. Another of my informants, a woman of thirty-eight, said she had only now agreed to marry her 'serious' partner of six years, though he had often asked. After all, she had her work, her flat, her sense of independence. It was only the thought that there might be children on the horizon that had convinced her the man she had long been living with might just be Mr Right-enough to warrant marriage.

Some of the young men I talked to gave another reason for delaying any commitment to marriage or monogamous fidelity. They didn't want to repeat the sins of the fathers and inflict the pain of separation on partners, so it was best to keep things casual. But of course, while postponing the moment of cohabitation or marriage, with its contemporary onus of fidelity, they had already in some instances enacted what they feared, and inflicted pain on a string of earlier partners. Meanwhile, adamantly independent young women, refusing what might be the maternal model, were partly taking revenge on long-suffering mother and unfaithful father by abruptly cutting off relationships with their own mates.

Marriage carries centuries of social baggage, alongside familial hauntings. In our risk-averse society, where economic independence for both partners is often the norm, it's hard to decide to take the plunge and harder still to feel buoyed by the everyday fact of it once the inevitable difficulties set in.

Back in 1918, the American humorist H.L. Mencken quipped that a husband was an indentured servant – all duties pertained to him, all privileges to the woman. With the undoubted benefits that have accrued from the growth of women's equality, it is too often forgotten amidst the sometimes noisy backlash that it has also benefited men. Liberated from the discipline of a social model that marked responsibility and the altar as the underpinnings of mature masculinity, men were freed to engage in serial or multiple relations with no stigma attached. They were also freed from being breadwinners and supporting a wife. In the fifties, when the average age at which a man married in the US was twenty-three, to be a bachelor was an indication of deviance. Even a successful writer like John Cheever, whose diaries show him to be self-avowedly attracted to men — a passion only irregularly indulged — sings the praises of the beneficial ideal of marriage and sub-urban home life to which he is tortuously committed. Now, for men, though still far less for women, there is no stigma attached to single-dom. Nor, conversely, are there those old-fashioned rewards from dependants for being a good provider.

The anthropologist Claude Lévi-Strauss noted that the heterosexual bond depends on a firm division of labour. A woman does X, a man Y — and they are branded female and male activity and considered a fair exchange. Over these last decades, when both men and women do a proportion of X and Y, the division of labour within the heterosexual bond, along with the bond itself and the constituents of what can be branded male and female, have had to be negotiated at each step.

Equality today is understood as the due of both partners. Each is entitled to emotional and sexual fulfilment and the space in which to actualize their potential. Each must have the freedom to pursue work or a profession in a world of increased job mobility where employers most often set the rules. Partners in the adventure of coupledom, both now also share responsibility for all facets of existence from decision-making to nappy-changing, stocking the refrigerator, keeping up the social contacts, building each other's self-esteem, while at least inter-mittently engaging in erotic play and providing satisfaction.

It is no wonder that commitment to the bond is an arduous step; and once made, difficult to hold on to. Never an institution that was free of them, these new strains have made the path of marriage a thorny one to navigate. In what the great sociologist Zygmunt Bauman has called our 'liquid age', where we are ever in pursuit of the next tantalizing product, it's onerous indeed not to cast one relationship aside with the lure of another and better in view.

Yet the motor of love is powerful, and people do commit. At first at least, they ride blindly and blithely enough along. But the road of expe-rience is full of stumblings and wrong turns. It is when the potholes gape, the abysses appear on either side, that the real challenges emerge. And that is where we have to test our understanding of what it means for two beings to carry on loving each other — happily enough ever after, or thereabouts.

Happily Ever After

What is it that we value about marriage and long-term cohabitation, value so much that they rank high amongst our pursuits of happiness? This union with another constitutes a major step into the wider social world. It is the space from which we undertake the projects of life, provide hospitality, find meaning. From here, too, we give new life, nurture new existence, extend ourselves beyond mortality. The homes we make with partners provide a shield against the ups and downs of the wider world, a place of belonging. Where else is there to feel safe, to put to rest that core helplessness that trails us from early childhood and which we once looked to mother or father to assuage? Where else is there to debrief, to construct a narrative of who we are and what we do, to put our feet up, to chat and exchange, to row and trust we can make up, to cry, to play, to laugh; to buoy the oft harried, lonely self, to refuel? Behind the frequently scoffed-at, sentimentalized Victorian version of home, there is after all what seems to be a fundamental human desire for an at-homeness in the world, as potent as that sexualized desire for the other, for the sublime rapture of passion. The home we create with another, create imaginatively out of love, is our best shot at it.

Our mate is the one 'other' on whom we can depend in times of crisis or illness, our comfort against 'the thousand natural shocks that flesh is heir to', our most intimate, trusted and cherished friend. To put power relations aside as best we can and for as long as we can is an abiding desire in a conflict-ridden world. Agape, that thoughtful and respectful form of affection, rather than flighty Eros with his youthful promise of bliss and short-lived ecstasy, governs many of the goods of marriage. These include facets of life which might find a place in that old word 'character' and are rarely voiced in our desire-driven world. Several of my younger interviewees mentioned the satisfactions of 'taking responsibility' for others, of 'serving' partners and children, of a mutual shaping. We are, after all, not only striving individualists, but also social beings for whom the sense of good character, of kindliness to our kindred, brings inner rewards and, yes, joy.

As for whether equality between partners in marriage has hampered the possibility of happiness, I would wager that the problem here is less with equality than with contemporary notions of happiness. Too often these last contain a slippage from mood states, the time-stopped 'highs' of drugs or the ecstasy of extraordinary moments. Gauging the 'happiness' of a partnership that unfolds through the peaks and pitfalls that time brings may bear more of a kinship with determining what makes up a good life with its inevitable highs and lows, its achievements and failures, than with a mood or gratification chart. An equal devotion to the life of the partnership, a valuing of each partner's talents, needs and necessarily changing role within it, may be more important than negotiations about strict equality in housework or childcare hours, however central these may sometimes loom. Compromise, which may be more of a virtue of the older than of the younger, rules the marital sphere. Which is why marriage, for many, may feel better second time round.

Many of the phrases in the old Christian marriage vows still maintain their resonance: to have and to hold, from this day forward; for better, for worse, for richer, for poorer, in sickness and in health, to love and to cherish – even if the divorce statistics put in question 'until death do us part'.

Against the liquidity of our age, it's good, when thinking of marriage, to remember Shakespeare's evocation of its ultimate existential basis:

> Let me not to the marriage of true minds
> Admit impediments. Love is not love
> Which alters when it alteration finds,
> Or bends with the remover to remove:
> O no! it is an ever-fixed mark
> That looks on tempests and is never shaken;
> It is the star to every wandering bark,
> Whose worth's unknown, although his height be taken.
> Love's not Time's fool, though rosy lips and cheeks
> Within his bending sickle's compass come:
> Love alters not with his brief hours and weeks,
> But bears it out even to the edge of doom.
> If this be error and upon me proved,
> I never writ, nor no man ever loved.

Contemporary literature, like the media, is far richer in evocations of the battlefield of marriage, its routs, betrayals and humiliations, its psychosexual droughts and bitter endings, than in portraits of loving, settled states. Fiction feeds on conflict and extreme emotion even more voraciously than does life. Meanwhile, therapeutic manuals necessarily focus only on problems: every couple emerges as a suitable case for treatment, harried by the conflicts between trusting intimacy and the unruliness of desire.

One of the few portrayals of a good and pleasurable marriage is to be found in Ian McEwan's novel, *Saturday*. At the core of its satisfactions is an unmodish view of desire and masculinity which sites its pleasures not in the anonymity and distance that cyber-sex or secret partners allow, but within a long-trusted intimacy. It is here that its hero can abandon himself to the ruthless self-absorption on which sexual excitement thrives. The middle-aged neurosurgeon, Henry Perowne, knows that he's not in tune with his times in remaining faithful to his lawyer wife, Rosalind. He wonders whether he's deficient in curiosity or in some element of masculine life force. Yet what he seems to need is 'possession, belonging, repetition'.

> By contemporary standards, by any standards, it's perverse that he's never tired of making love to Rosalind, never been seriously tempted by the opportunities that have drifted his way through the generous logic of medical hierarchy. When he thinks of sex, he thinks of her. These eyes, these breasts, this tongue, this welcome. Who else could love him so knowingly, with such warmth and teasing humour, or accumulate so rich a past with him? In one lifetime, it wouldn't be possible to find another woman with whom he can learn to be so free, whom he can please with such abandon and expertise. By some accident of character, it's familiarity that excites him more than sexual novelty.

When trouble comes into their lives, it is from the outside, and the solidity of their marriage helps them in facing it. Marriage, here, is a base for the rest of life.

Core to keeping the hopes we have of relationships alive and making them as successful as we can may be a re-estimation of habit itself. Our

world of plenty and constant stimulus, our enshrinement of the excitements of youth and novelty, shroud habit with a negative aura. Of
course, habit can be deadening and certain habits can prove irritating.
But any enduring love needs habits — those structuring and orches-
trating dailinesses which let us get on with the rest of life, with the
whole business of doing, of living as full social beings. A habit, as the dictionary tells us, is the protective garment we put on to go out into the
social world. Habits contain our excesses. Habit is also our 'habitation',
a space of security and our 'settled disposition', the way we prefer to live.
Enduring love needs a balance of mutually devised habits and excitements to create a cohabitation. It's perhaps not incidental that in our era
of agitated pursuits of ever new stimulants there has been a concurrent
rise of so-called obsessive compulsive disorder: to order their lives individuals create complicated rituals, ever more excessive habits which
introduce a repetitive order into their otherwise unmanageable lives.

A few other matters are fundamental to married love. These are iter-
ated by experts of all ilks, from the professional psychologists to those
who have simply learned from experience. An attentiveness to the emotions and interests of one's partner is key. A sense of the value of
separateness, a respect for the other's desire for it, play into that ever
shifting equation. Distance too easily topples into a sense of isolation,
and with it can come that demon of contempt who belittles and undermines. Remembering what we value and admire about the other,
keeping a hold on that through the everyday irritations of life, is at the
very basis of intimacy. Appreciation is crucial. This is what those supposedly romantic, but actually rather pragmatic, commemorations of
moments are all about. Anniversaries, birthdays, Valentine days, help to
concentrate us on what it is that drew us to the other in the first place —
their pluses, their kindness, their virtues.

Listening to our partners, hearing their words and reading their gestures, is important; as is not reconfiguring every ill, every negative
feeling or mood, as an attack on oneself, which can then too easily
translate into an attack on the other. Interpreting behaviour or tangible problems as a personality or character defect is invidious: we can
alter behaviour and solve problems far more easily than we can change
our selves. So if a partner comes home preoccupied by conflicts at work,

or is worrying about a child or parent or boss, saying 'That's ridiculous', 'You're a fool' or 'Get over it', and thus dismissing their emotions and them, will not make matters better. Nor will saying, 'You're such a weakling.' On the other hand, 'Tell me more about it,' or 'What will help us get through this?' or 'You're so good at putting up with all these problems' may. Humiliations, minor or major failures at work or home, are part of all lives: understanding, seeing them through and focusing on better or stronger suits, helps.

These days, our social sense of entitlement, shored up by a culture of rights and ardent equality – perhaps, too, by a growing-up in which parents were so intent on building self-esteem that they forgot to tell us that not everything about us was estimable – can translate into coupled life in insidious ways. We cannot be entitled to the best and to happiness every moment of the day. Life is full of discontents. We all commit wrongs, have weaknesses. A certain hard-eyed, honest look at our own failings has never hurt the ongoing life of a partnership. As for that competitiveness, whether for constant signs of affection or of admiration, which often enough creeps into twosomes, it needs an admixture of generosity and fondness. Though sometimes life makes a battleground of the couple, declaring truce, compromising, is often a greater victory than triumphalist winning – which as all conflicts show brings an aftermath of resentment and a rearming for future skirmishes and major battles. The ongoing life of marriage makes star negotiators of us all.

Finally, it's worth remembering that all human beings seem particularly adept at wanting incompatible things. Restless creatures, we're simply not all that rational. We want to be babied, succoured and simultaneously want to inhabit a respected pedestal. We want passionate sex, yet may feel no desire. We want our partners to look beautiful, yet are overcome by jealousy when someone else notices the fact. We want to possess, yet lose interest in our possessions. We may love our partners, yet be fatally attracted to someone else. So in the proximity of cohabitation, it's good to step back, take a deep breath and assess the measure of ourselves and our partners.

If all this brings with it the aura of relational platitude, it may nonetheless contain some truth. In *Must You Go?* Antonia Fraser notes that no matter how much she and her husband rowed, they always made up before night fell, which sounds as good a recipe for intimacy as thousands of others.

Trouble in Paradise

All marriages, all cohabitations triggered by love, like life itself, have their conflicts and disappointments. Sometimes the very weight of our expectations and hopes, or the very passion that ignited them, casts an admonitory aura over what follows. At other times, the very power we attributed to the other to assuage that childhood helplessness which haunts us all becomes a prison: we resent our own need, chafe against our bonds, which have become a form of bondage once willingly submitted to. We grow angry, projecting on to our mate all the inevitable grievances we had against our parents, and more. The once loved one becomes the hated one, cause of all our unhappiness.

The ways in which passionate love can turn into hate are many and various. Extreme emotions, the two have long been bedfellows. In marriage, the other can too easily become the mirror of all our failings – whether inside or outside the home. Once the supreme source of our satisfactions, he or she becomes the one who seems to prevent us from attaining them. The ties that bind in security have become the bonds that constrain. So we cut and slash, in verbal or physical violence, criticize and punish our mate, sometimes binding ourselves further in the process – though now in hate rather than love. The power struggles that ensue rarely produce an outright winner.

The battle of the sexes has raged ever since jealous Hera tried to constrain rampant Zeus from his myriad infidelities. Transported into all-too-human domesticity, the battle continued, waxing fiercer in periods when strong-minded women chafed or rebelled against inequality. The marital dramas of the turn of the 1900s revealed the psychosexual component of the power struggle. Love here is a sado-masochistic jousting to which both man and woman submit. In Strindberg's gruelling *Dance of Death* (1900), diabolical verbal jousting and malicious intrigues enact a master–slave dialectic between husband

and wife. Hatred proves as addictive as love. The failures of the misan-
thropic, tyrannical Captain in both outside world and bedchamber are
turned against him by his emasculating wife, once an actress, whose
freedom he has taken from her with her initial compliance. Both are
imprisoned in the claustrophobic fortress of a marriage from which
there is no escape, yet they are both compelled to repeat the struggle to
escape over and over again.

Edward Albee's *Who's Afraid of Virginia Woolf* (1962) replays the themes
in a darkly comic idiom for early 1960s America. George and Martha
(named after America's first presidential couple) needle and abase each
other and their dinner guests through the length of a drunken evening
which constantly verges on and once tips over into physical violence.
Games of 'Humiliate the Host', 'Get the Guests' and 'Hump the Hostess'
are played. The abyss of a marriage – where neither the desired child,
sign of female power and fulfilment, nor George's projected novel, ever
come – stands exposed, together with the pitiable extremes to which
partners can drive each other. Hell, here, is distinctly 'other people', as
Sartre's famous line in *No Exit* goes: they reflect and expose our weaknesses and our sins. Their very existence is a torment to us.

Ingmar Bergman's six-part television drama *Scenes from a Marriage*
(1973) – also written as a shorter two-hander for the stage and released
as a cinema film – reveals that the love–hate dynamic hardly vanishes
with social equality. Marianne is a lawyer married to Johann, and the
tensions, the sexual and affectional dissatisfactions in their marriage
gradually lead to adultery, divorce and remarriage to others. The rub is
that, once remarried, they engage in a secret affair with each other.
What they have together, they realize, may be the closest they'll ever
come to love.

Through a long, dark night of the soul during which his forty-
something scriptwriter hero, Jay, debates his resolution to walk out,
come morning, on his partner and their children, Hanif Kureishi's
Intimacy (2000) dissects the breakdown of a contemporary relationship.
Restless, teetering on the brink of depression, all pleasure and most sex
gone from his ten-year cohabitation with a successful and competent
woman, honest about his own and his partner's lacks, Jay wants more
from life than this lifeless marriage – even though he is devoted to his

children. Indeed, the only remaining passion he and Susan share is
their passion for the children. Is that enough?

It is clear that though he admires much in Susan, the kind of love
that covers over lacks has dissipated between them. Susan is a woman
infuriated and frustrated by others, and critical of him – of his silences,
his ability to do nothing, the lack of order in his life. 'I can't be in a room
with her for too long without feeling that there is something I must do
to stop her being so angry. But I never know what I should do, and soon
I feel as if she is shoving me against the wall and battering me.' He in
turn has had his casual infidelities and a more serious one, which he has
forced himself to give up, but which may go by the name of love. Which
may indeed underlie his sense of her battering.

Around him there are other marriages, bad and good, as well as disastrous splits. He interrogates all of them. He is taking his decision
seriously; and at any point, if Susan were (sexually) suasive, his mind
could be changed. Of his parents' marriage, a shaping example from an
earlier generation when men put loyalty, the family and responsibility
before desire and individual renewal, he thinks:

> What did Father's life show me? That life is a struggle, and that struggle
> gets you nowhere and is neither recognized nor rewarded. There is
> little pleasure in marriage; it involves considerable endurance, like
> doing a job one hates. You can't leave and you can't enjoy it. Both he
> and Mother were frustrated, neither being able to find a way to get
> what they wanted, whatever that was. Nevertheless, they were loyal
> and faithful to one another. Disloyal and unfaithful to themselves. Or
> do I misunderstand?

Kureishi leaves the way open for other understandings. Baby-boomers
who grew up in a time of individualist plenty, a desire for satisfied desires
as well as for social change and experimentation, have different understandings of the world and themselves from their parents. Yet one of the
characters he depicts, the teacher Asif, lives a good marriage. Jay values
it, but it isn't his. In the morning, he leaves for his new life. He has convinced himself that 'leaving someone isn't the worst thing you can do
for them'. The new beckons.

Will he find the satisfactions he seeks there? The narrative is not alto-gether optimistic. Kureishi's hero is aware of the dangers: 'I know love is dark work; you have to get your hands dirty. If you hold back, noth-ing interesting happens. At the same time, you have to find the right distance between people. Too close, and they overwhelm you; too far and they abandon you. How to hold them in the right relation?' But with Susan things have gone dead: there is nothing left to explore, to discover, as there might be after years in a good relationship. All they mirror are each other's lacks. So he takes the leap into betrayal and a new life.

Intimates, it is clear, can become our intimate enemies. If there is gross incompatibility or worse, we fortunate inhabitants of the twenty-first century can either see it arise in an initial period of cohabitation, or we have the recourse of divorce. We can walk out and start over again. There is, after all, rarely a single Mr or Ms Right in the course of a long lifetime.

That said, divorce — legally endorsed or simply a split after cohabita-tion — is no trifle. Tears, pain, anger, a will to vengeance, a sense of failure and, even if there is an immediate other waiting in the wings, a period tantamount to mourning and its accompanying depression, attend. When children are involved, the marriage is seldom altogether over. For better or worse, partners accompany us throughout our lives, as intimate ghosts or fractious negotiators. Or they're reignited in the faces or character traits of our children. So it's as well to recognize the pitfalls that seem to be part of the state of marriage itself as it unfolds in time and try to see them through if we can. After all, they may well recur with another partner unless we, too, have changed in the process and can learn to be alive to love in new ways.

The American philosopher Stanley Cavell puts the core difficulties with luminous precision:

Something evidently internal to the task of marriage causes trouble in paradise — as if marriage, which was to be a ratification, is itself in need of ratification. So marriage has its disappointment — call this its impotence to domesticate sexuality without discouraging it, or its stupidity in the face of the riddle of intimacy, which repels where it attracts, or in the face of the puzzle of ecstasy, which is violent while it is tender, as if the leopard should lie down with the lamb. And the disappointment seeks revenge, a revenge, as it were, for having made one discover one's incompleteness, one's transience, one's homelessness.

Where to begin to unravel these riddles that stalk the condition of marriage whenever the social, the affectionate and the sexual are woven into the state, compounded with high expectations of each? Is it possible to domesticate sexuality without discouraging it, prevent once desired intimacy from tumbling into contempt or loathing?

The psychic grammar of love is mysterious. We all decipher it and live with its consequences as best we can.

Two stories

Joanne, thirty-three, is a hardworking academic historian, full of brio and determination, elegantly dressed and with the animated features of a young Paulette Goddard. Just over two years ago, she and her now thirty-five-year-old partner Rob, a journalist, tied the knot. They had met at a book launch some four years back. The attraction had been instantaneous. Afterwards, she said ruefully, he had told her he felt like the aged man at the start of *When Harry Met Sally*, who states to camera that when he saw his future wife walk into a restaurant he had turned to his friend and said, 'You see that woman over there. I'm going to marry her.'

Rob and Joanne had a great many interests in common to bolster the initial attraction. They would talk about anything and everything, argue vociferously, and he could send her into peals of laughter. After a few months of dating – during which the sex, as she told me, was 'fabulous' – a rupture took place. She couldn't bear Rob's roving eye at parties, what she called his 'flirting', even though he insisted it rarely went further than that – perhaps only once, right at the start of their relations, when he was travelling. His excuse – that he liked women and they liked him, that flirting was a way of engaging with the world and made people sparkle – didn't wash. Plainly put, she was jealous. And his wandering eye and manner humiliated her. She wanted Rob to give up his gallivanting. He had promised he would, though he couldn't promise he could utterly change his social being. She, on her side, would have to learn to trust him. She was intelligent enough to realize that what had attracted her to Rob would attract other women too, and it was in part her own scepticism about relations – her father had left her mother when she was fourteen – that made her overly sensitive to the possibility of male infidelity.

They had moved in together, and after some six months had set a wedding date. They both knew that the social sealing of the bond was more important to her than to him: it buoyed her trust. Though they didn't like to use the word 'love', they got on so well, were so alive to each other, so sustained each other's sense of potential, that love was palpably in the air. And so it had continued until about six months ago. Then sex, which had already begun to grow routine and lose its imaginative edge, had become sporadic and dull. She knew from hearsay that this was in part inevitable, that the daily demands of work, tending to the house, engaging in a busy social life, the very texture of everyday intimacy, played against the adventure that sex between them had been. But she feared that if he wasn't yet, Rob would soon be seeing someone else and she didn't want to bring the child they had talked of having into a twosome that was already showing wear and tear, even if she loved him, perhaps more than ever.

Jasper is fifty-eight, balding, still relatively trim, and a successful corporate lawyer, though he has of late grown weary of his work and spends much of his time providing voluntary services for charities. He and Claire (fifty-two) have been married for almost twenty-six years and their two children have now both left home. For the last year Jasper has been engaged in an affair with a woman in her mid-thirties. He hasn't told Claire. He can't bear the suffering he knows he is going to cause. He loves her, but he thinks he may leave her, partly because he can't stand the pain of confrontation and the guilt, which makes him more rather than less punishing. He knows. He has been through this once before. Then, too, he's still 'in lust', as he says, with his lover, who makes him feel like a man in his prime, not just a tattered blanket to wrap oneself in on a wintry night. He doesn't feel he has much time left.

Jasper met Claire, who at that time worked as a television producer and now heads a small NGO, in his early thirties. He had lived with another woman before, but the relationship had floundered and they had agreed to split. They had simply, he says, been too young when they entered on their union, and had become different people. He and Claire were madly in love when they first met, he tells me with a smile. God, she was gorgeous. But now at home, she's grumpy and menopausal and interested only in her work. He might indeed be doing her a favour by going off, though she wouldn't see it that way, not at first, anyway. As for sex, they've more or less stopped. Even when he was still interested, some years back now, she would put him off, and sex became a site of fractious disappointment – to both of them, he imagined. He would have to fantasize madly, and not about her, to keep himself going. Probably she knew. Probably she had to do the same.

He had had his first significant affair when their daughter was thirteen. Some six months in, Claire had discovered it, but, as he had pointed out to her, she wouldn't have if he hadn't half deliberately left signs lying around. He had been in agony about cheating and didn't want to leave Claire, though they were having one of those fallow patches where everything in life was more important and more interesting than they were to each other. On top of that there were ageing parents and adolescent children to contend with, and home was a place of friction and daily problems. With his lover he felt alive, renewed, full of potential. That's all he had wanted, he now thinks. He wondered whether any men I had interviewed had linked the activity of their penises, not to some evolutionary mumbo-jumbo about spreading their seed, but to the waving of a magic wand whose use wards off death.

When Claire had discovered that first affair, she had talked of kicking him and his wandering and banal member out. She had raged and fumed. It came as a surprise to him, but suddenly sex between them had started up again: bed had once more become a place of excitement and exploration. Between rows, they had also had long intimate conversations: they had shared their lacks and frailties. She was even prepared to acknowledge that – though his was the far greater fault – she wasn't altogether unimplicated in his infidelity. And she had decided to give him a second chance, which he wanted to take. He really did love her. She was a fine woman. And he valued their family and everything they had made together. But roll on the years, and that newly refound intimacy had once more vanished into torpor. This time, he really thinks he will go, though he doesn't relish facing the children or the divorce lawyers. Yet he wants a future, not just a past.

In the course of my writing this book, Joanne and Rob were beaming with the arrival of a baby. Jasper and Claire were in the midst of that wrenching pain which is betrayal and separation, even when apparently desired.

That fleeting deity

> It is terrible to desire and not possess, and terrible to possess and not desire.
>
> W.B. Yeats

The annals of love are replete with paradox. The very security we seek in coupledom can diminish passion, child of unpredictability. Working at sex, donning that new negligee, creating that romantic moment, buying the latest sex toy or DVD, as the magazines and self-help books advise, rarely provides more than a momentary solution. Sex is not a work-out with quantifiable effects. Couples-porn and Viagra – 'late capitalism's Lourdes for dying marriages', as Laura Kipnis in *Against Love* aptly calls it – simply don't account for the complexities of the erotic, which engage our imagination, our phantoms, our very sense of ourselves and the other. Nor is there any necessary symmetry of desire between partners: they can be out of step, the disinterest of one provoking the interest of the other and so on, through the vagaries of time. Desire rarely plays by the rules of good citizenship to reward work or best intentions. It just isn't rational. It may return, but it won't be willed or reasoned with. Blaming oneself, one's mate or the nature of the couple serves only to exacerbate unhappiness.

So what is it that confounds our fondest hopes and makes of Eros a fleeting deity, often allergic to domestication? Analysts point to passion's excessive nature — those violent transports that make one out of two, beyond the reach of language and other than the mere bodies which enact its ecstasy. Within the archaeology of the individual, the only kindred state is that of the preverbal infant whose whole world is mother or carer: he merges with her, takes his bliss from her, without ever recognizing her separateness. Two are one. And then, the babe grows, becomes a 'self', and recognizes himself and his mother as separate beings. Ever after, he may be trailed by a ghostly memory of greater plenitude, when world and self were one, a time before the measurement of time itself, with its demarcated separations.

When two beings come together in passion, these archaic shadows of a lost past are revivified. The world revolves in and around the newly discovered other. Everything is exchanged, bodies, thoughts, feelings. The lovers become one another. Describing a tiff in the early months of Kitty and Levin's exemplary marriage in *Anna Karenina*, Tolstoy brilliantly evokes the blissful rapture of their union and the attendant nascent conflicts that merging brings in its wake.

> Only then did he [Levin] understand clearly for the first time what he had not understood when he had led her out of the church after the wedding. He understood not only that she was close to him, but that he no longer knew where she ended and he began. He understood it by the painful feeling of being split which he experienced at that moment. He was offended at first, but in that same instant he felt that he could not be offended by her, that she was him. In the first moment he felt like a man who, having suddenly received a violent blow from behind, turns with vexation and a desire for revenge to find out who did it, and realizes that he has accidentally struck himself, that there is no one to be angry with and he must endure and ease the pain.

The initial transcendent ecstasy of union may, some speculate, last for two years, perhaps more, in an echo of the time it takes for a child to acquire language. Then ecstasy dissipates. It is as if the passionate merger has become too much: the couple, the one that is made of two, now feels as if it may swallow up what has become a newly vulnerable because unbounded self, cannibalize it. If eroticism is a 'movement towards the Other', as Simone de Beauvoir writes, echoing Montaigne, 'in the deep intimacy of the couple, husband and wife become for one another the *Same*; no exchange is any longer possible between them, no giving and no conquering. Thus if they do continue to make love, it is often with a sense of shame', as if incest were taking place. In this incestuous sameness, the taboo of the sexual mother can re-emerge, and the very act of sex may feel frightening and breed impotence. Tenderness is possible in coupledom, but rarely the passion that confounds inside and outside, into which one feels one may disappear never to know separate boundaries again.

Of course, the passion doesn't go all at once or necessarily for ever. Rows that demarcate difference can reignite it. So, too, can exchanged memories of past lovers, or the eyes of a third party focusing on the beloved in a way which once more constitutes him or her as other – as that tantalizing, mysterious person first spied across a crowded room.

Yet gradually the passion that so forcefully drew two separate beings together and made them one, can seep away. Sometimes it may seem that this happens for only one partner, but in this coupling there is rarely only one, though only one may take the blame. For some, the tenderness, the fondness, the companionship and sharing that replace passion may be more than enough. For others, as sex diminishes in intensity or quantity, disappointment follows in its wake, and often enough irritation. The very differences that drew lover and beloved together, that made passion possible, now exasperate, seem too close to one. Every half of a couple has at one time or another felt shamed by the other's comments or actions in public, as if the other were oneself. Once admired energy seems to have become overbearing loudness; sweet spontaneity, babbling silliness; austere rectitude, punitive stiffness, and so on. Trapped in a 'we', the partners chafe against the chains that were once the bonds of ecstasy.

Domestic life inevitably requires some reformulation of early passion. Sexual intimacy can, of course, speak other idioms than that of obliterating passion. It can speak affection and tenderness. It can tease and laugh. It can speak the sensual and the playful. It can aspire to an erotic art. It can be a parenthesis for emotional recharging or be replete with a benign possessiveness. It can also be a site for power play, withdrawal, coldness and forms of deceit. In the lifetime of any couple, it can be all of these at different times. But to desire where one loves, to somehow incorporate the erotic with the familiar, is rarely straightforward. Love needs tending. It also seems to need a spirit of generosity and emotional intelligence in which the lines of privacy and togetherness can be redrawn. It may also need a cultural sense that the next available in a series of relationships won't necessarily provide a cornucopia of greater fulfilments.

The difficulty of sexual love in marriage is hardly peculiar to our own times: what is peculiar is that we have expectations of more and better and assume that this more and better will somehow be delivered by another cohabiting partner. Some 180 years ago, when the great French novelist Honoré de Balzac formulated his ebullient and wonderfully comic *Physiology of Marriage* (1830), he succinctly concluded: 'Marriage must incessantly contend with a monster which devours everything, that is, familiarity.'

> No man [Balzac advises] should enter his wife's boudoir. The man who enters his wife's dressing-room is either a philosopher or an imbecile . . . It is easier to be a lover than a husband, for the same reason that it is more difficult to be witty every day than to say bright things from time to time . . . To call desire into being, to nourish it, to develop it, to bring it to full growth, to excite it, to satisfy it, is a complete poem of itself.

The rituals of love, Balzac knew, need constantly and imaginatively to be reinvented.

Cultural traditions impact on the way we imagine sex, rarely a simple animal act. One of my youngest interviewees, who had spent some time living in France, noted that her French boyfriend always brought her flowers and gifts, and treated sex as an elaborate ritual to be prepared for as meticulously as for a banquet. Seduction and its arts were in the air. She felt pampered but not swept off her feet. Brought up in a British tradition, where romantic sexual spontaneity is understood as a proof of love, all this made her uncomfortable. She preferred her current American boyfriend, who allowed her to feel 'more equal, more normal'. In the long life of an ongoing relationship, however, sleep may end up coming far more spontaneously than sex. And the creation of rituals of erotic play allow the bedroom to be re-infused with imagination.

In *Mating in Captivity*, her fine book on the travails of sex in ongoing unions, the therapist Esther Perel punctures the myth of spontaneity. She cites the case of a gay couple who came to see her because their sex life, now that they were living together, had lost its lustre. She points out to them that when they lived in separate cities, they anticipated their reunions, imagined what they would get up to, planned their dates. There was a lot of imaginative foreplay, 'longing, waiting, and yearning', an intentionality to the seeming spontaneity and artlessness of their coming together. The art now goes into epicurean meals rather than loving. 'Is the titillation of seduction only the privilege of those who date?' she asks one partner in the couple. 'Just because you live with someone doesn't necessarily mean he's readily available. If anything, he requires more attention, not less.'

Too often in our target culture where the sex industry is rampant, Balzac's poem of erotic marital love gets infused with a work ethic. We install performance ratings in the bedroom, count the how many and how much, note outcomes. But sex as hard work loses its allure and becomes as dreary as composing an annual report for the ever vigilant appraisal team. How much better to engage in imaginative elaboration, to dream ourselves afresh, to abandon oneself in the company of our other, and play. Cupid, after all, is a plump child.

When Ian McEwan's hero Perowne thinks of the excitements of familiarity that life with his wife provides, he evokes a sexual site of freedom and abandon. In the inherited ethos, both Freudian and religious, of double sexual standards, which place the sacred in domesticity and emotional satisfactions and the profane outside of it in the passionate excitements of 'debased' sexual objects, this can sound counter-intuitive. Indeed, many grow shy and inhibited as soon as the bed moves into the marital chamber, and find themselves unable to enact an abandon available elsewhere – as if parental forbiddings now hovered over maritally sanctioned acts and we stood to lose our mates if we showed them our wild side. To bring the illicit home, both within ourselves and to our loved one, may be the ultimate challenge in domesticating Eros.

Reinventions

Pondering the mysteries of marriage and sexuality, Freud noted in 'The Taboo of Virginity' that 'it must strike the observer in how uncommonly large a number of cases the woman remains frigid and feels unhappy in a first marriage, whereas after it has been dissolved she becomes a tender wife, able to make her second husband happy. The archaic reaction [the discharge of immature sexuality on to the man who first has coitus with her] has, so to speak, exhausted itself on the first object.'

Though physical virginity is rarely these days the condition of women on entering a first marriage or cohabitation, it still remains the case that first unions may bring with them an 'immature sexuality', one that trails 'archaic reactions', fears of dependency or 'bondage'. These bear the whiff of Mummy and Daddy, a submersion or loss of oneself in and to the other from which second unions can be relatively free. In the classic formations, young women tie themselves to older men, finding in them the father (or mother, since gender here is less the issue than unresolved ties to the past which the self in flux carries within) they aren't quite ready to leave. At times, when this kind of union was less taboo, young men would regularly engage in passions with older women, a rite of passage that had the added benefit of putting the overpowering sexualized mother within them to rest.

In our era of independent working women, sometimes more successful than their husbands, certain difficulties can be exacerbated for both. Men can too easily find themselves infantilized by their partners (who may indeed 'baby' them). An attractive wife then takes on the aura of a critical, suffocating mother. When children arrive, this maternal aspect of the feminine comes quickly into the picture, and the attractions of the woman whom the man once desired prove difficult to reawaken. What then? The problem is a recalcitrant one, emphatically

so in an age where we put arguably far too high a value on sexual passion – ever short-lived in its intoxicating form. A rebalancing here
towards the value of other kinds of loving would not come amiss: tenderness, care, conversation, a shared history, mutual projects, and a
mutual investment in the good life a couple has constructed may serve
individuals far better than serial relationships in which the tail wags
the dog and sets him running.

In his analysis of what he calls the Hollywood 'comedy of remarriage'
of the 1930s and 40s, Stanley Cavell probes the ways in which marriage,
second time round, can be turned into an adventure, a romance, rather
than a tragedy or farce. Remarriage for him entails a reconstituting of
the self or a growth in self-knowledge, as well as a seeing of the other
afresh and an understanding of human frailty. The rupture – divorce or
split – helps: it marks an important point on the journey from illusion
to disillusion to re-illusionment. In *The Philadelphia Story* Katharine
Hepburn (Tracy) and Cary Grant (Dexter), having divorced over a
number of incompatibilities – her pride, rectitude, sexual fears, over-
attachment to (regulating) Mum and Dad, his drinking – find 'home' in
each other again on the very point of her marrying another.

Howard Hawks's *His Girl Friday* begins with the journalist heroine,
Rosalind Russell, telling her ex (and editor) Cary Grant that she is
poised to marry another: in other words, she has constituted her freedom from him, she is once more a separate, independent being. But
after a series of adventures, one of which entails her giving up the film's
mother-figure, the original couple are once more 'at home' together,
poised to re-enter a familiar union on revivified terms. Crucially, the
new union preserves something of an adventure, of the illicit – a 'moral
equivalent of the immoral'. It also holds out the promise of joint projects, a working life together.

What is it that makes these remarriages possible? Cavell underlines
the reawakened capacity in these couples to notice one another, to
remember that if familiar, they are nonetheless strangers. They may be
the same, but they are also different, together as a we, but also two distinct 'I's.

The philosopher of ethics Emmanuel Levinas, in a somewhat different register, deepens this understanding of love. He posits love as a uniquely ambiguous relation, at once possessive and deferential, between the self and the beloved. Though motivated by desire and need, love comes into authentic being only when a reciprocity is set up in the other: there is a simultaneous sense of needing without being able to bring the other into possession, the sense of being needed, but without surrendering to exploitation of one's self. One could say that freedom and bondage here coexist. 'Love remains a relation with the Other that turns into need, [a] need [that] still presupposes the total, transcendent exteriority of the Other, of the Beloved.'

In Cavell's understanding, an erotic remarriage is underpinned by the ability to experience dailiness as a comedy — a festive sense that human beings are complicated, neither angels nor beasts, neither heroes nor villains, but creatures prone to weakness and fragility. Playfulness is a plus, an antidote to the earnestness and idealizations of romantic passion. The constant conversation, the tender or rebarbative exchange between couples, flirtation, keeps the flow of desire and togetherness alive, keeps them connected and devoted one to the other. Jane Austen would have concurred, as would Charlotte Brontë, whose Jane in her last words emphasizes the constant talk that fills her and Rochester's days.

The romance of domesticity, with all its upheavals and occasional ruptures, its mingling of dream and dailiness, can triumph outside those luminous Hollywood comedies as well. Children, those intruding strangers, can sometimes help, at least at first. Sometimes, though it feels criminal to say it, so can affairs — the advent of a third party who makes us confront what we value most in love. At other times, in these days of wished-for fidelity, a therapist often enough provides that third party — the other with whom we can fall into 'transferential' love, emotionally re-enact our ways of loving and hating, and through whose triangulating presence we can realign our separateness and our togetherness.

In *Netherland*, his fine post-9/11 novel, Joseph O'Neill offers amongst much else a subtle portrait of a modern (re)marriage — one lived out in the generalized anxiety of the modern world and in the din of an advice culture which makes the trajectory of love banal, as chewed over as a second-hand sock.

Hans van den Broek, Dutch by origin, deeply introspective, is a high-flying New York-based oil analyst married to Rachel, a successful English lawyer. With their small son Jake they live in a loft in Tribeca until the destruction of the Twin Towers forces them to take up temporary residence at the Chelsea Hotel. Here they remain in a kind of paralysis until Rachel announces that she can't face the insecurity of New York any longer. She wants to take their son home to London. She has realized, too, that she no longer enjoys a pace of work that takes her away from her child. Other things become clear as well, to both of them. A tiredness has taken over their coupled life, a malign weariness which is both part of and more than the apocalyptic moment. The narrative of their union to the exclusion of all others just isn't right any more. It is Hans, not terror, that Rachel is fleeing: they have grown alone together. Love has turned into loss.

A separation ensues. Every two weeks or so, Hans flies to London to see his son. But without his family, he feels his life to be meaningless. He has no friends, no pastimes. A dullness which had already set in has become general. Only in one area does he find a rekindling of liveliness: cricket. The game allows him to revisit his childhood, and in a metaphoric way to come to terms with his mother's death, part of the background of his inner paralysis. Cricket also sparks the important and unlikely friendship with Chuck Ramkissoon, a Trinidadian Gatsby who dreams the big dream while engaging in small-time racketeering. Chuck is both friend and in some respects a replacement father figure for the one Hans never had. Larger than life, traditional in his views of women, Chuck has both a good wife and a mistress. His gambling reminds Hans of his mother's sometime lover. Through the friendship and the inner journey it allows Hans to undertake, he gradually comes back to life, though the coming back is to a new place, a subtly altered self.

The ongoing relationship with Rachel plays into the change. She has not been standing still either. On one of his visits to London, Hans realizes, through something his son says, that she has now engaged in a serious affair. He is angry, jealous. He sleeps with other women and eventually, after he has moved to London to be closer to his son, even enjoys it. Time, that proverbial healer, passes, and just when it seems that Hans has really at last left Rachel, that he can take his marriage or leave it, she announces that she has broken up with her lover.

> 'He's fucking someone else,' Rachel said.
> 'Good,' I said. 'That means I can fuck you.'

They do — with the 'minimum of variety and history: our old bag of tricks belonged to those other lovers and those other bodies'. They are new to each other, separated out from their old melded skins. They only kiss after two months — and in mid-kiss Rachel suggests, 'We should see a marriage counsellor.' They move into a house together as well.

When the marriage counsellor asks Rachel why she had stayed married to Hans, she doesn't answer as Hans fears she will — that she had tragically decided to settle for a reliable man, or as he hopes, that he bowled her over — but rather because 'she felt a responsibility to see me through life and the responsibility felt like a happy one'. Hans is overwhelmed by her response. It puts into words and into reality exactly how he feels, though with a subtle difference. 'Rachel saw our reunion as a continuation. I felt differently: that she and I had gone our separate ways and subsequently had fallen for third parties to whom fortunately we were already married.'

In O'Neill's version of the contemporary comedy of remarriage, love is a kind of omnibus. You can get on, then off. Fortunately, you can also get on again, though you'll have to have walked for a while along that road of life which is always full of blunderings and detours.

As for happiness, though we carry on seeking it in marriage and elsewhere, it is not what people do best. Yet if we didn't have its opposite, we wouldn't know how to gauge or recognize it. And marriage or long-term cohabitation — once we have learned to live generously with our own and the other's limitations, once we have acceded to the frustrations life and age inevitably bring — may be our best shot at it.

In his fine poem 'An Arundel Tomb', Philip Larkin examines an effigy of a noble couple and sees with 'a sharp tender shock' that the recumbent figures have their hands entwined. With the dispassionate gaze of

a modern, he expresses our unwilling, sceptical, yet 'almost true' hopes
of love.

> The stone fidelity
> They hardly meant has come to be
> Their final blazon, and to prove
> Our almost-instinct almost true:
> What will survive of us is love.

PART FOUR

Love in Triangles

A woman we love rarely satisfies all our needs, and we deceive her with a woman whom we do not love.

Marcel Proust

The laws of love are . . . . stronger than human laws.

Honoré de Balzac

Adulterous Passions

In the annals of love, adultery has ever played a raucous part. Being crazy about the 'you' who belongs to someone else unleashes a havoc that can reverberate through the generations.

Paris, in bedding and stealing away Helen, Queen of Sparta and wife to Menelaus, begets the destruction of Troy and brings down mass carnage on the victorious Greeks. Clytemnestra, lost to lust for her lover Aegisthus and maddened by her husband Agamemnon's earlier sacrifice of their daughter, murders him in the bath on his return from Troy. She is in turn murdered by her son, urged on by his sister's fury.

Born of passion and the irrational, adultery breeds more of the same, engendering, in its antique heroic mode, death and devastation which catapult through the generations. Eros and Thanatos are close kin, the Greeks tell us, well before Freud linked desire and the death-wish. Death, the dark side of oblivion, haunts passion untamed by the social constraints, the contractual arrangements and the daily habits of marriage. Making one out of two, possessing the other, is an annihilating business, all the more so if rules are being broken. *La petite mort*, as the French nickname orgasm and its temporary oblivion, can catapult into the larger one.

The Ten Commandments enshrine adultery as a major prohibition. Number seven of the Decalogue states: 'You shall not commit adultery', while number ten echoes it, doubling its force by moving inward from the realm of action to that of desire: 'You shall not covet your neighbour's wife.' The New Testament, always alert to the importance of policing thoughts, further elaborates: 'That whosoever looketh on a woman to lust after her hath committed adultery with her already in his heart' (Matthew 5.28). The strength of the prohibition against adultery, the severe punishment for the act which all the major religions pronounce, is a certain sign that the transgression was widespread – as, of course, it continues to be.

One might disingenuously ask why such a common human act is conceived as so fundamentally transgressive? The answer is simple enough. If marriage constitutes our primary social and legal bond, creating that unit, the home, through which society regenerates itself, then a breach of that bond is a 'criminal' act which challenges both social order and social cohesion. Adultery is both revolutionary and treacherous. Aeschylus in *Agamemnon* pinpoints the treachery by underlining that Paris violates not only Helen but the crucial rules of hospitality, a form of love that functions as a bringing together rather than a tearing apart. Paris is, after all, a guest, a stranger in Menelaus' house: that social love, which hospitality is, welcomes strangers, but in welcoming them incurs a debt of honourable behaviour, not theft.

> This was Paris: he came
> To the house of the sons of Atreus,
> Stole the woman away, and shamed
> The guest's right of the board shared. (Chorus, lines 399–402)

Having transgressed, having turned hospitality into hostility, Paris takes to Troy not only Helen, but a dowry which includes war and death.

Adulterous passion may be ecstatic, but it is also deadly, particularly for women. Guardians of hearth and home, their person long their husband's possession, women's passionate transgression is ever greater than the male's. It brings with it the danger of miscegenation, a bastard in the familial nest, poised like a cuckoo to endanger the hereditary line. The Greeks permitted concubinage. Up to a point, so did the Abrahamic religions. But wives were severely punished for even presumed infidelity. In Western literature, male adulterers fare far better than their female equivalents. Adultery, after all, doesn't mean 'sex for adults' as the worldly quip would have it, but takes its meaning from 'adulterate', to pollute or contaminate, by mixing the wrong combination of things together. 'If society depends for its existence on certain rules, governing what may be combined and what should be kept separate,' Tony Tanner writes, 'then adultery, by bringing the wrong things together in the wrong places (or the wrong people in the wrong beds), offers an attack on those rules, revealing them to be arbitrary rather than absolute.'

In our own Western, post-patriarchal and largely secular times, in which rules are looser and a certain hybridity championed, punishment is not quite so harsh. We draw the boundaries of the permissible differently. Yet some kind of punishment persists, particularly where public figures in the Anglo-American world are concerned. President Clinton and a variety of other American and British politicians have been persecuted for their affairs by the media and by opposition politicians, however forgiving their wives may have been. Persecuted, too, despite the evidence of rampant hypocrisy, given that so-called upholders of family values were often soon themselves outed as adulterers. Tiger Woods strayed and lost his sponsors, if not immediately his wife, and made a mind-numbingly long public apology. England football captain John Terry was stripped of his captaincy for allegedly bedding the wife of a team-mate: private pain was augmented by public humiliation, and social order was only partly restored by the intervention of the coach, Fabio Capello. And the tabloids could then blame England's poor performance in the World Cup of 2010 on their former captain's adultery! The personal transparency demanded of our public figures, full confessions of where they stray and betray, together with the public clamour scapegoating their acts, may be evidence of our own unease. We demand retribution all the more vocally when betrayals mirror, or are projections of, our own transgressive desires.

In the midst of the eighties backlash against single professional women, the film Fatal Attraction (1987) acted as a moral warning of the havoc adultery can breed. It turned a casual weekend infidelity between the married attorney, Daniel (Michael Douglas), and the publisher, Alex (Glenn Close), into a nightmare of bloody proportions. An increasingly deranged Alex stalks the straying Daniel, kidnaps his daughter and tries to murder his wife, only to be shot by her in a grotesque finale. The family must be kept intact against all odds, the

film loudly proclaims, all the while underlining the sexual danger of
voracious single women.

Despite early promiscuity, despite the prevalence of prior relationships before the moment of commitment, despite serial unions,
no-fault divorce and remarriage, we continue to believe or wish to
believe in sexual exclusivity and punish infidelity and adultery. A conviction seemingly born out of inner choice and idealization, rather than
strict convention, arguably calls for greater blame – as well as guilt and
self-and-other flagellation – when a partner strays.

But why are we prostrated by a partner's betrayal, when we know the
act is so common?

Betrayal calls upon our deepest feelings. It involves, the *Oxford English
Dictionary* states, 'A violation of trust or confidence, an abandonment' as
well as 'A treacherous giving up to an enemy'. Deceit, cheating, perfidy,
violation of faith, misleading, seducing – all fall into the purview of
betrayal. The philosopher Judith Shklar includes it amongst her 'ordinary vices', reflecting that there is 'an irreducible experience in betrayal:
desertion. This brings into play the greatest of childhood anxieties, the
fear of abandonment. In quitting a bonded group, an equally primeval
fear is stirred: of the failure to distinguish kin and stranger.' Betrayal at
the level of the couple, our primary social bond, is tantamount to trea-
son in state terms. Yet, as Shklar also points out, people invite betrayals.
'If one idolizes or imposes excessive moral demands . . . one may well be
betrayed unintentionally by the overburdened person . . . It is not the
idol's fault that he has feet of clay.'

Thorny contradictions rumble through our ideals of coupledom.
Our marriages are based on a romantic notion of passionate merger for
ever, an intimacy in which our inner lives are shared. Betrayal brings
with it the spectre of the dissolution not only of the couple, but of the
betrayed partner's very being. Losing the other becomes losing oneself,
as if we were all babes at the breast and had grown no thicker skin or
survival skills since. Simultaneously, we live under a cultural order that
tells us we're entitled to develop our own individuality and can continue to fulfil our unmet needs, those lacks left over from early
childhood, for the entirety of our lives. What more common way of
developing our individuality than falling in love or in lust? Would it not

be self-betrayal to renounce the passion that promises transformation in the name of a deadening or warring coupledom? In this thicket of inconsistencies, the perils of adultery loom, all the while giving off a sulphurous glow.

While people suffer and harm for their adulteries, they also continue to commit them and 'adulterate' their marriages. Perhaps because we grow up in triangles, we go on to recreate them, sometimes over and over again. Even our earliest blissful oneness with Mummy, first site of our romantic possessiveness, was, after all, shared – with Daddy or those other siblings in the wings. Third parties shadow our coupled lives in a variety of ways: old lovers or partners hover in the anterooms of our minds; women or men spied on streets or on Internet sites intrude into our minds and into our togetherness. In *Monogamy* Adam Phillips notes, 'The couple is a resistance to the intrusion of the third, but in order for it to last it is indispensable to have enemies. That is why the monogamous can't live without them. When we are two, we are together. In order to be a couple, we need to be three.'

The Way of All Marriage

In older worldly times, dominated by aristocratic patterns of marriage based largely on property, adultery was often conceived in a sardonic vein, whatever religious, moral or political edicts might (hypocritically) demand. Adultery was simply the way of all marriages that could afford it.

Balzac's *Physiology of Marriage*, a kind of guide to the wedded state written under the heady influence of Rabelais and Sterne, was begun when Balzac was only twenty-six. Here he plumbs, sometimes in cool, sometimes in hyperbolic, vein the secrets of both the male and the female mind to satirize the hypocrisies and expose the conventions which attended the institution. Still a seething, ambitious and relatively innocent provincial poised to take on *le tout Paris*, Balzac was granted insight into the feminine psyche by his generous mistress, Madame de Bernay, who at the age of forty-eight and after nine children took the young genius on as her lover. It was her last passion and his first. It's worth

noting here that in the paradigm of love between a married older
woman and a young man, which takes in all the romantic and courtly
tropes, the affair acts as a civilizing experience for the man, a kind of finishing school in life. In Balzac's case, in the writing of his book, a second
and younger woman about town also revealed her secrets to him. As for
men, he knew their ways only too well and had merely to look around
him.

In his preamble, Balzac suggests that the germ of his book on marriage lies in the word 'adultery', confronted during his studies as a
student of the French legal code put in place by Napoleon, who believed
that marriage was an institution of culture and not of nature, and could
thus be radically improved. Under the Code Napoléon, as already
noted, adultery for men occurred only if they brought a mistress into
the sanctity of the family home. For women, if the husband so wished,
it could lead to imprisonment for up to two years and constitute
grounds for divorce, though that could be obtained by mutual consent
as well, if the woman's adultery was kept private and concealed.

Balzac confesses that the word 'adultery' began by conjuring up in
his mind a 'mournful train of consequences. Tears, shame, hatred,
terror, secret crime, bloody wars, families without a head, and social
misery rose like a sudden line of phantoms.' But later on, when he
'became acquainted with the most cultivated circles of society, the
author perceived that the rigour of marriage laws was very generally
mollified by adultery. He found that the number of unhappy homes
was larger than that of happy marriages.' Everywhere men kept mistresses and seemed incapable of fidelity; while women, except the
religiously virtuous who ended up in Swiss spas, had lovers often stu-
pider than their husbands and certainly younger. These came from
amongst the scores of gallant and seductive young men who couldn't
marry during their most ardent years. 'The laws of love are simply
stronger than human law,' Balzac notes, himself amongst the most
ardent of young seducers. It may well be 'the rashest of all undertakings
to swear eternal love'.

Balzac's *Physiology* is a sardonic observer's guide to worldly mores.
The double sexual standard of Victorian England and America, which
exonerated men and punished women far more brutally for adultery,

and which prevailed in divorce laws that robbed straying women of home and children well into the second half of the twentieth century, has little place in the *Physiology*. Marriage, for Balzac, is merely a way of extinguishing passion and letting society reproduce itself – unless everything changes. To begin to pave the way for 'unadulterated' happiness in marriage, Balzac argues, would entail a social revolution in which girls were educated and free to love early, in concert with the young males' most ardent phase. This in turn would mean that they could later be faithful to their husbands and as wives no longer prey to the advances of desiring young males. Marriage itself would need to be based on passion as well as on property. And both parties would need to be as intelligent as philosophers and as inventive as artists. If in our own liberated times we have reached these first two points, we have scarcely arrived at the other two.

For Stendhal, that literary psychologist who is Balzac's near-contemporary, love is also, often enough, an adulterous matter. In his great novel of Romantic realism, *The Red and the Black* (1830), the young and ardent Julien Sorel engages in a passionate and formative relationship with the mayor's wife, Madame de Rênal. He is an ambitious young man, and rivalry, the displacing of a more powerful figure, inevitably plays into a passion that we might now label 'Oedipal'. The passion will be the death of him. First, however, after an interim of Parisian intrigues, it is Madame de Rênal he attempts to shoot for exposing him to the father of the aristocratic Mathilde, the woman the plebeian Julien has meanwhile fallen in love with and hopes to wed. But awaiting execution, Julien's first love for the maternal Madame de Rênal resurfaces and he goes to his death buoyed by her beneficent love. Three days later, she gives her children a final embrace and follows him, her heart having given way.

In his ground-breaking mid-twentieth-century study, *Love in the Western World*, Denis de Rougemont argues that nine out of ten times the great loves in Western literature take the form of adultery, as if ecstatic suffering and misfortune were bound up in our very understanding of passionate love and were constitutive of its force. 'It is obvious,' he writes, 'that Western Man is drawn to what destroys the happiness of the married couple *at least as much* as to anything that ensures it.'

Starting with the myth of Tristan and Isolde, de Rougemont points out how the desire for obstruction, for breaking rules, for finding obstacles, has become for us an intrinsic part of passion, that 'divine delirium'. By idealizing this ecstatic form of love we hide from ourselves the fact that the ultimate obstacle, death, is what this kind of 'passion has yearned after from the beginning'. Underlying Tristan and Isolde's transcendent desire for one another – a desire that takes them into exile, far from the rules of society, and then brings them back only to perish – is, de Rougemont claims, ultimately the desire for death – for that oblivion in which our very individuality is annihilated.

Some of the major fictions of adulterous passion would seem to bear him out. Arguably the world's two greatest novels are amongst them: Flaubert's *Madame Bovary* (1857) and Tolstoy's *Anna Karenina* (1877). It is worth pausing over them, since they provide such astute analyses of the dynamics of love and adultery. As if wishing instantly to signal that adulterous passion lies at the heart of marriage and shadows its lacks, both novels proclaim their heroine's married state in their very titles. The implication is that the whole project of bourgeois marriage is destined for failure. Passion and property simply won't be wed – and, in particular, if woman is part of the property. The odds are even greater if passion is understood as a form of quasi-religious transcendence, a beatitude which pays little heed to law or contract.

An ordinary sensuous woman

Young Emma Rouault is susceptible to literature. Books prepare her for passion. They provide her indoctrination into the exoticism of ecstasy. They move her, as the Greek *ekstasis* suggests, 'out of her place'. But so, too, does religion and the convent school this farmer's daughter enters at the age of thirteen.

Before her formal education begins, Emma has already read that Rousseau-inspired pastoral romance, *Paul et Virginie* by Bernardin de Saint-Pierre, set in a mythical Mauritius of sensuous and social harmony. Historical romances are soon added to her imaginative armoury. Sir Walter Scott and his heroic tales of ill-fated women – Mary Queen of

Scots and Joan of Arc – stir her fantasies. But it is the convent that completes Emma's sensuous education, both aesthetically and emotionally. Here she succumbs to the 'mystic languor exhaled by the perfumes of the altar, the coolness of the holy-water fonts and the radiance of the tapers', all of which play on her senses. Meanwhile, images of the pierced Sacred Heart and 'poor Jesus falling beneath His cross' awaken self-mortifying emotions which subtly combine with Christian metaphors of 'betrothed, spouse, heavenly lover, marriage everlasting' to awaken 'an unlooked-for delight' in the depths of her soul. Like any receptive adolescent girl, Emma has her senses and imagination awakened by the romances of her times, into which religion plays. When her religious ardour grows excessive, the nuns prohibit it.

Flaubert may ironize all this and highlight what is happening to his young heroine with a cool eye. Yet he is never less than ambivalent about her, as his later pronouncement 'Madame Bovary, c'est moi' makes clear. The education in sensibility which turns Emma into a romantic dreamer is not, in itself, a negative. It does, however, make her intensely susceptible to the heightening pleasure of secrecy itself – 'that condition of forbiddenness in the erotic life of women' which Freud links to the delay between sexual maturity and sexual activity. In her early teens, Emma's adolescent sexuality is fed by the secrecy so fundamental to the pleasures of the imagination, of reading and religious transport. This condition of prohibition is reawakened in her secret affairs.

Her early transports also make her susceptible to the disappointments of a marriage in which she had placed much hope. This, despite Charles Bovary's love, is too limited, too meagre, unadorned and dull in its daily unfolding to fulfil her wishes. She tries to allay the tedium by making her home beautiful. But the satisfactions are few and she grows increasingly nervous – thin, ill, despairing. Some have diagnosed Emma as a 'hysteric'. The psychiatric diagnosis 'Bovarysme' has been named after her: a marked tendency to escapist daydreaming. The prerogative to see the world as other than it is, belongs, of course, to all writers and all people dissatisfied with their condition. Emma yearns: she longs to travel or to go back to the convent, to die or to go to Paris.

The move that does take place is to another small town, Yonville, near Rouen, and when it takes place, Emma is pregnant. But there is no money to feed her maternal fantasies. Charles Bovary's medical practice doesn't thrive. Emma vests her hopes in having a strong son, a male who is free to live out adventure and passion, who can afford her 'a kind of anticipatory revenge for all her past helplessness'. But there is no son, only a daughter, another being to be trapped like herself between desire and convention. Emma takes little interest in her child. A dreaming sensualist, with hankerings after a finer life and with no activity or projects in which to deflect (or sublimate) her desires, she is prey to the advances of men who speak of a wider and deeper experience than her parochial husband seems able to provide. One might say that Emma wants nothing more than to be ecstatic – displaced, either by rapture or by martyrdom, from the petty world into which fate has cast her.

Believing that love 'must come suddenly, with thunder and lightning, a hurricane from on high that swoops down into your life and turns it topsy-turvy, snatches away your will-power like a leaf, hurls you heart and soul into the abyss', Emma does not at first recognize that the sensitive and poetical lawyer, Monsieur Léon, who woos her with poetry and fine sentiment, is in love with her. When she does and finds that she returns that love, she tells herself she is first and foremost a 'virtuous woman' and imposes a domestic martyrdom on herself which casts her into the 'nervous' abyss of unrequited love. Despair and frustration make her hate her poor husband all the more, so that when the worldly upper-class Rodolphe appears on the scene, she is all the riper for the plucking.

In the famous scene of the agricultural show, with its pervasive authorial irony, Flaubert sets the small-town republican virtues of industry, trade, service and duty against Rodolphe's more aristocratic code – one to which Emma aspires. Prizes for manure, rams and pigs, culminating in a prize for fifty-four years of domestic service, are counterpointed with Rodolphe's wooing: 'Duty again! . . . I'm sick to death of the word . . . To feel nobly and to love what is beautiful – that's our duty. Not to accept all the conventions of society and the humiliations society imposes on us.'

So Emma joins 'that lyrical legion of adulteresses' and becomes 'a part of her own imaginings'. 'Love, so long pent up within her, surged forth at last with a wild and joyous flow.' Her life of secret letter-writing and illicit encounters begins in high adventure. But soon enough, intox-ication wanes: Rodolphe grows careless in his love. The tender words and tempestuous embraces vanish and when she redoubles her love, he waxes increasingly indifferent. Emma, in turn, becomes a slave to pas-sion. When ultimately Rodolphe reneges on their – or principally her – plan to elope together, she contemplates suicide, then succumbs to a state of nervous prostration. Meanwhile poor Charles, ever more in debt because of her extravagance in purchasing finery, contends with creditors and the depression and illness of a wife whom he continues innocently to love.

When Emma finally rallies, it is to engage in another doomed passion with the law student Léon, her first admirer. But the increasingly sexual frenzy of what had started as an affair of heart and mind, alongside attraction, tires Léon before it tires her, and once more she is confronted by the vanity of her dreams: 'All was lies! Every smile concealed a yawn of boredom, every joy a misery. Every pleasure brought its surfeit; and the loveliest kisses only left upon your lips a baffled longing for a more intense delight.'

Emma is confronted by the elusiveness of her pursuit of satisfaction: rapturous love through time ever eludes the lover's grasp. Like so many engaged in a passion which initially seems grand, she comes to redis-cover in adultery 'all the banality of marriage'. Torn apart by the spiral of debt for which she has only herself to blame, she takes poison. Charles, bereft, continues to love her despite the revelation of her infi-delities. He dies of a broken heart. Orphaned, their daughter is reduced to earning her keep in a cotton-mill. The fate of the passionate dreamer and adulteress is to wreak havoc on the lives around her.

But Flaubert judges his heroine – if he judges at all – less severely than the pettiness of the society of which she is part. In this quintes-sentially modern novel, the adulteress's punishment comes neither from religious power – as it does, say, in Hawthorne's *The Scarlet Letter* (1850) – nor indeed from the society around her. It comes from her very condition as a woman, which allows her no dreams of transcendence apart from those of love; and from the nature of adultery itself – doomed to become as dull as marriage. The very obstacles which contribute to passion, Flaubert the psychologist demonstrates, are not enough to sustain it through time. Born out of fertile illusions, it is bound for disillusionment. Ever even-handed in his ironies, however, Flaubert posits little hope for domestic love either: Charles's idealization of Emma, his willing, indeed uxorious, recognition that this beautiful woman is cut from finer cloth, does not mean that he is capable of the imagination that might even briefly satisfy her desires. Desire may indeed be doomed, but without it, there are only the chemist Homais's empty platitudes and comically provincial self-satisfaction. Human heavens are brief and self-created, but they're heaven for all that.

If Emma's story has a tragic dimension, her male counterparts in continental fiction tend to be treated in a comic idiom. Unmarried men may woo and love older married women, with meaningful passion – like Stendhal's and Balzac's heroes – but married men pursue their lusts by rote and with a degree of social acceptability, whatever the moralizing of the Church or the malice, ever mingled with envy, of gossip. Mondanity rules.

Unhappy families: Anna Karenina

Despite the passage of time and shifting social conventions, Tolstoy's *Anna Karenina* remains the richest psychological elaboration of love, marriage and adultery fiction has given us. The tragic passion of Tolstoy's iconic heroine is so vivid in cultural memory that it can make us forget that the book in fact begins with its comic counterpoint: the marital plight of Anna's worldly brother, Stepan. An upstanding and much loved member of the Russian aristocracy of the 1870s, Stepan Oblonsky is a charming, pleasure-loving, happy-go-lucky philanderer. It is *his* family that is the first case to follow from the most famous opening line in fiction: 'All happy families are alike; each unhappy family is unhappy in its own way.'

Stepan's family is unhappy because his wife, Dolly, has discovered his infidelity with their former French governess. Dolly feels that she can neither forgive him nor go on living with him. Her palpable pain suffuses the household and unleashes disorder: the smooth running of

family life grows impossible. Recognizing this and suffering its consequences, Stepan, *homme moyen sensuel* that he is, can nonetheless feel little
guilt for his infidelity: 'He could not deceive himself into believing that
he repented of his behaviour. He could not now be repentant that he, a
thirty-four-year-old, handsome amorous man, did not feel amorous
with his wife, the mother of five living and two dead children ... He
repented only that he had not managed to conceal things better from
her.' Although he understands the gravity of the situation and pities
Dolly, Stepan is quintessentially a man of his time. Indeed, he encapsu-
lates the double standard inherent in a particular type of masculine
pragmatism, whatever the period. He has never thought through the
question of his infidelities clearly, 'but vaguely imagined that his wife
had long suspected him of being unfaithful to her and was looking the
other way. It even seemed to him that she, a worn-out, no longer beautiful woman, nor remarkable for anything, simple, merely a kind
mother of a family, ought in all fairness to be indulgent.'

Dolly isn't. It takes the intercession of Stepan's sister, the charismatic
Anna Karenina, to smooth matters between husband and wife. With
her force of presence, as much as with the force of her argument, Anna
convinces a Dolly whose heart and pride have been wounded to forgive
her husband. There are different kinds of love, she argues: Stepan's for
Dolly is a love of the soul, he has called her 'remarkable', she has been
a 'divinity' for him; while his love for the governess is a mere sexual
exploit – 'infatuation'.

Soon Anna herself will be caught up in a passion that challenges
any easy separation between the values of the sacred and the profane;
and as an adulterous *woman*, forgiveness will be far harder to find.

Stepan, the kind but fundamentally amoral pleasure-seeker, provides one pole of the novel's exploration of morality in love; his deeper
and more troubled friend, Levin, provides another. Tolstoy's own stand-
in, Levin is reflective, austere, idealistic, tied to the land and to
overarching religious values, yet racked by unconscious impulses and
his own inability to understand or indeed control himself, particularly
where passion is concerned. Like everyone else, except momentarily
Dolly, he loves Stepan: but he can't viscerally grasp his friend's wayward, childlike greed and undisciplined desires.

When Stepan says to him: 'Suppose you're married, you love your wife, but you become infatuated with another woman . . .', he responds that he doesn't understand, just as 'I don't understand how I could pass by a bakery, as full as I am now, and steal a sweet roll.' Stepan, decidedly a man with the makings of a modern consumer, counters that the sweet roll may be so fragrant you can't help yourself, even if it is a theft and engenders lamentable consequences. Not a man driven by passing desires, Levin advises him simply not to steal sweet rolls. But, remembering his own past sins in this area – before he formed a pure and overarching love, a love that leads to higher areas of the soul, for Dolly's sister, the delectable Kitty – he blurts out that he simply hasn't the answer to these problems of love.

Stepan will go on chasing 'sweet rolls', whatever his wifely ration of daily bread. And Levin will continue to agonize. There are, Tolstoy shows, simply differences of character. These play themselves out in the arena of love. There are also fundamental incompatibilities between desire, morality (here, the social institution of monogamy) and indeed the very desire for morality. These produce the conflicts with which humans struggle. The charming, philandering adulterer may, like a sensuous child, be forgiven by a kind and caring, one might say maternal, wife; whereas the stern, austere, more reflective character will experience his own straying from his high ideals as a sin and flagellate himself for it, though this may not always stop the straying. Nor will his guilt necessarily make him any kinder to his wife. It would be a little, if one dares to leap from fiction to political life, like comparing an Alan Clark with a Gladstone, or a Clinton with a Lincoln.

When Levin, after much delay and soul-searching, does get his idealized Kitty, the way of marriage is never smooth, for all that.

Tolstoy's own marriage to Sophia Andreevna Bers, sixteen years his junior, as the radiant and pure Kitty is Levin's, may have begun with intense passion. She served as his loyal secretary, reading and copying his major books, managing his financial affairs and bearing him thirteen children. But Tolstoy, again like Levin, torn by the struggle between his idealist hopes and the reality of his debauched past – what Nabokov has called his 'sensual temperament and his supersensitive conscience' – was rather less than tactful when it came to Sophia's own sensitivities:

for one thing, he felt duty-bound to show his innocent eighteen-year-old bride the diary of his lusts on their wedding night. Revelation and self-confession trumped care for the other.

After reading the first part of *Anna Karenina*, Sophia is recorded as having said to Tolstoy that Levin was him, minus the talent; and that he was an impossible man! Over the long years of a tempestuous marriage, in which five of their thirteen children died before their tenth birthday, Tolstoy and Sophia see-sawed from love (and lust) to hate and back again. At the last, he seemed to prefer his acolytes to his family, abandoning Sophia to die amongst them. Wild with rage and jealousy, she had several times attempted suicide.

In imagining Anna, his adulteress, Tolstoy had initially wanted to judge her as morally reprobate. Her punishment for her sin was a pre-determined suicide. But in the final version of the novel, based like *Madame Bovary* on an incident from life, Anna gains in psychological depth so that her destiny is less moral punishment than a matter of desperate choice. She becomes a person we feel we have known more intimately than our intimates. Viewed from inside and out, speaking what she does not intend to say, prey to unconscious forces beyond her control, derailed and tormented by a love she can neither abandon nor enjoy, cast out by society, separated from her son, Anna's journey towards her fate takes on the grandeur of tragedy. Amongst the destinies of the other 'unhappy families' interwoven with hers, her own emerges as particularly pitiable. By telling us that Anna was handed over in marriage by her aunt to a man twenty years older than her, by making that man the rigid, righteous, bullying and unappetizing Karenin, Tolstoy has us wanting Anna to sin, to *live*, whatever the social and spiritual consequences. And if Count Vronsky, her lover, as Nabokov judged, is 'a blunt fellow with a mediocre mind', with none of Anna's brilliance and depth, he has charm and energy on his side.

Then, too, Tolstoy's art is such that he leaves no doubt that neither of his lovers is in command of their actions. They are propelled by the electric charge of a blind passion which from the first seems to have death as its inexorable shadow. No sooner have they met on the train that brings Anna and Vronsky's mother from Petersburg to Moscow than a watchman is found dead on the tracks: 'a bad omen', Anna murmurs with trembling lips. During the ten months of Vronksy's wooing, sheer physical attraction, a sexual imperative, sways far more than any inconsequential words that are spoken. The two are driven towards each other by a force that frightens by its sheer quantum of desire. Anna in love glows with the 'terrible glow of a fire on a dark night' and when at last she succumbs, it is as if the man she has desired and who now has every power over her is also her murderer. The 'sole person in her life', her great love, Vronsky is also her doom. On his account Anna will be ostracized from all else – her husband, her son, society as a whole, and indeed from herself, for she can never stop judging her own actions.

Anna's attachment to Vronsky bursts beyond the bounds of an acceptable 'secret' liaison between a young officer and a married woman. Unlike her peers, unlike Vronsky's mother who has tallied up lovers in her youth, Anna's love cannot be managed. She lives it in perpetual anguish, tossed between desire and hapless guilt, between a passion that gives meaning to her life and conventions that mark her out as depraved and guilty. She doesn't want to and can't give the love up, yet she can't live it happily. Unable to dissimulate, she can't play by the rules of the worldly game. She simply feels too much. 'Love,' as Horace Walpole observed, 'is a comedy for those who think and a tragedy for those who feel.'

Nor can Tolstoy allow Anna's to be a redemptive passion, the kind he gives to Levin and the innocent Kitty. It is just too sexual. The carnal is always in play: Vronsky's white teeth, Anna's beauty and quick hands, the dark hair curling above her white neck. In a metaphoric signal of the doom that is to be unleashed by the dark forces of ungovernable passion, Tolstoy has Vronsky accidentally break the back of his equally subjugated mare in a long-awaited race played out before all Petersburg. Anna, already pregnant, is similarly broken. In her distress at Vronsky and the mare's fate, she blurts out the fact of her affair to Karenin.

First Karenin, the 'administrative machine', feels jealousy; then he sees Anna as depraved. He considers a duel, but is too cowardly; finally he reflects on divorce or separation, both of which would bring social shame and the terrible side-effect of setting Anna free to follow her passion. Karenin reasons that Anna should pay and be unhappy, while he, who is not guilty, should not be unhappy. So he determines to punish her by keeping their marriage intact, at least in appearance, and by allowing her to repent – all under the aegis of his magnanimity. This is a man whose desires are all to do with reputation and morality.

'He's right ... he's always right. He's a Christian, he's magnanimous! ... the mean, vile man!' Anna bursts out when she hears his decision. Karenin is 'mean' and 'vile' because under the cloak of rectitude he is, as he has been through their eight years of marriage, stifling everything that is alive in her. Yet she, too, is entangled in his 'lies and deceits', since Karenin knows that she cannot willingly abandon their son and live as a 'criminal'.

Hardly a tract promoting easier divorce, the book teases out the torments that attend the unravelling of any marriage, its impact on the new 'adulterous' attachment as well as on the family left behind.

Trapped between her love for her son and her love for Vronsky, aware of the plight of her son in having to judge between the competing parental narratives, Anna begins to question her love for Vronsky. In that generalizing of paranoia which so often attends love's moments of greatest permeability, she no longer altogether trusts Vronsky or her love; she finds herself constantly having to readjust her image of him, to re-illusion it. She grows jealous, which has the effect of making Vronsky increasingly indifferent. His bond to Anna grows into a prison. He is more fully enmeshed than he has appetite for in a liaison which has put paid to his ambitions together with his income from his disapproving mother. When his love was stronger, he reflects, 'he might have torn that love from his heart ... but now, when he felt no love for her, he knew that his bond with her could not be broken'.

The birth of Anna and Vronsky's daughter and the puerperal fever which follows it unleash a new stage in this adulterous passion. In her delirium and on the cusp of death, Anna asks for Karenin's forgiveness. He gives it: the feeling and expression of compassion bring him a joy he has never known. But for Vronsky, Karenin's forgiveness engenders humiliation. Abased, Anna lost to him, his life is emptied out, meaningless. He tries to shoot himself.

But neither he nor Anna die. This is only the first step in the elaboration of their grand passion.

As she convalesces, Anna experiences her existence with the newly lofty and doubly repulsive Karenin as a death-in-life. In that constant counterpointing of family stories that Tolstoy so expertly dovetails, it is Anna's brother, Stepan, who now miraculously engineers Karenin's release of her to Vronsky, just as she had so well orchestrated his reconciliation with his wife Dolly. Anna and Vronsky leave for their coupled life together, for happiness, just as Levin embarks on his rapturous married life with Kitty. But the fate of the two couples will be very different.

After travelling through Italy with their baby girl, though separated from Anna's beloved son Seryozha, Vronsky and Anna set up house in a small town. The brief honeymoon over, Anna is faced by a new anxiety. Vronsky is so dear to her, makes her so happy both in himself and in his attentiveness to her, that she is plagued by an anxiety that he will stop loving her, that he will become aware of just how much he has given up for her – his military post, his ambition, his vocation for statesmanship, his whole life – worthless as she now is in comparison to her earlier social status. And indeed Vronsky, though he knows his wishes have come true, also recognizes that their realization has given him 'only a grain of the mountain of happiness he had expected'. The freedom to love has robbed him of both his other freedoms and his desires. The pleasures of society, of meaningful work, are gone and, 'as a hungry animal seizes upon every object it comes across, hoping to find food in it, so Vronsky quite unconsciously seized now upon politics, now upon new books, now upon painting'. Both he and Anna, left with only each other, suffer from too much freedom. Boredom, and then worse, sets in.

Meanwhile Karenin, the abandoned, friendless husband, suffers such a deep sense of humiliation that he can barely carry on with work or daily life. The intervention of Countess Lydia Ivanovna, one of the new Petersburg spiritual enthusiasts, shows him that his lofty magnanimity towards Vronsky and Anna, which so shames him, was God working through him. He has no reason to feel dishonoured. Karenin, though he thinks this rapturous faith silly, turns to it and its proponent to reorder his life. Part of that reordering is to tell Seryozha that his mother is dead.

Back in Petersburg, Anna is tormented by the need to see her son. Her baby daughter cannot make up for the child that is lost to her. Since permission to visit Seryozha is refused, she steals in to her old home for a heart-breaking encounter and must too soon steal away. That night, in an agitated state and against Vronsky's wishes, she dons her finery to flaunt herself at the Opera, before all Petersburg. Shunned and insulted, she challenges Vronsky to give her the love for which she has forfeited everything: her son, her relations, her social place. Though he is dutiful and makes the gestures, he is no longer capable of it. The forces set in train by passion and adultery will soon drive her to her death.

A brief respite far from society, in their country home, sees Vronsky revive amidst projects that absorb him. He remodels his old house, builds a hospital for the locals. Anna takes an informed and active interest. Yet it is as if they are both playing at their coupled roles without quite inhabiting them. Vronsky suffers from the fact that his daughter, and any future children, will not legally be his, but Karenin's. He also suffers from Anna's jealousy of his 'male independence' – the political and social activity that takes him away from her. Her anxious love, in its need for constant expressions of worship, collides with his need for freedom. A dark struggle for power ensues.

Simone de Beauvoir's scathing analysis of 'the woman in love' and the grand passion which begins in generosity and ends in exigence parallels the process of Anna's and Vronsky's love. At first the woman in love, de Beauvoir writes, 'takes delight in gratifying her lover's desire to the full; later on . . . she applies herself to awakening this desire so that she may have it to gratify. If she does not succeed in this enterprise, she feels so humiliated and useless that her lover will feign ardours he does not feel. In making herself a slave she has found the surest means of enchaining him.' The love that began as a gift becomes an insatiable tyranny, as master and slave grow enmeshed, each taking on opposing roles in turn.

'Man's love is of man's life a thing apart,/ 'Tis woman's whole existence,' Byron wrote – apparently with Madame de Staël in mind. In her social isolation, the words take on especial weight for Anna. She narrows her eyes so as not to allow too much reality in. She cannot bear

Vronsky's absences. Nor at first can she bring herself to write to Karenin to demand the divorce he promised: it would mean giving up her son utterly. She cannot have both Vronsky and Seryozha. The two loves are irreconcilable. Torn between them, she takes more and more morphine to dull the pain. When she does finally ask for the divorce, Karenin refuses it.

An increasingly demanding Anna and an increasingly trapped Vronsky quarrel bitterly, and at the slightest provocation. They say what would be best unsaid. After what is their final quarrel, the words, 'I want love and there is none', go round and round in Anna's mind. In their repetition, the thought of death surfaces. She imagines Vronsky's feelings after she is dead, how her death will punish him. In that brilliant stream of consciousness Tolstoy gives a delirious Anna as she rushes towards Vronsky and death, the world metamorphoses into an ugly, dirty place in which contact with others is impossible. 'He has long ceased loving me,' Anna thinks. 'And where love stops, hatred begins . . . I have become his unhappiness and he mine.' So she jumps on to the train tracks to her death. That death is also a murder enacted not only on herself, but on Vronsky. In the wake of Anna's suicide, he leaves for certain death on the battle front in Serbia.

One way of thinking of the various kinds of love Tolstoy gives us, outside the socio-legal contract which demarcates legitimacy and illegitimacy, is to posit some fundamental ways in which two can become one. In one template, two different beings become one by an act of possession or incorporation. One eats the other up, cannibalizes, dissolves the other's difference into him or herself – like Stepan's sweet rolls, or the babe at the breast, or Proust's Marcel feeding off his mother's goodnight kiss. The other's resistance to incorporation or refusal of it, like Vronsky's resistance to Anna, unleashes hatred or the possessive jealousy that sends the lover in vigilant pursuit of the other, wanting more and more of the caresses, the proofs of love that grow less and less.

Another model of love – though the two are rarely absolutely distinct, but rather fluctuate into one another – functions through identification. We become one with another by identifying with them or with one aspect of them which becomes both all of them and what we want to become in and through them. Madame Bovary's adulteries are based on this kind of passionate identification, which is also in her case a kind of mimetic envy: through Rodolphe she wants the ease, finery and glamour of the upper-class world he represents; in Léon, the poetry, sentiment and romantic chivalry she has always desired.

As for Levin, in Kitty he sees a kind of purity, a truth and truthfulness he feels he lacks. By becoming one with her, he also takes on what she has. Her forgiving him for his past debauchery on the eve of their nuptials means that he can forgive himself, become truthful, attain, though gradually, an inner peace. When she strays from that spiritual perfection he identifies with her — for example, through her infatuation with Vronsky he is abased, humiliated, and his love momentarily turns to hate.

Anna's attachment isn't founded on identification, but is far more elemental. It is carnally incorporative — one might even say cannibalistic. There is nothing in Vronsky that she wants, except all of him. She wants him, not his qualities. That is why, when she commits suicide, she is killing him, too.

Adultery today usually wreaks somewhat less havoc than in societies where divorce was rare and women bound by constraining convention. Anna and Emma are not modern women, free to pursue life paths they choose and to play an equal role in marriages they are free to leave. But the toll in individual pain remains great, and those rampant nether passions of hatred and jealousy as biting as ever.

The Green-eyed Monster

Love and hate

Love and hate walk hand in hand, the poets have long told us. As Oscar Wilde mournfully repeats in the 'Ballad of Reading Gaol', each man or woman in various measures 'kills the thing he loves':

Some do it with a bitter look,
Some with a flattering word,
The coward does it with a kiss,
The brave man with a sword!

Some kill their love when they are young,
And some when they are old;
Some strangle with the hands of Lust,
Some with the hands of Gold:
The kindest use a knife, because
The dead so soon grow cold.

Freud postulated that there exists an inherent ambivalence in our passions. Love and hate, seeming opposites, live side by side, feed off the same fuel. We want to possess. We want to take in the beloved fully. It needs only the slightest resistance on her or his part to provoke hatred. That resistance can manifest itself as the attention paid to a third party. Jealous hatred erupts. As Sartre put the paradox: inherent to the object we want to love is that she chooses us freely. There is no love, if that freedom doesn't exist. But if she has freely chosen us, she could also choose another, perhaps already has. And that fact, or even the suspicion of that fact, thrusts jealousy and hatred into play.

In his late and dark romance *The Winter's Tale*, Shakespeare shows us this inherent ambivalence in love in stark action. King Leontes is happily married to Hermione, his pregnant, virtuous and outspoken Queen, already mother of his son. His dearest and oldest friend, King Polixenes, has been visiting from Bohemia. As the play opens, Leontes is trying to convince him to stay on. Polixenes insists he needs and wants to return home. But when Leontes exhorts Hermione to persuade him and she succeeds, everything shifts with sudden abruptness. In the flick of a gesture, Leontes suspects an affair between his wife and his best friend. Love turns to instant hatred, a murderous, jealous rage, a vindictive madness which will listen to no reason. He doubts whether even his son is his own and brutally interrogates the child. He issues a secret command for Polixenes to be executed. He has his virtuous wife imprisoned. The poisonous plague of Leontes' ambivalent passions will run its course, in time. Eighteen years later, reparation is made. But in the interim, his son has died as a result of his actions.

It is out of the proximity of love and hate that the 'green-eyed monster' jealousy is born. The fact or even suspicion of betrayal may unleash it in a marriage. But the hint of any third party in our passions may equally let it loose between the adulterous or secret lovers themselves.

Secrecy

In that continuity of emotions we see throughout history, passion waxes ever greater in the presence of the real or imagined antagonism of others from whom love must be kept secret. Secrecy propels the twosome into a hothouse, marking them with a sense of criminality, whether self-imposed or imposed by their policing watchers – who may be real, imagined or internalized. Indeed, triangles in whatever configuration can both invent and augment passion. Coded signals that secret lovers engage in, covert glances, freighted double meanings – all add a frisson to passion. Adulteries flourish because they exist in an endangered space dedicated solely to passion, from which the rest of the pressing world is barred. Once secrecy is removed, passion often wanes.

Within the marriage, the adulterous partner's secrecy creates greater and greater distance between the couple. The safe terrain for talk – in which slips about the secret lover won't emerge – grows ever more restricted, until children and the weather are all that is left to the spouses. While the temperature rises in the hothouse of secret passion, it cools markedly, even if unintentionally, in the home.

Even in our permissive times, adulteries are generally carried on in secret; the secrecy is often one of the conditions of their rapture and also of their eventual rupture. A romantic sensualist, Madame Bovary carries the secrecy through to her doomed end. Anna, a woman of greater moral heft, cannot live with the lie for long and braves convention. But once that secrecy is divulged and the doors of the secret room opened to other social relations, love quickly changes.

What makes secrecy so potent a stimulant to passion? The answer may lie in the fact that love and sex, both before and after we have experienced any couplings, are such active components of our secret fantasy lives. Indeed, the very whiff of the whole murky terrain of sex amongst adults can establish a space of secrecy, a closed door, within a child. Henry James's precocious Maisie in *What Maisie Knew* closes a door within herself on the couplings of the adulterous adults around her so that she can maintain her innocence, while still intuiting the 'corrupt' facts of life and letting them rumble on within her. This kind of inner splitting can easily persist into later life, establishing secrecy and the forbidden as the prerequisites for sexual passion. Sometimes this may entail secrecy from oneself. Like sleeping beauties, women, even today, often enough need to be awakened into desire, taking their stimulus from the desire of the other and attributing it to that other person. Meanwhile, both men and women accompany sex acts with their legitimate partners to the secret unfurling of fantasies – those third parties who may make the act itself more pleasurable or possible.

Secrecy is, of course, also about keeping others out, establishing a guarded perimeter. First of all against the spouse, ever a key player in illicit loves. Without that dangerous third presence to provide a sense of imminent danger and permanent rivalry, the heat of the adulterous passion can fizzle out. Indeed, the sense of the other at the gate is essential. Only in its shadow can the lovers literally be 'out of control', beyond the regulation that governs marriage. Secrecy itself acts as a transgressive liberation. Yet the hovering of the other at the perimeter also provokes a host of attendant hostile emotions and ambivalences. Jealousy, envy, greed and grief stalk the worlds of secret adulterous lovers and of those against whom they guard themselves.

Beasts in the nursery

These primal emotions in both betrayer and betrayed catapult the players back into the nursery of their lives, where powerful nameless beasts roamed, provoking tantrums, rage, gestures, feelings, omnivorous appetites which had few of the pacifying restraints of language. Jealousy may be the most unbridled of these passions. And it comes in as many shapes as love itself, sometimes inspiring it and keeping it alive, at others murdering both love and lovers.

Like some contemporary psychologist, Saint Augustine noted in his *Confessions*, 'I have myself seen jealousy in a baby and know what it means. He was not old enough to talk, but, whenever he saw his foster-brother at the breast, he would grow pale with envy.' The child is jealous of the rival who displaces him with his beloved mother, wants to be him, and is also envious of the milk and love he is getting in his stead. Teasing out Augustine's childhood scene further, one could also conjecture that the child values and loves his mother more in the light of her love for another; or, in that mimetic faculty that love and jealousy are also prone to, loves her *because* another, whose characteristics the child admires, also loves her. Passionate relations ever combine a host of other internalized relations. As the old adage goes, when we make love there are always at least four people present.

In the influential child psychoanalyst Melanie Klein's schema, the dynamics of envy and jealousy find a primary place amongst the earliest of childhood psychic structures. The infant's first relations with the world are with his mother and her breast (or the bottle which is its stand-in), source of nourishment and thus of love and life itself. Taking the breast in, the baby takes in the whole of his mother – what Klein calls 'introjection' – and she becomes part of him. He takes in both what is good, that is gratifying and life-giving, and what is bad or frustrating and destructive. The experience is in part dependent on the child's constitution, in part on the mother herself and the environment. Helpless, the baby is also inevitably shadowed by anxiety, which grows greater if the breast is not available or if evidence of maternal love and warmth is erratic.

Envy comes into being when the baby feels that 'the gratification of which he was deprived has been kept for itself by the breast that frustrated him'. It is an 'angry feeling that another person possesses and enjoys something desirable – the envious impulse being to take it away and spoil it' by putting bad parts of the self into it, first of all excrement, and thereby to destroy it. Jealousy, for Klein, is based on envy, but involves a relation with at least two other people: the love, the good that the subject feels is his due, has been taken away by a rival. It does not, as envy does, necessarily involve despoiling the loved one, though it can. The slippage between the feelings is frequent enough.

Configurations of jealousy

Shakespeare's tragedy *Othello* makes jealousy the stalking partner of envy. Even before we meet Othello, we learn that he has incurred his ensign Iago's invidious enmity by preferring Cassio to him. The act has unleashed the fatal envy that poisons everything. Before bringing Othello on stage, Shakespeare also lets us know that the Moor has taken Desdemona away from her father, Brabantio, by stealth – not unlike, one might say, an adulterer invading the play's primary and regulated twosome. Jealousy is therefore already embedded in the dynamic of the play's relations. Brabantio impugns Othello with having used a magic potion to woo Desdemona away. In fact Othello has won her with that other convention of romance – storytelling, ever a swaying prop in love's seductive armoury.

Envious Iago bears Othello a double hatred: 'it is thought abroad, that 'twixt my sheets/ He has done my office'. Even though Iago doesn't quite believe it, the publicly held suspicion of his cuckoldry adds fuel to his malice. Plotting against Othello, whose 'free and open nature' makes him easy prey to 'lead by the nose', cunning Iago pours his contemptuous poison into his ear, insinuating the need for suspicion and jealousy of Desdemona and Cassio by warning Othello against the self-destructiveness of the very passion he has implanted in him.

> Oh beware my Lord of jealousy;
> It is the green-eyed monster which doth suck
> The meat it feeds on . . .

At first Othello resists Iago's own 'green-eyed monster': he is not intrinsically an envious soul and will not easily succumb to the venom Iago skilfully injects. But the poison of suspicion has only to be lodged for it to spread, whatever Othello's conscious determination. As her maid

Emilia states, when Desdemona exclaims that there is no cause for Othello's jealousy:

> They are not ever jealous for the cause,
> But jealous for they are jealous: 'tis a monster
> Begot upon itself, born on itself.

Once Desdemona's handkerchief comes into play – the purported 'evidence' of her tryst with Cassio – jealous passion overcomes Othello. It literally drives him mad. His words break up and he falls into a 'trance', only then to be prodded further, by 'honest Iago's' insidious ploys, into murdering Desdemona.

Othello may be a noble soul, his tragedy – as he says of himself before taking his own life – that 'of one that loved not wisely but too well', his jealousy wrought by another who had him 'perplex'd in the extreme'. And indeed, the dynamics of the play are propelled by the unbridled envy of Iago. But – and this may be an interpretation too far – Othello himself is contaminated in that emotion. That evidential prop which is the white handkerchief is no mere 'napkin': Othello gives it a provenance that brings us back to that crucible of the emotions, the nursery. It was his mother who gave the handkerchief to him on her deathbed. It has magical properties, through its connection to her. The thought that Desdemona, now herself in possession of this magical object steeped in mother love, would pass it on to a rival she speaks so highly of is what spells her doom. The passionate rivalries of infancy have been brought into play. And with them love turns into murderous hate.

In *Anna Karenina*, Tolstoy gives us several possible configurations of jealousy and envy.

Dolly's is perhaps the most common of these, and is nonetheless violent. Learning of Stepan's infidelity with their former French governess, Dolly suffers from sleepless nights. She all but locks herself in her room, gives up the running of the household and is poised to leave her husband, though she simultaneously knows that, because of the children, she cannot. Nor can she give up on loving him, despite wanting to punish and shame him, to take revenge. She screams at Stepan who is trying to make it up with her: 'You are vile, you are loathsome to me! ... Your tears are just water! You never loved me; there's no heart, no nobility in you! You're disgusting, vile, a stranger, yes a total stranger to me!'

Like a child cast out from the parental pride of place, the confirmed centre of attention and emotion, Dolly is racked by jealousy at the arrival of a younger and more beautiful object who she feels has displaced her. She is also humiliated: the object of Stepan's love is a mere governess, a woman of lesser rank. She is doubly humiliated because the woman is a familiar, someone in her own home. Envy for the younger woman's attributes is compounded by the degradation of Stepan's idealized image in her eyes. Like the powerful parent in the displaced child's eyes, Stepan will never quite attain his idealized or powerful status again. But Dolly will, of course, forgive him and go on, in part swayed by Anna's conviction that Dolly's status remains for Stepan superior to that of the governess.

Despite our radically different times, contemporary surveys on jealousy iterate Tolstoy's understanding. In one such, respondents were asked, 'Are you a jealous person?' Fifty-four per cent responded in the affirmative, but the 46 per cent who had answered no to the question described their experience of betrayal in the same terms as those who had judged themselves as jealous people – and in much the same way as Tolstoy portrays Dolly. Those who considered their partners' choice of love object to be of lower social rank and a passing liaison tended to forgive them and were often stimulated into taking a new interest in their relationships.

In another instance of jealousy in *Anna Karenina*, Levin, recently married to his beloved Kitty, receives a visit from her brother-in-law Stepan and the handsome young Vasenka Veslovsky, the object of jealousy. The scene Tolstoy sets up is redolent of the play of jealousy and rivalry triggered by a family atmosphere which always brings old childhood feelings to the fore. To make this clear, Tolstoy has Levin hoping that the sound of the carriage will announce the arrival of his beloved and respected father-in-law, indeed something of an admired father to him: he is palpably disappointed. Levin's own brother, an old rival, is also present, as are other members of Kitty's family, including Dolly. At dinner, before the arrival of the two men, Levin and the pregnant Kitty had been particularly amorous and in the merriest spirits. But no sooner do the two newcomers arrive than everything changes.

Levin sees Veslovsky warmly kissing Kitty's hand, and, in that slippage unconscious responses are prone to, reacts by thinking darkly, while Stepan kisses his wife Dolly, 'Who did he kiss yesterday with those lips?' He hates the manner in which the sisters' mother welcomes Veslovsky, 'as if she were in her own home'. His own brother suddenly seems unpleasant to him. In particular, he is enraged by Kitty's 'special smile' to Veslovsky. He leaves abruptly. By the next day, his jealousy has progressed by leaps and bounds and he suspects that Kitty is already in love with the handsome young man. He imagines himself as a deceived husband, 'needed by his wife and lover only to provide them with life's conveniences and pleasures'.

One could conjecture that Levin's speedy descent into jealousy, in part sparked by the family configuration, is also due to the knowledge he carries within himself of his own past, filled with a colourful variety of liaisons. His own buried guilt and knowledge have him projecting passions of a similar kind on to his imagined young rival and his wife. Levin's jealousy here is, of course, quickly eased. His suffering and sense of humiliation are dispelled. Meanwhile, Kitty quietly rejoices at the palpable strength of his love that has expressed itself in this way.

Anna's unbounded jealousy of Vronsky shares a structural pattern with Levin's. She, too, is guilt-ridden – far more markedly so since having abandoned her beloved son and her husband. She projects her own excessive passions, her own inner dividedness, on to Vronsky. She imagines the loved and now hated Vronsky constantly betraying her with other women who endanger their union. This is a replay of the way she betrayed her own with Karenin, whom Vronsky made 'disgusting' to her, just as she imagines she is to Vronsky now. The power of her emotion is compounded by envy. She is not only jealous of the imagined other women Vronsky may have, but also envies the power he has as a male to walk freely in the world while her own ostracized position chains her in passivity. She both wants to be Vronsky and to be the object of his once undiminished passion.

Anna's case elaborates the truth of that old conundrum that the opposite of love is not hate, that equal and opposite passion often spurred by jealousy, but indifference. Karenin tips quickly into indifference. His emotions, Tolstoy stresses, have been stultified by a parentless childhood. His initial sense of rivalry towards Vronsky, his inability to challenge him to a duel, his wish to see Anna dead, are all sparked by social humiliation. But as soon as he finds a way to assuage that sense of humiliation – first by the power that resides in forgiveness, then by allowing a God who governs all into the frame – his jealousy of Anna and of his rival abates. His love, his very being, has little of a passionate base and passes quickly enough into indifference.

The fall-out of the adultery for Seryozha is more severe. When Anna first falls in love, the boy, without quite understanding the circumstances, feels that he has a rival in Vronsky. He is hostile towards him when they meet: he senses how everyone in the household, apart from Anna, treats Vronsky with 'horror and loathing'. Faced by Seryozha's uncertainty towards him, Vronsky, too, is filled with an 'inexplicable loathing'. Child and lover battle for primacy in Anna's love and Vronsky wins, at least in the initial foray. Meanwhile, the boy is faced by his father's cold severity, since Karenin hates Anna in him. With his father, Seryozha is mute, his mind jumbled, his aliveness stifled. When his mother steals in to see him on her secret visit, the child is overwhelmed by joy. But her second disappearance, a double betrayal, makes him ill. Absence and the passage of time, which place him in a school environment, then combine to make his feelings for his mother into a secret and shameful place. He experiences this as a girlish place of sentiment that needs to be repressed. In the last scene in which we see him with his uncle Stepan, Seryozha is unable to feel anything for Anna, except a confused embarrassment. He doesn't want to, perhaps no longer can altogether, remember her, nor the emotions she aroused in him. Tolstoy, with a dark irony, has him rush off and play with trains in which people fall, just as his mother will.

Children are the innocent pawns in the trials of love and death that adultery can produce. The Greeks have them enact savage and unconscious revenge: Oedipus slays the father who tried to murder but only succeeded in banishing him, then marries his mother. Orestes and Electra murder their adulterous mother and her lover in revenge for having murdered their father. In jealous rage, Medea murders her betraying husband's next bride-to-be, and also the four children she herself has borne him.

At best, we moderns usually – though not always, given the incidence of domestic murders – live out our passions internally, in fantasy, but they take their toll on us and through the generations, nonetheless.

Amongst the many configurations that our emotions can take, it is clear that some lovers need triangulation, an imagined adultery (or third presence), a suspicion of betrayal, for passion to exist. Indeed, for them, echoing Saint Augustine's much cited 'He that is not jealous is not in love', passion can be born only in jealousy. In Proust's great novel it takes only a missed appointment, an absence when presence was anticipated, a chance remark opening the gates to a host of imagined other lovers of whatever sex, for a moderately tedious relationship to be transformed into an obsessive passion. 'There is no doubt that a person's charms are a less frequent cause of love than a remark such as, "No. This evening I shan't be free",' Proust writes.

The pattern of jealous love that Marcel, his narrator-hero, enacts is deeply rooted in childhood emotions and rituals. The peace, the sensuous beneficence – one might say the post-orgasmic calm – that he can obtain only from his mother's kiss, and then only briefly since she partly belongs to another (his rivalrous, also loved, but frightening, father, who won't let her stay long), never materializes when there are guests present in the childhood home. But little Marcel is explicitly aroused by that 'hostile, inexplicable atmosphere ... that used to float up to my bedroom at Combray, from the dining room in which I could hear, talking and laughing with strangers amid the clatter of knives and forks, Mamma who would not be coming upstairs to say goodnight to me'.

The world of strangers stimulates desire, which in Proust's world is always pan-sexual – roving freely across nostalgic memories, hawthorn flowers, men, women, even children – and able to find its object, though only temporary satisfaction, in each and any. The underlying dynamic is the same whether the object choice is hetero- or homosexual, narcissistic or perverse. 'Envy, suspicion, rivalry, nostalgia', as Malcolm Bowie points out, 'these are the elements which, in varying combinations, give any sexual life whatsoever its characteristic grain and coloration.'

Marcel's relationship with Albertine, subject of *The Captive* and *The Fugitive*, begins as a mere summer infatuation with a band of adolescent girls met on holiday. But when Albertine, whom he is about to give up, mentions that she has been friends with the two women the boy Marcel had spied in a transgressive lesbian scene, passion springs into being. Albertine suddenly develops a past in which she was loved by others and a future in which others will also play parts. She becomes an undiscovered country that the narrator must possess in every detail. He takes her home to Paris with him, promises marriage, monitors all her activities, effectively imprisons her, and yet she continually eludes him. Time, with its shifting kaleidoscope, the new it brings in each moment of its passing, is simply not on his side. He knows that total possession, total knowledge of the other is impossible, all the more so here because what Albertine experiences in her lesbian loves is not available to him as a man. Yet the desire to know persists.

For Proust, love and knowledge are ever entwined. The obsessive detective work and the rampant fantasies that jealousy brings into being, the need to know and possess everything about the other, past and present, is akin to the voracious curiosity of the child faced by the mystery of adult sexuality. It also parallels the curiosity of those other searchers after knowledge, the philosopher and the scientist. The Proustian lover is a taxonomist of desire.

Amongst the structures of love he designates, one harks back, albeit in a different register, to Plato's Socrates in his pursuit of Diotima. The love Marcel initially feels for Albertine is less about her specificity as a person than for that occult force of which she is an emanation and with which she puts him in touch.

> . . . the mistresses whom I have loved most passionately have never coincided with my love for them. That love was genuine, since I subordinated everything else to seeing them, keeping them for myself alone, and would weep aloud if, one evening, I had waited for them in vain. But it was more because they had the faculty of arousing that love, of raising it to a paroxysm, than because they were its image . . . I

am inclined to believe that in these relationships ... beneath the out-
ward appearance of the woman, it is to those invisible forces with which
she is incidentally accompanied that we address ourselves as to obscure
deities ... The woman herself, during our assignation with her, does
little more than put us in touch with these goddesses.

But as soon as the woman is imagined as desiring another, everything
shifts. Jealousy imbues her with an unknown specificity and reawakens
a lost part of himself. She is now both inside and outside himself. This
new Albertine 'penetrates to the depths of my lacerated heart': she
generates both suffering and an imperative need for discovery.

For Proust it is the desire and pursuit of the fleeting beloved in her
(suspected and imagined) relations with others that constitute love.
This is the erotic force that drives all other pursuits. The woman made
desirable by the imagined love or attention of others arouses the jealous
suffering, that possessive passion which gives meaning to everything in
an otherwise dormant universe. Fantasy, pleasure and pain, under the
aegis of jealousy, become inextricably linked and follow their object
beyond death. For Proust, as for La Rochefoucauld, 'Jealousy is always
born with love, but does not die with it' (*Maxims*, no. 361).

Proust's narrator, as Malcolm Bowie has so aptly put it, is 'one of
European literature's most engaging monsters – a protagonist who is by
turns a Lothario and a spoiled child, a visionary and a pathological case,
a hero of the speculative intellect and a paragon of self-defeating folly'.
But the elaborately analysed arc of desire and jealousy, pleasure and
pain, which Proust describes, touches on many ordinary lives. Morbidly
vigilant Marcel may be, but he makes crystal-clear the voyeuristic core
of passionate jealousy. His jealous love for Albertine leaps into being
when she mentions Montjouvain: it was here that the young Marcel
spied on a forbidden sexual scene. This included the desecration of a
father's image by its lesbian protagonists. The very mention of the place
name evokes the scene vividly. And his pursuit of Albertine is characterized by the same graphic imaginings. Like a child, he remains
fundamentally passive in his jealousy, preyed on by images which consume him.

The images are important. The leap of jealousy – like passion itself, and like trauma and its replay in memory — happens in a part of us where language, reflection, indeed the passage of time, seem to have only a secondary force. Describing a bout of jealousy he experienced when he was eighteen, while acting in American repertory theatre and in love with a young actress, the journalist Alex Linklater underlines how jealousy made him prey to recurring images of her enlaced with his rival:

> of all animal emotions, jealousy is the purest excruciation. It is watching as someone else enjoys what you most desire on earth. The watching is important, whether real or imagined, because jealousy works its cleverest tricks with visual distortions ... In the time that immediately followed this introduction to a world of conspiracy, shame and consuming jealousy, something peculiar happened to my eyesight. I would get on stage or go for a walk and my vision would flicker in black-and-white. It was like watching a movie with sections filmed intermittently in negative. Briefly, the curiosity of this delusion would take my mind off what was actually happening.

The therapist-hero in HBO's engrossing television series *In Treatment* erupts into jealousy when his wife tells him she has been sleeping with someone else, although his interest in her has long been quiescent. He insists on knowing, on eliciting graphic detail of every aspect of her sexual encounters with her lover, even though that knowledge contributes to his pain. With that sexual curiosity so common to the experience of jealousy, he then confabulates, expands and elaborates on what his wife has barely hinted at, so that his vilified rival can render him more abject. The intensity of his jealousy and abjection is made greater because he hasn't yet permitted himself to engage in an affair with a patient who lubricates his fantasies and claims she is in love with him. This relationship has lasted as long as his wife's affair, along with the inevitable unconscious guilts.

Obsessive jealousy needs no more than a hint to erupt and engender pain that can feel far more powerful than love itself. Timing is important here. The art critic Catherine Millet, in the second of her autobiographical narratives, *Jealousy*, records the inferno she was cast into on the discovery of her husband's affairs. Her pain was all the odder and more mysterious because, as a self-styled 'suffragette in the cause of libertarianism', she and her husband had an open marriage in which it was agreed that both could and did conduct affairs. Love at home, she has said, was what freed her from having to find it in her other sexual pursuits.

Millet had had a long history of partitioning her life – indeed, even her understanding of her body – into split-off parts, each living its own existence with little accountability to the others. The promiscuous body occupies a zone akin to dream: fantasies intersect it and are occasionally spied upon. Then there is a married, loving body, a body in the social world. Her life, pleasurable and productive, takes shape as 'a series of layers, as densely packed as the earth's crust, and likewise permeable'. Yet, when she finds in her husband's study a nude photograph and a diary entry suggestive of desire, jealousy leaps and stabs: the various permeable layers of the self are sharply penetrated. She succumbs emphatically to 'the timeless and universal malady' that jealousy is.

In the background to this sudden onslaught of jealousy, one might speculate, is a recourse to an age-old childhood configuration, akin to the one Proust brings into play, though, of course, specific to her own life. Parental ghosts haunt, and leave a residue in, all our passions.

Catherine's mother has recently committed a violent suicide, thrusting her daughter back, as all parental deaths do, to infancy, that time when we were helpless dependants – but now she is also orphaned. A childhood sexual curiosity, it could be said, now comes into play, turning her into an obsessed detective of her husband's/parents' secrets: and all the more violently because her parents' coupled lives already included other lovers – those intruders on the home front. Her husband, adult keeper of the stable home, now becomes unstable, mysterious. The world has turned topsy-turvy. She is racked by physical pain, finds herself like a child, on the floor, a powerless creature, unattended, no longer the centre of attention. She can't breathe, her heart and mind race, she is reduced to a pair of snooping eyes, an ignominious detective of the other's life. Creeping around on all fours, reading letters and diaries, her imagination is overwhelmed with an obsessive need to know.

At the core of obsessive jealousy is a kind of childlike murderous impotence, turned, depending on the person, against the rival, the betrayer and their progeny, or against the self – often enough all three at once or in sequence. Language can rarely encompass the pain of betrayal and the loss or distortion of the 'us' that was invested in the lover. Such primal emotions propel us into a world where images come first. This is perhaps why, as in Millet's case, writing, talking therapy, articulation, as well as time itself, help the passage towards a new state where jealousy has passed. Her marriage stays intact.

Other jealous lovers, of course, lash out. Violence is enacted: for a long time the legal systems of France and other countries maintained a special category for the *crime passionnel*: murder either of the loved one or of the displacing rival. In the USA a crime of passion could constitute a defence of 'temporary insanity'. Passionately jealous, we are less than responsible beings.

Jasper, an interviewee we met before, recounted a not untypical configuration of the jealous passion and its timing. Not particularly a philanderer – a character whose greed, or call it 'love of women', needs voraciously to be fed and who finds it difficult to combine love and sexuality in one site – he sought out other women when his marriage, and he himself, felt dead. And these were serious liaisons, not the casual one-night stands which so often attend work trips or conferences far from home, for both men and women. Each adultery was precipitated by an atmosphere of internal crisis or shift – a mid-life crisis, one might say, though the timing of these crises is postponed as people grow younger, and they often enough recur.

His first affair, in his forties, coincided with his adolescent son's first forays with women and his daughter's early-teen rebellion. We could speculate about a background rumble of mild unconscious rivalry with his son and a sense of growing disappointment that he was no longer the predominant male in his daughter's life. If there was any jealousy here, it was of the mild kind directed at his children. As they moved out of the family group, so did he. At work, he had begun to grow bored with his lot. So when an admiring businesswoman strayed across his path, he took the leap. The affair was short-lived: his wife's unexpected jealousy helped to rejuvenate the marriage.

The second affair came after a bout of illness that frightened him, and brought thoughts of death close, not least because his father had recently died and his wife was embroiled in her own menopausal difficulties. She had lost interest in him. Clocks were ticking. *Carpe diem*: a sense that the day had to be seized became imperative. Just then, as timing would have it, Jude entered his world. (How he had loved the Beatles song! And now he wanted to take the advice and let this female Jude under his skin.)

Jude was a much younger lawyer who had joined his firm some years back. Amongst her many attributes that Jasper spoke of, the one that had his eyes gleaming was her sexuality. It was simply supremely uninhibited, in talk and fact, and Jasper found himself feeling not only rejuvenated, but young in a way he had never been young before. He was riding high. He moved out of the family home into a rented loft, bore his wife's storms, even his children's cold sneers, and happily gave over the house. All he wanted was Jude; and Jude, miraculously, it seemed, wanted only him – though they were moving into the cohabiting life slowly, spending only part of the week together for the time being.

A text message he happened to see on her phone changed everything. He discovered that there was another man in Jude's life, had been since soon after they had started their affair. At first he couldn't quite believe it. When he realized that he knew the other man, a barrister of high repute who at university had been an admired acquaintance, jealousy forked through his life with a savage vengeance. Passion had already made him labile, by turn omnipotent and vulnerable, and his jealousy took on a primal, untempered force: he was no longer his recognizable self. The threatened loss of Jude, on top of the loss of his stable home life, was tantamount to a loss of himself. He had never experienced anything like it.

Jude told him she was extricating herself from the other man, but he could no longer allow himself to trust her. He was overwhelmed by suspicion. Everything she had ever said to him, everything he had felt, was now in doubt. He retraced every moment of their love. He started to spy on her, to snoop on his rival as well, trawling the Net for references to him, for photos. The activity debased him. He felt alternately suicidal and murderous – occasionally felt, too, that Jude had preferred him when he was solidly married and something of a parental figure.

Jude's loving provided only momentary solace. His rampant fantasies of her and her other lover together plagued him. They had so taken over his mind that the real woman was a mere, often hated, chorus to that solitary activity, though he continued to want her with a boundless passion, wanted explicit detail of what she and the other man got up to. One day, he waited for the hated barrister to come out of his chambers. He accosted him with murderous rage, just hidden beneath a veneer of icy coldness. The man paid him little heed. He said he was due in court and rushed off before Jasper could land the punch he so much wanted to deliver. Jasper pursued him again, but his one-time friend refused to meet him.

Unable to concentrate on work, unable to sleep, eat, or talk to his wife who was his oldest and best friend, Jasper felt he was cracking up. His skin felt thin, his body shorn of defences. His children seemed to hate him. With that incipient paranoia which so often gains strength from the labile condition of jealousy, he sensed that his colleagues had turned against him. They had all grown critical. He felt humiliated, and chastised himself mercilessly. He arranged to take a long break and throw himself amidst strangers by signing up for a sailing expedition. He had to extricate himself from the arms of Circe, he said, or he might wake up not only a pig, but dead; but he kept delaying the moment of departure.

Jasper's dismantled state is hardly an unusual one in times such as ours, which value sexuality and the 'happiness' that is meant to reside there above loyalty, and the measure of stoicism that tolerates the downs of ongoing partnerships and the ageing process itself. The tide of cross-generational unions has, it would seem, risen, though I would wager that it may not be all that much greater than in epochs when women died young as a result of complications in childbirth. The difference is that our culture seems to give permission to ageing men to enact not only their sexual, but their marriage-breaking, urges far more than, say, the fifties did. The sense of permission comes in part from the workings of envy as much as from copycat mimicry based on media stories: if X – and there are so many Xs in our media – can engage in cross-generational passions, that is my due, too. What is less often recounted is how, in the crucible of our passions, envy and jealousy feed into each other and fly off in a variety of directions. If Jasper's story is anything to go by – and there is much anecdotal evidence from other cases of ageing men and young brides – the plague of jealousy, the split loyalties, the suffering of former partners and the possible vengefulness of children may seldom make for a greater harvest of happiness.

For all its madness, Jasper's jealousy is quite normal, which hardly makes it the more endurable. Time and that other old remedy, distance, may be the only doctor.

Those repeated stories of cross-generational love in which the older partner is thrust into agonies of jealousy for the younger, is envious, too, of his or her tantalizing and unpossessable youth, may serve as admonitory exempla in the history of rampant emotions – though they rarely seem to stop lovers themselves. There is a kind of psychic vampirism at work in all this, the old lover feeding on the energies of the younger to revitalize himself. Some rejuvenation may indeed take place, but often with eerie sequelae. A young woman who loves an older man for his father-like properties may feel an urge to compete in the illness stakes, just when her lover needs her to step in as the caring nurse he may subliminally have hoped for while feeding on her desirable youth. In order to carry on being daughter, she falls ill, and the ailing, ageing man finds himself uncared for, having, instead, to look after *her*. Enviable illness, instead of enviable youth, now encircles the couple. In an alternative and too familiar scenario, the besotted old lover cuts off his own children – the embodiment of his mortality – in his will, leaving everything instead to the envied life force his new beloved seems to be. In the process, he hopes to buy his young lover, fully possess her, so that her (potential) straying and his jealousy can be put to rest. But it is only he who is put to rest. Death makes fools of us all.

In writing about jealousy, Freud posits three layers, or grades: competitive or normal, projected, and delusional. Normal jealousy, however, he adds, is by no means completely rational, in other words 'derived from the actual situation, proportionate to the real circumstances and under the complete control of the conscious ego'. He describes it as being rooted in the 'earliest stirrings of the child's affective life'. It can also share aspects of the other forms of jealousy – projected or delusional. Made up of grief, the 'pain caused by the thought of losing the loved object and of the narcissistic wound', jealousy is compounded by enmity for the rival. Some people, he also notes, experience it bisexually: a man will feel pain about the woman he loves and hatred of the rivalrous man, but also grief about the man, whom Freud states he 'loves unconsciously'. In this unconscious scenario – one elaborated in Harold Pinter's *Betrayal* – it is the woman who becomes the hated rival for the other man's affections. Some men go so far as to imagine themselves in the position of the faithless woman with their rival. The sense of helplessness makes the pain unendurable.

Projected jealousy Freud describes as being derived from the sufferer's own actual unfaithfulness in real life or impulses towards it that have been repressed. The jealous person achieves some alleviation of the repression by projecting faithlessness on to his partner. Delusional jealousy, which shares much with paranoia, functions in the same way, but the impulses that have been repressed are towards the third party of the same sex: in a man the formula would go '*I* do not love him, *she* loves him.'

The adamant disavowal of same-sex love can hover over many of our couplings, inspiring the most vehement jealousy and the most ardent philanderings. Friends pursue the other's partner, finding rapturous passion only in a friend's mate. In a comic vein Sir Harcourt Courtley, in Dion Boucicault's *London Assurance* (1841), quips that when his wife left him for his best friend, it was the friend he really missed. Alternatively, the most potent of relations for Don Juan, that icon of seductive masculine promiscuity, seem to be with the fathers or husbands from whom he pilfers the women on his ever lengthening list – and certainly with his servant, Leporello.

Contemporary Infidelities

During the first wave of women's liberation in the 1970s, infidelity was often understood as a necessary journey towards independence, at once a way of constituting female desire and owning it. Traditional feminine dependence on marriage had to be shed, together with its psychological constraints. This came hand in hand with an attack on romantic love. Its mythical exaltations were exposed as mere sex and masochistic postures. Its idealizations of the transgressively domineering, seductive male, whether sung in the pages of women's magazines or in D.H. Lawrence's novels, were debunked and exposed as power politics.

Erica Jong's hilarious *Fear of Flying* (1973) charts the journey of her writer heroine from a constricting marriage gone cold, through dreams of a great and anonymous 'zipless fuck', into a passionate, but not as passionate as she'd hoped, affair with Adrian, a Laingian-style English psychoanalyst. Through the process, her *femme moyenne sensuelle* discovers a self that is stronger and more capacious, one who doesn't try to adapt herself to the theories men have of women. She also recognizes the fallacy underlying her vision of romantic love. Sitting in a Paris café after Adrian has left, she watches a couple kissing on a street corner.

> They were gazing into each other's eyes as if the secret of life were to be found there. What do lovers see in each other's eyes anyway? Each other? I thought of my crazy notion that Adrian was my mental double and how wrong it had turned out to be. That was what I had originally wanted. A man to complete me. Papageno to Papagena. But perhaps that was the most delusional of all my delusions. People don't complete us. We complete ourselves. If we haven't the power to complete ourselves, the search for love becomes a search for self-annihilation; and then we try to convince ourselves that self-annihilation is love.

She doesn't want to 'screw up' her life in another great self-destructive passion. So she returns to her husband, not her lover, though it's an open-ended question whether she will stay with him.

Some forty years have now passed during which women's sexual and social freedoms have grown far greater. Our hopes of romantic love leading to marriage have acquired a healthy scepticism, without ever being altogether obliterated or undermining passion's existence, even if short-lived. Yet our own times of greater equality with their later commitments have re-emphasized the value of fidelity in a new way, internalizing it, so that it becomes an inner moral injunction for each member of the couple – as if belief in fidelity could itself sanctify the endangered institution of marriage that we so want to preserve as an island of coupled safety in a lonely world; to preserve alongside the individualist desires for ever more love and experience, so palpably antagonistic to long-term fidelity. This has had the result of making male adultery as havoc-inducing an act as it was historically for straying women: marriages break down on the basis of infidelity, creating the attendant fall-out for children. Though in that private rebalancing of relationships which couples have ever been prone to whatever the social aegis, people may also forgive, realign and go on.

Yet, despite the increasingly liberal social consensus in the West – one in which acceptance of homosexual unions, cohabitation and pre-marital sex has risen dramatically in recent decades – infidelity remains an act that garners large-scale disapproval. In fact, it would seem that the more emphasis we put on the value of marriage as a key life relation – one that fulfils our desires of love, companionship, sexual pleasure and family life – the less tolerant we publicly grow of infidelity.

In 1951, Geoffrey Gorer found that infidelity was infrequently perceived to be the worst 'crime' that a spouse could commit, and only a small minority of his sample thought it should trigger the end of a marriage. In Britain, a YouGov and *Sunday Times* poll of January 2007 showed that 84 per cent of men and women considered infidelity always or mostly wrong, much the same as in the early 1980s, though more than in the less liberal fifties. If men were slightly less disapproving than women, the young were slightly more condemnatory than the over-forties.

A 2008 Gallup poll in the US revealed that almost two-thirds of Americans would not forgive their spouse for engaging in an extra-marital affair, while 62 per cent claimed they would get a divorce if they discovered their spouse had been cheating. The International

Social Survey Program, which monitors attitudes in twenty-four largely Western and industrial countries, had most people stating that extramarital sex was 'always wrong', with the US coming near the top of the charts at 80 per cent, a figure comparable to conservative Catholic populations such as Ireland (80%), Northern Ireland (81%) and the Philippines (88%). Other countries were less adamant in their condemnation: Australia (59%), Austria (67%), Bulgaria (51%), Canada (68%), Czech Republic (43%), Germany (data reported separately: East Germany, 60%, and West Germany, 55%), Great Britain (67%), Hungary (62%), Israel (73%), Italy (67%), Japan (58%), Netherlands (63%), New Zealand (75%), Norway (70%), Poland (74%), Russia (36%), Slovenia (57%), Spain (76%) and Sweden (68%). Most people – a majority of Russians apart, it would seem – today support sexual exclusivity between husbands and wives: an average of only 4 per cent of respondents believed that extramarital sex was 'not at all wrong'.

Moral attitudes about monogamy, however, are hardly in synch with the figures for actual infidelity. As ever, it seems, our publicly expressed wishes and hopes exceed our ability or desire to live up to them. Investigating adultery in post-war Britain, the historian Claire Langhamer noted that 'a hardening of attitudes towards infidelity accompanied increasing incidences of it'. So, too, for our own times. In America, if politicians act as indicators of the people they purportedly represent, then the harder the line on fidelity and marital values taken, the more likely it would seem that potentially scandalizing infidelities have been engaged in.

In a 2006 BBC survey of forty-six thousand respondents, 43 per cent of them married, one in five men admitted to straying, as did one in ten women. The smaller percentage for women, though not altogether to be trusted, may argue that women still bear a larger responsibility for children and the security of home life, so stray less. As for America, experts agree that despite the emphasis on Christian values, infidelity is even more prevalent. The consensus for the US is that between 50 and 65 per cent of husbands and between 45 and 55 per cent of wives become 'extramaritally involved' by the age of forty. Statistics here are inevitably inexact and to be treated with some scepticism, since we are often dealing with secret matter, hardly always to be revealed, even anonymously.

According to *Vanity Fair* journalist Melanie Berliet, when you factor in the number of unmarried people in committed relations who are cheating on their mate, the percentage increases to between 75 and 80: 'If you take an average of the infidelity studies, statistics, surveys and polls from the last 5 to 7 years, it becomes clear that infidelity in one form or another (physical or sexual infidelity, emotional infidelity, online or internet infidelity, female infidelity, same-sex infidelity, work-place infidelity) affects an estimated 80% of all marriages and committed relationships today.'

In France, where sex is rarely in the first instance a moral category, straying politicians rank high in approval ratings, unlike their kin in Britain and the US. Here there is a long tradition of relatively acceptable adultery, while the arts of seduction rank amongst life's pleasures. According to the French Institute of Public Opinion, however, only an estimated 39 per cent of men and 25 per cent of women cheat on their partners, though the figure for women has tripled since the seventies. Again, the first of these figures – relatively low – may say more about in what circumstances it is honourable to lie in France than about real infidelities, while the rise of the second statistic may have as much to do with the growing culture of public revelation as it does with actual figures. Figures are higher for those who engage in illicit virtual romances, where imaginary pornography is lived out at a click: 'Infidèle' is a common pseudonym. French lawyers report a growth in divorce cases citing Internet infidelities. This rush to divorce is a recent phenomenon on the French scene: traditionally, divorce counted as a far graver sin than straying.

In the US, one-third of divorces are apparently sparked by online affairs. Virtual betrayals can have real consequences – hardly surprising, perhaps, given the obsessional nature of our fantasy lives and the old-fashioned spur of secrecy they feed on, which nonetheless sparks altogether real jealousy in partners. Adultery social-networking sites have sprung up in America to follow on the success of singles sites, which it appears already find 30 per cent of their users amongst the married. Having had an affair she relished with a married man for two years, Melanie Berliet posed as a wayward wife and signed up, under a pseudonym, with Ashley Madison, a site whose tagline reads 'Life is

Short. Have an Affair.' The entrance cost was $49. She wanted, as her *Vanity Fair* article on the experience states, to find out what kind of men went in for illicit relations online; whether adultery could be a way of fulfilling one's needs without alienating one's partner; and whether cheating was really as bad as society makes it out to be.

Her mailbag numbered a hundred within a few days: she later discovered that the ratio of men to women on the site was nine to one. It is worth noting that on singles sites the balance sways in the other direction: there seem to be more attractions for men in a contractually delimited affair than in a relationship between unattached beings in which 'commitment' hovers in the background.

After getting to know a few select respondents through email, Melanie met one in the flesh: a fetching young Englishman who was a 'big believer in monogamy through adultery' — an attitude he said he shared with his wife. Though the affair went on pleasantly enough, Melanie Berliet decided not to take it to its sexual conclusion, but it proved to her that it was perfectly possible to 'have an affair cavalierly, rationalize it easily, and live happily'.

Her second chosen partner was more problematic. Handsome, well educated and successful, as his profile had suggested, he was however intensely guilty about cheating. He had three children he was devoted to. The problem was his wife simply didn't want sex and had never been very good at it. He told Melanie he had singled her out from the other women he had met on the site because they were weird: wanted to have their husbands watch, or wanted to be peed on. Melanie didn't take up his offer for a weekend away together but consented to a few rounds of real-time cybersex.

Her final 'test subject' was a non-starter. He had lied on his profile and he turned out to be 'arrogant and clueless'.

Without wanting to champion adultery, Melanie concludes from the experiment and from her prior experience that the 'notion that strict monogamy is the right path for everyone strikes me as narrow-minded, even holier than thou ... affairs don't have to destroy the lives of everyone involved. A successful dalliance, if such a thing exists, requires candor and discretion — two things Ashley Madison specializes in.'

A brief trawl through the private world of the Internet provides an instant sense that the old Catholic sin of adultery in the mind, not only in the body, is alive and well. And the real-life partners of these virtual cheats may suffer from their solitary sex escapades just as much as those of non-virtual adulterers do. The partner's experience of absence and non-attentiveness is the same. The caveat may be that the fantasy world the Web provides never offers the three-dimensional challenges and resistances of an embodied other. So Web affairs can last longer and be far more addictive than embodied ones, even though these latter, need-less to say, contain like all loves, an element of fantasy.

Amongst my cohort of married or once married interviewees, all pro-fessionals, many, particularly those in a first marriage, had engaged in infidelities: the longer the marriage, the more likely the occasional sur-reptitious straying. Most of these 'affairs' were short-lived, a casual instance of away-play during a time of dearth in togetherness. Few had told: it was simply a way of fulfilling a lack in themselves as much as in the couple, a short-term reinvention of the self and a way of re-establishing a needed separateness. Most assumed or knew that their partners had too, and an equalizing of the partnership entered into the inner dynamics.

In one case, the woman had engaged in an affair with another woman, though her long-term partner was a man. The lover was a new friend, a woman of her own mid-years, and one thing simply led to another. She thought the timing might have had something to do with the fact that her mother had recently died and she felt a need for the 'softness' she didn't get with her husband.

If short-term affairs didn't result in break-up, longstanding arrange-ments with another emphatically did — though in two cases, after a period of separation, the couples came together again. Interestingly, the timing of the break-ups coincided with the children having left home.

If many continue to disapprove of affairs within established relationships based on a promise of monogamy, it is not only because they can provoke rampant sexual jealousy and the possible break-up of the couple. Trust is the fundamental glue of all partnerships. In a long-running secret affair a breach of allegiance, of primary loyalty, has taken place: the betrayed partner can no longer trust the other. In an insecure and isolating competitive world where trust is already at a premium, betrayals within hearth and home make existence even lonelier and more precarious. The betrayed feels she has passed her sell-by date and can be disposed of in the dustbin of life, no longer even recyclable. She is catapulted into a retrospective agony of hunting out the chapter and verse of duplicity: 'So when we were celebrating Anna's birthday, you were busy texting X and setting up a meeting'; or 'When you insisted on taking a holiday in Cornwall, it was because X was nearby'; or 'When I rang you to say Anna was ill and you couldn't come home early from your sales conference, it was because there *was* no sales conference' – and so on and on, until every moment of settled life and the betrayed one's place within it becomes a wasp's nest of lies. All security is gone. Vertigo ensues; the ground opens up. Rage, vindictiveness, despair follow. If a separation ensues, the betrayed partner enters a state akin to mourning, but the partner is still alive, so peace of any kind can be hard to find; for some, even after years.

The paradox here is that we want freedom, the sexual satisfactions that ever unpredictable Eros can bring and that so many others so publicly seem to enjoy. In our post-traditional culture, we feel they constitute part of the quest towards self-fulfilment. Affairs, great or casual loves, make the story we tell ourselves about our lives rich and varied. They proffer meaning. And the pleasures of passion.

Yet we also want a predictable steadfastness, security, that path of continuous intimacy with its satisfactions of history and progeny, its promised gift of exclusive specialness to the other. Perhaps that exclusive specialness does not always and ever have to run alongside total possession. After all, the love that sees us through life is a gift freely given by the other, not a form of enslavement.

Truth and lies

Truth, lies and deception circle adultery like vultures waiting to feed on the body of intimacy. Can there be a just measure of transparency about affairs? And what measure feeds what purpose? Our confessional culture prompts individuals to be truth-tellers, though few have totally open arrangements; and spouses, unlike priests, find it difficult to forgive. Most therapists believe in disclosure, but then in certain cases they share a redemptive agenda with religion.

Men, it seems, prefer their settled partners eventually to find out about their straying: they leave signs to be found, as if unconsciously they want their wives, perhaps now maternal figures, to admire their prowess. A new conquest, they seem subliminally to feel, adds to their status and desirability. As the old joke goes, 'Better a 50 per cent share in a good business, than a 100 per cent share in a bad one.' Others want discovery because they simply can't bear the guilt of their treachery and a secrecy which in time has utterly distanced them from their home, their 'real' lives. Straying wives, though also some men, seem to prefer secrets and lies, a state which adds to the desirability of their affair and produces additional excitements. Others, who have drawn different lines between privacy and togetherness, seem quite happy not to know about their partner's extracurricular doings, particularly if sexual interest has run its course.

The balance of truth and lies will work its way out differently in every couple that becomes a threesome, and can change through the life of a marriage, just as it has done historically. In the 1940s the *Woman's Own* agony aunt regularly advised her straying women readers that 'far more harm is done by morbid "honesty" than by sane concealment'. Thirty years later, in more individualist times and with divorce more accessible, agony aunts were advising openness, talk, and visits to the Marriage Guidance Council.

After many years of marriage and as many in the consulting room, Freud, who as a jealous young lover had insisted on full honesty at all costs from his fiancée, grew rather more measured about the value of truth. On 10 January 1910, he wrote to his younger colleague Sándor Ferenczi, who was enmeshed in complicated affairs, that when it came to sexual honesty in marriage he had become more pragmatic: 'Truth is only the absolute goal of science, but love is a goal of life which is totally independent of science, and conflicts between both of these major powers are certainly quite conceivable. I see no necessity for principled and regular subordination of one to the other.'

Never a great one for absolute principles, Freud also belonged to an older social order than Ferenczi. Here, the weather of marriage had different storm patterns. Straying was a given for men in return for a stable security for wives. The more experimental Ferenczi looked forward to different kinds of sexual and marital settlements. Indeed, his work has been taken up by contemporary therapists who focus on the relational and intersubjective underpinnings of our lives. Here honesty within intimacy is key.

Bucking the therapeutic tide for total transparency in relationships as the only possible ground for 'rebuilding intimacy', Esther Perel evokes cultures where 'respect is more likely to be expressed with gentle untruths that aim at preserving the partner's honor. A protective opacity is preferable to telling truths that might result in humiliation. Hence concealment not only maintains marital harmony but also is a mark of respect.'

Young and old

Today, if those who grew up in the tide of sixties permissiveness aren't dependably certain that what they most want from their partners (or from themselves) is predictable steadfastness, their children and perhaps grandchildren definitely know they want it from their parents – and project this wish on to their own future committed partnerships.

Amongst my interviewees in their twenties, disapproval of infidelity was unanimous and adamant. Georgia, a high-spirited young graduate, explained to me that her generation had 'normative ambitions': of course, they might not live up to them, but that didn't make them the less important. They were children of 'sixties generation' parents. So they had grown up with the sequelae of parents who had disastrous affairs from which they, the children, had to pick up the pieces. Gallivanting fathers whose girlfriends were always twenty-one, no matter how old and pot-bellied those fathers grew; distraught, weeping mothers, left to take care of children who then had to take emotional care of them; meetings with dumb paternal girlfriends who would rather drown one than meet; a slew of short-lived stepsiblings, each unhappier than the last. None of this was the way to run a life, all her friends, women and men alike, agreed – although the men might not be so resolute about the horror of future infidelities, fearing that they might somehow trip up and slip into their father's footsteps. But that fear didn't lessen their condemnation of their fathers, whose behaviour was treacherous and altogether unseemly.

Her generation, Georgia told me, knew that children were more important than sex. They'd had enough of it young to realize that much. Affairs had transgenerational repercussions and, for some mysterious reason, their parents didn't seem to have considered that. As for girlfriends who got involved with men old enough to be their fathers, or simply with fathers of young families, that was just stupidity or madness. Didn't they know that they'd be dumped as soon as their boobs began to sag! And meanwhile the poor wife, the poor children forced to shuttle between home and their father's new set-up . . .! The whole thing was irresponsible and destructive.

So, she concluded, far better to have normative ambitions about fidelity, which put the family before personal desires. With a sweet, softening smile, she added, 'Of course, we're grateful to your generation for opening the doors and allowing us to have sex before marriage, sex before ultimate commitment. Best to get all that promiscuity out of the way and maintain fidelity once we have families.'

Georgia may well be right and her generation may well establish more successful, long-lasting unions. There is wisdom in the notion that some early promiscuity may lead to more grounded marriages – as if they were already remarriages.

Nonetheless, she made me think of a scene in *Philadelphia Story* in which principled, idealistic Tracy has laid down the law and told her mother she is to have nothing to do with her philandering, unfaithful father. Cowed into not allowing her husband home, her mother is not totally convinced. When Tracy's father returns, to reassert his conjugal claims on his wife and his paternal role in the family, there is a wonderful scene of confrontation between young and old – between him and Tracy in the presence of her mother. The family drama, the tugs and pulls one generation exerts on another, are all to be found here. Tracy asks what he's doing at home and upbraids him for his dancer friend. He states vehemently that his straying – if that's what it is – has nothing to do with *her*, nothing to do with *them*.

Men have a reluctance to grow old, that's all. And their best mainstay should be a daughter – a devoted young girl who gives her father the illusion that youth is still his. A girl of his own, possessing warmth, an unquestioning affection, an understanding heart. Tracy hasn't given him that, so he went to look for it elsewhere.

'So I'm to blame for the dancer!' Tracy says, enraged. And her father, undoubtedly a little unfairly but underlining the Oedipal point, acknowledges that in a way she is. Echoing Dexter's earlier comments about her personal sense of inner divinity pre-empting any regard for human frailty, he calls Tracy a prig, a 'perennial spinster no matter how many marriages'. Worse, he tells her, she has been behaving like a jealous woman.

And so she has.

By the end of the film, having recognized her own human failings, Tracy has developed a more 'understanding heart'. 'I'm glad you've come back,' she says to her father. 'I'm sorry I'm a disappointment to you.' And he answers, 'I never said that, daughter. I never will.' Tracy can now remarry Dexter, following her father into his own 'remarriage' with her mother. The Oedipal jealousy – which, it has to be assumed, runs both ways – is put to rest. One might go so far as to say that both Tracy and her father have grown up – never, after all, a once-and-for-ever process.

The values of the young rarely remain untainted through the vagaries of life. Though, without their 'normative ambitions', we might well be in a sorrier state.

Georgia's ambitions also reminded me of another film, one set not amidst the disappearing upper crust of America's East Coast but in the less than glamorous post-war Midlands. David Lean's *Brief Encounter* (1945) is a slice of ordinary life raised to the level of tragedy by the incursion of romance and unconsummated sexual passion. Laura Jesson (Celia Johnson) meets Dr Alec Harvey (Trevor Howard) at a railway station. Both have families and children. They talk, they meet again, they fall in love. They kiss. They dream of togetherness, but the real beckons and constrains. And in that constraint – not the denial but the conscious refusal of romantic passion – they achieve a kind of grandeur, a heroism beyond the mundane. Zadie Smith puts it well. It is not that Laura and Alec are 'morbidly repressed'. 'The film offers a different hypothesis: that the possibility of two people's pleasure cannot override the certainty of other people's pain. *Primum non nocere* is the principle upon which the film operates. As a national motto, we could do a lot worse.'

It is heartening to think that at least some of our idealistic young have a will to make the underpinning of love reside in that first principle of doing no harm to others, rather than in the *carpe diem* of instant gratification.

The answers to why people commit adultery are as various as the people themselves. Some will do it because they feel satisfaction is their due and it hasn't been provided by their existing partner. Others will fall into it, simply because the opportunity presents itself: the thrill is too great to be resisted. Some want a new intensity, a new meaning in their lives: in the self-absorbed excitements of secrecy far from the mundane cares of bills and children, the ordinary self flourishes in the eyes of the other. Still others find their home lives have grown imprisoning, sex has grown stale or vanished, or partners no longer show them the needed affection or attention. The reasons for the latter are various, too. One is too great a preoccupation with work: according to one report, the recent 'credit crunch' has apparently made wives disenchanted with preoccupied husbands and provoked them into secret flings. Alternatively, a young mother's attention to a new baby displaces her interest in 'Dad'. Or attentiveness to ageing parents or even social life can make a partner feel removed from the core relationship. Or like Tracy's father, a man may simply need a sense of renewal, and find it in the adoration of the young. Or it may be several of these at once.

People, Adam Phillips says, have affairs because there is some deprivation in their primary union, or a deprivation in themselves – one that may have followed them from childhood's unmet needs. The problem is that they believe that the next woman or man will do the trick, as if they inhabited a magical universe that carried rewards, as if the deprivation weren't also already a part of them. Though we may think there is one, there is no simple solution to the fact of human frustration.

Looking In

In *Couples*, his hugely popular novel of 1968, John Updike, like some zoologist graced with mordant irony, traces out the ingenious nesting habits of the residents of Tarbox, a small New England town where extramarital couplings come in dizzying permutation. Frank Appleby is having a fling with Marcia little-Smith. Janet Appleby is at it with Harold little-Smith. Through the vehicle of wife-swapping, Eddie Constantine and Roger Guerin are in fact working out homosexual desires. Meanwhile Piet Hanema . . . and so on, in a version of musical beds which brings some sexual rapture, some divorce, some remarriage and a great deal of child negligence. In this corner of American civilization, all couplings are intramarital.

What this particular zoology leaves out of the equation of adultery is the solitary third party: lover or mistress. Historically, lovers have been young unattached men, uninterested in displacing the husband in the married couple. This is a less usual pattern today, since changing sexual mores have made unmarried women more accessible than their married sisters. For those who may be worried about 'commitment', the latter may, however, seem fair game, though the initiating party is more likely to be the woman than the man.

The Balzacian code of the woman providing the youth with a 'school in life' is also sometimes still in play, though rarely. Unlike the French, the Anglo-American axis resists thinking of sex in terms of an *ars erotica*. The slang word 'milf', meaning 'mum-I'd-like-to-fuck' and much in use by my children's cohort, is a case in point, with its smutty, derogatory associations. It's somewhat diminishing to think of Stendhal's Madame de Rênal or Madame de Staël as mere sex objects — milfs — when they are palpably women of substance who give their young lovers lessons in sensibility and more.

In his short story 'Strangers When We Meet' Hanif Kureishi dissects a contemporary love affair between a slightly older married woman,

Florence, and a young working-class actor, Rob. Florence advises Rob on his acting, initiates him into cinema, helps him put words to his 'melancholy'. Though he has wept over and hated her inaccessibility, he has assumed that he doesn't care enough about her 'to worry about her husband', who seems irrelevant to the twosome that they are. But when instead of joining him to take a holiday together, she appears on the train with a man he recognizes from a picture as her husband, everything changes. Finding himself in the planned-for hotel in the room next to them, despair looms. He listens obsessively through the wall. 'I want her to want me – and me alone. I must play the lead and not be a mere walk-on,' he thinks. As Florence's husband takes on substantial life for him, jealousy, rivalry and love enter the adulterous dance in varying permutations. And Rob realizes that for reasons he can't altogether understand, though one of them is security, Florence, however much she may want him alone, will not leave her husband.

Far less uncommon – if anything can be measured with certainty in this field of rampant human vagary – is the continuing presence of mistresses, or simply single female lovers, as the triangulating party to a marriage. The historic lists of great royal mistresses, such as Madame de Maintenon, Madame du Barry, Madame de Pompadour, supplied the Sun King with children and often functioned as courtly advisers. But aristocratic examples hardly translate easily here into contemporary mores, emphatically less so if one remembers that these 'affairs' were conducted openly. In the nineteenth century, the 'mistresses' of the French social elite were also openly 'kept'. The contractual rules which bound the famous *horizontales* to their roles as erotic playmates were firm. Paid for the 'entertainment' they provided, they might work their way up the social ladder and, if they were lucky, eventually find their position regularized with another man.

If the French are still more tolerant of the position of the mistress as an adjunct to marriage – as the revelations about various politicians make clear – it is in part due to this long tradition of keeping marriage and the erotic in relatively separate spheres.

The doublings of secret 'bigamy' which so haunted the Victorians, the shocks of two separate families emerging at a man's death, still occasionally occur. But most 'mistresses' today are, in fact, likely to be wives-in-waiting: a shift of the kaleidoscope, and the roles change. Many women at some point in their lives have been 'the other woman'. Usurpers from the wife's point of view, from their own they are the sexual partners of men whose marriages are erotically, but sometimes also otherwise, lacking. They may well be rapturously in love, though sometimes they hide it, and are waiting for the oft-promised divorce – which comes rarely enough.

Kathy Lette, whose comic novels trace the ways in which love and sex go right – though mostly wrong – through the various phases of women's lives, stated in an interview:

> In Sydney when I was in my twenties, all the men were married or gay, or married and gay . . . It was impossible to find a man who didn't think monogamy was something you made dining room tables out of. So you invariably found yourself, at some stage, having an affair with a middle-aged married man . . . Of course you didn't know he was married until you found the teething ring in his pocket. But by that time it was too late because you were in love and believed him when he said that his wife didn't understand him. Which simply means he wants you under, not standing. I thought love was in the air – but it turned out to be the exhaust of his Meno-Porsche as he sped back to his wife.

Women who are hardly interested in cultivating the role of mistress can easily find themselves on the outside of a marriage looking in. Once they have reached their late twenties or thereabouts and haven't settled into long-term coupledom, or have separated from an earlier union and have a child, that hoary age differential between the sexes rears its head. Despite social change, being in love with another who 'belongs' to someone else still happens to women more often than to men, who continue to have access to ever new generations of women. Gay men repeat the same generational scenario.

In *Where the Serpent Lives*, Ruth Padel depicts a single mother who is passionately in love with a married man, a philanderer, so enthusiastic about women he can't keep his hands off any of them – except his own wife. Naive, faithful, romantic, this mistress believes his repeated exclamations that she is 'the only one' and that he will marry her. She also believes over the years the various excuses he makes for not being able to disengage from his wife, about whom, post-feminist that she is, she also feels guilty. She puts up with perpetual lateness, with broken engagements and desolate holidays. The sex is so great, she convinces herself, that he can only eventually be hers. Only when the tissue of lies is dramatically revealed does she pick up the reins of her own life ... eventually to find a man who isn't attached elsewhere.

In the merry-go-round that modern marriage is, people get on or off at various points. Meanwhile, unless she loves her liberty more than her man and prefers independence to the messy dailiness of intimacy, the single woman is prey, erotic satisfactions apart, to all the downs of love – plus loneliness. There is rarely anyone there at the end of the telephone.

'Sure, there were times when I felt lonely, exploited, and neglected,' the journalist Melanie Berliet says of her affair with her married lover. 'But I knew what I was getting into.' Others don't, and wait and hope. The odds, apparently, are against them. In *Quiet Desperation: The Truth about Successful Men*, Jan Halper investigated 4100 men from the Fortune 100 lists and found that only 3 per cent eventually married their lovers. Seventy-five per cent of these went on to divorce them. The old adage, most recently attributed to Jimmy Goldsmith, that men who marry their mistresses automatically create a job vacancy, has its truth.

Yet there are few easy answers to coupled life in a world saturated both with sexual temptation and a wish for a forever of monogamous fidelity. It may be as well to remind ourselves that the triangle is always present in one way or another in our twosomes – even in that publicly vowed social contract which is marriage. It's there in our memories, in our flirtations with others, in our fantasies, in our desires, in the books we read and the films we watch. Imaginative beings are not by nature monogamous, or not for long, even under the aegis of romantic passion. The presence of the shadowy third can help reinvent the distance that keeps the erotic sparks flying. It can, of course, also destroy.

It's as well to remember that, although in our society we tend to think of sex as a good, it is also a force that consumes. Robert Stoller concluded a chapter of his *Sexual Excitement* on the pungent note:

'Humans are not a very loving species, especially when they make love. Too bad.'

But people also try to make good of the bad. They weave their own paths through the difficulties of relationships, and negotiating the twists and turns as they come. A proportion endure the pains of infidelity, the anguish of mid-life crises, and find a way back to each other in a new settlement. Home, after all, can be a warm and capacious place, far more resilient and capable of transformations than we sometimes imagine.

In other quarters, some, like those ardent nineteenth and early-twentieth century utopian seekers who set up colonies where love and sex were differently lived, are trying to reinvent conjugal models. Gays are experimenting with new codes: couples in civil marriages talk of a mix of emotional exclusivity, a committed relationship admingled with a degree of sexual freedom.

Welcoming in the third, where possible, may make us more generous to our partners and to ourselves.

It's rarely easy. In a cultural regime that champions marriages triggered by an ever-fleeting romantic passion, one that will allow each partner to be transfigured, realize individual as well as coupled hopes and last in fidelity for ever, even less so. Couples in trouble these days often enough turn to that other third party, the counsellor or therapist. Here all the configurations of love can be lived out and sex talk can displace the straying fact of it. The biographical narrative can be reconstructed in the presence of another who isn't quite a lover. In a different historical moment with other social arrangements, the priest would have played a similar role: every virtuous married woman of a certain class had one to hand, or to dinner.

Yet the couples therapy that so many turn to – and there are some fifty thousand couples therapists in the US – can sometimes exacerbate the difficulties of married life, as much or more so than a straying infidelity. Picking at lacks and faults, putting these into language that always has its own performative aftermath, can be as damaging as it is illuminating. Words hastily spoken take on their own substance and rumble through our coupled lives with unintended consequences. It's hard to pick yourself up off the floor after a verbal attack and get on merrily with the joys of sex – if it's still a possibility – or with the laughter at your own or the other's foibles which helps enliven daily domesticity. Working at relationships, as the jargon goes, can turn married life into a 'domestic gulag', as Laura Kipnis deftly names it in her bracing invective *Against Love*. And where there's a regime of hard and earnest relational labour complete with production and success targets, it's hard to re-imagine or re-create either the romance or more often the playfulness and interest that keep coupledom alive.

Luckily for many loving couples, the first marital triangle is completed by the arrival of that most generally welcome of intruders and today, arguably, the most romantically endowed: his majesty, the child.

PART FIVE

Love in Families

Once one is married . . . one lives rather with each other for some third thing.

Sigmund Freud

The family is the little-sung crucible of our passions. We learn to love within it, whatever its configuration. It is here that our capacity for loving and the ways we live love – in all their specificity and particularity – are shaped or misshaped. Mothers, fathers, siblings, grandparents and other relations play into the picture. Their characters, their memories, fantasies and hopes leave indelible marks on us, though not always ones we can see. The social environment and the cultural moment, with their shifting conditions, fears and expectations, provide the grain of this canvas of domestic love, and some of its hues.

Site of our most intense and durable emotions, collective artist of our contents and our woes, the family is remade afresh with each new life. So what is this thing called love as it cascades through the family? It's best to begin at the beginning . . .

Babies

It is a truth universally acknowledged that love attends the arrival of new life. Plump or papery, still or squalling, the newborn turns all around her into the three biblical kings gazing in rapturous awe at the heralded babe who holds in her tiny body a whole world of promise.

In *The Millstone* (1965), her ground-breaking novel of single motherhood, Margaret Drabble gives us a heroine who had expected little of her newborn: she had been told of their ugliness, 'their red and wrinkled faces, their waxy covering, their emaciated limbs, their hairy cheeks, their piercing cries'. Yet when she looks at her daughter, she is beautiful: 'I sat there looking at her, and her great wide blue eyes looked at me with seeming recognition, and what I felt it is pointless to try to describe. Love, I suppose one might call it, and the first of my life.' 'What did my fingers do before they held him? What did my heart do, with its love?' one of the three women in Sylvia Plath's radio play of that name wonders, as she looks at the 'shiny and strange' creature to whom she has just given birth.

When Levin, in *Anna Karenina*, wakes from the torment of Kitty's anguished screams during labour, that 'mysterious and terrible, unearthly world in which he had lived for those twenty-two hours', to the fact of birth, 'to this new human being who had appeared incomprehensibly from somewhere', he feels he has been catapulted into a radiant new sphere of happiness, so intense he can hardly bear it. Wavering 'like a small flame over a lamp' is a life 'who had never existed before and who, with the same right, with the same importance for itself, would live and produce its own kind'. Unforeseen sobs and tears of joy rise in him, 'with such force, heaving his whole body', that for a long time he simply cannot speak.

'Love set you going like a fat gold watch,' Sylvia Plath writes in her 'Morning Song'. Just as in the greatest of passions, the intoxicating love affair with this new creature releases a redemptive hope – and this time it really feels, and it may indeed well be, for ever. This new being embodies the promise of a future.

The rapturous new love affair which parents, and particularly mother and child, are wrapped up in is as bodily as it is of the imagination. That delicious skin, those luscious folds at knee and arm, those bubble-blowing lips, those seemingly omniscient eyes staring only at you, captivate us. We gaze and stroke, listen for the sound of their breath and cry, sniff and nuzzle, cuddle and rock, nibble and tickle, gathering them up into ourselves. We devour them. We're infatuated, besotted.

Hardly surprising that Eros, or Cupid, is pictured as a plump, joyous babe. Plenitude has entered the world and for the mother, in particular, the relationship can feel, and indeed in part is, symbiotic. Two are one. After all, this squidgy new life in which love seems to inhere is utterly dependent on us, on the love of others for milk and warmth

and movement. Helpless, vulnerable, destined to a protracted immaturity, this little being calls on all our resources of loving care.

But who are these miraculous babies who would perish without us
and who throughout their lives will bear the imprint of our ways of
loving?

It is only in the last hundred years or so that babies, once prone to
early mortality, have become the focus of significant study and expert
discourse. The Jesuits' old motto of 'Give me a boy of seven, and I'll have
him for life' was premised on the importance of reason, of thinking, as
the predominant force in shaping character. This has been displaced:
the first five years of a child's life are now seen as being crucially formative. Not surprising, perhaps, that the weight given to these early years,
traditionally the mother's sphere, also coincides with the rise of
women's importance in shaping our ways of thinking.

In the last decades, physiological and neural research has shown that
the newborn is at first akin to an external foetus. The baby may carry
her own unique set of genes which provide a blueprint for the complex
being she will become. But these are activated by experience and environment. The carers' touch, smell, movement, voice, excitement or
despondency all impact on the babe's circuitry and chemistry, working
to establish the kind of individual she will become.

'Physiologically, the human baby is still very much part of the
mother's body,' Sue Gerhardt writes in *Why Love Matters*. 'He depends on
her milk to feed him, to regulate his heart rate and blood pressure, and
to provide immune protection. His muscular activity is regulated by her
touch, as is his growth hormone level. Her body keeps him warm and
she disperses his stress hormones for him by her touch and her feeding.
This basic physiological regulation keeps the baby alive.'

In some scientific research, this early sensuous love has in part displaced genes as a significant shaper of future health and character.
Scientists working for the Canadian Institute of Advanced Research
have stressed that genes are not 'the weavers of our fate, the sole deter-
minants of our destiny'. The new field of epigenetics studies the way
environmental and social factors influence children's health and well-
being: it has shown that children with identical DNA can follow
different patterns of development, depending on their experience in

earliest life. A mixture of neuro-imaging and non-invasive techniques brings to light that certain genes regulating the stress hormone cortisol and others associated with inflammation, for example, are less or more active in babies, depending on early conditions. An adverse environment, such as that associated with poverty, leads to a lifelong rise in the risk of a number of chronic diseases.

If love isn't there, if it is nowhere in a small child's environment and instead all touch is violent and there is hate, abuse, deprivation, trauma, then the emotional cauldron that he is boils over. Untempered, unregulated by the carer's stroke, sound and attention, the child grows mad: psychotic ideas take over. Empathy, putting oneself in another's shoes, imagining another mind, becomes nigh impossible.

In *The Philosophical Baby*, her tour of the recent findings of cognitive science about the first five years of life, those years all but shrouded in amnesia or layers of forgetting, Alison Gopnik paints an enthusiastic picture of the complexity of the infant mind before the age of five. This is the point at which autobiographical memory comes into play and this miraculous alien being is transformed into a person continuous with the adult. So babies and toddlers really are radically different from older humans, as their carers have long known.

Nearly all the hundred billion neurons in our nervous system may already be in place from birth. But through early childhood, synapses – the points of contact between neurons that transmit information and thereby fire memory and sensation – are produced in far greater quantity than later. The infant brain is thus poised to make connections, wild or pedestrian. Infants, like scientists, Gopnik argues, make causal maps of the world, posit links between things and make predictions on the basis of their hypotheses. They have theories on the nature of their surroundings and the universe as heady as those of dreaming scientists. They speculate on origins, on birth and the facts of life. Like poets and novelists, they confabulate, treat the imaginary as real. Their fantasy life is rich, inhabited by monsters, angels and imaginary friends who follow them through their days, serve as playmates or persecuting ghouls demanding to be placated. To the adult, their minds seem to work in mysterious, uninhibited ways.

Maturity, in fact, the neuroscientists now tell us, consists in a neural

trimming, leaving adult consciousness with only what is most expedi-
ent for conducting our everyday lives. The prefrontal lobe, which plays
a part in blocking out stimuli from other facets of the brain, doesn't, it
seems, come to full maturity until we are in our twenties. This leaves
small children less capable of internally driven attention, but far more
fully alert than adults to external stimuli; far more open to the full
panoply of their sensory environment and the imaginative and speculative elaborations this sets in motion. Such findings may make us
wonder whether 'attention deficit hyperactivity disorder', so liberally
diagnosed in recent years, may in part mark an adult unwillingness to
countenance the very essence, the *difference*, of early childhood. As poets
have long known, one is simply more alive to the world in childhood
than in adulthood.

Given the very young's extreme sensitivity to their environment, to
stimulus, the love parents or carers offer their children radically affects
the way they mature – neurally, physiologically, emotionally, mentally. 'It isn't just that without mothering humans would lack
nurturance, warmth and emotional security,' Gopnik writes. 'They
would also lack culture, history, morality, science and literature.'

Neuroscientists and cognitive psychologists give us an evidence-based
discourse for ideas about the exceptionality and importance of early
childhood. But these ideas are not altogether discontinuous with certain
aspects of a Christian tradition, or of a Romantic or a psychoanalytic
one. All accord a special place to the extraordinary creature the infant is.
In the first, the innocent, vulnerable child has a privileged access to the
Kingdom of God: the child is not only a gift, but a teacher of virtue,
spontaneous love, and receptiveness to the Word of God. Rousseau and
the Romantic poets also acknowledged the unique imagination and
curiosity of the child, his particular aptitude for wonder, his other-
worldliness. Nature and sensuous experience – his environment, one
might now say – were better teachers than stultifying institutions,
which also corrupted. In *Émile* (1762), Rousseau, echoing a Lockean
empiricism, noted: 'Since everything that comes into the human mind
enters through the gates of sense, man's first reason is a reason of sense-
experience. It is this that serves as a foundation for the reason of the
intelligence; our first teachers in natural philosophy are our feet, hands,

and eyes.' Rousseau even convinced middle-class mothers of the desirability of nursing their own babies, then an unusual occurrence.

Ever since Freud set out to excavate the residues of early childhood
experience in the adult – experience that was later obscured or
repressed and therefore 'unconscious', not available to the adult except
in dreams or flashes of imagistic memory – psychoanalysts, too, have
been particularly alert to the infant's uniquely rich and responsive
world – a world before later inhibitions or 'neural trimmings' came
into being. In the 1890s Freud worked as a consultant neurologist at the
Children's Hospital in Vienna. As an analyst he never practised directly
with children, but he observed his own children and grandchildren, and
theories about early childhood became crucial to his speculations. In
part, these theories were based on the childhood memories he elicited
from his patients. Such memories seemed to reside as much in their
bodies – as symptoms or gestures or as sense-experiences unrelated to
a context – as they did in the mind. The Freudian unconscious was
thus a residue of early childhood: it was also always individual, whatever
generalizable patterns might then be extrapolated from it.

The Freudian baby and toddler is a pleasure-seeking creature driven
by libidinal appetites, 'a cauldron of seething excitations', seeking satisfaction for her 'polymorphous perversity'. Her demands for love are
always immoderate, and coexist with a 'powerful tendency to aggres-
siveness'. Indeed, the more passionately a child loves its mother or first
carer, 'the more sensitive does it become to disappointments and frustrations'. The infant's ego – transposing discursive languages, one could
say its autobiographical self – is not yet in place, not integrated.
Thinking and feeling occur at this early stage through what Freud calls
the 'primary process', characteristic of the unconscious system. These
intense primary processes are obscured to adult consciousness during
waking hours, but they come into prominence in dreams, hallucina-
tions, mystical moments, fantasy and imaginative work. Then, like
infants, our thoughts are 'unbounded' by the reality principle.

Freud's descriptions of the child's early psychosexual development
now seem commonplace. As he grows, the babe's interests and satisfactions seem to concentrate on key areas of the body, first the mouth, the

so-called oral phase, then the anus during toilet training, then the genitals. Difficulties, deprivations, excessive stimulus at any stage shape
later character and can produce what Freud called 'fixations' on particular erogenous zones.

One of the resonant effects of the Freudian revolution is to have
made the child the father of the man: our early and largely forgotten
childhoods, we now acknowledge, remain with us to echo through
our lives. This gives particular and shaping force to our first instinctual
loves and attachments.

Mother, for Freud, is the first object of infant pleasure, the site of a
symbiotic plenitude, a fusion which is ever both momentary and for
ever, since the infant has no sense of time, only of want or lack. Into this
space of lack, the darker, death or aggressive instincts also tumble. That
early plenitude, in any case, is soon to be lost, when father, a rival in love
and the representative of the law and of prohibitions, steps into the
frame.

Freud's first inklings of the power of the Oedipus story came out of
his own self-analysis, conducted in the years after his father's death. On
15 October 1897, he wrote to his friend Wilhelm Fliess:

> I have found, in my own case too, [the phenomenon of] being in love
> with my mother and jealous of my father, and I now consider it a uni-
> versal event in early childhood ... If this is so, we can understand the
> gripping power of Oedipus Rex, in spite of all the objections that reason
> raises against the presupposition of fate ... the Greek legend seizes upon
> a compulsion which everyone recognizes because he senses its existence
> within himself. Everyone in the audience was once a budding Oedipus in
> fantasy and each recoils in horror from the dream fulfillment here
> transplanted into reality, with the full quantity of repression which sep-
> arates his infantile state from his present one.

Before I had a child of my own, I used to think that Freud's Oedipal
scenario was wild speculation, as tenuously grounded in the real as any
other writer's imaginative conjectures. The young adult I was certainly
didn't feel, or remember feeling, any particular desires for my balding
Dad or any more than the usual antagonism towards Mum. As for the

sexuality of children, it felt like a slightly repugnant theoretical trope. Enter my infant son, kicking and squalling, tender and smiling in turn, and as philosophical as any babe. He was garrulous, too, once language took hold.

One day when he was about four and I was driving him home from nursery, he adamantly demanded a pair of scissors. 'What for?' I asked him, from the front seat of the car. 'I need them,' he insisted, and when I probed once more, he announced he needed them for his Dad, eventually revealing, before he burst into peals of laughter, that he needed them to cut off his Dad's willy. After a momentary sense of shock, I assured him that that was hardly a good idea, and of course, by the time we'd got home he'd forgotten all about it. He greeted his father in the ordinary way and went off merrily to dismantle some robotic monster instead.

The fact that children have ungovernable fantasy lives should, on reflection, hold little surprise. Why else should they be so attuned to the intrinsic savagery of fairy-tales, with their gobbling witches, vengeful stepmothers and abusive fathers — frightening narratives contained and mastered by the sheer fact of repetition? Why else, too, should past centuries have spent so much effort in disciplining their unruliness both at home and at school?

We now recognize the family as the hothouse in which children learn the whole repertoire of human emotions from love to hate and all the complex recombinations in between. The parents' role in containing these, and negotiating their passage from rampant fantasy to some kind of recognition of the real and all the social forms it entails, is central. It's in these early years, after all, that children learn about absence and presence, that all desires can't be satisfied and certainly not instantly, that other people exist and have needs, wishes and minds of their own; that they may be loved, but that all their acts aren't pleasing and some aren't permissible, that conflict exists and compromise is no bad thing.

Mothers have ever played a dominant role here, and despite a century of struggles for independence and attempts in the last forty years or so to rebalance the equation of family and work for both sexes, it is still women who emerge as the child's primary carers, the bearers of mother-love.

Responsibility in this area has grown increasingly complex as we have learned more and more about a child's early life – from psychologists, analysts and now neuro- and cognitive scientists. To a historically knowledgeable Martian it might even seem that the exponential growth in theories about early childhood is oddly coincident with the rise of feminism from the late nineteenth century on – with particular points of emphasis after each of the world wars and in periods when middle-class women have been seen as too prominent in the workplace. It is as if educated women needed to be convinced by science of the very real interests of their babies, and as if mother-love were not altogether or always that maternal instinct we would also like it to be.

Mother-love

I remember distinctly the night after my daughter was born listening to her soft snufflings at my side. A sense of what I can only call beatitude filled me: I felt blessed. When she opened her pink little mouth and let out a soft mewl, a sublime happiness flowed through me. The narrow, shadow-strewn bed where the street lights crept through greying blinds, the alien cacophony of hospital noises, vanished as she opened her eyes to stare up at me. I read deep knowledge there and beneficence, despite my everyday scepticism. This was definitely love at first sight.

The arrival of my equally gorgeous son, my first-born, initially roused different feelings. It had been such a long delivery, the pain so much more intense than any woman is led to expect or can imagine. The midwives – barking out their orders of 'Push!' while I was trying to remember the useless instructions I'd been given about types of breathing – had appeared to me in that half-conscious state of labour like Macbeth's witches, their cauldron my vast tum in which trouble was bubbling and boiling. Afterwards, I was exhausted and I suspect my son was, too. His blindly flailing arms, his very helplessness, filled me with fear. Who was this tiny stranger? How would I and his father manage? Panic threatened. He didn't speak and couldn't be reasoned with, ever a shock to some of us. Then, too, his utter vulnerability seemed to awaken my own.

When the team of chief doctor and silent students, all male, all eyes cast downwards, made their way to my bed and issued more orders, this time about breast being best, no matter how sore, no matter how many hours it took, I baulked and said I'd never be able to manage. Of course, I would, I was told. Women in Africa did. (This was a long time ago, when 'Breast is best' was a newish mantra and my lead doctor had worked in Africa.) But we weren't in Africa, I protested. And I would soon have to go back to work.

Well, it took some weeks of fuming and fussing and getting used to those breasts and this new being who was my son as well as this second new being who was myself as mother before I fell a little reluctantly in love and realized that of course my son too, now plump and pink, was, like so many other first-borns, most definitely a Messiah.

That new being, who was mother-me, by the way was decidedly different from the woman I had been before, and she coexisted alongside the old one. Films or television programmes about children instantly brought tears to my eyes — though I'd never been particularly sentimental. If they were endangered children, anxiety overwhelmed me; more than that, pain: I walked out or switched the television off. Even now that they've grown, I find such media content difficult and immediately have the impulse to ring the children just to make sure they're still there and intact. As time passed I also developed a thick skin and would go to battle for them when necessary, though I had never before been either brave or forthright. I started to intervene when I saw children fighting on the street. I put on a convincing show of being a grown-up when talking to headmasters or mistresses, though they continued to frighten me, as they always had. I even learned to ring doctors, those other authority figures.

Parenthood does really change many of us, matures us, as the cliché goes, though our earlier selves continue to hover in the background, creating obstacles here and there along the way when they meet up with those parenting bits. If I recount these tales from my children's first years it is simply because all births while similar, are also different, even to the same mother — as are all childhoods. A complexity of emotions comes into play with each new arrival. Mother-love may for some shine like a bright sun after the storms of labour. Milk and gladness may flow without a hitch and the babe seem as bonny as the best gift from heaven. Here, indeed, is that famed symbiotic plenitude.

For other women, depleted by the ordeal of labour, feeling as help-less as the newborn whom they are meant to tend, laid low by anxieties about how to cope with the alien, squalling being who gnaws at and enflames their breasts, side by side with the endless stream of advice from mothers, mothers-in-law, partners, experienced friends, nurses, doctors, guidebooks – the much vaunted maternal instinct may feel like another stick with which to beat their sense of inadequacy. So it's as well to note that, as with other forms of falling in love, this one needn't come all at once; and when it does, it too will have its ups and downs and bring in tow parts of ourselves we didn't know we possessed. The baby will grow and develop even if maternal rapture isn't instanta-neous. Indeed, since they're freed from anxiety and the often competing cares of work and babe, grandmothers may delight more ardently in the new arrival than new mothers.

Given that everywoman and indeed, man, knows much of this, how is it that we continue to believe in the cultural myth of an idealized mother-love and its accompanying maternal instinct?

In the biblical tradition, Eve's punishment for allowing herself to be seduced by the serpent and for eating of the prohibited tree of knowl-edge was to bring forth in pain – an early admonition to women, one might say, to stay in their place, keep their eyes and ears fastened only on their husbands and leave knowledge to authorities higher than themselves.

Theologians tell us that the New Testament Mary redeemed Eve's transgression. A faith based on love and human vulnerability, Christianity gave the world an ordinary woman as mother of an indi-vidualized, embodied God. No other religion in its foundational narrative confers such significance on a small family nucleus. No other turns us all into children of a merciful father and provides an embodied merciful mother, 'meek and mild' as the traditional hymn declares, who may intervene on any ordinary mortal's behalf.

Through the narrative of Mary and baby Jesus, through repeated images and retold tales of the nativity and the holy family, our culture has underscored the value of mother-love as at once transfigurative and eternal. The tender, watchful Mother and her holy child are imbued with an authority which casts the really existing paternal figure into the background. Joseph is a mere adjunct to the miracle of the messianic birth.

The New Testament and the Church Fathers went to some lengths to make Mary exceptional by her virgin birth, untarnished by the sins of the flesh and wife only to the Holy Spirit. But the nativity story, alongside her countless images painted over and over again through the centuries, speaks of the domestic idyll of any ordinary mother and the miracle of her child. Leonardo's gentle and graceful Madonna Litta gazes down at the buxom infant at her breast as attentively and tenderly as any enraptured Mum cradling her own child's pudgy flesh. His Benois Madonna smiles lovingly at the playful creature in her arms, who clasps at her hand and stares at the flower she holds up to him.

These are familiar scenes of domestic love, reinvented in myriad chapels across Catholic Europe, and now the world, by local artists. Amidst gods gendered male, the Madonna emerges as an understanding receptacle for shared daily cares, a potent intermediary for women's prayers. She also enjoins all ordinary mothers submissively to love their miraculous babies. If the Church Fathers had trained as propagandists, they couldn't have found a more homely exemplum to popularize a faith based on love and simultaneously provide a model of woman's most important task. Sublime maternal love emerges as woman's path to redemption.

In *Alone of All Her Sex* (1976), the historian Marina Warner points out that the figure of Mary has served through time to entrench a set of desirable feminine characteristics: submissiveness, compliance, docility, virtuous purity, humility, obedience. All of these have abetted women's confinement to a subsidiary sphere which supports patriarchal power. Simone de Beauvoir, in her energetic demystification of women's condition, *The Second Sex* (1949), had already stressed that motherhood, unless freely chosen, was the primary cause of woman's secondariness; a vehicle of her disempowerment, chaining her to her biology, to fecundity, to nature. Crucially, too, de Beauvoir underlined that a woman's subservient state could pervert her love for her child and threaten its future, since the child became the vehicle through which she sought to compensate for all the frustrations of her trapped secondary state.

> Like the woman in love, the mother is delighted to feel herself necessary; her existence is justified by the wants she supplies; but what gives mother love its difficulty and its grandeur is the fact that it implies no reciprocity; the mother has to do not with man, a hero, a demigod, but with a small prattling soul, lost in a fragile and dependent body. The child is in possession of no values, he can bestow none, with him the woman remains alone; she expects no return for what she gives, it is for her to justify it herself. This generosity merits the laudation that men never tire of conferring upon her; but the distortion begins when the religion of Maternity proclaims that all mothers are saintly. For while maternal devotion may be perfectly genuine, this, in fact, is rarely the case. Maternity is usually a strange mixture of narcissism, altruism, idle day-dreaming, sincerity, bad faith, devotion and cynicism.

Young women in the liberation movement of the seventies criticized their mothers for a subservience which made them both overly controlling and over-identified with their children, given their frustrations in the confined sphere of the home. These new women simultaneously questioned and rebelled against the primacy attributed to their role as the reproductive sex. They set out to show that their vaunted 'maternal' traits were hardly innate, but rather the products of patriarchal wish and power. Freed by the pill which had given them control over reproduction and liberated their sexuality, they could now choose to have children if they so wished, and to do so in co-parenting arrangements with men which would equalize responsibility and free both members of the couple to work – to enter the sphere of knowledge and power. The characteristics that made up mother-love were not those which Mary 'meek and mild' enshrined: nor was the care of children women's domain alone. It could be shared with men, newly liberated to express their softer, caring sides, long trapped in templates of conquering, dominant malehood.

By the early eighties a new 'Madonna' had entered the sphere of popular iconography and partly overshadowed her earlier namesake, to give the world a 'material girl' whose only interest in virginity was to lose it. But the pop-cultural desacralization of Mary and her motherly qualities was never altogether secure. Throughout that decade, while the battle for equality and rights at work went on, and 'having it all' seemed a possibility worth aiming for, various forces once more came together to essentialize women's difference in terms not only of her biology, but of the attributes that biology was purported to give rise to.

Back in the 1870s, Charles Darwin had extrapolated from animal observation and women's primary and most culturally cherished activities during the Victorian epoch to argue that women with their small brain size, intermediate between child and man, were, owing to their maternal instincts, more tender and less selfish than men and had greater powers of intuition and rapid perception. They extended these properties, grounded in the biology of mothering, to those around them.

Some of these premises echoed through the essentialist and initially American wave of the women's movement during the 1980s and 1990s, the high point of identity politics. This coincided with a renewed interest in evolutionary thinking and the (re)invention of evolutionary psychology, a discipline that understands human psychology as a direct product of our biology. Within these optics, woman in her maternal guise was effectively naturalized; her 'natural' motherly properties, her 'nesting instinct', foregrounded. She emerged as more caring and less egotistic than the male of the species, more attentive to the vulnerable, the relational and the specific. As such, in the feminist literature of the period, she became a moral model, indeed an ethical ideal, for both sexes. The care model first took hold in an America that had never had a welfare state, or what the French call, with the full force of Christian values despite their adamant republicanism, a 'providential' state. The model is a laudable one, as are the ethics of care which have grown out of it.

However, a difficulty arises when care is essentialized as feminine. The closeness to older thinking invoking the 'maternal instinct' boomerangs back on women, particularly when married to evolutionary premises. Held up as a moralizing ideal, the model of woman as naturally a maternal carer locks men out of the pleasures of the nursery while liberating them from the burdens of care. For mothers, who are cut from many different cloths, it can provoke anxiety, it can stigmatize, particularly when the individual woman may have few overriding maternal impulses, or if her initial feelings for her baby don't coincide with the desirable norm.

The last twenty years have seen something of a re-enshrinement of women in their motherly loving role. This has been abetted by the rise and rise of the new neuroscience, ever quick to leap to adventurous cultural pronouncements from the evidence of microscopic events in the brain translated by algorhithms into brightly appealing computer images. The difference between the genders has once more been essentialized to reinvigorate the kinds of hoary stereotypes John Stuart Mill objected to over a hundred and forty years ago. In *The Essential Difference: Men, Women and the Extreme Male Brain*, the leading Cambridge psychologist Simon Baron-Cohen writes: 'The female brain is predominantly hard-wired for empathy. The male brain is predominantly hard-wired for understanding and building systems.' This makes possessors of female brains pre-eminently suited for such tasks as caring, counselling and teaching primary school children. And, of course, mothering.

In pop culture, the motherly role is now rendered covetable by its paradoxical twinning with sexiness, as if the latter in our hypersexualized culture conferred the ultimate value. Stars with rounded tums increasingly appear in glossy mags. Hollywood's Demi Moore launched the trend in 1991 when, nude and seven months pregnant, she graced the cover of *Vanity Fair*. The pregnant sex symbol provoked controversy: some attacked this newly demeaning objectification of women; others hailed it as a sign of women's empowerment.

In the two decades since, babies have increasingly appeared with their celebrity mothers in the glossies, marking a new line both in fashion accessories and in marketing tools. But they also signal a return to the pre-eminent importance of maternity. To indicate her participation in the reborn faith of mother and baby which Madonna had already joined, a pregnant Britney Spears — once America's most cheekily slutty virgin — featured pornographically semi-nude in *Harper's Bazaar* in August 2006. The spread blatantly evoked the iconography of Virgin and Child. Loving motherhood now seemed to have once more become supremely important even to the most liberated and famous of women.

Air-brushed pictures are pictures, and life is life. Few heavily pregnant women feel particularly sexy; mothers with newborns, even less so. But the circulation of these images in our public sphere turns these into a desirable, though rarely attainable, norm. They also simply advertise maternity, something our politicians, too, are now increasingly prone to do, trotting out their children for the cameras far more than they ever did. The pressure has been mounting, particularly on working women, to breed – ever more so because those who have sought a career first are constantly reminded of the ticking of that now media-noisy biological clock. Babies have emerged as both increasingly covetable and increasingly delayed, because the wanting of them is such a major enterprise.

All this has taken place against a background of long-term falling birth-rates in most countries throughout Europe – until very recently when, particularly in Scandinavia, they have been rising. This is not surprising, given that Norway and Sweden have the best provision now for both partners on parental leave and on early childcare. The picture in America is slightly different. Though the secular middle class fails to reproduce itself altogether adequately, the religious and the poor make up the numbers.

It seems that, given the choice, plus a liberated sexual ideology prioritizing the pleasures of youth, which makes men in particular loath to take on the responsibilities of commitment – women have over the last decades chosen work first – out of desire or financial need. In Britain, almost two-thirds of women with children work. Now, failing economies and unemployment or low wages, which generally induce women back into the home, are marking a swing. And the pressure is on from various sources, popular and 'scientific', for mothers to give up work for ever longer periods so that they can tend adequately to the important task of child-rearing. Mother-love has reasserted its cultural centrality – even if many women, judging from the statistics, are not particularly eager to take on motherhood, or to take it on too soon.

Those who do may be caught up in a cult of idealized motherhood so assiduous and competitive that it might have disconcerted even their Victorian forebears. The toll in guilt and anxiety, which can easily percolate into their children's lives, is great. If there is indeed no more important and wonderful task than making new lives, the weight of advice which now bears down on parents, the tick-lists that monitor good and bad parenting, can make love itself — never conducive to quantification and targets — a chore. Working at love, here, may be as joyless as it is in adult relationships.

Indeed, mothering today can appear more challenging than running the World Bank — perhaps because so many of the women who undertake it once more or less did, or could have. It seems in any event to require equivalent investment, time and skill. The list of middle-class maternal tasks and duties in the name of love is formidable and calculated to rob mothering of its pleasures. There's an onus on stimulating the child, on providing extra lessons, on keeping her ever busy with a schedule that would challenge executive diaries. There's the added imperative of bolstering, at every possible instant, the child's self-esteem — a notion rolled out from the delusional positive-thinking and well-being industries—so that children develop a false sense of life and themselves. There's the task of precluding any possibility of boredom — a state which, arguably, feeds both imagination and thought. And so on and on, even before the worries about risk and danger — of unsafe streets and playgrounds, of poor schooling, of 'unsuitable' friends. Advice once acquired in the local park, in the nursery and in face-to-face chats between mothers now also comes from science (ever-changing in its recommendations) and from that global powerhouse, the World Wide Web. Sites such as Mumsnet and Netmums are just a click away, to provide guidance, support, online conversation and experience-sharing. Yet, however helpful they may be, the conflictual and competing voices on these sites, as Lucy Cavendish, a mother of four, attests, can induce more rows and anxiety than a coven of visiting mothers-in-law. In Britain, Mumsnet also functions as a lobbying site, hosting visits from leading political contenders. Women as mothers are now a powerful force, and not only in the home.

One of the many areas of maternal contention is breast or bottle, and for how long. Ever a symbol — though never a fact — of instinctual mother-love, the flow, value and long-term attributes of mother's milk have now even generated their own science wars.

The French philosopher Élisabeth Badinter has argued that the rise and rise of the 'breast is best' movement has coincided with a modish evolutionary biology – which sees all animals' primary task as that of reproducing the species – to promote women's full-time return to the home. Biology with its reductive imperatives has once more emerged as the best destiny for women.

Badinter charts a history of La Leche League to underline how ideology can, with some help from science, become the potent ally of 'nature' and thus influence our understanding of maternal love. La Leche began in a meeting of like-minded, breast-feeding mothers in a Chicago suburb in 1956 – a time when 80 per cent of American babies were bottle-fed and the word 'breast' could not easily appear in newspapers. The initial seven members were Catholic and adherents of the militant Christian Family Movement. Making links with doctors propagating 'natural' childbirth, the League grew to become a worldwide movement with chapters in sixty-eight countries, its precepts gradually adopted by the medico-scientific establishment and eventually by Unicef and the World Health Organization. The guiding tenets of the movement are:

> Mothering through breast-feeding is the most natural and effective way of understanding and satisfying the needs of the baby.
>
> Mother and baby need to be together early and often to establish a satisfying relationship and an adequate milk supply.
>
> In the early years the baby has an intense need to be with his mother which is as basic as his need for food.
>
> Breast milk is the superior infant food.
>
> For the healthy, full-term baby, breast milk is the only food necessary until the baby shows signs of needing solids, about the middle of the first year after birth.
>
> Ideally the breast-feeding relationship will continue until the baby outgrows the need.

The fact that the League's principles – with their subtle moral undertow of encouraging mothers back to the home and their sidelining of partners to the role of protective onlookers – now seem commonplace and are recommended by most doctors, is evidence of the distance the movement has travelled. In the early 1970s only 24 per cent of American mothers breast-fed; by 2010 this had risen to nearly 75 per cent. In the Scandinavian countries, from the same low, the percentage is now between 95 and 99 per cent, with Germany lagging only slightly behind; Britain comes in at about 70 per cent, while France and Ireland have proved most recalcitrant and have reached only 50 and 30 per cent respectively. Largely gone is the moment when co-parenting from a babe's earliest days was heralded as an ideal. Gone, too, is any element of choice. Working mothers, who constitute the majority, are catapulted into a state of permanent guilt-ridden conflict, deemed somehow unnatural if they don't continue breast-feeding for the recommended span of at least a year. Pump rooms (where mothers can express milk) in large workplaces in the US have been campaigned for and won.

But must love flow mainly through milk?

Major scientific claims have been made to underpin the 'breast is best' message. Some of these are indubitably proven. During the first few days after the child's birth, mother's milk is less milk than colostrum, a substance rich in antibodies which help develop immunities in the child as well as stabilizing his blood sugar and lining the gut. But that the child's eventual psychological well-being as well as his or her intellectual accomplishments can be linked to the single fact of mother's milk, as some of the claims contend, is very doubtful. In 2006 British scientists published the results of a longitudinal study of 5475 children, the offspring of 3161 mothers, compared siblings with the same DNA and conclusively showed that despite propaganda to the contrary, there were no links between a child's IQ and his history of breast-feeding. If breast-fed middle-class children had better cognitive development, it was likely to be linked to a host of other factors.

Loving may figure amongst these. Infants, of course, benefit hugely from touch, skin-to-skin cuddles and affection, but the breast is only part of a much wider environment. Those seven out of ten British mothers who give up the breast for a variety of factors after six weeks have not failed in their 'natural' duty or proved themselves less loving than those who carry on feeding for a year or three. Nor is breast-feeding for women as 'natural' as the eulogies make out; certainly, at the outset, many women experience difficulties. New mothers are not unnatural if the symbiotic plenitude with babe at breast is something they fail to live out in ideal fashion. Nor have they failed in parental love which feeds the child far beyond its first infancy.

The natural paradigm, which in any case shifts its attributes through history, is rarely an altogether useful one for the cultural beings humans are. The animal life that evolutionary psychologists so like to compare us to provides a very distant template for human mother-hood. There are continuities of course: all young animals need nurture, and in most species the female will provide it, though often both parents are implicated. Sometimes, too, as Darwin himself tells us, the instinct for self-preservation may take over from maternal care: the swift's migratory instinct triumphs over her maternal instinct and she takes off in the appropriate season, whatever the age of her brood. That said, animals do not take a year of tending before they can get up on their hind legs, another before they can learn the basics of language, and some eighteen more years before they (may) leave home. So the long immaturity of humans – and their vast and malleable brains continually shaped and reshaped by childhood experience – calls upon capacities for loving which are great, complex, and subject to change through a child's life.

Expert Knowledge

> Before I got married I had six theories about bringing up children; now I have six children, and no theories.
>
> John Wilmot, (2nd Earl of Rochester)

Until this recent wave of instinctual motherhood, middle-class babies were rarely breast-fed by their own mothers. Facts are not the easiest to come by in this area, but it is clear that until the twentieth century an infant's proximity to mother was not understood as an indication of future happiness or accomplishment. Nor was it, necessarily. Jane

Austen was farmed out from birth for some five years, as were her siblings, to a woman who lived miles away. Balzac, as custom then had it, was similarly sent to a wet-nurse and spent four years away from home. Historians will undoubtedly also discover that some lovingly breast-fed babes matured into unloving, murderous tyrants.

One of the difficulties attending parental love in our cultural moment is that the child, and first of all, the baby, has become the focus of so much expert know-how alongside so many redemptive hopes. Bringing up children now often seems to require a concentration of programmatic activity and consumerist expenditure so intense that love can flip into frustration and disappointment, though this may have little to do with the child's own individuality. The pleasures of love too often seem to have been displaced by a work and production ethic in which parental achievement is judged by effort and by the honed product at its ever receding terminus.

Though the advice of the experts may be well meant, the generalized repertoire of dos and don'ts is difficult to abide by, since every child is so different — as are family constellation and circumstance. Nor is the effort particularly conducive to the ineffable appreciation of another that love also is.

In *The Child in Time* (1987) Ian McEwan's hero, a writer of children's fiction and member of a government commission on childcare, humorously reflects that over three centuries, generations of experts — priests, moralists, social scientists and doctors — mostly men, have provided ever mutating instructions, dressed up as facts, for the benefit of mothers. Each generation, of course, has paraded its own as the apogee of common sense and scientific insight.

> He had read solemn pronouncements on the necessity of binding the newborn baby's limbs to a board to prevent movement and self-inflicted damage; of the dangers of breastfeeding, or elsewhere, its physical necessity and moral superiority; how affection or stimulation corrupts a young child; the importance of purges and enemas, severe physical punishment, cold baths, and earlier in this century, of constant fresh air, however inconvenient; the desirability of scientifically controlled intervals between feeds, and conversely, of feeding the baby whenever it is

hungry; the perils of picking a baby up whenever it cries – that makes it feel dangerously powerful – and of not picking it up when it cries – dangerously impotent; the importance of regular bowel movements, of potty training a child by three months, of constant mothering all day and night, all year, and elsewhere, the necessity of wet-nurses, nursery maids, twenty-four-hour state nurseries; the grave consequences of mouth-breathing, nose picking, thumb-sucking and maternal deprivation, of not having your child expertly delivered under bright lights, of lacking the courage to have it at home in the bath, of failing to have it circumcised or its tonsils removed; and later the contemptuous destruction of all these fashions; how children should be allowed to do whatever they want so that their divine natures can blossom, and how it is never too soon to break a child's will; the dementia and blindness caused by masturbation, and the pleasure and comfort it affords the growing child; how sex can be taught by reference to tadpoles, storks, flower fairies and acorns, or not mentioned at all, or only with lurid, painstaking frankness; the trauma imparted to the child who sees its parents naked, the chronic disturbance nourished by strange suspicions, if it only ever sees them clothed; how to give your nine-month-old baby a head-start by teaching it maths.

Sifting through the welter of oft-conflicting advice, parents will inevitably follow dollops of what suits their needs best within the aegis of their own time's cultural imperatives, and give their behaviour the name of love.

Having somehow made my way through decades of motherhood with all its ups and downs, its rows and pleasures, the competing needs of children, partners, work and oneself, I now sometimes think that, basic care apart, children thrive best on imaginative understanding. Though it can't be there at every minute of the day, and sometimes fails, regular applications of it will see them and you through. Love, after all, is more of an art than a rigorous production line with targets in place at each step of the way. And like art, it asks of us both form and freedom, attentiveness and its relaxed suspension.

Because of his attempts to understand the child first rather than focus on a programme of care, D.W. Winnicott (1896–1971) remains interesting: one could say there's a strong anti-expert expert in him. Winnicott's ability to enter a small child's very particular sphere is legendary. Play was Winnicott's therapeutic tool. Play, here, is not a question of sophisticated toys bought to assuage parents' guilts or a child's often momentary and shifting demands — stand-ins for desires or lacks they can't place (and are rarely given the quiet time, the necessary and creative boredom, in which they might). Play, for Winnicott, is serious activity. It exists within its own suspended time, engages the imagination and hones our ability to think symbolically. It helps to locate a child's desires. A train or a ball or a rag doll can stand in for a host of emotionally charged events or people and situations. The writer John Berger, who had a small top-floor studio in Winnicott's house during the late 1940s, told me that he has never forgotten the striking sight, on coming in, of Winnicott sprawled on the floor of his living room, which doubled as a consulting room. The door was always kept open and Winnicott could be seen absorbed in playing with his small clients. He was so imaginatively engrossed that he might himself have been a somewhat oversized child, or indeed a stand-in for his ideal of the good-enough mother.

In Freud's wake, a host of analysts had turned their attention to the child — his own daughter, Anna Freud, amongst them. Britain became a fertile centre for the study of infancy and the kind of love under which children thrive. Here, a romantic tradition of childhood, elaborated in a wealth of literature, had long existed. From the turn of the nineteenth century on, play, too, had been seen as something of a child's foundational and privileged right, as Antonia Byatt so well elaborates in her novel *The Children's Book*.

The analyst Melanie Klein, who established herself in London in 1926, used play to understand infants: her theories focused on the forces at work in the child before language developed. The infant who emerges from her writings is a dramatic creature whose inner landscape is the site of warfare between conflicting passions — aggressive and libidinal demands — all of them at first focused on the mother's breast, which stands in for his whole life. Site of his satisfaction, or lack, the baby fantasizes the breast as good, loved, idealized; or bad, persecutory, destructive. This split cannot be reconciled until the infant is old enough to integrate his 'self' as a whole; in other words, to become another, a separate person. In some, the split is never reconciled. Klein's followers suggested that this depends, in large part, on the kind of love the mother provides. Unlike Freud, whose work reflects his time's patriarchal pre-eminence, Klein and her followers shifted the psychological focus within the family to the mother. In that spirit of scientific inquiry which always seems to propel searchers back to an understanding of earliest forces and origins, early mothering displaced castrating, disciplinary fathering as the crucial shaping influence on the child and on the formation of mind and inner life.

Klein's theories about the earliest life of the infant fed countless practitioners. Principal amongst them was Winnicott himself, who added psychotherapy with children to his practice as a hospital paediatrician. In the course of his working life Winnicott saw some sixty thousand children and their mothers, fathers and grandparents in his 'paediatric snackbar'. Here he gathered a wealth of observations which fed his writing, much of it in common, comprehensible and playful language. Ordinary doctors and parents were his public, not only fellow professionals; and his BBC talks on childhood spoke to the nation, informing notions of childhood and good parenting.

The Winnicottian baby is a bundle of ruthless instinctual forces utterly dependent on mother (or primary carer), without whom existence would not be possible. In this sense, mother and child are a couple. Yet she is primarily part, if the central part, of a facilitating environment. And she needs to trust herself to be responsive to her baby's needs: simply put, to be interested in him, 'to see the human being in the new-born infant'. Winnicott posits that in the last stage of pregnancy and in the first few weeks of a baby's life, the mother inhabits a trance-like state of heightened sensitivity. This 'primary maternal preoccupation', a lulling attention in which she feels herself into the child's place, is a crucial component of maternal love.

Concerned to free mothers from the anxiety-inducing pressure of guidebooks and the conflicting advice of doctors, nurses, grandmothers and friends, Winnicott constantly reassures the mother that she will know just what to do 'spontaneously' in order to be 'good enough' — not perfect. Striving for perfection, her anxiety infiltrates the baby, provoking his. Given good-enough mothering, good-enough love, the baby will go on to create what it is within him to create and contribute. In a BBC broadcast of 1949, Winnicott stated:

> In each baby is a vital spark, and this urge towards life and growth and development is a part of the baby, something the child is born with and which is carried forward in a way that we do not have to understand. For instance, if you have just put a bulb in the window-box you know perfectly well that you do not have to make the bulb grow into a daffodil. You supply the right kind of earth or fibre and you keep the bulb watered just the right amount, and the rest comes naturally, because the bulb has life in it.

The baby needs attentiveness: she needs to be held and fed, more or less when she likes, and changed, perhaps not too soon, since she enjoys the warmth, and indeed the excitement, of producing and sometimes retaining excrement. Excited by feeding, which is also a sexual activity, she may turn away or prove aggressive, but eventually she will be satisfied, at least for the time being — which isn't long. Babies cry and can be a downright nuisance. But Winnicottian babies are allowed, often enough, to shriek and scream: every mother will soon recognize which cries are to do with hunger or pain and which are simply a mark of what the baby is living out internally — for the baby has his own fears and fantasies to live through, which produce inner conflicts.

Feeding difficulties are common amongst all children at one point or another, and can return periodically, Winnicott notes, thus calming his listeners. So, too, are orgies — of sex, food or excrement. This needn't worry mother. There is a tug-of-war going on in the infant between inner and outer reality: destructive thoughts go along with excitement, and these frighten him. Growing fond of the person he gradually recognizes as mother, he may worry that he will destroy her in the very act of eating her, so he stops eating. As long as the good-enough mother (or her partner) doesn't panic, shows the baby that she can withstand his attacks; as long as she is reliably there, alive and breathing, the baby will grow happily enough, sensing that his rampant needs and conflictual desires are somehow being held — and held together — as he moves towards that integration which marks his existence as a bounded self.

Parents don't need to know everything that goes on in the minds of their small children, any more than they need to know everything about physiology. (The analogy here might be with the state: we want it to provide basic security, but rebel against invasive surveillance.) Winnicott says: it's not the head, but the heart that counts. Parents simply need 'to have the imagination to recognize that parental love . . . is something which a child absolutely needs of them'. Above all, he needs mother to be 'real' for him, to provide security, so that he can hate her, bite, stab, kick, without destroying her. Gradually he'll move from a state of illusion – that omnipotent, magical time when the imaginary world dominates – to 'disillusion', a recognition that there are other beings in the world, that satisfactions are dependent and may be sporadic and limited.

Mother-love is what sees the child through and shapes the kind of being he will become.

Winnicott is well aware that mothers grow despondent and also depressed, are sometimes absent even when physically present, perhaps because their baby evokes dimly flickering events from their own infancy. The child may follow suit, give up in some way, as children in institutions do when there is no one to hold them – to respond to their ruthless needs which are also a primitive form of love. Time can be made up, someone else may be able to step in. But when there is no rallying on the mother's part, the consequences, Winnicott's work with deprived and delinquent children showed him, could be harsh.

> . . . without the initial good-enough environmental provision, this self that can afford to die never develops. The feeling of real is absent and if there is not too much chaos the ultimate feeling is of futility. The inherent difficulties of life cannot be reached, let alone the satisfactions. If there is not chaos, there appears a false self that hides the true self, that complies with demands, that reacts to stimuli, that rids itself of instinctual experiences by having them, but that is only playing for time.

This false, compliant self will eventually feel futile and inevitably at some period of later difficulty, break down.

In all the schools of relational therapy that stem from Winnicott, the analyst, by providing or mimicking a good-enough childhood environment where trust and continuity reign despite the patient's anger or aggression, tries to make good or at least bring into awareness the many permutations of lack and deprivation from early childhood. The hope is that failures in loving are not perpetuated through the generations.

In the therapeutic models, much hangs on mother's or a first carer's love. It is hardly surprising, then, that contemporary young women may feel daunted by the prospect of babies. When they do engage in the challenge, often at a later age than their mothers, they're determined somehow to make a consummate success of it. So it's as well to put things in perspective, to underline that 'good enough' may be far better than perfect, and that children have blossomed under many and varying regimes, some in which they were considered as diminutive adults, others in which childhood was separated off as a special sphere of innocence.

The Child in History

The place of the infant within the family has shifted greatly over the centuries. In historical agrarian societies, extended families constituted a team, sharing work. Children – conceived in large numbers although only a small percentage survived into maturity – were understood as an eventual part of the labour force. Once out of their swaddled state and past their earliest game-playing infancy, they took part in the tasks of the household. According to the seventeenth-century French cleric Pierre de Bérulle, childhood was 'the most vile and abject state of human nature, after that of death'. Even unweaned children were enjoined to learn the catechism, while a special four-hundred-page version existed for the tutoring of five-year-olds. Shaping unruly children into disciplined adults, by means of either religion or the rod, was a primary preoccupation for Catholics and Puritans alike.

Ushering in the Enlightenment, John Locke counselled that reason and education should guide child-rearing. In *Some Thoughts concerning Education* (1683) he drew on his experience as a tutor to advise on children's diet, stool, clothes and cleanliness. He also drew attention to parents' psychologically formative influence. Though each child had its own 'natural Genius and Constitution' and all should be 'tenderly used . . . and have Play-things',

> parents, by humouring and cockering [pampering] them when *little*, corrupt the principles of nature in their children, and wonder after-wards to taste the bitter waters, when they themselves have poison'd the fountain. For when their children are grown up, and these ill habits with them; when they are now too big to be dandled, and their parents can no longer make use of them as play-things, then they complain that the brats are untoward and perverse; then they are offended to see them wilful, and are troubled with those ill humours which they themselves infus'd and fomented in them; and then, perhaps too late, would be glad to get out those weeds which their own hands have planted, and which now have taken too deep root to be easily extirpated.

The 'Principle of all Vertue and Excellency,' he continued, 'lies in a power of denying ourselves the satisfaction of our own Desires, where Reason does not authorize them'.

Locke's 'nature' is a reasonable human nature, not the sublime one of the Romantics. That reason also advises that parents teach their children by example: their beatings incur more of the same in their children, as do their lies and gluttony. Though restraint is necessary, imperiousness only leads the child to ask the question, 'When will you die, Father?'

While the Romantics imagined childhood as a privileged, innocent space where the principles of a beloved and wild nature took their own shape, the Victorians brought that nature, at least for middle-class children, into a disciplined garden where happiness was intended to reign. This was the era of tough love and the inculcation of a rigid sense of duty. School became compulsory from 1870: the wealthy sent their sons off to board, far from mother-love, from a young age. Indeed, as Philippe Ariès argued in his classic *Centuries of Childhood*, for the rising middle classes from the seventeenth century onwards, schooling confined childhood within 'a severe disciplinary system, which culminated in the eighteenth and nineteenth centuries in the total claustration of the boarding school'. Though it inflicted what was tantamount to the punishing life of a convict on the child, all was done out of an 'obsessive love'. Rigid restraint and demand for obedience prevailed, both for the privileged middle-class and for the working child, bound in apprenticeship or in menial, repetitive toil. Corporal punishment was everywhere in use, as were those anti-masturbating devices that bear a close relationship to torture instruments. Throughout the latter part of the nineteenth century, reformers campaigned to put an end to child labour and protect children from the adult sphere of work and responsibility.

Though named the 'century of the child', the twentieth has seen as much cruelty to children as earlier ones. Nonetheless, expectations of how children should be treated have risen hugely. In the West, this has come in tandem with welfare provision for health, care and schooling to at least sixteen, and with various theorizations of infancy and childhood, each of which has drawn up its own guidelines for rearing. Alongside the rise of psychoanalytic theories like Winnicott's emerged the influential ones of John Bowlby and his 'attachment' school. Based in part on animal observation, attachment theory even more emphatically prioritized the importance of mother-love, understood as a warm, intimate, secure and continuous relationship with the mother. Maternal deprivation caused the child to protest, then despair, and finally to enter a state of denial, the damaging effects of which would resurface later in life.

Towards the end of the twentieth century and into our own, the values placed on childhood and on mother-love have both increased. This has coincided, perhaps not unexpectedly, with a generalized anxiety that children are everywhere in danger. Images of children under attack from famine or war feature regularly in the media. Statistics about child poverty, on the increase in our ever more stratified Western world, sit alongside sensationalist reports of abuse in the family: torture, and paedophilia. Teenagers unrestrained by parents seem ever to be on the rampage – at least on the news – though rarely at work in the universities which nearly half of them at least manage to attend. Divorce and lone or dysfunctional parenting are regularly elided with such problems, though poverty rarely plays into the same statistics-gathering and has a far greater impact. In such an environment, the pressure for perfect mother-love and calls for father-love looms ever larger. All of it sits uneasily with women's need or desire to work, even though equality for women in all spheres is rightly championed and enshrined in law. Meanwhile little provision is made, except in the Scandinavian countries, for a life–work balance that might meet family needs.

Probing the forces underlying the difficulties in love, marriage and parenting in our competitive capitalist world, sociologists Ulrich Beck and Elisabeth Beck-Gernsheim have pointed in the first instance to an economic model which undermines the stability of families. During the second half of the twentieth century, they note, an increasingly mobile job market has meant that individuals must follow the demands of work *first*. In thrall to economic forces, families have grown increasingly atomized, rarely living near potentially supportive kin. With both partners in a family needing or wanting to work, the birth-rate has fallen. Meanwhile, given our cultural habit of serial monogamy, lone parenting, at least for part of a child's life, has increased. In the UK in 2004, one in four children lived in lone-parent families, up from one in fourteen in 1972. Despite this, we continue to assume marriage to be based on love and intimacy. And the nuclear family, with so much evidence to the contrary, persists in appearing as a secure haven.

Bred in ever smaller numbers, children, Beck and Beck-Gernsheim argue, accrue greater and greater value. While the world of work trains one to behave rationally, to be efficient, quick and disciplined, the world of childhood emerges as its utopian opposite – enticingly green and golden. Play, the imagination, the love a partner can't altogether or has failed to satisfy, all come to be located in the child. The baby holds out the promise that, through him, we may rediscover some of the lost sides of ourselves, express and fulfil all the needs that we fail to satisfy in the rest of our high-tech lives. For women in particular, motherhood may take on the glow of a refuge and fulfil the deepest private needs of home and love.

When we do at last make the difficult decision to have this precious child, his very value marks him out as a site of demands and expense. He becomes 'a focus of parental effort, a carefully tended plant, a work of art, a cult object'. Childhood is transformed into a 'programme' requiring careful surveillance and monitoring. Each of the child's phases

becomes heavy with meanings learned from the psychobabble industries, as well as a site for parental squabbling. The more changing of
partners there is, the more special the child becomes, to emerge as the
parent's only alternative to loneliness, 'a bastion against the vanishing
chances of loving and being loved', a bulwark against utter disenchant-
ment, a stand-in for a more equal partner or, indeed, a compensation
for that partner's lacks. With such an investment of hopes, loving can be
volatile and may quickly deteriorate into bitter disappointment and
even cruelty.

Enter the new technology of assisted reproduction: the glow of science now attends the making of babies, giving them an extra dimension
of specialness. But this further complicates parental love. Like virtual
dating and porn, AR seems to have expanded our sphere of possibilities
and choice, at the same time making what once belonged more or less
to the province of the uncontrollable into a rational, self-determined
matter. Fertility is no longer a question of fate. Women can choose to
have the desired children alone, independent of embodied males. They
can store eggs and manipulate time. This can feel like a form of empowerment. But like all choices, it can also increase anxiety. Equally, the
very fact of AR can resonate to reduce the value of being gendered
female to that old reproductive function.

Parthenogenesis – women conceiving without the help of a male – is
a symbolically freighted matter. Ever enraged at the philandering Zeus,
who had given birth to wise Athena from his brow, the goddess Hera set
out to match him. In Flora's garden, one of the stories goes, she is
shown a rare seed which, once swallowed, has her pregnant with Ares –
god, of course, of war. Typhon, the monster with the savage jaws, father
of Cerberus and the Gorgon, is another offspring conceived without the
help of a male. Lame Hephaestus follows: Hera throws him down from
the heavens. Breeding without a mate seems here to introduce rather
unenviable progeny.

But science, like miraculous religion, pays little heed to pagan prece-
dent. As he did for Mary, the Holy Spirit, now in the figure of a
lab-coated doctor, can intercede to give any of us the possibility of a
miraculous child, with no intervention necessary from a really existing
male. This extraordinary change has been naturalized within just a few

decades. So highly prized are children today, so enshrined has the right to fertility (with a little help from medical science) become, that some young and emancipated women – whether gay or simply single – prefer to engender donor babies than have a child with a man. Others have surrogate babes or make use, with their partners, of the various other available forms of reproductive technology.

It might be said that all this extends the simple continuum created by the invention of the contraceptive pill, which did so much to enable women to control reproduction: their children, whose unconscious was shaped in the homes of liberated mothers, find no great difficulty in taking the leap into assisted reproduction. Yet the shift is a remarkable one, and inevitably accompanied with some unease and residual apprehension. Its attendant anxieties can percolate through generations of siblings – in the way that old-fashioned arrangements did when secret loves brought children fathered outside into the family. Now children conceived with donor sperm, once they grow up, can and do seek out any number of donor kin and establish sometimes large horizontal kinship networks. New meanings of 'father', 'mother' and 'sibling' tug against the old, forcing conventional notions of family love and responsibility into frames that often don't fit. Little wonder that the whole notion of 'family', already endangered and in question from both outside and in, renders traditionalists shrill in their attempts to sanctify it, while others live out its many permutations of gender and stepparenting.

Unconditional Love

Having a child always calls into being a host of fantasies and fears, many of which are barely conscious. Inside that swelling tum there's a whole imagined future, a dreamed-of bond with another, a gift to one's partner or parent, a transforming other who will fashion one anew or be a narcissistic replica of one's best self. There's also a terror that one's life will be utterly out of control, that a partner will give up on this swelling and preoccupied maternal and therefore asexual self, that domineering parents (the ones we may yet replicate) will take over, that we're ourselves babies and can't cope with another, that we'll be forever tied and tied down and that all of it may go drastically wrong.

A few days before my son was born, I had a vivid dream that I had given birth to a nicely roasted chicken, complete with platter. My parents and husband oohed and ahhed and immediately sat down to consume it, though I didn't, as I remember, partake. I woke in a nightmare sweat.

Evidently a great many grandparental hopes rested on this forthcoming child, alongside my own terror of what kind of creature he might be and how we might treat him. There was also perhaps something of my own fear of becoming my mother, who at that time, I felt, was nothing if not carnivorous and would happily have eaten the chick I also was in the dream, my legs splayed in the way that those birthing images sometimes show. Most women worry about becoming their Mums, good or bad, and conduct a dance with the conflation through much of their lives.

Looking back, I think I was also fearful of the term 'unconditional love' that attends all our motherhoods. It's a Christian term, of course, and comes from the presumed love of God for all his creatures, whatever their acts or dispositions. The term is freighted, and being a sceptical sort – sceptical of my own powers, above all – I didn't really think I could live up to it. What if I simply didn't like the creature my child was?

Of course, once he appeared, all such considerations vanished in the sheer trance-like ardour of tending to a new life. He was alive and kicking, he was ours, and he needed us, our reliable presence alongside all our hopes and worries. Roll on many years and another child later, and I've begun to think that what the unconditional in parental love means is not that you'll engage in that over-zealous parenting so fashionable today; not that you'll never say no, since you'll often be saying no and sometimes loudly. Nor that you'll never criticize or have rows, of which there'll inevitably be and need to be a good number, since we hardly live in an unconflicted world and even our very special children have to learn to live with that, too. What unconditional love means, simply, is that you'll be there when they need you, listen, pay attention and help them get through, because to you, whatever their failings, they're special, and specially loved – even when they have no time for you. And in that love there is great and abiding pleasure, the very pleasure of an ongoing bond in another's life. With luck, they'll take pleasure in it, too.

One of the things the tick-list advice books seem rarely to mention is that *enjoying* one's children and taking time to enjoy them, to appreciate them, to laugh with them, to talk, is one of the cornerstones of parental love. Parenting may involve work, but the work ethic doesn't underpin it: there are seldom any material rewards at the end. Children are in no sense smoothly honed products off the assembly line of parental labour. They're ever a surprise and often a pleasure, though like all our loves, they also make us weep, just as we make them weep. For what feels like a long time to them – though to us not long enough – they think their parents are the most important people in the world; and they learn to love the world through us, step out into it, relish it, empathize with kin and friends, become social beings. Like A.A. Milne's James James Morrison Morrison Weatherby George Dupree, they can be far more possessive than lovers, unwilling to allow mother to go to the 'end of the town' without 'consulting me'. They're also sometimes more entertaining than any lover, with their first babblings, their questions and insights and tales, their engrossing imaginative play, their fresh responses to the world. But their love will always ask more of one than we can ask of them.

The baby grows up. Children have their own complicated lives. They go to school, come under the influence of teachers and peers. They provoke worry, instil in mothers in particular an abiding and easily triggered anxiety. Like all loved ones, they also make us suffer. Too quickly, from the parental vantage point, they become secretive, surly adolescents, inevitable rebels, not always easy to love. Though they need that secure flow as much as, arguably more than, babes, they now judge us. Fallen one-time gods that we are, they often do so harshly, lashing out at us since we're closest to hand. It's tough to have to take it, but our being there to understand and help sort out their emotional jumble if only by listening, to set limits which may be under siege but are nonetheless internalized, is a necessary part of love's unconditionality.

Then they leave home. Parents must needs be left behind. Gone are the days of the large traditional Victorian family in which the youngest daughter all too often took on the care of parents, particularly Daddy; though in these days of expensive housing, we may find a young adult making use of the parental home (and maternal servitude) well beyond the approved date. As Oscar Wilde has Mrs Arbuthnot quip in *A Woman of No Importance*, 'Children love their parents. Eventually they come to judge them. Rarely do they forgive them.' So our immoderate hopes of children, our unconditional love for them, are subject to a necessary betrayal through time, that greatest of betrayers. As E.M. Forster, in bittersweet mood, has a character remark in *Where Angels Fear to Tread* (1905) '. . . a wonderful physical tie binds the parents to the children; and – by some sad, strange irony – it does not bind us children to our parents. For if it did, if we could answer their love not with gratitude but with equal love, life would lose much of its pathos and much of its squalor, and we might be wonderfully happy.'

There is no single formula for mother-love. If there were, we'd all be clones of one another. And, just as with our partners, our love for our children needs frequent reinvention. They may in parents' eyes always be adorable three-year-olds, but they're also all the other ages they become, each with its own needs of separateness, of responsibility, and one hopes, too, of occasional re-engagement with that 'home' that parents provide. But, given our long lives, the nest is likely to be empty for several decades. This may be another good reason for holding the rhetoric of idealized full-time maternal love at arm's length and for women to maintain at least some relation to the world of work.

Undoubtedly, a measure of selflessness and service, of availability and, above all, understanding and tenderness are crucial to parental love. But maternal self-surrender beyond school age, a wholesale identification with a child's wished-for achievements and a deep sense of failure if they don't meet one's desires for them are rarely wise attributes. Somewhere along the way, children also need to learn about conflict, about the fact that their loved ones are not ever-available servants, about absence which evokes a return but yet is not a constant presence.

It was only some fifty years ago, after all, that America was caught up in a discourse about 'momism' – an outpouring of vituperation against powerful and clinging mothers who undermined their sons' and daughters' lives, who sought to control, who identified their own ambitions too closely with those of their offspring – like Paul Morel's archetypal cannibalizing mother, both loved and hated, in D.H. Lawrence's *Sons and Lovers*. Needless to say, that form of mother-love was born out of a cultural imperative that women give themselves utterly to children and home: in some sense 'jailed' during their offspring's childhoods, they repeated the favour by trying to jail them in later life. As in all our other loves, it's as well to recognize and enjoy the child's separateness from us, which also revivifies love far more emphatically than does smothering.

Some psychologists have recently warned against the dangers of over-zealous mother-love and the limitations of the attachment-theory model, which allows no necessary separation between mother and child and engenders a fusion which can provoke its own anxieties. The child's psyche becomes structured on a dualistic basis, permitting no entry into the world of others, an outside which the father, the third party, who traditionally demarcated a limit to blissful bodily plenitude, provided. When mother and child are one for too long or too intensely, the child can develop a sense of being overwhelmed from the inside: there is no regulation of his desires or fears, no safeguards, no learning to live with the lacks and limits that underpin life. Without a prohibiting third of whatever gender, we never grow up, or we remain children seeking an all-powerful state or saviour of whom salvation is expected and with whom we can merge.

Erotic Intruders

The arrival of that delicious Cupid of a babe in the familial nest with his demands for unconditional mother-love usually means that all other libidinal desires promptly fly out of the window. Passion may have ushered him in, but once he's there, most mothers report that passion with their partner is one satisfaction too many. In that 'maternal pre-occupation', in that vaunted early plenitude, all sensual satisfactions are spent. Father is displaced. And even if, for some, the babe's skin, suck, wide eyes and coos don't actually in fantasy altogether stand in for Sean Penn or husband, then exhaustion, sleepless nights, the round of nappy changes and health visitors, the juggling of time and responsibility that the new arrival demands, will rarely leave much imaginative space for those old desires.

Women's sexuality, Esther Perel notes, echoing the long line of analysts from Freud on, 'is diffuse, not localized in the genitals, but distributed throughout the body, mind and senses. It is tactile and auditory, linked to smell, skin and contact; arousal is often more subjective than physical, and desire arises on a lattice of emotion.' Babies, those 'dangerous rivals', can for a while displace the partner, even when that questionable new fashion for co-sleeping – which places his majesty the infant squarely in the family bed, supposed site according to our latest mother cult of all benefits: nurturing security, lowering stress, raising self-esteem and cognitive ability – isn't part of the family pattern.

Marginalized by the new erotic couple, the traditional father's role here is ideally that of secure and understanding provider and occasional helpmate. Displaced, dispossessed of his one-time lover, it would not be surprising if he also sometimes felt a pang of jealousy. Perhaps more. We know that key moments of our adult lives can reawaken earlier, unconscious ones. If the new father was an older child in his own family constellation, his present jealousy might gain the added heft of an earlier displacement from his own Mum when a new sibling arrived. Fatherhood can kindle a cauldron of emotions, difficult to control.

Two men amongst my informants had begun affairs while their children were babes at the breast. They simply couldn't bear the advent of this latest rival. For one of them the situation was repeated in a second marriage, making it clear – whatever was actually said or rationalized – that it was hardly his choice of wife that was amiss. Plainly, the new arrival called up unresolved aspects of himself which kept him locked in an unbearable moment from infancy. His third, childless union was long-lasting, and once the children he had left behind had passed earliest infancy he proved himself a fond and loyal father.

For other men – and they're hardly few in number – once their lovers turn into mothers, they also take on the aura of their own mother. The old incest taboo looms into prominence: while they may still love their partners, and indeed be warm and caring, the very possibility of passion, which often has a rapacious edge, flees. This may suit the partner perfectly for the span of her love affair with her babe – or, indeed, if she's fond of protective Daddies, for ever after. But rekindling that old sexual spark may prove a daunting challenge. Passion, ungovernable, unpredictable, often fanned by the illicit, is rarely altogether amenable to domesticity, which can provide other, more durable, satisfactions. It's just as well for the children, you might say: they can suffer from the inattentiveness of parents who are erotically embroiled only with one another. This may also be why children can be so averse to the appearance of new partners, indeed downright nasty. After all, they have their own love affairs with their idolized parents to protect.

Patterns of love lived in the family cascade through the generations, whether we like them or not, so it's as well to be aware of these patterns rather than blindly repeat them. As for new fathers, if they allow themselves, or are allowed and encouraged, to engage with their silken babes, they may be just as good at passionate mother-love as working Mums.

Father-love

Once solidly authoritative in their position as head of the family, fathers were traditionally imagined as the dispensers of tough love. They had little to do with children until language and 'reason' came within their grasp. Enunciator of the prohibitive No, it is the father, in Lacanian discourse, who ushers the babe into the world of language and what Lacan calls the symbolic, the arena of religion, culture and the social.

Up until the late 1970s, a middle-class male presence in the nursery was less than usual. Nor were men often seen playing with a small child, the occasional weekend foray apart. A friend of mine, born in the early 1920s to an upper-class German family, told me that at birth he had been presented to his father, who took one glance and promptly responded, 'Good, now bring him back to me when he's fifteen.' If such an attitude was hardly universal and many look back with adoring fondness at their relationship with their fathers (perhaps because they were less present than mothers), the family division of labour saw mothers as mistresses of the nursery and fathers as interlopers or occasional visitors. 'To be a successful father,' Ernest Hemingway said, 'there's one absolute rule: when you have a kid, don't look at it for the first two years.' Perhaps unsurprisingly, two is the moment when language arrives.

Though Mediterranean cultures sanctioned the hugging and kissing of small ones by males, children everywhere belonged primarily in the women's and then the school's domain, until adulthood beckoned. On the way, fathers were distantly omnipotent, often disciplinary figures, brought in when punishment was due or arguments needed settling; or in the case of girls, to admire their accomplishments. Indeed, in the various permutations of the family romance that Freud shaped out of observation and his patients' accounts, it is the father's approving gaze that moulds the little girl into the sexed creature she becomes. She interiorizes this gaze, to be transformed into the being who is always looked at, the object of desire or its lack.

In her *Memoirs of a Dutiful Daughter* Simone de Beauvoir recounts how, on being displaced from her mother's lap by her baby sister, she found solace in wooing and winning her father's and visiting males' attention, sometimes dressing up to engage in a performance of femininity for their eyes. Mother, here, emerges as her rival in father-love; one who, it seems from the little girl's vantage point, is less difficult to displace than she is to come to terms with as the bearer of a comparable femininity.

It's a commonplace that fathers develop special relationships with their ever admiring daughters, guard them jealously as they enter the world of sexuality, and loathe to give them over to other men whose designs they know too well. In Victorian fiction, where mothers are so often dead, patriarchal fathers turn their growing daughters into all but overtly sexual partners, while daughters willingly comply out of love and duty, sometimes maintaining their primary bond even after marriage. At its simplest, Henry James's *The Golden Bowl* (1904) is the story of a young woman who recognizes that in order to save her marriage and win over her straying husband, she must somehow give up her primary allegiance to her rich and powerful father. She needs to become a woman, not simply a daughter, and take the reins of her life into her own hands.

Women as various as the psychoanalyst Helene Deutsch, Simone de Beauvoir – both of whom regularly ensconced themselves under their fathers' desks, sites of knowledge and power – and Margaret Thatcher, long idealized their fathers, with whom they shared a whole sphere of aspiration. This active identification with father brought in tandem a spurning of mother. To the latter the first two attributed a suffocating world of either materialism or narrow conformist religiosity, together with a focus solely on their daughter's eventual marriage. Helene Deutsch noted that during adolescence, when a 'powerful sensual current' takes the father-identified girl over, she may need to split the father in two, to find a father figure who is also a lover. Alternatively, she may sublimate the erotic capacity altogether to pursue altruistic ideals. 'The danger of such a relation to the father,' Deutsch further elaborates, may be that when the father, often prompted by the mother, recognizes that his daughter should have more feminine interests, 'he refuses to have "active" communion with her. Very often his own subsequent anxiety drives him to repudiate this relation.'

A son's relationship with his father has different outlines. In sons' accounts fathers are regularly experienced, at least until sons grow into fathers themselves, as admonitory and punishing. They are opponents, initially for mother-love and then for a place in the world. For the father, as Tolstoy describes so well in the scene where Levin's babe is born, the son, in representing generational continuity, also signals his own death, his replacement.

Franz Kafka graphically evoked the torments at the heart of the patriarchal family. In his gnomic writings timid sons are singled out for cruel and unusual punishment by ruthless fathers or their authoritarian stand-ins, all the while acquiescing in their terrible fates. Never quite rising to the challenge of rebellion or totemic murder, they remain hapless children, confined like the metamorphosed Gregor Samsa to his room, to be tended by mother and sister until he reverts to mere dust. In his short story 'The Judgement' Georg Bendemann is arbitrarily sentenced to death-by-drowning by a wilful father, and remains obedient and loving for all that. Kafka's view of the traditional patriarchal family is a sobering one. 'All parents want to do,' he wrote to Felice Bauer in 1912 at the age of twenty-seven, 'is drag one down to them, back to the old days from which one longs to free oneself and escape: they do it out of love, of course, and that's what makes it so horrible.'

The contradiction inherent in this family model is that the son will grow up, become a man emancipated from the family, by following the father's example, yet the obedience and gratitude that are demanded chain him to the position of an eternal child – not the limitless all-desiring, narcissistic infant of the mother–child couple before the paternal rival has arrived implacably on the scene, but one whose desires have been forcibly suppressed in an Oedipal conflict with an authoritative paterfamilias.

Kafka's 'Letter to His Father' (1919) details the conundrum and the ambivalence that shadows all our loves. A grown man of thirty-six, he still lives in fear of the 'hot-tempered', commanding, threatening father he describes as a 'true Kafka in strength, health, appetite, loudness of voice, eloquence, self-satisfaction, worldly dominance, endurance, presence of mind, knowledge of human nature'. He, in contrast, remains infantilized, unable to marry, still prey to the memory of himself as a timid child, ever fearful of the punishment meted out when he whimpered one night for a glass of water and was promptly carried on to the balcony and locked out in cold, solitary isolation, reduced as it were to a nothing, a no one. Instead of encouragement, a little friendliness for the person that he was, there was only denial, an attempt to compact him into the fatherly mould. When his father, regularly only present for dinners or punishment, takes him swimming and makes him undress in the same bathing hut as his huge self, the boy Kafka feels like a miserable specimen. 'When we stepped out of the bathing hut before the people, you holding me by my hand, a little skeleton, unsteady, barefoot on the boards, frightened of the water, incapable of copying your swimming strokes', he feels humiliated. Yet in his unobserved anguish, he is still 'proud of my father's body'.

A sense of failure, an inner anxiety combined with self-contempt, follows Kafka, self-avowedly, through his days, and prevents his attempts at marriage: the women in question are cheapened and dirtied by his father's casual slurs on sex. He is, he suggests, emasculated, rendered at least metaphorically impotent, eternally a son. It's worth noting that Freud's discourse of repressed sexuality and the boy's fear of castration by the ever huge and prohibiting paterfamilias — a fear that also sets up in his psyche that superego which is conscience and duty — grows out of this traditional regime of patriarchal command.

Traditional fathers hover over the household, their great symbolic function a direct outgrowth of their remoteness and their social power. The Great War, the modern moment, the Freudian revolution, all combined to abet the gradual and always spasmodic decline of their power. When new, slightly looser, sexual and marital forms came into being in the post-First World War epoch, the father's role vis-à-vis his children began very slowly and unevenly to shift. Loving took on softer contours.

In the idealized family of the 1950s, paternal love still manifests itself primarily in the provision of security. Fathers may regularly engage in weekend or holiday ball games, sport and outings with their growing children, but contact is seldom daily or necessarily prolonged. There's a laconic element to it. Themselves the children of depression and war, this generation of parents were often indulgent, fathers treating their young to the goods they themselves had never enjoyed. In the remembered childhoods of my cohort, the period at its best often emerges as a nostalgically ordered world, both hierarchical and caring. Fiercely possessive early mother-love and protective father-love are both in place, though ever shadowed by parental memories of war and austerity.

A fierce disillusion with parental limitation and choices followed, in part occasioned by a Cold War that had grown too hot in its nuclear capability and in its manifold eruptions, notably in Vietnam. The baby-boomers vociferously rebelled against the conventional bourgeois family. 'They fuck you up, your mum and dad/ They may not mean to, but they do,' Philip Larkin wrote in 1971, crystallizing the sentiments of a generation and several since. Fucked-up themselves 'by fools in old-style hats and coats', parents visit their faults on their children, handing on misery. The only way to halt the cycle of generational wretchedness, Larkin counsels, is to get out early and not have children yourself.

This is precisely what the coming of the oral contraceptive permitted. With it came women's liberation and the dawn of a new parental settlement, often more wish than fact. Women's greater voice and power ushered in a more tender epoch, one alert to the vulnerable and the relational. Dual, hands-on parenting, once children were had, now emerged as not only desirable but necessary. Men began to be seen showing an interest in the birth process, walking babes, playing with toddlers, waiting at school gates. In a good many instances the responsibility awakened men to that tenderness they had earlier only shown when they reached grandparenthood. None of it happened uniformly, all at once, or without contention, but gradually affectionate and early father-love took on a normative cast, though one ever questioned by traditionalist and clerical forces.

The Academy Award-winning film *Kramer vs Kramer* (1979) captured the moment and also distilled some of the attributes of contemporary father-love. Tracing the process and fall-out of a divorce between a couple and their four-year-old son, the film begins with Joanna Kramer (Meryl Streep) saying goodnight and 'I love you' to a sleepy Billy (Justin Henry), before packing a bag. She is poised to leave her husband Ted (Dustin Hoffman), a workaholic advertising executive, who is late home. It is clear when he arrives that the couple don't know how to speak to one another and that love has foundered. Long depressed, Joanna is leaving so that she can become a functioning person again. Her love for her son, though palpable, is doing neither of them enough good.

Left to the duties of childcare on top of demanding work, Ted flounders and is at first barely attuned to his son's needs, all the more intense given the sudden absence of his mother. But gradually through the eighteen months that the film spans, he learns to listen and to communicate, to play and shop, to provide the requisite food and appear at the school gates. Mutual love, care and attentiveness blossom between father and son, changing Ted in the process into a far more attractive and textured being. Egocentric high-flier becomes sensitive daily cuddler. Parenting begins to take precedence over the demands of work, and when Ted is late for a key meeting, his boss, who has never heard of that thing called work–life balance, asks him to go.

The moment coincides with a custody hearing. Joanna wants her son back. She's been living in California, had therapy and is now back in New York with a well-paying job. She loves her son and is now ready to raise him.

In order to have a chance of keeping a Billy he now can't bear to be parted from, Ted has to get a new job, and quickly. He moves down the hierarchy and settles for a lower-paying post, proudly taking Billy to see the new premises, which offer spectacular views of Manhattan. The court, we have been told, is predisposed to rule in favour of mother-love, according to the so-called tender-years doctrine, a default legal position which at the time was already being contested. So Ted, at the hearing, has to do particularly vigorous battle to keep the son he so wants: he knows, too, that a second adaptation to new circumstances would hurt Billy deeply. Nonetheless, the new man that he has become is aware that the picture Joanna's attorney paints of him was once accurate. It is only through the process of enforced hands-on fathering that he has actually learned to love his son fully. He has also, it is made clear, learned to understand Joanna: while wanting to contest her claim, he is alert to her needs. When the judge rules in Joanna's favour, he decides not to appeal: it might mean putting his son on the stand and forcing him to make the impossible choice of one parent over another. He prepares, painful as it is, to give his son over to his former wife. In the last scene we see that Joanna, too, has recognized not only the change in her former husband, but that a second rupture would do Billy no good, and she abandons her claim.

For all its inevitable sentimentality and its underscoring of the need to put the child's interest first, *Kramer vs Kramer* points to a cultural shift, often more wished for than lived. A new parenting balance between the sexes is in play. Ruthless macho man and subjugated wife have given way to the tender, paternal male implicated in the daily life of his children, and the working mother: a woman whose life is now larger than home and children. In the film's last shot, the hope is even raised that the estranged couple may come together again in a more harmonious constellation.

The new man – though perhaps not altogether as equally as some women may wish – at least aspires to sharing in the tasks of child-rearing, even when mothers choose to be at home. If the balancing act between partners in the new domesticity is rarely altogether unfraught, men's interest in small children and this tenderer version of paternity can only be a good.

Some, however, not least on the psychological side, have worried about the decline in the father's symbolic function as the bearer of authority, compounded in the cultural sphere by a general postmodern suspicion of authority and power as a whole. In combination with an advice culture particularly intent on ensuring that a child shall suffer no lack of self-esteem, this decline in what was once paternal clout can result in the shaping of individuals who have no sense of boundaries and no recognition of bad behaviour. With lives premised on a feeling of self-entitlement, little heed is paid to the needs of others. In a nutshell, we appear to have been breeding a generation of uncontrolled toddlers who have become unbounded, grasping adults. Anxious, restless in their dissatisfactions, they are nonetheless certain the cause lies not in themselves but elsewhere.

It matters little what gender, male or female, generates the parental limits, but evidently they need to come from somewhere. This, too, is part of parental love.

So, too, is the fraught task of keeping in touch with children if separation or divorce takes place. In the period of enmity and high emotion that accompanies divorce, children become trapped in each parent's contesting and hateful view of the other, often dragging along a sense that somehow they, once so important, are the cause of the fray. There are no simple rules here, except to repeat that the child isn't at fault, and for both parents to carry on recognizing and acknowledging what it is he or she feels, which may be quite contrary to what they themselves experience. The psychoanalyst Enid Balint writes of the importance of this recognition: it is what gives the child a sense of his own reality. And it is another aspect of parental love, far more crucial than spirited weekends with ever guilty absentee fathers or, indeed, mothers. Without it, children's thinking or feeling is never joined up with what they live, and a false sense of themselves comes into being, covering over a core emptiness.

Love's Crucible

Each in our own idiosyncratic way, we learn to love in the family. Though it can sometimes provide a sentimental idyll, the family is also the site of tempestuous drama. All shades of love from bright to dark are there. It's a school in intimacy and power, hierarchy and democracy, passion and ambivalence.

The ancient myths shine a dazzling Mediterranean light on the powerful subterranean emotions that hurtle through life in the family. Like tragedy and opera, they enact the passions on a grand scale. If Oedipus still speaks to us – and not only in Freud's interpretation – it is because his story embodies the turbulence of family relations. Consider: fathers want sons, as Laius, King of Thebes, so desperately does – even though in some versions his desires are homosexual. But the arrival of sons also signals the death of the father and a new lover for the mother. So Laius sends his infant son Oedipus, destined to displace him, out to die on a mountaintop. But the generational fate, time's deadly arrow, can't be stopped. Unbeknown to him, Oedipus, now caught up in the conflicts of adoption, leaves his adoptive family: in a scuffle over pre-eminence on a country road, he kills the man who is his blood father. As if to underline that this father-murder is part of the human condition, Oedipus then proceeds to solve the riddle of the sphinx: 'What is the creature that walks on four legs in the morning, two legs at noon, and three in the evening?' To which swollen-footed Oedipus answers, 'Man'. We may be the same creatures throughout, but at different points in our lives, we get about in different ways, first on all fours, then upright, then with the help of a stick.

The doors to Thebes open to him, Oedipus is presented with and married to Jocasta, the mother he originally lost when she succumbed to paternal wish, and becomes her lover/husband. When the gamut of cross-generational sins – old against young and young against old – finally comes to light after much resistance, Jocasta hangs herself, and Oedipus puts out his own eyes, a punishment which no longer allows him to see the havoc he has helped to engender. He is then utterly dependent on his daughter and half-sister, Antigone, who in that sense displaces Jocasta. Antigone provides him with a metaphorical third leg and loyally guides him through the years to Colonnus, where he will die.

First, however, he learns that his two sons, to whom he has granted the throne of Thebes to occupy in yearly rotation, have risen against each other. Legacies ever generate jealousy and turmoil. Asked by his brother-in-law/uncle Creon, to bless Eteocles in single succession, Oedipus refuses. Both sons, Eteocles and Polynices, have been negligent towards him, he deems. The warring brothers thus slaughter each other in a battle for single inheritance. Creon, who has stepped in as King, allows only Eteocles official burial, since Polynices was effectively a rebel against the law of the land, having raised help from a foreign power.

Enter ever loyal Antigone, upholder of family honour and kinship ties above any contractual duty of citizenship to the state, keener than ever, we might say, given her family's taints, to uphold that honour. Polynices, too, must be appropriately buried. She asks her sister Ismene for help, but Ismene refuses: she isn't as brave as her sister, she says. So Antigone carries out the burial rites alone. She is caught and condemned to be interred alive. Now, Ismene, in retrospective loyalty to her sister, tells Creon that she too is guilty of this 'illegal' burial. Meanwhile, Creon's son, betrothed to Antigone, pleads for her life to his father, is refused, and when he learns that Antigone has hanged herself he, too, commits suicide. Creon's wife, learning of her son's death, does the same.

This is, we might say, family dysfunction on a grand scale. Equalling it are the passions in Shakespeare's tragedies: the sins of fathers or mothers rebound on their children. Hamlet avenges his ghostly father, replacing him in rank jealousy of Gertrude, a mother sexualized through her marriage to the one-time King's brother. His thoughts poisoned by his mother's sexuality, Hamlet turns on Ophelia. His actions lead to her death, his mother's and his own.

Such patterns find their partial equivalents in so-called honour killings today in which daughters (and mothers), who stand in for paternal and familial reputation but count for little in their own right, are expendable in the purification of family virtue.

King Lear unleashes tragedy by partitioning his territory in response to public and competitive testimonials of love from his daughters – an exchange of money for love, one might say. While the elder two,

Goneril and Regan, greedy and worldly, know how to flatter, the youngest, his favourite Cordelia, is tongue-tied. She simply can't traduce the intimate nature of her feeling in a public contest: her love is more 'ponderous' than her tongue: it weighs too heavily for easy speech. Heaving her heart into her mouth is an impossibility; all she can say, her words echoing marriage vows in a scene in which her future husband is present, is 'I love your Majesty/ According to my bond, nor more nor less.'

When Lear, insatiable in his demand, asks for more, she responds in judicious fashion that his claim on her is inappropriate. He is asking for more than natural affection can give.

> Good my lord,
> You have begot me, bred me, loved me. I
> Return those duties back as are right fit,
> Obey you, love you, and most honour you.
> Why have my sisters husbands if they say
> They love you all? Haply, when I shall wed,
> That lord whose hand must take my plight shall carry
> Half my love with him, half my care and duty.
> Sure I shall never marry like my sisters,
> To love my father all. (I. i. 98–106)

Vain, tyrannical, incapable of giving up the power he so ostensibly seeks to shed, Lear avoids his favourite's plea, abdicates love, throne, and eventually reason. He disowns her. Perhaps he thinks her suitors won't have her without her dowry and she'll remain all his. When the King of France is moved to take her just for herself, Lear proclaims to Cordelia: 'Better thou hadst not been born than not to have pleased me better.' His private love has turned to public hate, and his curses on her will fall on many heads, his own amongst them. Casting out Cordelia, Lear too becomes an outcast, a poor naked wretch on a blasted heath. The insatiability of his love brings on her death.

If murderous passions within the family are now mostly not enacted on a grand scale – though the sordid, abusive and traumatizing instances of parent and vulnerable child incest provide their demotic underside – it's clear that emotions in the family run the whole gamut from love to hate, and all the affection, kindness, pride, envy, jealousy and grief in between. These emotions also hurtle across the generations. How our parents behave towards one another and towards siblings and ourselves, as well as what they say – inevitably not quite in keeping with what they do – impacts on the love patterns, the conscious and unconscious wishes, that we then proceed to enact in a variety of ways. Growing up, the child identifies with parts of one or t'other parent – absent or present – rebels against the identification, yet often holding on to it in some way, then finds it revivified at one moment or another in life's ever variegated journey. His status amongst his siblings, his loves and rivalries, play into these patterns.

In his memoir *My Lives* (2005), Edmund White evokes that shaping trajectory through family life. His mother, Delilah Mae Teddlie, had lost her own father when she was still a child, and thought that this had instilled in her 'a floating, but permanent dread, of being abandoned by a man, a crucial man, or just by men, men in general'. Her husband left her for his mistress when little Edmund was just seven, though the marriage had endured for twenty-two years. She then took a post as a state psychologist testing children who were 'very bright or very slow', work she had long been training for. She also tested Edmund and his sister frequently, detecting in her son 'signs of a great soul and highly advanced spirituality'. A larger-than-life character, who the children later determined bore a kinship to Tennessee Williams's Blanche Du Bois, she was prone to rages, fits of weeping and self-dramatizing. She also loved her bourbon and her extravagant clothes, and was always on the lookout for the right man. Young Edmund was her most constant one, and would daily tie her girth into a gargantuan girdle and act as her reader on long car journeys – 'hopeful, deep books, that would sometimes cause her to look dreamy'. She hoped and feared for a 'strange destiny' for her son, giving him Nijinsky's *Life* when he was nine or ten.

Having grown up during the fifties when homosexuality was seen as an aberration to be cured, young Edmund continued to be obsessed by men and drawn to betraying them. Somewhere in his reading of and visits to a variety of analysts, he came across the theory that homosexuality was caused by an absent father and a suffocating mother. Perhaps my mother herself had been the one to suggest that my father's absence had queered me, for she was always eager to work out the multiple ways in which his desertion had harmed us all . . . I was sent to live with my father for one year back in Cincinnati, but he ignored me – and I had sex on a regular basis with the neighbour boy.

His father was a man who, though privately eccentric, even violent, 'wanted to appear, if not actually be, irreproachable', so despite his view of psychoanalysis as a form of 'soak-the-rich charlatanism', he paid for the teenage Edmund to see an analyst. Needless to say, his sexual orientation didn't change: it was society, rather than him, that needed to, and eventually did.

Neither, for many years, did his *ways* of loving change – or not altogether – though he had in part internalized a childhood moment of homophobia. Like his mother, who suffered from self-loathing and was prone to make drunken, coquettish demands, 'I alternate between low self-esteem and a prickly sense of my own importance.' Like her, he sobs for long periods when a lover leaves him. And like her, he is always 'pursuing one man or another', though his love affairs last longer.

More tales from family life

Amy, by contrast, grew up with parents who were enmeshed in that unusual constellation, a lifelong love affair with each other. In her narrative, she and her sister hardly count: they are barely visible witnesses to their parents' ever manifested ardour. Always holding hands, their first allegiance is to each other and is palpably physical. So she and her sister form a parallel, secondary universe and find their succour in one another. They play, they chat, they imagine, they shore each other up, they wonder at their parents' indifference to them. If neither girl becomes the apple of her father's eye or mother's favourite, they're not unhappy. They often think of their parents as 'simple', as their children, rather than the other way round. When she grows up, a rebellious Amy is interested only in intellectual love. She marries a mathematician.

Sex is unimportant. When she and her husband have a daughter, unlike her parents she is devoted to her child. Yet soon she is quite happy to leave her for long periods in the care of others. And when she travels for work reasons, her closest links are with other women. Sometimes these are sexualized, particularly after she and her husband divorce. It is with other women in her circle of friends that she finds her strongest bonds. They give her the kind of attentiveness her childhood relationship with her sister helped to put in place.

When Paula, twenty-six, describes her childhood, it is also a narrative of parents in love, herself on the outside looking in, bringing them her accomplishments which in the course of time grew considerable. Her mother, once an actress, was and continues to be by Paula's own account rivetingly beautiful, flirtatious, ever the centre of male attention, including her adoring husband's. Paula, an only child, joined her father in that adoration. In a sense she made the choice of not competing with her mother in the womanly stakes. Instead, she opted for her father. He became her companion, her pal, her fellow spirit, the person with whom she discussed life, interests, books: together they treated her mother as the incarnation of the feminine. Growing into adolescence, Paula actively rebelled against her mother's wiles, her mantra that a woman must hold back and play hard to get, her sexualized conception of womanhood. She felt plain, ill at ease in her female skin. She wore boyish clothes, had cropped hair. She shunned flirtation and sexualized play. She didn't know how to engage with boys, except as friends; though she participated in a number of the kind of casual sexual encounters that tend to characterize the urban young, she never fell in love. She was a self-avowed feminist. Yet her father remained the measure for her of what a man, indeed what a human being, should be. He was the most important person in her life, and she sensed that when she was paid attention by boys of her own age he felt eclipsed, displaced. When she recently at last fell in love, it was with a young man she clashed swords with intellectually. But she continues to worry that she has somehow betrayed her father, let him down. She still hasn't introduced her new love to her parents.

Proprietary and adoring, fathers' relationships with their daughters can run far more smoothly than relationships with their sons, at least until adolescence brings other men on to the scene and they begin to have to consider their little girls as sexed women. The moment that girls leave home can prove a thorny rite of passage for them both. Indeed, fathers love their daughters so much that in order to replace them, they may seek out other younger, adoring women. This may well end by turning their daughters against them and propelling the girl at last into an identification with her spurned mother, a mother she may have violently rebelled against and hated during her early teenage years. Now bound up masochistically with her mother, the daughter may later repeat aspects of the family tangle in her own life.

Peter and Sophie's story reveals some of these familial processes at work.

Peter grew up in a large Canadian family. He was the second-youngest of four boys, a defiant son of a stern, high-ranking clerical father and a mother committed to good works. Both parents expected best behaviour from their children. In the busy family, little enough attention was paid to him and he sought it out in a variety of alternative ways, bad and good, the first often reaping the reward of instant interest in the form of blame and discipline. Rebellious, always at loggerheads with paternal dicta, he became a fine public speaker, and in the late sixties a student leader. Though more radical than his father, he internalized the paternal recti-tude. He needed to be good and he sought approval for his goodness in crowds and in individuals. Over the years he became a prominent and much respected figure in the world of NGOs and human rights.

Sophie was the elder of two daughters in a military family, where regular habits and a certain coldness of relations were the order of the thoroughly regimented day. Her father abandoned the family, without any articulated explanation, when she was seven. He returned when she was fourteen and, though it was never spoken of, everyone knew that he had set up with another woman during those missing years. Stiff-lipped, her mother grimly accepted him back, though never ceased to criticize and upbraid, often by her mere expression of sullen discontent.

A clever and pretty young woman, Sophie blossomed at university law school during the late sixties. She never, however, managed to keep her always serious boyfriends: two left her in turn and promptly married others. On the rebound, she consciously made herself over, changing her prim clothes for the velvets and bright colours of the day. It was then that she met Peter, the most popular man in her circle. Something meshed. They were in love. They set up house together and eventually had two daughters, Sophie working only part-time in order to tend to them.

An intriguing set of relations developed within the couple. According to Peter, who travelled a great deal for work reasons, Sophie from almost the beginning of their partnered life grew suspicious of him, habitually accusing him of engaging in affairs, of being a philanderer. Though he wasn't at the outset, he became one. If recrimination was the name of the game, he half told himself, he might as well inhabit the persona he was given and reap its benefits. Much later, it became clear to him that he had needed the blame, the reproach, the constant allegations, the repeated diminishing of him, just as Sophie seemed to need his guilt and the repeated reasons for finding fault. She created a circle of haughty perfection around herself: it gave her the power to counter Peter's power and popularity in the wider world. Despising that, she shored herself up.

And so it went on, with increasing rigidity and lessening satisfaction on both sides, until the children left for university. Then Peter fell in love with another woman, easier in her ways, comfortable in her body, happy to take pleasure in him and his achievements. This time he decided to leave his wife. He could no longer bear what had become the joyless trap he and Sophie had fallen into. But if there are fifty ways to leave your lover, there are few clean breaks. Sophie just wouldn't allow their relationship to end, holding on to property and to the power that the potent tie of continuing blame and recrimination gave her. Almost in mirror image of her mother's behaviour during her childhood, she now proceeded to turn the children against Peter, so that they too unleashed the full force of their scorn on him.

Both partners were in part repeating patterns of love and hate established in childhood. More aware of them now, Peter is struggling to break out, particularly pained at the way these patterns have also entangled his daughters.

Bobbie's story is different. Ever alert to her New England family's constraining paradoxes, secrecy and general coldness, she vowed not to repeat the maternal saga of rectitude and self-abnegation in the face of a loveless marriage. A feminist in the seventies, defiant, she lived her life to the full. Eventually settling into marriage, she had a daughter. It seemed to suit both partners for the father, who was freelance, to be the stay-at-home parent. When the marriage ran dry, Bobbie and her partner parted amicably, against her own mother's vocal wishes. She still felt and was young, and she engaged in a series of intense, short-lived affairs, always telling at least part of the truth of them to her daughter Natasha, a bright and beautiful girl, who was herself by now adolescent and engaging in sexual encounters.

Natasha's father had remarried and proceeded to have other children who, she felt, had displaced her in his affections. Her beloved grandmother, who had helped look after her in her childhood, had died when she was fifteen. When her grandfather followed, Natasha began to develop an eating disorder: food, that bearer of mother-love, had grown tainted and she would have none of it. Once bubbly, she became austere, pure, as squeamish about female sexuality as her grandmother had been. She would, it seemed, neither compete with her mother in the sexuality stakes nor take in food, which had become as ambivalently dangerous as her mother. The latter now, paradoxically, gave up everything to tend to Natasha. Defiantly ill, Natasha had all the love and attention she both wanted and rejected. She was, she felt, the only adult in the family, while once again being a small child.

And finally, Marion. She had grown up in London, one of two children of an academic father and an artistic mother. When Marion was thirteen her mother, whom she describes as flaky and all over the place, upped and left the family to pursue her talents and a bohemian lifestyle. She also became a vociferous lesbian. In rebellion, Marion pursued fatherly ideals. She grew into a studious young woman and diligently followed a scientific path, making a name for herself in her chosen field. She left the UK for the US, where she married and had a child, bringing him up with textbook correctness; while ambitiously, though always with an unhappy edge of nervousness, making her way up the professional hierarchy. Just after her mother, with whom she maintained distant and disapproving relations, died, Marion left her husband and child. Despite the radicalism of the act, she blossomed, suddenly growing beautiful. Her loves were now other women.

A cautionary note. There are many ways of telling such stories other than by focusing on family patterns internalized in childhood and perpetuated with variations through generations. But our post-Freudian twenty-first century, with the Christian narrative at its helm and abetted by countless writers and novelists, has an (auto)biographical impetus. It is through such individual narratives of the percolations of love and lack in the family, and perhaps redemption in the setting-up of new ones, that we largely make meaning of our lives. But if the telling of stories can give the early underpinnings of life a deterministic weight, there is no absolute necessity to this, any more than there is to hereditarian or genetic discourses or explanations based on physiology or chemistry. People do break through and out. With a little self-awareness, they make new patterns out of old.

Siblings

The horizontal line in families is as formative of our loves and hates as the vertical one. The passions of children for their siblings run deep: the Egyptian myths of Isis and Osiris with their tales of murderous rivalry as well as incestuous love provide a world of early paradigms alongside the biblical stories of Jacob and Esau, Cain and Abel.

First-borns, certainly early on, can loathe the baby who arrives to displace their pre-eminence. Writing to Freud, Carl Gustav Jung reported a conversation with his four-year-old daughter, Agathli, on the evening before his son's birth. 'I asked her what she would say if the stork brought her a little brother. "Then I shall kill it," she said quick as lightning with an embarrassed, sly expression, and would not let herself be pinned down to this theme.'

My own family lore has it that just after I was born, my brother tried to smother me with a pillow, so intense was his loathing for this squalling creature who had usurped his centrality in the family. No

particular monster, he was only enacting the passion St Augustine had
so astutely observed and which finds so many instances in police annals.
A friend's four-year-old daughter, when her little sister was born, was so
palpably troubled that she did her best to imitate the newcomer who
had stolen her place at mother's breast and lap. She lost her considerable grasp of language and lolled about sucking her thumb, only
regaining age-appropriate speech when her sister began to speak.
Another friend's child decided to give her loathed and crying sibling a
good shaking. Translating into the real a gesture she often performed
with her doll, she shook her and heaved her out of her high-chair, con-
cussing her in the process.

   Freud never theorized sibling relations. But in his paper, 'A
Childhood Recollection', he focuses on a passage in Goethe's memoir
where the latter describes his pleasure at breaking the family crockery
at the instigation of friends. Freud is convinced that for the incident to
feature in Goethe's memory, it must be linked to other matter that is
screened from his view. Through a patient who had experience of the
same rebellious behaviour, but timed with the birth of a sibling, Freud
postulates that this might have been the case for Goethe, too. Dr
Eduard Hitschmann gave Freud a list of Goethe's siblings, together with
notes:

> Goethe, too, as a little boy, saw a younger brother die without regret. At
> least, according to Bettina Brentano his mother gave the following
> account: 'It struck her as very extraordinary that he shed no tears at the
> death of his younger brother Jakob who was his playfellow; he seemed
> on the contrary to feel annoyance at the grief of his parents and sisters.
> When, later on, his mother asked the young rebel if he had not been
> fond of his brother, he ran into his room and brought out from under
> the bed a heap of papers on which lessons and little stories were written,
> saying that he had done all this to teach his brother.'

Throwing the crockery out on the street, smashing it, was for Goethe,
as it was for Freud's patient, Freud concludes, a magical act which gave
violent expression to his wish to get rid of the little interloper.

   Pondering the tumult that the arrival of a new baby created in a sibling, Freud observed that the child grudged the 'unwanted intruder and rival' all the aspects of maternal care:

> It feels that it has been dethroned, despoiled, prejudiced in its rights; it casts a jealous hatred upon the new baby and develops a grievance against the faithless mother which often finds expression in a disagreeable change in its behaviour. It becomes 'naughty', perhaps, irritable and disobedient and goes back on the advances it has made towards controlling its excretions. All of this has been very long familiar and is accepted as self-evident; but we rarely form a correct idea of the strength of these jealous impulses, of the tenacity with which they persist and of the magnitude of their influence on later development. Especially as this jealousy is constantly receiving fresh nourishment in the later years of childhood and the whole shock is repeated with the birth of each new brother or sister. Nor does it make much difference if the child happens to remain the mother's preferred favourite. A child's demands for love are immoderate, they make exclusive claims and tolerate no sharing.

Yet, in time, many children do make accommodations and learn to love their siblings. The way love unfurls depends on any number of contingencies: from their own place in the family hierarchy to the new arrival's nature and, indeed, to the parents' absence and presence, as well as their actions and discourse about the children. Much of this complex nest of processes then shapes the child's relations with the rest of the world.

The early feminist sociologist Harriet Martineau, the sixth of eight children, was a frail child in a family of rambunctious boys and a scolding elder sister. When a baby sister was born, she recounts in her *Autobiographical Memoir* (1877), she resolved that 'she would never want for the tenderness which I had never found'. Her little sister became a new life to her, on whom she could lavish love. Forty years on, she still remembered 'lifting her out of her little crib, at a fortnight old, and the passionate fondness she felt for her, which has ever since "been unlike anything else"'. The child became 'a pursuit', as well as an 'attachment': through her, Martineau felt, as she told a young woman at the time, she could 'see the growth of a human mind from the very beginning'.

Simone de Beauvoir, after a first jealous phase, accommodated herself well to the fair and pretty sister, two-and-a-half years younger, whom the family nicknamed 'Poupette' or little doll. She convinced herself, with her parents' help, that the advantages of being older were many. She had her own room, a big bed, and it was she who accompanied her mother when she went to visit her father doing military service. Ever aware of rankings, little Simone thought of Poupette as 'secondary', almost a superfluous being who was always, at school and at home, being compared unfavourably to her own pre-eminence. But her sister also provided an exemplary and docile playmate, one who was ever ready to take orders from Simone, and in their secret imaginary play would enact whatever role was allotted to her. Nearly a half-century on in her *Memoirs of a Dutiful Daughter* (1959), de Beauvoir writes that she owes her sister a great debt: that of helping her 'externalize many of my dreams in play'. Poupette also saved her 'daily life from silence'. Through her, de Beauvoir took on the habit of wanting to communicate with people, a habit that stood her in good stead in her later teaching and writing life. In Poupette's presence, too, words took on meaning, but not the gravity of deeds, which words with parents did. Recounting the day's incidents and emotions to one another, 'they took on an added interest and importance'. One could speculate that de Beauvoir's later relationship with Sartre, grounded in the way they regularly 'sifted' each other's experiences and ideas, had its origins in sisterly ways.

In *The Interpretation of Dreams* (1900), Freud, ever emphatic about the jealousy of older siblings towards new arrivals, describes an early formative and intense quasi-sibling relationship with a nephew who was a year *older* than himself.

> Until the end of my third year, we had been inseparable, we had loved each other and fought each other, and this childhood relationship ... had a determining influence on all my subsequent relations with contemporaries. Since that time my nephew John has had many re-incarnations, which revived now one side and now another of his personality, unalterably fixed as it was in my unconscious memory. There must have been times when he treated me very badly and I must

have shown courage in the face of my tyrant ... All my friends have in a certain sense been re-incarnations of that first figure ... They have been 'revenants' ... My emotional life has always insisted that I should have an intimate friend and a hated enemy. I have always been able to provide myself with both, and it has not infrequently happened that the ideal situation of childhood has been so completely reproduced that friend and enemy have come together in a single individual.

Where some may re-enact early family bonds in a variety of constellations and splittings, other sibling ties may run so deep that in certain circumstances they stay together for life. In traditional societies it wasn't unusual for unmarried or widowed sisters to set up home with siblings, either as adjuncts to their families or as part of a lifelong pair. Jane Austen's sister Cassandra remained her closest friend and confidante until her death. Charles Lamb and his older sister Mary formed a lifelong near-symbiotic couple and writing team. She was his 'never-alienable' friend. He took care of her after she murdered her mother in a fit of mania, and watched over her recurrent illnesses. She in turn ran their home and the vibrant literary *salon* they held, while tending to him when his alcoholism got the better of him.

In societies where mothers died young leaving behind a brood of children, siblings often enough – and particularly, it seems, if they had been separated in childhood – formed abiding ties of love. The theme of sibling incest, of course, runs through Egyptian myth and history. In literature and recorded life, it seems to reach a peak in the Romantic moment. Two kindred souls unite, sometimes also in body, forming a love bond in which the natural world, raised to mystical heights, conspires. Bernardin de Saint Pierre's bestselling *Paul et Virginie*, which Madame Bovary reads, tells the pastoral love story of two young people raised as siblings. Byron, 'mad, bad and dangerous to know', had a passionate affair with his half-sister Augusta Leigh and fathered a child by her, an episode which fuelled the secret past of his rakish hero Manfred, who longs for his Astarte. Thomas Babington Macaulay, the great Whig historian and politician, was deeply attached to his two sisters, Margaret and Hannah. On 6 April 1831 he wrote to Margaret, 'the affection which I bear to you and Hannah is the source of the greatest enjoyment I have in the world. It is my strongest feeling. It is that which will determine the whole course of my life.' Margaret's wedding not long after this letter so affected him that, even after a year had passed, he was writing to Hannah in terms of deep dismay. 'Whether I am in London or Calcutta, she is equally lost to me. Instead of wishing to be near her, I rather shrink from it. She is dead to me, and what I see is only her ghost' (23 December 1833).

Shelley, who had no sisters, invented libidinal soulmates in *The Cenci* (1819) and *Epipsychidion*, where brother and sister unite in a transcendent union. This is the oceanic feeling raised to poetic heights.

> Let us become the overhanging day,
> The living soul of this Elysian isle,
> Conscious, inseparable, one . . .
>
> Our breath shall intermix, our bosoms bound,
> And our veins beat together; and our lips
> With other eloquence than words, eclipse
> The soul that burns between them, and the wells
> Which boil under our being's inmost cells,
> The fountains of our deepest life, shall be
> Confus'd in Passion's golden purity,
> As mountain-springs under the morning sun.
> We shall become the same, we shall be one
> Spirit within two frames, oh! wherefore two?
> One passion in twin-hearts, which grows and grew . . .

William Wordsworth and his unmarried sister, Dorothy, created a comparable lived bond. Like Mary and Charles Lamb in their loyalty to one another and in their literary intermingling, the sibling psychology at work had its own pattern. The Wordsworths' mother had died when Dorothy was seven and William eight. There were two younger brothers and another older one. Dorothy, the sole girl, was immediately sent off to live with relatives and never again saw her father, who died when she was twelve. Throughout that period she yearned to return to a home that took on increasingly idyllic proportions. Neither her mourning nor her profound longing was ever altogether acknowledged, and a sense of emptiness trailed her days, undermining her perception of her own value.

When the siblings were reunited, at first only during the boys' school holidays, William and Dorothy began to take on increasing importance for each other. Gradually, a symbiotic closeness developed, fuelled by their temperamental similarities, their conversations, their walks, their love of nature. When they set up house together in Grasmere, this in some measure reconstituted that early childhood home, for which both longed. The journal Dorothy kept was both a way of controlling her passionate nature, of subduing it, and of training herself, like a mystic, in the observation of the natural world around them. Her writing fed directly into her 'beloved' William's poetry, which she, both muse and amanuensis, noted down and transcribed for him. Intimately bound to him, when William was away Dorothy felt a threatening void open up inside her. She longed for him, yearned, with the same ardour and reverence she had for the natural life around them. This yearning which looks forward is also nostalgia for a lost state; the absences of past and present are confounded.

'It was a strange love,' Virginia Woolf, who knew not a little about sibling patterns, notes in her essay on Dorothy:

profound, almost dumb, as if brother and sister had grown together and shared not the speech but the mood, so that they hardly knew which felt, which spoke, which saw the daffodils or the sleeping city; only Dorothy stored the mood in prose, and later William came and bathed in it and made it into poetry. But one could not act without the other. They must feel, they must think, they must be together.

In 'Tintern Abbey' Wordsworth describes something of the twinship that his sibling, as attuned to nature in their ramblings as he was and perhaps even more dedicated to precise observation, provided:

For thou art with me here upon the banks
Of this fair river; thou my dearest Friend,
My dear, dear Friend; and in thy voice I catch
The language of my former heart, and read

My former pleasures in the shooting lights
Of thy wild eyes. Oh! yet a little while
May I behold in thee what I was once,
   My dear, dear Sister!

For William, arguably a great narcissist, Dorothy evokes facets of his
former self: her response to the sublime aspects of nature is directly akin
to his when he first experienced the scene.

Sibling intimacy, emotionally if not actually incestuous, here takes
on what Camille Paglia calls 'a supersaturation of identity': two become
one, blend into one another, in an apogee of romantic love. The anthropologist Claude Lévi-Strauss has pointed out, as Frances Wilson,
Dorothy's biographer, notes, that the obsession with sibling incest in the
culture of sensibility is 'at some level related to a wish, not on the existential level of a desire for mating with actual relations, but on the level
of memory and nostalgia for a primal state in which no revulsion from
incestuous acts or longings was felt'. A nostalgic yearning for an originary home, a childhood oneness, underpins all romantic passion: the
twinned souls of brother and sister may give it its ultimate expression.

However, brother-and-sister merging is no easier to maintain in the
quotidian than any other kind. The skewered power relations between
a Dorothy, who is both vulnerably sensitive and 'wild', and her idealized
poet brother call to mind, as Frances Wilson so aptly sees, the relations
between Narcissus and Echo. Dorothy's subordinate state, her inability
to conduct an independent life, has a double effect on her ways of
loving – one common enough to her time, but one which also still
lingers on, despite our own moment of greater equality. On the one
hand, like many mothers, she admirably deflects personal desires and
aspirations into altruistic care: she lives for and through her brother,
whose narcissism embraces her. But this means letting go of him so that
he can court and eventually marry her friend Mary – a treacherous
psychological business, leaving her alternately tied up in painful knots,
then emptied out. Nor, in tandem, is it easy for him to throw off her
controlling ties, both emotional and literary. After his marriage, some
have argued, Wordsworth never again matched his greatest work.

Dorothy's sometimes hidden, sometimes open, resentments boiled over or burned inwardly. Tormented while he courted Mary, she suffered from terrible migraines, grew very thin and was repeatedly ill, sometimes in synchrony with William. Talented, by many accounts exceptional, she breaks down when William and Mary finally marry. Though she may lose herself, in her mad state the one thing she never forgets is William's poetry. With few other social choices and fewer psychological ones open to her, Dorothy carried on living with her brother's family and made herself indispensable, a veritable second wife to William. Idealizing her nephew, she took out her bitterness, it seems, on the niece that was named after her, undermining the girl's evident intelligence and criticizing her pride, until this little woman, too, bowed under, and became yet another 'wife' in service to the adored family poet.

Adult sibling love, libidinal if not overtly sexual, can, like other kinds of love, tumble into hate, acknowledged or obscured.

In our own times, when siblings rarely cohabit during their elsewhere partnered lives, such passionate relations are rarer, though they may simmer beneath the surface. Older brothers rarely feel benevolent, at least at first, towards younger sisters' admirers. Sisters, particularly in youth, replay childhood rivalries and often enough steal each other's boyfriends. When parents are present, even with mature siblings, the intense emotions of childhood surface: this is what can make Christmas or other ritualized family gatherings such an ordeal. Infantilized once more in the company of parents, early patterns of jealousy, rivalry, envy and demands for love may resurface and erupt, taking everyone by surprise. The death of parents, the divvying up of possessions, exacerbate matters once more. A mother's necklace, a father's preferred painting, can take on a near-magical value, as aged toddlers scrabble over the relics of favouritism.

Good-enough parenting, the kind that allows siblings to remain affectionate, extends well beyond the grave and seems to demand the wisdom of Solomon.

Grandparents

If the family is the environment in which children first gather their sense of others – our earliest social space – then some sense of the rich palette of the real is a useful part of it. One of the reasons children so love their grandparents is that they introduce into the family an added vertical dimension, a sense of history and time, as well as a parent-plus.

For parents, grandparents may present tricky terrain to negotiate, particularly as they grow older, crotchety and dependent. Lear-like they may still insist on their primacy, and the debts of love grow heavy. But for children they introduce a rich, new, sometimes usefully quirky element into family life. Grandparents can bring a breath of much desired freedom to children suffering from a sense of enclosure within the vigilant family nest.

Recalling her grandmother, Nell Dunn writes: 'Ever since I first remember seeing my maternal grandmother I knew I was like her: that narrow face, those worried eyes. When I was about seven, she asked me who was the most important person in the world to be friends with. She eventually told me the answer was, "Yourself". I loved being with her and with my mother and my sister.' Outings with Granny are visits into an eccentric world of others. On one foray into a grand house, Dunn meets a woman who is always horizontal, because lying down 'preserves a woman's beauty'. Stories from earlier generations trickle down, describing strange, superannuated customs, other social codes, war and exile.

Though I found my own ageing mother a handful and bridled at her sense that she always knew best — that she carried on being mother even when the generational power balance had been reversed and she was the one who needed looking after — she was much loved by my children. I suspect they were more than a little pleased that their own mother wasn't an ultimate authority on everything. They listened to their gran's endless stories, loved the food she so carefully prepared for them and carried on visiting her even when dementia had got the best of her mind. Her tales gave them a lived sense of history stretching deep into that foreign country that the past is. Eventually, and in part through her, they learned a little about human vulnerability and the duty of care.

One of the reasons children can create such a deep bond with grandparents is that grandparents love them with such attentive profuseness. Having passed through that time of life which is so bound up with the travails of ambition and the daily strife of getting and spending, they have the space to focus on these new beings absolutely, but with no urgent need to shape their lives. In that sense, they're more childlike themselves. A grandmother Nell Dunn interviewed attests:

> What Cato [her grandson] gives me is the sheer pleasure of living. He reminds me that there isn't so much to it all, that actually a good breakfast, a nice walk, a new word, good weather, a new hat – everything – is just outrageously delightful, and that it's as simple as that, and all those things that take enormous effort are not necessarily where our satisfaction comes from. The greatest surprise for me is that after seeking satisfaction in so many places it can be so easy, so before my nose . . .

Grandfathers, and indeed those ageing fathers who are of grandparental age, share this sense. They have a new-found ability to play and get down on the floor with their grandchildren, as if there were nothing more important in the world, though that leisure, that freedom, that time, never existed when their own children were young. And grandparental spoiling, often free of those unwitting demands that can turn gifts into bribes when they come from parents, provides a reparative space for children.

Changing Families

Up until the Great War, traditional families were large, not only in numbers of siblings, but in their extensions. The arc of experience that children underwent was far wider than today, even though our virtual world supplies far more information about other lives. Not only grandparents, but mothers, like Dorothy and William Wordsworth's, might die while children were young. The death of siblings, too, was a regular occurrence. Ghosts were a felt presence in the family. Pain and mourning attended young life. Sometimes stepmothers appeared and produced a new brood of siblings, which brought a repeated panoply of rivalry and tensions in tow. The small child was quickly tossed into a miniature society, only partially protected by the walls of home.

Virginia Woolf's writings bring to life the storms and loves that inhabited this particular kind of extended family. Her parents had both been previously widowed. Laura, the daughter of her father Leslie Stephen's first marriage, was mentally unstable and, despite best parental efforts, was institutionalized when Virginia was nine, leaving behind her a trail of shame and grief, as well as a little relief. Virginia's beautiful mother Julia, so hauntingly evoked in *To the Lighthouse*, had three children by her first marriage, George, Stella and Gerald Duckworth. When Virginia was thirteen her mother died, followed two years later by her stepsister Stella, who had helped to look after the young ones: Virginia herself, her older sister and brother, Vanessa and Thoby, and the youngest, Adrian. Around this time, and perhaps emotionally not unconnected to it, Gerald began to molest his two stepsisters. In 'A Sketch of the Past', Virginia recalled the horror of it. 'I can remember the feel of his hands going under my clothes; going firmly and steadily lower and lower, I remember how I hoped that he would stop; how I stiffened and wriggled as his hand approached my private parts. But he did not stop.' In the same memoir she also recalls her father's rages, sinister, blind, animal, savage, though this alternates with memories of him as kindly, comforting and grandfatherly.

The range of a child's experience within the family was both painfully and blissfully broad, and bonds were formed which lasted a lifetime. Virginia and Vanessa, with all their ups and downs, remained intimate. Their parents and siblings in their various recreations people Virginia's fictions: the family had become what Wilde called 'that dear octopus from whose tentacles we never quite escape'. Indeed, one could say that the Bloomsbury circle itself was a lateral extension for the Stephens, as it was for the Stracheys, of their originary, already large family circles.

We think of our own families, today, as nuclear. Parents and adult children often live at great distances from each other. Our single child or two have a special and heightened importance. We work hard in the name of love to shield them not only from harm, but from those very conflicts and disappointments which, arguably, shape richness of character. We try to keep conjugal rows hidden or alternatively, if divorce or separation takes place, we're quick to split off good from bad, demarcating everything on one side as good and loading all the bad on to the other. Whereas, in fact, both inevitably inhabit each. The difficulty of lone parenting is simply that it takes place alone: there are no others of whatever sex or age for children to build up other allegiances with, other models of trust, other forms of argument and resolution. There can be too little sense that conflict necessarily inhabits the world inside as well as the outer world, that there are always limits to satisfaction, that frustration exists and that we can live with it and still love.

The extensions that our long lives, divorce and separation rates have introduced into our contemporary families can, for siblings, parallel those of older, traditional societies when dead parents were replaced and new broods came along. In Britain today, according to Relate, 'a third of people find themselves in a step-family at some point in their lives'. A twenty-five-year-old can easily enough have a stepbrother ten years younger, and two stepsisters from a different mother who arrive when he himself is old enough to be starting his own family. Harbouring residual anger at former partners, we may guard our children jealously and think of these extensions as part of a negative experience. Certainly, there are difficulties: ex-partners quarrel, shadow the life of the new family, cause tugs of affection, split loyalties, guilts. The very sense that one needs to fall in love with all of a new partner's familial baggage, or on a child's part that one somehow needs to love a parent's new partner, adds to the burden.

Yet from the child's point of view, these additional family members can also offer new attractions and benefits. An alternative mother or father, if wise enough not to make too many competitive demands of love or acceptance, can grow into a kind of aunt or uncle and provide the child with a different possibility of what an adult can be, perhaps even an extra ear to listen to problems. A range of step-siblings, alongside the inevitable rivalries and jealousies, can also provide new interest and give love other shapes, grow the range of affections and ways of caring.

None of it is necessarily easy. Little in our ways of loving is. Yet, for all their bad press in the annals of literature, families are the seedbeds of our social world and any hopes we have of it. It is in the family that we learn how to love and to hate and everything in between. It is here that we first experience grief and loss. It is here, too, that we learn to trust, and how to temper at least some of our rampant desires. Here, that we derive at least some of the hopes that keep our world together. When, in adolescence, as Adam Phillips writes, we become excessive, too much for ourselves, and 'definitely too much for other people, so much so that we have to leave them', we usually — even if we also find an institution, a leader or a god — also eventually discover someone else with whom we form a family.

Love in families may often be hate. Its path is pitted with misunderstandings and pain, that experience which leads to deformations of the heart. It may not offer up the immediate pleasures that passion and commodified sex advertise (though so rarely deliver through time). But it enmeshes the originary couple, their parents, their children and all the many possible extensions in ways that draw upon all sides of ourselves. Reliance, kindness, fortitude, stoicism, loyalty, generosity — all the ordinary virtues — are forged here, alongside the nether passions. And our kindred, in this atomized world, may be the only ones to follow us from cradle to grave. When they are gone, we mourn them, our love once more as idealizing as it was in childhood.

At the root of the word 'kindness' is the word 'kin'. The first definition in the *Oxford English Dictionary* for 'kindness' is 'kinship; near relationship; natural affection arising from this'. This sense of the word is obsolete, which is perhaps not altogether unrelated to our historically developed ambivalence about families — those familiars not of our own choosing. In our culture of individualism we're prone to feel queasy about the attributes of kindness, most particularly in our families, and prefer to sing of the love of strangers. But for these strangers to become friends, we have first to prime our tenderness, our fondness, our affections, our recognition of our own and others' vulnerability — our 'kindness' — in that primer that is family life, which is also the memory store of the selves we become.

PART SIX

Love and Friendship

My friends are my 'estate'. Forgive me then the avarice to hoard them.

Emily Dickinson

Friendship catapults us out of the sphere of kin and binds us into a world of others. It does so without engaging carnal passions and thus in its ideal form – if not always in the vicissitudes of the real – has a greater hope of durability. It is also one of the fundamental building-blocks of society.

The Greek word for friendship, *philia*, means 'love'. *Philia* forms part of the word 'philosophy', the love of wisdom or knowledge, and the love that informs friendship and philosophy have long walked arm in arm. Playing with the words, the French philosopher Jacques Derrida commented in an interview that this *philia* entails an 'affirmative desire towards the Other – to respect the Other, to pay attention to the Other, not to destroy the otherness of the Other'. This 'yes' to the Other – in all his or her difference and without the cannibalizing instinct which sexual desire can often bring in its train – will engage one in questioning. So the very process that underpins philosophy was also in ancient Greece a dialogue between friends who admired each other's qualities. Friendship has a high calling. It is one based on an appreciation of attributes, and in that it is markedly different from the elemental thunderbolt of passion.

Through Western history philosophers have continued to stress friendship's value. Arguably, until the twentieth century it trumped passionate love and even marriage as a desirable relation. In the ancient world, C.S. Lewis noted, 'friendship seemed the happiest and most fully human of all loves'. Edmund Burke went so far as to talk of a human instinct for sociability as fundamental as the instinct for self-preservation. Today, sociologists urge that companionship is an essential way of making good the loss of happiness regularly reported in market democracies, which have long overemphasized the dominance of the self-interested individual. The love of friends can be more enduring and satisfying than our tumultuous passions. Affectionate friends shore up the self in times of upheaval, and provide the companionship we humans can rarely do without.

So friendship remains one of the key aspects of a good life, all the more important in highly mobile times when families can be quickly dispersed. The worldwide popularity of the American sitcom *Friends* is part witness to the significance that friendship has once more taken on. The programme, which ran for ten years (1994–2004), appeared in adapted form in various countries and is repeated over and over in its original version everywhere. *Friends* became a formative model for a generation. As its creators stated in their original treatment for the series, 'When you're single and in the city, your friends are your family.' Yet in our globally interconnected times, when each of us may number thousands of 'friends' on Facebook or MySpace and 'tweet' intimate details to virtual hordes, what can friendship mean?

Adolescence has always been a time of fluctuating group cohorts, when the turbulent, isolated young mass their identities under various political or cultural banners, often to change them as quickly as they first embraced them. It is the young who maintain their virtual networks most assiduously. But quantity, in friendship as in other domains, may displace quality. Having vast numbers of 'friends' can express a very real need of friendship, masking a core loneliness and an inability to engage fully with another. 'A sign of health in the mind,' Donald Winnicott wrote in 1970, 'is the ability of one individual to enter imaginatively and accurately into the thoughts and feelings and hopes and fears of another person; also to allow the other person to do the same to us.' Even if the imagination is in some respects already a virtual sphere, exposure in words and images to a loose network is not the same as engagement with an individual who, at times, may be less than compliant. 'Better be a nettle in the side of your friend than his echo,' argued the great American transcendentalist, Frank Waldo Emerson.

Friendship in the contemporary world is further complicated by the fact that the dividing lines that used to separate the private from the

public – what you revealed to intimates and what you told the world –
have grown increasingly blurred. 'Outing' the secrets of the rich and
famous was once a matter for the tabloids. Now every man and woman
aspires to self-initiated celebrity status on a global stage. The young, in
particular, insouciantly 'share' confidences with thousands. Gossip on
the village green has become a matter of self-publicity to a network of
disembodied contacts. The bounds of the self, already conceived as shifting and unstable, grow dauntingly porous in consequence, and may
soon give us a differently constituted individual. After Freud, the ego
was unseated as master in its own house; today what is inside that
house, and what out, defies definition. This confusion about the nature
of the intimate self challenges the very nature of friendship.
Narcissistically bloated on our virtual contacts, we forget or never learn
how to 'enter imaginatively and accurately' into the world of another
and allow her or him to do the same for us. Quantity, here, may be a
sign of impoverishment.

There is more. Our competitive, individualist world of selfish genes
and narcissistic self-promotion heralds the erotic as a principal key to
the good life – even though sex can be less pleasurable than its triumphalist exposure. With this emphasis on carnal bliss as the primary
happiness to pursue, alongside wealth and ever more acquisitions, we're
in danger of emptying out what has long been that most fundamental
of human delights and the facilitator of the trust that binds society:
loving friendship. Thomas Jefferson, the very man who enshrined the
'pursuit of happiness' as an inalienable right in the Declaration of
Independence, also noted: 'The happiest moments [my heart] knows are
those in which it is pouring forth its affections to a few esteemed characters.' If the pursuit of happiness has made a great many unhappy, it
may be that what we have pinpointed as happiness and the good life is
simply mistaken.

The Most Fully Human of All Loves

In French, as in other Romance languages, the words for love and friendship – *amour* and *amitié* – share a common root in the word for soul – *âme*.

The *Oxford English Dictionary* gives as its primary definition for the word 'love' not the feelings we associate with passion, but those which characterize friendship: 'A feeling of deep affection or fondness for someone, typically arising from a recognition of attractive qualities, from natural affinity, or from sympathy, and manifesting itself in concern for the other's welfare and pleasure in his or her presence'.

Indeed, loving friendship, a meeting of souls, was long thought a far more significant bond than the kind of love that involved carnal relations. An attachment of soul or mind trumped one based on self-gratifying sexual desire in whatever configuration. After Darwin and Freud, we've grown suspicious of such ties: all love tends to appear as rampant reproductive urge or camouflaged desire and its distortion. Yet neither Darwin nor Freud would have welcomed a human world where love was reduced to mere reproductive drive or blind instinct. After all, as Adam Phillips has written, 'We depend on each other not just for our survival but for our very being. The self without sympathetic attachments is either a fiction or a lunatic.'

Given the importance of loving friends, it's worth pausing over some of the classical and humanist ideals of friendship and exploring how they have shifted through time.

In his *Rhetoric* (367–322 BC) Aristotle, that most capacious of early philosophers, defines the activity involved in *philia*, or friendship, as wishing for the friend 'what you believe to be good things, not for your own sake but for his, and being inclined, so far as you can, to bring these things about'. Mutual well-doing, here, is a fundamental good.

Philia can, of course, exist between lovers, kin, cities, fellow voyagers, soldiers, neighbours. But in its highest form, as Aristotle interrogates it in the last two books of his *Nicomachean Ethics* (350 BC), genuine friendship is more than either pleasurable conviviality or mutual usefulness, or indeed relations of respect or care. Genuine friendship is itself a virtue *and* a relationship involving virtue. Even more than generosity, wit, truthfulness and intelligence, friendship is something that we would not choose to live without, 'for no one would choose to live without friends, even if he had all the other goods'. Friendship is core to our happiness. For Aristotle, it is the happiest and most fully human of all loves, the apogee of life and the very school of virtue.

Arriving at this genuine friendship, which assumes equality and character as its base, is a matter not only of acts, but of reciprocal words, of getting to know each other through shared conversation. In his fascinating gloss on Aristotle in *Cities of Words* (2004), Stanley Cavell writes that the highest form of friendship comes into being by 'granting and overcoming inequalities as [the friends] study themselves in each other . . . The friend becomes, as it were, my next self.' And at the heart of this friendship is conversation: 'friends are each other's pasture, providing indispensable food for thought'. And this thinking together, Cavell goes on to say, is a stepping-stone to the constitution of political life: 'Listening to each other, speaking one's judgment with a point that matters to others who matter to you, is the condition of the formation of a *polis*, the reason Aristotle makes language the condition of the highest of human formations.' So through friendships incorporating conversations about what might be involved in living the good life, we develop a shared idea of the good and how to pursue it. With loving friends we envision the kind of society we want and develop our hopes of it.

Making liberal use of earlier philosophers, the Roman statesman and orator Cicero wrote a major analysis of friendship, *De Amicitia* (c. 44 BC). Here, it is a given that friendship can only truly exist between 'worthy' men, and can be a matter of neither self-interest nor profit since the friend is a second self: 'For everyone loves himself, not with a view of acquiring some profit himself from his self-love, but because he is dear to himself on his own account; and unless this same feeling were transferred to friendship, the real friend would never be found; for he is, as it were, another self.' In view of the instability and perishableness of mortal things, Cicero continues, we should be continually on the lookout for some person to love and by whom to be loved, 'for if goodwill and affection are taken away, every joy is taken from life'.

The Christian exhortation to 'love thy neighbour as thyself ' grows out of such classical treatments of friendship to become *caritas*, or benevolence. The generalization from a particular and worthy friend to a universal rule, while attempting to bind society in kindness, arguably hollowed out some of the value of individual friendship. With Jesus as a friend, it's not clear that others can make the grade. Then, too — as the

French psychoanalyst Jacques Lacan quipped – the injunction to love thy neighbour as thyself must be ironical, since it's quite clear that people hate themselves. Arguably, they may have hated themselves less before selfishness – having become, with Thomas Hobbes, an irrefutably universal, though unlovely, attribute – grew into capitalist modernity's defining driving force.

Montaigne, that most astute and self-analytically modern of Renaissance thinkers, left Christianity out of his essay 'on affectionate friendship' – a relationship he valued above all other loves. His thoughts on *parfaite amitié* are based on his own bond with the political philosopher Étienne de la Boétie, cut short by the latter's early death at the age of thirty-three. The loss haunted Montaigne throughout his life and he carried on championing his friend's controversial writings. He compares this affectionate friendship with other kinds of love – familial, carnal, marital. He reflects that the 'congruity and affinity' that existed between himself and La Boétie made for greater love than is usual between brothers or between fathers and sons. Kin may be 'of totally different complexions'. Their needs and ours 'must frequently bump and jostle against each other'. Commanded by both law and nature, familial affections also have less 'willing freedom' about them. Put simply, you don't choose your family.

The passion men feel for women, though also born of choice, suffers in comparison to friendship. Montaigne speaks as a connoisseur of Eros's darts and flames. 'Sharp and keen' they may be, but they are 'only a mad craving for something which escapes us': subject to 'attacks and relapses', passionate bodily love soon gives way to satiety. Friendship has none of this fickleness. It is a meeting of minds which lasts beyond the death of a friend. And in the practice of friendship, souls are purified, nourish each other and grow.

As for marriage, Montaigne is pragmatic about its limits. Unlike affectionate friendship, marriage is a bargain struck for other purposes. Nor are women, he reasons, normally able to respond to the 'familiarity and mutual confidence' that friendship feeds on. They are simply, it seems, not educated enough: if they were, the possibility of a union of soul and body – where the whole human being is involved – would indeed be a 'perfect love', a *parfaite amitié*. And though he holds up the union of body and soul as the highest form of love, Montaigne brushes aside the ancient world's example of homosexual union. Not only is it 'rightly abhorrent to our manners', he writes, but in its practice by the Greeks, the disparity of age and favours made it an unequal form of love. Did any of the Greeks fall in love with a youth who was ugly or with a beautiful old man? No. The friendship Montaigne cherishes is more equal, equable and equitable: 'souls are mingled and confounded in so universal a blending that they efface the seam which joins them together'.

Montaigne's thinking on affectionate friendship between men, its equality and permanence, emerged as something of a humanist ideal at a period when the feudal family and kinship networks were losing their hold and modern notions of individuality were in the making. A male friend becomes the trusted second self, the other through whom individual identity can be mirrored, measured and constituted. And as in so many other spheres, women hardly figure in these reflections on friendship: bound as they are, legally and socially, to fathers and husbands, they haven't the freedom to be considered as equal 'others' who can be true friends. There is something of a historical irony here. As a ruthless capitalism takes hold in the nineteenth century and the solitary conquistadorial male emerges as hero, the affections are gendered female: 'true' friendship, grounded in conversation, gradually and increasingly becomes women's sphere.

Without friends, 'the world is but a wilderness', Francis Bacon, that keen observer of men and matter, both statesman and philosopher of science, wrote in his essay 'Of Friendship' (1612). A vivid fear of loneliness colours Bacon's essay: man alone, without fit society, topples from reason into brute animality. Those unfit for affection and friendship are more akin to beasts than humans. 'It is a mere and miserable solitude to want true friends.' Bacon's is an uneasy, changing world where familial as well as political instability haunts all relations. Shifts in power abut on instrumental friendships and clubbable associations, one-time friends are ostracized in preference for the new. Cities may burgeon, but 'a crowd is not company'. Bacon's thinking seems already to herald the insecure world that his last amanuensis, Thomas Hobbes, brings to life in *Leviathan*, that reflection on legitimate government written during the strife of the English Civil War.

Like some contemporary therapist urging the advantages of talk to purge discordant passions, Bacon underscores the healing value of friendship:

A principal fruit of friendship, is the ease and discharge of the fulness and swellings of the heart, which passions of all kinds do cause and induce. We know diseases of stoppings, and suffocations, are the most dangerous in the body; and it is not much otherwise in the mind; you may take sarza [sarsaparilla] to open the liver, steel to open the spleen, flowers of sulphur for the lungs, castoreum [secretion of castor sacs] for the brain; but no receipt openeth the heart, but a true friend; to whom you may impart griefs, joys, fears, hopes, suspicions, counsels, and whatsoever lieth upon the heart to oppress it, in a kind of civil shrift or confession.

A friend, it seems, is superior to a priest. Not only does the 'communicating of a man's self to his friend' redouble joy and cut grief in half, but a friend also engages one in the kind of argument that clarifies thought. This second fruit of friendship 'is healthful and sovereign for the understanding', just as the first is for the affections. 'For friendship maketh indeed a fair day in the affections, from storm and tempests; but it maketh daylight in the understanding, out of darkness, and confusion of thoughts.' Furthermore, if a friend can provide wise counsel, he can also act as a better second self. He can deputize for one, speak one's case and one's merits to others. He can often do so more objectively and persuasively than one can oneself, particularly where one's existing role, such as husband or father, clouds vision. With a true friend, a man can also rest secure 'that the care of his works will continue after him'.

Shakespeare probes this humanist ideal of friendship on stage. Hamlet and Horatio, Prince Hal and Falstaff, provide two distinct trajectories.

Horatio is Hamlet's only confidant. Self-avowedly 'more an antique Roman than a Dane' (V.ii.346), he has the classical attributes of learning, bravery, virtue and good judgement. He is not afraid to stand up to the ghost and question him in the opening scene. He listens to Hamlet's tortured thoughts and emotions with marked sympathy and self-control. By acting as a reliable witness to Hamlet's extremes, Horatio enables us to enter into them without judging Hamlet too harshly. Trusting Hamlet, he allows us to trust the Prince as well. It is Horatio's sound philosophy that anchors Hamlet's searing consciousness of self and world.

'Horatio, thou art e'en as just a man/ As e'er my conversation cop'd withal' (III.ii.56–7), Hamlet says, admiring in him the stoicism and strength of mind he himself does not possess. A little later, he adds:

> Give me that man
> That is not passion's slave, and I will wear him
> In my heart's core, ay, in my heart of heart,
> As I do thee. (III.ii.65–70)

Hamlet's libidinal attachment to Ophelia and to his mother propels disaster, but his friendship with Horatio lasts beyond his own death. Horatio's loyalty is such that as Hamlet lies dying, he is prepared – out of duty and honour – to take his own life. Hamlet dissuades him. 'Report me and my cause aright/ To the unsatisfied,' he pleads.

> If thou didst ever hold me in thy heart
> Absent thee from felicity awhile,
> And in this harsh world draw thy breath in pain,
> To tell my story. (V.ii.357–60)

And good Horatio will, indeed, be Hamlet's representative, bearing his voice to the world and explaining Hamlet's actions after his death. It is he who judiciously apprises rash Fortinbras, Prince of Norway, of the 'plots and errors' that have led to this sorry tragedy. By doing so, he fulfils the bonds of ideal friendship and reinstates Hamlet's 'noble heart'.

If this is Shakespeare's portrait of classical friendship at its best, then Prince Hal and Falstaff in *Henry IV* Part 1 provide its counterpart in what the critic Allan Bloom has called a 'parody of Aristotelian friendship'. Rather than augment his young friend's virtue, Bacchic Falstaff, no equal, educates him in vice. Prince Hal's honour is restored only once he rejects his Rabelaisian friend. Yet the rejection is not effected without

some regret. When Hal believes Falstaff dead towards the end of the first
part of their conjoined dramas, he mourns:

> What, old acquaintance! Could not all this flesh
> Keep a little life? Poor Jack, Farewell!
> I could have better spar'd a better man. (V.iv.102–4)

A better man would not have provided Prince Hal with half the school
of common, yet excessive, life that Falstaff brings to him. If not quite an
ageing sage in a Socratic, homoerotic academy, Falstaff does gives Hal
some of the demotic wherewithal with which to rule in unruly times.

In their pairing, Shakespeare offers an early instance of those friendships with charismatic others that characterize the turbulence of
adolescence. Forged in the sowing of wild oats, formed in companion-
able activity more than through conversation, such friendships may
end when the responsibilities of more sedate maturity call. Yet, for all
that, they remain emblazoned on the mind. And Falstaff, in some measure Prince Hal's libidinal alter, provides a necessary transitional
identification for the man who would be King, the responsible ruler
whose body symbolically incorporates the many aspects of the state.

With the growth of cities and the development of a competitive commercial and industrial society, new pressures and pleasures attended
friendship, as did new configurations of loving. In *The Wealth of Nations*
(1776) Adam Smith worried that the increased division of labour in
manufacture would have a damaging impact on relationships and
impoverish human personality. Alone in an impersonal city, the poor
labourer would be 'sunk in obscurity and darkness'. Unobserved by
friends or family, he would begin to neglect himself and his conduct.
Friendship, Smith suggests, provides a mirroring effect, that recognition which bolsters character and a sense of self-worth. For the
lonely urbanite, Smith urged the joining of associations and
churches. Here companionship and mutual purpose would provide
the solitary with the recognition that strengthens the self. Social
policy planners today mirror such thinking and insistently align
friendship with well-being.

Concerned by the decline in civic and communal spirit that a newly market-driven society based on contract might engender, Adam Ferguson, a leading figure in the Scottish Enlightenment, stressed that benevolence was a primary source of human happiness. Malice, fear, envy, greed, jealousy, all the nether emotions prompted by rivalrous competition, he argued, promoted no felicity. 'To abstain from harm, is the great law of natural justice,' he wrote in his *Essay on the History of Civil Society* (1767), 'to diffuse happiness is the law of morality.' Loving friendship came high on Ferguson's list of social goods. Stressing the sociability of human nature, he draws on Pope's pithy formulation in the *Essay on Man*: 'Man, like the generous vine, supported lives;/ The strength he gains, is from th'embrace he gives.'

For David Hume, who based his ethics on feeling rather than on abstract moral principles, urban life offered more optimistic prospects than it did for Ferguson. The city, after all, fostered 'urbanity', a growth of a new sociability and politeness. Friendship and kindness sparked more of the same. Human psychology, Hume observed, was character-ized by a reciprocal flow of passions. Sympathy with another led to love and to the good of social benevolence:

It is remarkable, that nothing touches a man of humanity more than any instance of extraordinary delicacy in love or friendship, where a person is attentive to the smallest concerns of his friend, and is willing to sacrifice to them the most considerable interest of his own ... The pas-sions are so contagious, that they pass with the greatest facility from one person to another, and produce correspondent movements in all human breasts. Where friendship appears in very signal instances, my heart catches the same passion, and is warmed by those warm senti-ments, that display themselves before me. Such agreeable movements must give me an affection to every one that excites them.

This is the case with every thing that is agreeable in any person. The transition from pleasure to love is easy: But the transition must here be still more easy; since the agreeable sentiment, which is excited by sym-pathy, is love itself; and there is nothing required but to change the object. Hence the peculiar merit of benevolence in all its shapes and appearances.

Known as the great enlightening Age of Reason, the eighteenth century in its last four decades is also often dubbed in England the Age of Sensibility. After the long civil unrest and the wars of the previous century, overseen by a dour, punishing and omnipresent God, peace broke out and the heavens gave way to a newly interpreted, kinder, more distant and reasonable deity, happy to allow his subjects to get on with the pursuit of science, to dream more equitable regimes, do business, and engage in affectionate, companionate marriage. The times emphasized the faculty of feeling as a mark of civilization. Sensibility was understood as the capacity for refined emotion. It was both a physical, sometimes sexual, susceptibility *and* a mental and moral one. A quickness in displaying compassion was seen as a good, as was reflecting on sentiment. Generous hearts were praised, as were quick minds and tongues.

Exaggerated, however, sensibility could topple over into its own parody. The adjectives used to describe it change as the century turns. Janet Todd charts the movement from Addison's 'exquisite sensibility', Hume's 'delicate sensibility' and Sterne's 'dear sensibility' to Austen's 'acute', Coleridge's 'mawkish' and Byron's 'sickly'.

Friendship was extolled throughout the period, between and across the sexes. Wives and women, too, could now be friends. Amorous friendships flourished in the French Enlightenment *salons*, sometimes drifting into the realm of the sexual but often enough stopping short at the pleasures of flirtatious conversation. For the early Romantics, feeling, fellowship and friendship ranked equally high, whatever their extolling of the sublimities of solitude. The young poets banded together, worked and argued and created a movement in the same way, if not with the same effect, that the Revolutionaries had done across the English Channel. At their gatherings Mary and Charles Lamb entertained a host of artists, politicians and poets, Coleridge amongst them. Letters teemed, extending affectionate and intellectual dialogue in times of absence. Goethe wrote thousands, dedicating some three hours before the start of the working day to correspondence. Bettina von Arnim poured out her rebellious heart to the poet-scientist-statesman, who was some thirty-five years her senior: published, her letters influenced Emerson and the tenor of American transcendentalism. Voltaire's letters – witty, amorous, philosophical and, yes, networking – fill 102 volumes.

In her subtle essay on the long, often rebarbative, friendship between two of America's founding fathers, John Adams and Thomas Jefferson, Judith Shklar probes the way different kinds of political regime colour the nature of friendship. Despotisms and civil unrest, she argues, foster the 'one soul in two bodies' kind of friendship, such as Montaigne describes in his *amitié parfaite* with La Boétie. The friends form a 'private polity', a 'moral universe' in which 'freedom and spontaneity reign while oppression and hypocrisy are the universal rule in the larger society'. If your friend is in trouble with the law, since there is an affinity between friends not just of feelings and opinions but of personality, the claims of friendship trump the claims of the state. 'To love one's friends more than one's rulers may be morally and emotionally the one way to have a worthwhile life at all.'

Free societies, in which friends may in the course of a lifetime take up different political causes, produce potentially combative friendships. Many may fail irreparably in the contest between private affection and political will or expedience. Adams and Jefferson, though temperamentally altogether dissimilar, maintained a friendship that was forged in politics and later became personal, despite a falling-out that lasted a dozen years. After both had retired, the two old gentlemen began a correspondence which, though it skirted an intimacy that the more passionate Adams may have wished and the more restrained Jefferson resisted, built an ever closer friendship grounded in 'affection, common memories, shared experiences, and continued lively interest in books and ideas'.

At its start, Jefferson having joked of his 'senile garrulity', Adams responds: 'My Senectutal Loquacity has more than retaliated your Senile Garrulity.' They discuss politics, grandchildren, walks, books, and agree to disagree on religion and much else. They could love one another despite their divergent views. Towards the end, on 15 February 1825, Jefferson, ever the composed eighteenth-century gentleman, signs off a letter with 'Nights of rest to you and days of tranquillity are the wishes I tender you with my affect[iona]te respects.' They died on the same day, the Fourth of July 1826, fifty years to the day after their finest hour, the signing of the Declaration of Independence.

Female Friends

It may come as something of a surprise at a time when the ability to relate is specifically gendered female that women were long thought – by men, of course – too frivolous, fickle and lacking in that refined moral sense which would permit the highest forms of virtuous friendship, based on steadfastness and intelligence. But gradually, intimate friendship, like all affairs of the heart, was feminized. By the Victorian era, men's friendships largely revolve around the companionship of clubs, pubs or workplace, or the solidarity of politics, soldiering or trade unions. The dominant image of an emotionally reticent and competitive masculinity, armoured in duties and cares, in part fearful of any homoerotic current, leaves less space for Montaigne's idealized *amitié parfaite*, with its mutual intimate outpourings of mind and heart.

Amongst women, this note of intimate revelation continues into our own time. Both the first and second waves of the women's movement gave a particular emphasis to female friendships, bonding women in a solidarity of shared bodies, shared problems and shared interests. The 'sisterhood is powerful' moment of the 1970s both allowed and encouraged women to love one another in a new way, by also learning to love themselves. Shaking off the stigma that historical secondariness had imposed on them, they revealed their fears and lacks, the shaming matter of their needs, the details of sexual and power relations, in consciousness-raising groups or in female friendships which sometimes extended into sexual terrain. Solidarity was forged.

By the 1980s women were widely considered to be more emotionally aware and articulate, more capable of reciprocity, and just better at the whole domain of relationship, than men. This female 'specialization' in emotion, held to have grown out of women's childhood conditioning in the need to please and nurture, to listen and be attentive to others, to intuit and empathize, to mask their own needs and desires and put the other first – all characteristics Simone de Beauvoir attributed to women's secondary status – did indeed make them more attentive to friends and the whole tangled business of relating to others.

In *Between Women*, Luise Eichenbaum and Susie Orbach characterized the social agility that attends an encounter between two women who find they share a mutual interest.

> Their conversation takes account of the emotional climate of the subject matter. Thoughts and feelings about work, children, husbands, boyfriends, lovers, about mothers, entertaining, cooking, politics, sex, music, about aspirations, sports, fashion, suffuse their conversation. Their emotions are intrinsic to the contact. They make up a patois – a distinctively women's language. Confidences are readily and easily shared, assumptions made about difficult emotional states, disappointments acknowledged, and solutions sought. Women unguardedly confide in each other with an ease that often astounds men. Sharing is not a concession, a particularly difficult struggle, an extraction; rather it is part and parcel of women's relating. It is second nature, a habit, a way of being. *Not* sharing feels odd, a holding back that feels almost like a betrayal.

Compassion, sympathy and identification, the authors note, are core elements of all women's relationships, which are often considered to be primary ones, outlasting sexual entanglements or even marriage. But this special ability to relate doesn't inevitably trump envy, jealousy and anger whenever lovers, competition or problems at work enter the picture. These, indeed, are the subjects that *Between Women*, written at a time that was already considered 'post-feminist', explores. A single woman may envy her married friend's stable family and children, while the latter envies the first's sexual adventures. In the workplace, competition is rife. A woman hitherto supported by her colleagues is shunned or attacked, once she proves successful. A powerful public woman can provide a role model, someone to emulate, but can also arouse hostility in other women, quick to vote or talk her down. Single women or indeed single parents, who depend on friendships far more than coupled ones, find themselves lonely and aggrieved over too-long weekends and holidays spent on their own. The attendant anger, often hidden, is hard to bear.

Sadly, too, sociologists have recently observed that once women are as much engaged as men in the workplace and in careers, the business of juggling work, family and friends becomes as difficult for them as it has long been for men. Gender stereotypes are rarely altogether stable, nor wholly consistent.

Friendship, though not always as intensely as passion, has ever been subject to our unruly emotions and riven by conflict and split loyalties. Long tied to lives which centred on the home, with a primary duty to father, husband and children, women would sometimes engage in intimate friendships only to betray them – then, when circumstances changed, take them up again. In Shakespeare's *As You Like It*, Celia abandons her tyrannical father to stay true to her best friend, Rosalind. In *A Midsummer Night's Dream*, the friendship between Hermia and Helena is ruptured by love entanglements. Rivalry in the marriage market and abandonment of friends on account of the calls of sexual passion, or estrangement through the cares of marriage, are constant themes in life as in literature. For women who didn't marry or whose marriages were ended by the death of the husband, long-lost or ever present friends might provide fine living companions. 'Boston marriages' – committed partnerships which may or may not have had an active sexual component – became common as soon as women developed some legal and financial independence. Henry James's novel *The Bostonians* (1886), in part inspired by his sister Alice's experience, gave birth to the term used to describe a relationship in which two 'new women' engage in a friendship which is also a living arrangement.

Jane Austen's life and work provide a panorama of female friendships. After her father died, she, her sister, mother and Martha Lloyd, a long-time friend, set up quarters together – an arrangement which provided companionship and also helped stretch their always limited finances. When young, the teenage girls had frolicked, danced and read together, and also schooled themselves in that feminine religion of self-denial. Jane was later at times in awe of Martha's selfless virtue in 'physicking little children' and providing 'mental physick' for the ailing old, though she never could altogether restrain herself from gentle mockery of her own and others' all-too-human ways: she might have garnered a rather good scene out of the fact that, ten years after her death, ever single Martha, at the age of sixty-three, married Jane's widowed brother Frank.

Female friends tumble through Jane Austen's fiction, taking a trait here and there from the women in her own entourage. Her older and adventurous cousin Eliza, Comtesse de Feuillide, whose French husband met his end on the guillotine, brought foreign climes to the parsonage. Her character echoes in the slightly corrupt urbanity of Mary Crawford in *Mansfield Park* and in the vivacity of an Elizabeth Bennet.

Lizzy herself has an intimate friend in Charlotte Lucas, a serious young woman, slightly older, with whom she shares confidences and argument. In part, the women rely on this kind of exchange to work out who they are and what they think. But their views on marriage and the suitability or not of partners diverge: when Charlotte, already twenty-eight and facing the prospect of a single and impoverished future, accepts an offer from fawning Mr Collins, a man Lizzy knows she doesn't respect, the two women fall out. Lizzy's aunt, older and wiser, provides the receptive ear of friendship and sound advice and support in Charlotte's stead.

Displacing her own ambivalence about marriage, Jane Austen's Emma concentrates on finding a husband for her new friend Harriet, mistakenly importing her own class bias – and her naivety about passion as well, perhaps, as an unconscious jealousy – into singling out unsuitable partners.

Amongst Austen's juvenilia is the burlesque, *Love and Friendship*, written when she was fourteen and signalling the centrality of friends, despite the overarching importance of marriage to the women's lives. Here, she takes several digs at the culture of over-heightened sensibility. When the heroine, Laura, elopes with penniless Edward, she is more than grateful, having been 'deprived during the course of three weeks of a real friend', to find Sophia at the house where she and her new husband arrive:

Sophia was rather above the middle size; most elegantly formed. A soft languor spread over her lovely features, but increased their Beauty. – It was the Charectarestic [sic] of her Mind – . She was all Sensibility and Feeling. We flew into each others arms and after having exchanged vows of mutual Friendship for the rest of our Lives, instantly unfolded to each other the most inward Secrets of our Hearts –.

The satire, of course, takes as its butt the self-indulgent sentimentality and spurious instant emotion of the popular novelettes of the time, as well as the effusions of fashionable teenagers in their friendships. Some things at least seem not altogether to have changed. Austen's understanding and views on female friendship are no more uniform than they are on love and marriage. Sometimes malice and envy dominate, as in Miss Bingley's hypocritical friendship with Jane; sometimes there is genuine engagement, as between Charlotte and Lizzy.

In *A Room of One's Own*, Virginia Woolf bemoaned the fact that literature largely gives us women ever and always 'lit by the capricious and coloured light of the other sex'. Men's fantasies of women, as objects of love, of sexual attraction, or of hate, inevitably dominate novels by men. She asks us to imagine how impoverished literature as a whole would be if men were only lovers, and never 'the friends of men, soldiers, thinkers, dreamers'. She allows, however, that Jane Austen and Charlotte Brontë gave us more capacious women, women as friends.

Indeed, Charlotte Brontë offers a portrayal of a singularly formative friendship – the one between schoolgirls. The intimacy between Jane Eyre and Helen Burns, who is fourteen to Jane's ten at their school, Lowood, delineates that process of identification with a friend which is so crucial to the eventual shaping of the woman she becomes.

Orphan Jane comes to Lowood, having suffered the injustice of her Aunt Reed's punishing treatment. Lonely, spirited, desperate to be loved, Jane's rebellious soul is partially tempered by gentle, daydreaming Helen, who has deep faith in a benevolent almighty Father, a parent for the lonely or orphaned children the girls are. From her faith Helen draws a talent for endurance. After Brocklehurst, the vindictive headmaster of Lowood, shames Jane in front of the whole school by depicting her as a lying ungrateful wretch, she reveals her sad trajectory of arbitrary sufferings to her new and supportive best friend. Helen's recognition of Jane as the wrongly calumnied being she is, soothes and bolsters her. In the process, Jane also learns how to be a little more like her friend. When Helen dies in her arms, it is as if Jane has taken into herself some of her loving friend's qualities. Helen's good-natured patience will abet Jane's survival in a world which is less than amiable to impoverished single women. What Brontë brings to light in this depiction of a friendship between schoolgirls is the way in which friends shape the individuals that we are.

Shaping Friendships

Psychoanalysts think of personality as being constituted through a series of identifications. Like Jane with Helen, the subject – unconsciously and rarely without ambivalence – assimilates an attribute or an aspect of another and is thereby partly transformed according to the model the other provides. Growing up, the child takes in various properties of its parents – gestures, habits of mind, ways of seeing the world and their own bodies and genders. Close friendships with admired others play a significant part in this process of shaping personality. If the friend, or indeed a lover, dies, is lost for ever, the incorporation of the friend (or lover) can have a more fundamental impact: they become part of one. The death of La Boétie seems to have had this kind of effect on Montaigne. Montaigne internalized his friend and continued to carry on 'a conversation' with him throughout his life. They had indeed become one.

In *The Psychology of Women*, the analyst Helene Deutsch draws on the case of a woman she names 'Mrs Smith' to explore the workings of a particular kind of remedial identification between friends. Mrs Smith was incapable of bringing a pregnancy to term. She had had numerous miscarriages and suffered a stillbirth when a baby was born a month too early. The problem, as Deutsch saw it, was that Mrs Smith's 'identification with her aggressive mother had filled her with almost conscious horror': this made taking on female matter problematic. Also, her mother had wanted a son, and the birth of her daughter had been met with long-term hostility.

Mrs Smith was eventually able to have a child, but only by the intercession of a friend with whom she could identify – a friend who had a mother whose maternal warmth embraced both of the younger women. In her memoir, Deutsch makes it clear that Mrs Smith is in fact herself. By a happy coincidence, she and her friend, 'a goddess of serenity', had become pregnant at around the same time. An identification with her meant 'my motherhood changed its character. Through a psychological impact on biological forces, my desire for a child was fulfilled.' Her friend gave birth one month later than she had expected, just when Deutsch's pregnancy had reached full term.

We develop, become the adults we are, with and through others – both real and imaginary. Even when they have real playmates, toddlers invent imaginary friends who sustain them. They become partners in pretend play, serve as vehicles for elaborating their fears and desires, provide a repository for secrets and wish-fulfilments, as well as help them to differentiate between right and wrong. They also help them to deal with problems and with loneliness: fantasy, after all, is one of the ways humans have of making good the stresses and strains of everyday life. One little girl who played the piano a lot was accompanied by Mozart, Beethoven and a musical retinue when she went off to pre-school. A three-year-old boy, who had just had a baby sister, invented an older brother for himself, who kept him fine company while his mother focused on the new arrival.

In a recent UK study, eighteen hundred children were asked about their past or present experience of fantasy friends. Forty-eight per cent had one or had had several. These children, as well as many observed by other researchers, displayed greater creativity than their peers, were more competent at language, were better able to imagine the minds of others and read their expressions – were in other words better at making 'real' friends and better at relations with adults. They also had a better grasp of symbolic thought, important to their subsequent intellectual abilities.

In one gender-based study, researchers found that while girls tend to 'have' a companion, boys tended to 'be' their companions. In other words, rather than having Spiderman as their friend, they became him. Boys also tended to make their imaginary companions better at everything, stronger, more powerful; while the little girls made their friends less strong and powerful, and then helped them. Since children take their cues from the culture around them, it's unsurprising that even where imaginary friends are concerned they fall into our time's stereotypes: women today are still valued for the care they can provide, while what is demanded of men is action and power.

Our epoch affords increasing possibilities for virtual make-believe. Individuals well past toddlerdom can fantasize any number of personalities for themselves while interacting with cyber-friends. We celebrate numerous remakings of the self, masquerade the performance of various gender identities and metrosexuality. In this environment, some psychoanalysts have begun to say that they are seeing an increasing number of 'as if' personalities in their consulting rooms: people who mimic others wholesale, imitate what they latch on to outside themselves, rather than identifying in an imaginative and reciprocal way. In other words, they don't engage. They simply repeat or double others, passively don personae without ever building up any emotional links. In one case, a man becomes a lawyer after having befriended a successful advocate. When that relationship ceases, he happens on a sailor and joins the merchant navy, and so on, without ever querying or doubting his choices and actions. Breakdown can ensue when the object of their imitation disappears. This distortion of personality is akin to what Winnicott calls a 'false self' — a self built in utter compliance with the environment, with deprivation at its genesis. If 'human kind/ Cannot bear very much reality', as T.S. Eliot says in the first of his *Four Quartets*, 'Burnt Norton', too much fantasy leads to its own forms of suffering.

Past toddlerdom, virtual friendships have the potential for encasing us in prolonged immaturity. We over-idealize our 'imaginary friends', provide them with 'angels' wings': they're easy to love since they don't frustrate us by not complying with our wishes in the way that embodied others do. When the latter are engaged with and then, being real, inevitably thwart our grandiose desires and expectations of them, love too quickly turns to hate. People lash out, unable to control their impulses and their rage. Anxiety can set in. This latter can also be a defence against a sense of fundamental weakness: the helpless inner child has never grown up enough to bear the contrariness of really existing others.

For Better or for Worse

The friendships of the years after toddlerhood provide the first we can fully remember. Like first loves, they imprint themselves on us. A best friend becomes someone we can share with and be recognized by. She or he can also possess wished-for aspects of ourselves: abundant curly hair, the ability to ride or swim or to talk back to teacher. Her family may present a hugely informative contrast to our own – an at-home or working mother, brothers, pictures on the walls, books, exotic food. The friend's family can indeed be a major component of the 'bestness' of our friend. Alternative models of love and living arrangements stretch the child's vision of the world and may also provide succour if life is difficult at home.

In the flux of the playground, early friendships also mark out our first wounds outside the home. The rivalries of school, the loss of best friends, the pain of rupture, may play into our sense of injustice: a demand for equal treatment for all.

During those labile and libidinally charged years which are adolescence, the young grow notoriously promiscuous in their friendships, locating in each often short-lived relationship something that they lack and as a result idealize in the other and will defiantly defend if they encounter parental opposition. Winnicott attributes this to the fact that teenagers are basically 'isolates', in part repeating a stage of earliest omnipotent, excited, yet utterly helpless infancy, before the recognition of fully existing others had come into being. In an essay entitled 'Adolescence: Struggling through the Doldrums', he notes that adolescence is characterized by a radical combination of 'defiant independence and regressive dependence', the rapid alternation between these states, and 'even a coexistence of the two extremes at one moment in time' – a description struggling parents will recognize.

These isolates collect together, finding comfort in shifting numbers. Themselves as yet unformed, without moorings, yet propelled to break away from the family, they find their anchors in a group where identities are forged on the basis of partial identifications. A shared activity or interest, love of a particular band or star, a mutual interest in a political issue, a mutual injustice, provides a group identity, often under a leader who, as Freud might say, represents an ego ideal, a combination of the desired characteristics. In the aura of the charismatic leader or the cultural ideal, individual rivalries can be put to rest. Pop stars often serve the purpose admirably.

Winnicott also posits that in the libidinal defiance of the adolescent there is an antisocial core, which most young won't live out for themselves in any radical way. But if a member of their group is indeed wildly antisocial, 'delinquent', and enacts a 'crime', they will bond around him, since he has given expression to their defiance. Through his act, they 'feel real'. Even if individually they may not approve of the act, they will remain loyal to him and defend him.

Like all our emotional attachments, early friendships have their dark sides and bitter sequelae. Pre-adolescent groupings, like later ones, are often consolidated by marking out an enemy or a scapegoat on whom all our own undesirable or spurned characteristics – our very helplessness – are projected. The narcissism of small differences takes hold: tiny divergent properties of dress or appearance stand in for our own often unconscious fears and hates. These are suddenly made living flesh in another whom we can detest. Vicious bullying may ensue.

In *Cat's Eye*, Margaret Atwood details a girl's friendship in the 1950s with devastating accuracy and shows its lasting force.

Eight-year-old Elaine moves from an enchanted, wandering rural existence with her entomologist father, unconventional mother and dear older brother to take up life in a half-finished house in a conventional 1950s suburb of Toronto. The rituals of school and the whole complex, ordinary world of 'girls and their doings' await her. She has not been well prepared. Her parents have been keeping things from her. Other families, she quickly realizes, when she makes her first tentative friendships with Carol and Grace, are not like hers. Nor does she know how to be a girl. She is both tomboyish outsider and vulnerable misfit.

Enter Cordelia who lives in a large two-storey house, with egg cups, napkin rings and a powder room. Her mother not only has a cleaner, but paints. Cordelia's two clever older sisters banter, as she does, in a mocking way. Elaine adores her brazenness and certainty, her scornful tones, her wild impropriety.

But Cordelia, who has the other girls, too, in her thrall, declares that Elaine needs improvement. A reign of terror is unleashed in its name. The girls mock the way Elaine dresses, eats, walks and laughs.

They draw attention to her failings, her looks. They enact her burial. They torment her. Persecute. Elaine submits: 'I am not normal, I am not like other girls. Cordelia tells me so, but she will help me ... It will take hard work and a long time.' Terrified of losing 'my best friends', wanting to please, to hold even their perverse attentiveness, Elaine with increasing desperation endures a final long winter of nightmarish cruelty. 'Hatred would have been easier,' she later reflects. 'With hatred, I would have known what to do. Hatred is clear, metallic, one-handed, unwavering; unlike love.'

Out of this thing called love, in her desire to please and appease, Elaine succumbs to a self-annihilating task. Devilish Cordelia has thrown Elaine's 'stupid' winter hat into a steep ravine where 'the bad men are' and the girls are forbidden to go. Elaine is ordered after it. She overcomes a last vestige of inner resistance and creeps down the hillside, into the half-frozen creek. Icy water fills her boots, weighs down her snowpants. She reaches for her hat and when she looks up at the bridge, her 'friends' have gone. She is alone. The cold chills her to the marrow. She can't move. She lies down at the edge of the stream, her head 'filling with black sawdust'. Death invites, 'peaceful and clear'. A woman appears, holds out her arms to her, urges her up, wraps her in warmth, tells her: 'It will be all right. Go home.' Elaine knows the woman who has saved her is the Virgin Mary. When she returns to school, freed in a sense because the old submissive self who wanted to be loved has died in the ravine, she finds she can now stand up to the bullying. It's easy. If they're not her friends, nothing binds her to them. She recognizes that they have needed her to enact their dominance and now she doesn't need them. She is indifferent.

In that indifference, Elaine is strong. In high school, the balance of power shifts and it is Elaine who knows how to get on with boys, who grows cruel towards an increasingly helpless and friendless Cordelia. The last time she sees Cordelia as an adult, her one-time friend and persecutor is confined in a 'discreet private loony bin'. Behind her 'locked, sagging face' is a 'frantic child'.

It is her friendship with Cordelia that haunts Elaine's return at the age of fifty to Toronto as an accomplished and successful artist embraced by young feminists. In her canvases, it is her childhood friends and their shared world that figure large.

Buried early friendships with their see-saws of love and hate, power and helplessness, under this spotlight, are as formative as later sexual passions. They endure within us. In Elaine's case, her relations with Cordelia make her distrust women: 'Women collect grievances, hold grudges and change shape,' she reflects. 'They pass hard, legitimate judgments, unlike the purblind guesses of men, fogged with romanticism and ignorance and bias and wish. Women know too much, they can neither be deceived nor trusted. I can understand why men are afraid of them.' Yet Cordelia is her twin, the one who holds a key to her reflection, and at the novel's end, when the Cordelia she was hoping she would once more confront fails to turn up — may indeed be dead — Elaine addresses her aura: 'This is what I miss, Cordelia: not something that's gone, but something that will never happen. Two old women giggling over tea.'

CODA: The Love You Make

The ordinary virtue of friendship, the ability to laugh at life's vagaries over a cup of tea with a compatible other, is what many, once early passions have been spent, hail as one of life's great gifts. Amongst my interviewees, one fifty-five-year-old man confessed – as if it were a deep secret, so unfashionable that it was difficult to share – that after the break-up of his first and only marriage, he had decided he was simply better at friendship and enjoyed it far more than any libidinal pursuits.

In fact, long-standing couples, after the hurly-burly of those days of getting and spending, lusting and rearing, also attest that it is the friendship between them that counts for most. Kindness, loyalty, the pleasure of having one's views or outrage shared, reflected, replied to by a familiar, buoys one through life. Cupid's searing arrows, the turmoils of passion, can feel, in retrospect, like rampaging tornadoes that lifted one savagely up and away from the more beneficent calms of steady companionship. Love here may be a more temperate zone, but it is love for all that.

It may be a wish to rebalance the prevailing contemporary ethos which makes me want to stress and end on this temperate zone of love. We are what was once called 'old' far longer than earlier generations. The assumptions underlying our world are that we are isolated, selfish, self-gratifying creatures, with rampant needs that demand satisfaction and protection. Yet looking around, it is also clear that what makes life worth living, what makes us feel alive and gives us hope from day to day, is the ordinary kindness to one another that we are capable of. It is unromantic civility and quotidian generosity that encourage our intimacies to endure. If in the name of love, we long for Himalayan peaks of rapture and find ourselves enmeshed in grand and unruly passions and their accompanying anguish, it may not come amiss if, in the name of common humanity, we also stretch our ways of loving into those foothills where it's good to walk and talk with friends.

There is more, though it is perhaps the subject of another book. In our imagining of the good life – a society worth living in and in which we and our children flourish – it is not only the fundamental rights of security and freedom the state is able to enshrine that are essential. We also need love. We need to give as well as take it. We need solidarity with our fellow beings. Happiness is not the question here. Love can bring that, but often does not. We need love because it confronts us with the heights and depths of our being, shows us what we can and cannot endure and reconciles us to what we discover in ourselves and others. We need love so as to be the human creatures that we are at our best, at once great and greatly fragile.

Notes

ABBREVIATIONS

SE   *The Standard of the Complete Psychological Works of Sigmund Freud*, 24 vols, ed. James Strachey in collaboration with Anna Freud, assisted by Alix Strachey and Alan Tyson (London: Hogarth Press and Institute of Psychoanalysis, 1953–74)

PART ONE: OVERTURE: THE RIDDLE OF LOVE

p. 17   *or failure*   See, for example, Helen Fisher, *Why We Love: The Nature and Chemistry of Romantic Love* (New York: Henry Holt, 2004) and *Why Him? Why Her?: Finding Real Love by Understanding Your Personality Type* (Oxford: One World Publications, 2009)

p. 19   *or heterosexuality*   Sigmund Freud (1920), 'The Psychogenesis of a Case of Homosexuality in a Woman', in *SE*, vol. 18 (1920–2), p. 170

PART TWO: CONFIGURATIONS OF PASSION: FIRST LOVE, YOUNG LOVE

p. 27   *may provide*   Stendhal, *On Love* (London: Penguin Books, 1975), p. 50

p. 28   *Is that normal?*   Peter Fonagy, 'A Genuinely Developmental Theory of Sexual Enjoyment and Its Implications for Psychoanalytic Technique', *Journal of the American Psychoanalytic Association* 56. 1 (2008), pp. 18–19

p. 29   *at their core*   Part of this formulation comes from a personal interview with the psychoanalyst and writer, Adam Phillips, 17 June 2009

p. 30   *has come*   Miriam Lichtheim, *Ancient Egyptian Literature*, vol. 2: *The New Kingdom* (Berkeley: University of California Press, 1976), pp. 182–93

p. 30   *with joy*   Bronislaw Malinowski, *The Sexual Life of Savages in North-Western Melanesia* (London: G. Routledge & Sons, 1929), p. 283

p. 31   *parental features*   See, for example, website on Face Research, available at http://www.faceresearch.org/ and Suzi Malin, *Love at First Sight* (London: Dorling Kindersley, 2004). For information on resemblance to parents, see T. Bereczkei, P. Gyuris, P. Koves and L. Bernath, 'Homogamy, Genetic Similarity, and Imprinting: Parental Influence on Mate Choice Preferences', *Personality and Individual Differences* 33.5 (2002), pp. 677–90

p. 32   *always blurred*   Marcel Proust, *Remembrance of Things Past*, vol. 1, trans. C.K. Scott Moncrieff and Terence Kilmartin (London: Penguin Books, 1981), p. 528

p. 34   *painful intermesh*   Simone de Beauvoir, *The Second Sex*, trans. H.M. Parshley (London: Picador Classics, 1983), pp. 418–19

p. 38   *appropriate passage*   Proust, *Remembrance of Things Past*, vol. 1, p. 214

p. 40   *as his Fate*   John Updike, 'More Love in the Western World', *Assorted Prose* (Harmondsworth: Penguin Books, 1965), p. 170

p. 42   *completeness*   Samuel Taylor Coleridge, *Shakespearean Criticism* (Hebden Bridge: Pomona Press, 2008), pp. 430–1

p. 43   *life again*   Simone de Beauvoir, *Memoirs of a Dutiful Daughter*, trans. James Kirkup (London: Penguin Books, 1984), p. 345

p. 46   *prostration*   Alice Munro, *Open Secrets* (London: Chatto & Windus, 1994), p. 10

p. 46   *element*   Daniel Bergner, 'What Do Women Want?', *New York Times Magazine*, 22 Jan. 2009

p. 47   *winged state*   See Martha Nussbaum's discussion of *Phaedrus* in *The Fragility of Goodness: Luck and Ethics in Greek Tragedy and Philosophy* (Cambridge: Cambridge University Press, 1986), pp. 213–23

p. 49   *simple idyll*   Carson McCullers, *The Ballad of the Sad Café* (Boston: Houghton Mifflin, 1951), p. 26

p. 50   *were love*   Howard Jacobson, *The Act of Love* (London: Jonathan Cape, 2008), pp. 12–13

p. 53   *blinding myself*   Roland Barthes, *A Lover's Discourse*, trans. Richard Howard (London: Vintage, 2002), p. 24

p. 54   *delirium*   Ibid., p. 39

p. 55   *sense of self*   Ethel Spector Person, *Love and Fateful Encounters: The Power of Romantic Passion* (London: Bloomsbury, 1990), p. 57

p. 58   *in play here*   See Natasha Walter, *Living Dolls: The Return of Sexism* (London: Virago, 2010)

p. 60   *planning centres*   Neir Eshel, Eric E. Nelson, James Blair, Daniel Pine and Monique Ernst, 'Neural Substrates of Choice Selection in Adults and

Adolescents: Development of the Ventrolateral Prefrontal and Anterior Cingulate Cortices', *Neuropsychologia* 45.6 (2007), pp. 1270–9

p. 61   *disappointment*   Quoted in Rebecca Camber, 'Why You Should Forget Your First Love: The Memories "Can Ruin All of Your Future Relationships"', *Daily Mail*, 18 Jan. 2009, which references Malcolm Brynin and John Ermisch (eds), *Changing Relationships* (London: Routledge, 2009)

p. 63   *if they could*   Luisa Dillner, *Love by Numbers: The Hidden Facts behind Everyone's Relationships* (London: Profile Books, 2009), p. 177

p. 64   *instantaneous*   John Berger, *G.* (London: Chatto & Windus, 1985), p. 142

p. 64   *dreams or art*   Robert Stoller, *Observing the Erotic Imagination* (New Haven: Yale University Press, 1985), p. 47

p. 64   *hormonal patches*   Martin Portner, 'The Orgasmic Mind: The Neurological Roots of Sexual Pleasure', *Scientific American Mind*, 20 April 2008

p. 66   *towards thirty*   See 'Facts on American Teens' Sexual and Reproductive Health', Guttmacher Institute Report, Jan. 2010, available at http://www.guttmacher.org/pubs/fb-ATSRH.html; 'Sex Uncovered', *Observer*, 26 Oct. 2008, available at http://www.guardian.co.uk/lifeandstyle/series/sex-uncovered; 'Facts and Statistics: Sexual Health and Canadian Youth', 2009, available at http://www.guardian.co.uk/lifeandstyle/series/sex-uncovered

p. 67   *earlier period*   See, for example, Peter Laslett, Karla Oosterveen and Richard M. Smith (eds), *Bastardy and Its Comparative History. Studies in the History of Illegitimacy and Marital Nonconformism* (Cambridge, Mass.: Harvard University Press, 1980), passim

p. 68   *things turn*   Michel de Montaigne, *The Complete Essays*, trans. M.A. Screech (London: Allen Lane, 1991), p. 968

p. 69   *relational proclivities*   See Walter, *Living Dolls*, for an excellent review of such material

p. 71   *how to compromise*   Anthony Giddens, *The Transformation of Intimacy: Sexuality, Love and Eroticism in Modern Societies* (Cambridge: Polity Press, 1991), p. 11

p. 72   *domestic violence*   See 'School Lessons to Tackle Domestic Violence Outlined', *BBC News*, 25 Nov. 2009, available at http://news.bbc.co.uk/1/hi/uk/8376943.stm, and 'Teen Girls Abused by Boyfriends Warns NSPCC', University of Bristol: School for Policy Studies, 1 Sept. 2009, available at http://www.bristol.ac.uk/sps/news/2009/34.html

p. 75   *school buses*   Susie Orbach, *Bodies* (London: Profile Books, 2009), p. 112

p. 76   *everyone else*   Adam Phillips, 'Insatiable Creatures', *Guardian*, 8 Aug. 2009. See also Franz Kafka, 'A Hunger Artist', in *The Basic Kafka* (New York: Pocket Books, 1979), p. 90

p. 77   *them to have*   Adam Phillips, *On Balance* (London: Hamish Hamilton, 2010), pp. 1–39

p. 84   *on weddings*   John Cloud, 'Americans Love Marriage. But Why?', *Time*, 8 Feb. 2007

p. 87   *share of vexation*   Jane Austen, *Pride and Prejudice* (London: Penguin Books, 1985), pp. 68, 163, 69–70

p. 87   *over-forties*   Deirdre Fernand, 'Mr and Mrs: The Marriage Report', *Sunday Times*, 14 Jan. 2007, from YouGov report, *Marriage and Divorce*

p. 87   *to be sure*   'Marriage Rate Falls to Lowest Level Since Records Began', *BBC News*, 11 Feb. 2010, available at http://news.bbc.co.uk/1/hi/uk/8510431.stm

p. 88   *their partners*   US Census Bureau, 'America's Families and Living Arrangements: 2007', available at http://www.census.gov/, and Pamela Smock, 'Cohabitation in the United States', *Annual Review of Sociology*, 26 (2000), pp. 1–20, which also notes that 55% of those cohabiting do actually marry

p. 94   *delicious rapture*   Quoted in Lawrence Stone, *The Family, Sex and Marriage in England 1500–1800* (London: Penguin Books, 1979), p. 190

p. 104   *as possible*   Sigmund Freud (1907), *Delusion and Dream in Jensen's Gradiva*, in *SE*, vol. 9: pp. 1–96 (22)

p. 104   *love to him*   Ibid., p. 88

p. 104   *Norbert Hanold*   Ibid., p. 27

p. 105   *the doctor*   Ibid., p. 90

p. 106   *with mine*   Sigmund Freud, letter to Martha Bernays, 14 Aug. 1882, in Ernst L. Freud (ed.), *Letters of Sigmund Freud 1873–1939*, trans. Tania Stern and James Stern (London: Hogarth, 1970), p. 41

p. 106   *the truth*   Sigmund Freud, letter to Martha Bernays, 25 Sept. 1882, in ibid., p. 47

p. 107   *you will be*   Sigmund Freud, letter to Martha Bernays, 23 Oct. 1883, in ibid., pp. 85–6

p. 107   *nursery*   Quoted in Ernest Jones, *The Life and Work of Sigmund Freud*, vol. 1 (New York: Basic Books, 1953), p. 154

PART THREE: LOVE AND MARRIAGE

p. 109   *by marriage*   Stanley Cavell, *Pursuits of Happiness* (Cambridge, Mass.: Harvard University Press, 1981), p. 74

p. 112   *and secure*   Montaigne, *Complete Essays*, p. 961

p. 113   *the question*   Alan Macfarlane, 'Kinship and Marriage Lectures', available at http://www.alanmacfarlane.com/kin/audiovisual.html

p. 114   *love in marriage*   See, for instance, P.G. McC. Brown, 'Love and Marriage in Greek New Comedy', *Classical Quarterly* 43 (1993), pp. 189–205

p. 114   *married life*   Peter Walcot, 'Romantic Love and True Love: Greek Attitudes to Marriage', *Ancient Society* 18 (1987), pp. 5–33

p. 115 *as husbands*   Quoted in Philippe Ariès and André Béjin (eds), *Western Sexuality: Practice and Precept in Past and Present Times*, trans. Anthony Forster (Oxford: Basil Blackwell, 1985), p. 124

p. 116 *East today*   Yossef Rapoport, *Marriage, Money and Divorce in Medieval Islamic Society* (Cambridge: Cambridge University Press, 2005), pp. 2–6

p. 118 *of ways*   Stone, *Family, Sex and Marriage in England*, pp. 29ff.

p. 119 *inheritance*   Ibid., p. 30

p. 121 *power of his*   Quoted in Marilyn Yalom, *A History of the Wife* (London: Pandora, 2001), p. 122

p. 121 *adversity*   Stone, *Family, Sex and Marriage in England*, p. 103

p. 122 *happiness*   L.H. Butterfield, Marc Friedlaender and Mary-Jo Kline (eds), *The Book of Abigail and John: Selected Letters of the Adams Family 1762–1784* (Cambridge, Mass.: Harvard University Press, 1975), p. 121

p. 123 *companionate family*   See Stone, *Family, Sex and Marriage in England*, passim, and R. Trumbach, *The Rise of the Egalitarian Family: Aristocratic Kinship and Domestic Relations in 18th-century England* (New York: Academic Press, 1978)

p. 123 *Productions*   'Of Popular Discontents' originally appeared in 1701 in the third volume of Temple's essays published after his death by Jonathan Swift. Quoted in David Lemmings, 'Marriage and the Law in the Eighteenth Century: Hardwicke's Marriage Act of 1753', *Historical Journal* 39.2 (1996), pp. 339–60 (p. 339). I am indebted to Lemmings for his judicious analysis of the Act

p. 123 *the rule*   Stone, *Family, Sex and Marriage in England*, pp. 181–2

p. 124 *marriages*   Quoted in Lemmings, 'Marriage and the Law in the Eighteenth Century', p. 347

p. 125 *marry her*   Quoted in ibid., p. 351

p. 126 *dearest friend*   Mrs Hester Chapone, quoted in Stone, *Family, Sex and Marriage in England*, p. 218

p. 127 *Church will do*   Richard Ellmann, *Oscar Wilde* (London: Penguin Books, 1988), p. 583

p. 127 *a misery*   Stone, *Family, Sex and Marriage in England*, p. 214. For more on this source, see also Norman Scarfe, *Innocent Espionage: The La Rochefoucauld Brothers' Tour of England in 1785* (Woodbridge: Boydell, 1995)

p. 128 *Relationships*   See Montaigne, *Complete Essays*, pp. 205–19

p. 128 *abundant*   Ibid., pp. 209–10

p. 130 *their choice*   James F. McMillan, *France and Women 1789–1914: Gender, Society and Politics* (London: Routledge, 2000), pp. 33–4

p. 131 *over it*   Napoléon Bonaparte, letter to Joséphine de Beauharnais, 19 Feb. 1797, in Rafe Blaufarb (ed.), *Napoleon: Symbol for an Age: A Brief History with Documents* (Boston: Bedford/St Martin's, 2008), p. 40

p. 132 *their fate*   McMillan, *France and Women 1789–1914*, p. 38

p. 132 *for girls*   Madame Romieu, *La femme au XIXième siècle* (Paris: 1859), p. 13

p. 134 *took place*   Lytton Strachey, *Queen Victoria* (London: Penguin Books, 1971), p. 92

p. 135 *imposed*   See, for instance, Patricia Jalland, *Women, Marriage and Politics, 1860–1914* (Oxford: Oxford University Press, 2002), p. 47 and passim

p. 136 *as a woman*   Ibid. p. 258

p. 137 *admired*   Ibid., pp. 76–7

p. 138 *in circulation*   John d'Emilio and Estelle B. Freedman, *Intimate Matters: A History of Sexuality in America* (New York: Harper & Row, 1988)

p. 139 *would have been*   *Dearest Child: Letters between Queen Victoria and the Princess Royal*, ed. Roger Fulford (London: Evans Bros, 1974), p. 90, and quotes below from pp. 94, 99, 254

p. 142 *substantial part*   Judith Surkis, *Sexing the Citizen: Morality and Masculinity in France, 1870–1920* (Ithaca, NY: Cornell University Press, 2006). I am indebted to this excellent book for these insights on Third Republic France

p. 145 *than two*   D'Emilio and Freedman, *Intimate Matters*, p.174

p. 147 *an illness*   Sigmund Freud, 'Civilized Sexual Morality and Modern Nervous Illness' (1909), *SE*, vol. 9, pp. 177–204 and passim

p. 148 *children*   Friedrich Engels, *The Origins of the Family, Private Property and the State*, chapter 2, online version http://www.marxists.org/archive/marx/works/1884/origin-family/ch02c.htm

p. 151 *me alone*   Quoted in Judith Thurman, *Secrets of the Flesh: A Life of Colette* (London: Bloomsbury, 1999), p. 343; and in Colette, *The Vagabond* (London: Penguin Books, 1960), pp. 226–7

p. 157 *Autobiography*   H.G. Wells, *Experiment in Autobiography* (London: Victor Gollancz and Cresset Press, 1934), pp. 464–5

p. 158 *intention*   Sigmund Freud (1912), 'On the Universal Tendency to Debasement in the Sphere of Love (Contributions to the Psychology of Love II),' *SE*, vol. 11, p. 179

p. 159 *inconspicuous one*   Ibid., p. 183

p. 161 *parents*   Robert Wohl, *The Generation of 1914* (London: Weidenfeld & Nicolson, 1980), pp. 5–47 and passim

p. 161 *before the Fall*   Ibid., p. 161

p. 162 *law of novelty*   Quoted in ibid., pp. 28–9

p. 164 *best wives*   'Good Brainless Wives', *Time*, 31 Mar. 1923

p. 164 *female body*   Quoted in Virginia Nicholson's excellent *Singled Out: How Two Million Women Survived without Men after the First World War* (London: Viking, 2007), pp. 38–9

p. 165 *over the world*   Quoted in 'Women v. Dictator & Earl', *Time*, 23 July 1928

p. 166 *out to her*   Ibid.

p. 167 *as a nation* Anonymous, *Every Woman's Book of Love and Marriage and Family Life* (Cambridge: Icon Books, 2003), p. 13. Original date of publication unknown

p. 168 *come from it* Ibid., p. 17

p. 168 *serious nature* Ibid., p. 20

p. 169 *man's part* Ibid., p. 55

p. 170 *risen again* Claire Langhamer, 'Love and Courtship in Mid-twentieth-century England', *Historical Journal* 50.1 (2007), pp. 173–96

p. 172 *thirty-one years* Stone, *Family, Sex and Marriage in England*, p. 56

p. 172 *exclusivity* Geoffrey Gorer, *Exploring English Character* (London: Cresset Press, 1955) and *Sex and Marriage in England Today: A Study of the Views and Experiences of the Under-45s* (London: Thomas Nelson & Sons, 1971)

p. 174 *employment* Yalom, *History of the Wife*, p. 359

p. 178 *all divorces* Margaret Brinig and Douglas W. Allen, 'These Boots Are Made for Walking: Why Most Divorce Filers Are Women', *American Law and Economics Review*, 2 (1), 2000, pp. 126–9

p. 178 *now returned* Betsey Stevenson and Justin Wolfers, 'Marriage and Divorce: Changes and Their Driving Forces', *Journal of Economic Perspectives* 21.2 (2007), pp. 27–52. This article provides the best summary of marriage and divorce figures in the US and Western Europe that I have come across

p. 178 *thirty-five* Arlie Hochschild, 'The State of Families, Class and Culture', *New York Times Book Review*, 18 Oct. 2009

p. 178 *in 1862* 'Marriage Rate Falls to Lowest Level since Records Began', *BBC News*, 11 Feb. 2010, available at http://news.bbc.co.uk/1/hi/uk/8510431.stm

p. 179 *the union* Louise Carpenter, 'The Myth of Wedded Bliss', *Observer*, 20 June 2010. The article cites a study by Chris M. Wilson and Andrew J. Oswald, 'How Does Marriage Affect Physical and Psychological Health?: A Survey of the Longitudinal Evidence', *Warwick Economic Research Papers*, Department of Economics, University of Warwick, available at http://www2.warwick.ac.uk/fac/soc/economics/research/workingpapers/publications/twerp728.pdf; and research by Kathleen Kiernan, Professor of Social Policy and Demography at the University of York

p. 179 *will marry* John Cloud, 'Americans Love Marriage. But Why?', *Time*, 8 Feb. 2007

p. 186 *excitement thrives* See Esther Perel, *Mating in Captivity: Sex, Lies and Domestic Bliss* (London: Hodder & Stoughton, 2007), pp. 122–3, for an excellent discussion of sexual ruthlessness

p. 186 *sexual novelty* Ian McEwan, *Saturday* (London: Jonathan Cape, 2005), pp. 39–40

p. 188 *suits, helps* See, for example, John Gottman, *Why Marriages Succeed or Fail* (New York: Simon & Schuster, 1994) and John Gottman and Nan Silver, *The Seven Principles for Making Marriage Work* (New York: Crown, 1999)

p. 191 *battering me*   Hanif Kureishi, *Intimacy* (London: Faber & Faber, 1999), p. 9

p. 193 *homelessness*   Cavell, *Pursuits of Happiness*, pp. 31–2

p. 196 *not desire*   Letter to Olivia Shakespear, quoted in A. Norman Jeffares, W.B. Yeats: *Man and Poet* (New York: St Martin's Press, 1996), p. 257

p. 196 *of time*   See, for example, Bettina Arndt, *The Sex Diaries: Why Women Go Off Sex and Other Bedroom Battles* (London: Hamlyn, 2009)

p. 197 *the pain*   Leo Tolstoy, *Anna Karenina*, trans. Richard Pevear and Larissa Volokhonsky (London: Penguin Books, 2001), pp. 481–2

p. 197 *language*   See Susie Orbach, *The Impossibility of Sex* (London: Allen Lane, 1999), pp. 166ff.

p. 198 *of shame*   De Beauvoir, *Second Sex*, p. 265

p. 200 *not less*   Perel, *Mating in Captivity*, p. 215

p. 201 *first object*   Sigmund Freud, 'The Taboo of Virginity' (Contributions to the Psychology of Love III), *SE*, vol. 9, p. 205

p. 203 *the Beloved*   Emmanuel Levinas, *Totality and Infinity: An Essay on Exteriority*, trans. A. Lingis (Boston: Martinus Nijhoff Publishers, 1979), p. 254

PART FOUR: LOVE IN TRIANGLES

p. 210 *and death*   Aeschylus, *Aeschylus I: Oresteia*, trans. Richmond Lattimore (Chicago: University of Chicago Press, 1953), p. 47. See Tony Tanner, *Adultery and the Novel: Contract and Transgression* (Baltimore: Johns Hopkins University Press, 1979), pp. 27–9, to whom I am indebted for this point

p. 211 *absolute*   Ibid., p. 13

p. 212 *feet of clay*   Judith N. Shklar, *Ordinary Vices* (Cambridge, Mass.: Harvard University Press, 1984), pp. 139, 142

p. 218 *the abyss*   Gustave Flaubert, *Madame Bovary*, trans. Alan Russell (Harmondsworth: Penguin Books, 1972), p. 113

p. 218 *imposes on us*   Ibid., p. 157

p. 221 *indulgent*   Tolstoy, *Anna Karenina*, p. 3

p. 227 *enchaining him*   De Beauvoir, *Second Sex*, p. 666

p. 232 *even today*   See, for example, Daniel Bergner, 'What Do Women Want?', *New York Times Magazine*, 22 Jan. 2009 on the work of contemporary sexologists investigating female desire

p. 233 *with envy*   Saint Augustine, *The Confessions*, trans. R.S. Pine-Coffin (London: Penguin Books, 1961), p. 28

p. 233 *destroy it*   Melanie Klein, 'Envy and Gratitude', in *Envy and Gratitude and Other Works* (London: Vintage, 1997), pp. 180–1

p. 236 *In one such*   See Ayala Malach Pines, *Romantic Jealousy: Causes, Symptoms, Cures* (London: Routledge, 1998), pp. 23ff.

p. 238 *but indifference* See Sigmund Freud, 'Instincts and Their Vicissitudes', *SE*, vol. 14, pp. 109–40

p. 239 *goodnight to me* Proust, *Remembrance of Things Past*, vol. 2, trans. C.K. Scott Moncrieff and Terence Kilmartin (London: Penguin Books, 1987), p. 1158

p. 240 *coloration* Malcolm Bowie, *Proust among the Stars* (London: HarperCollins, 1998), p. 230 and passim

p. 241 *goddesses* Proust, *Remembrance of Things Past*, vol. 2, pp. 1164–5

p. 242 *happening* Alexander Linklater, 'Dangerous Liaisons', *Guardian*, 22 June 2001

p. 243 *permeable* Catherine Millet, *Jealousy: The Other Life of Catherine M* (London: Serpent's Tail, 2009), p. 42

p. 248 *loves him* Sigmund Freud, 'Some Neurotic Mechanisms in Jealousy, Paranoia and Homosexuality', *SE*, vol. 18, pp. 223–5

p. 249 *is love* Erica Jong, *Fear of Flying* (St Albans: Panther, 1974)

p. 250 *marriage* Geoffrey Gorer, *Exploring English Character*, p. 145

p. 250 *over-forties* See Deirdre Fernand, 'Mr and Mrs: The Marriage Report', *Sunday Times*, 14 Jan. 2007, from YouGov report, *Marriage and Divorce*

p. 250 *cheating* 'Most Americans Not Willing to Forgive Unfaithful Spouse', Gallup, 25 Mar. 2008, available at http://www.gallup.com/poll/105682/most-americans-willing-forgive-unfaithful-spouse.aspx, 14–16 Mar. 2008, cited in *USA Today* and elsewhere

p. 251 *all wrong* For data, see 'Infidelity: Cross-cultural Perspectives', *Marriage and Family Encyclopedia*, available at http://family.jrank.org/pages/883/ Infidelity-Cross-Cultural-Perspectives.html

p. 251 *incidences of it* Claire Langhamer, 'Adultery in Post-war England', *History Workshop Journal* 62 (2006), p. 105

p. 251 *ten women* See 'High Infidelity: BBC Three's UK Love Map', BBC Press Office, 13 Feb. 2006, available at http://www.bbc.co.uk/ pressoffice/pressreleases/ stories/2006/02_february/13/map.shtml. See also accompanying website, bbc.co.uk/relationships

p. 251 *anonymously* For one set of figures, see 'Facts and Statistics About Infidelity', *Truth about Deception*, available at http://www.truthaboutdeception.com/ cheating-and-infidelit/stats-about-infidelity.html. See also 'Infidelity Statistics', Menstuff, available at http://www.menstuff.org/issues/ byissue/infidelity/stats.html; and Melanie Berliet, 'The Cheaters' Club', *Vanity Fair*, 28 Aug. 2009

p. 252 *relationships today* Berliet, 'Cheaters' Club'

p. 252 *infidelities* Delphine Peras, 'La tentation de l'infidélité dans le couple', *L'Express*, 19 May 2009

p. 252 *on-line affairs* 'Infidelity Statistics', Menstuff, available at http://www.menstuff .org/issues/byissue/infidelitystats.html

p. 256 *concealment*   Quoted in Langhamer, 'Love and Courtship in Mid-twentieth-century England', p. 103

p. 256 *Guidance Council*   Ibid., pp. 103–5

p. 256 *one to the other*   Letter from Sigmund Freud to Sándor Ferenczi, 10 Jan. 1910, in E. Brabant, E. Falzeder and P. Giampieri-Deutsch, *The Correspondence of Sigmund Freud and Sándor Ferenczi*, vol. 1, *1908–1914*, (Cambridge, Mass/London: Harvard University Press, 1993), p. 123

p. 257 *mark of respect*   Perel, *Mating in Captivity*, p. 186

p. 260 *a lot worse*   Zadie Smith, *Changing My Mind* (London: Hamish Hamilton, 2009), p. 196

p. 263 *to his wife*   Quoted in Rachel Johnson, 'Pity the poor (other) woman', *Sunday Times*, 30 Nov. 2008

PART FIVE: LOVE IN FAMILIES

p. 270 *of my life*   Margaret Drabble, *The Millstone* (London: Weidenfeld & Nicolson, 1965), p. 102

p. 270 *cannot speak*   Tolstoy, *Anna Karenina*, pp. 215–16

p. 271 *baby alive*   Sue Gerhardt, *Why Love Matters: How Affection Shapes a Baby's Brain* (East Sussex: Brunner-Routledge, 2004), p. 22

p. 272 *chronic diseases*   Marla Sokolowski and Thomas Boyce, 'Why Is Destiny Not in Our Genes?', Canadian Institute of Advanced Research, available at http://www.cifarnbq.ca/questions/why-is-destiny-not-in-our-genes/

p. 273 *literature*   Alison Gopnik, *The Philosophical Baby: What Children's Minds Tell Us about Truth, Love and the Meaning of Life* (London: Bodley Head, 2009), p. 15 and passim

p. 273 *Word of God*   Dr Rowan Williams, Archbishop of Canterbury, 'Good Childhood Report: Afterword', 2 Feb. 2009, available at http://www.arch bishopofcanterbury.org/ 2159

p. 274 *and eyes*   Jean-Jacques Rousseau, *Émile*, available at http://www.gutenberg .org/dirs/ etext04/emile10.txt

p. 274 *frustrations*   Sigmund Freud, *New Introductory Lectures* (1933), *SE*, vol. 22, pp. 122–3

p. 275 *present one*   Freud, letter to Wilhelm Fliess, 15 Oct. 1897, in *The Complete Letters of Sigmund Freud to Wilhelm Fliess: 1887–1904*, trans. Jeffrey Moussaieff Masson (Cambridge, Mass.: Belknap Press, 1985), pp. 270–3

p. 281 *cynicism*   De Beauvoir, *Second Sex*, p. 528

p. 282 *around them*   Charles Darwin, *The Descent of Man, and Selection in Relation to Sex*, 2nd edn, 1897 (New York: Barnes & Noble, 2004), p. 506

p. 282 *of the period*   See, for example, Carol Gilligan, *In a Different Voice: Psychological*

Theory and Women's Development (Cambridge, Mass.: Harvard University Press, 1982); and Nel Noddings, *Caring: A Feminine Approach to Ethics and Moral Education* (Berkeley: University of California Press, 1984), pp. 3–4

p. 283 *systems*   Simon Baron-Cohen, *The Essential Difference: Men, Women and the Extreme Male Brain* (London: Allen Lane, 2003), p. 1

p. 283 *children*   For an exhilarating critique of neuroscientific work on gender, see Cordelia Fine, *Delusions of Gender* (New York: W.W. Norton, 2010)

p. 285 *four, attests*   Lucy Cavendish, 'The War at Home', *Observer* magazine, 28 Mar. 2010

p. 286 *to the home*   Élisabeth Badinter, *Le Conflit: La Femme et la Mère* (Paris: Flammarion, 2010)

p. 287 *message*   Ibid., pp. 108–9, for a round-up.

p. 287 *breast-feeding*   Geoff Der, G. David Batty, Ian J. Deary, 'Effect of breast-feeding on intelligence in children: prospective study, sibling pairs analysis and meta-analysis', *British Medical Journal* 333.7575 (2006), pp. 945–50

p. 290 *teaching it maths*   Ian McEwan, *The Child in Time* (London: Jonathan Cape, 1987), pp. 80–1

p. 293 *has life in it*   Quoted in Madeleine Davis, 'The Writing of D.W. Winnicott', *International Review of Psychoanalysis* 14 (1987), pp. 491–502 (p. 492)

p. 294 *needs of them*   D.W. Winnicott, *The Child, the Family and the Outside World* (London: Penguin Books, 1964), pp. 128–9 and passim

p. 294 *for time*   D.W. Winnicott, 'Primary Maternal Preoccupation' (1956), *Through Pediatrics to Psychoanalysis* (London: Hogarth, 1958), pp. 304–5

p. 296 *extirpated*   John Locke (1693), *Some Thoughts concerning Education*, in *The Works of John Locke*, vol. 8 (London: 1824), paras 35 (and 38 below), p. 28 – available on www.gutenberg.org

p. 297 *obsessive love*   Philippe Ariès, *Centuries of Childhood* (Harmondsworth: Penguin Books, 1962), p. 397

p. 297 *responsibility*   See Hugh Cunningham, *Children and Childhood in Western Society since 1500* (Harlow: Longman, 2005) and *The Invention of Childhood* (London: BBC Books, 2006)

p. 299 *even cruelty*   Ulrich Beck and Elisabeth Beck-Gernsheim, *The Normal Chaos of Love*, trans. Mark Ritter and Jane Wiebel (Cambridge: Polity Press, 1995), pp. 107–9, 122–3, 137–9 and passim

p. 304 *underpin life*   See Paul Verhaeghe, *New Studies of Old Villains: A Radical Reconsideration of the Oedipus Complex* (New York: Other Press, 2009)

p. 305 *emotion*   Perel, *Mating in Captivity*, p. 132

p. 308 *this relation*   Helene Deutsch, *The Psychology of Women*, vol. 1 (London: Research Books, 1946), p. 196

p. 309 *so horrible*   Quoted in Franz Kafka, *The Sons* (New York: Schocken Books, 1989) 'Introduction', by Mark Harman

p. 309 *human nature*   Franz Kafka, 'Letter to His Father', in *The Sons*, ibid., p. 117

p. 323 *this theme*   Carl Gustav Jung, letter to Sigmund Freud, 19 Jan. 1909, in William McGuire (ed.), *The Freud/Jung Letters: The Correspondence between Sigmund Freud and C.G. Jung* (Princeton: Princeton University Press, 1994), p. 198

p. 325 *no sharing*   Sigmund Freud, *New Introductory Lectures*, SE, vol. 22, p. 122

p. 327 *individual*   Sigmund Freud, *The Interpretation of Dreams*, SE, vol. 5, pp. 424, 483

p. 328 *only her ghost*   Thomas Babington Macaulay, letter to Margaret Macaulay, 23 Dec. 1833, in Thomas Piney (ed.), *The Letters of Thomas Babington Macaulay*, vol. 2 (Cambridge: Cambridge University Press, 1974)

p. 329 *must be together*   Virginia Woolf, 'Dorothy Wordsworth', in *The Second Common Reader* (London: Hogarth Press, 1986), p. 169

p. 330 *was felt*   Frances Wilson, *The Ballad of Dorothy Wordsworth: A Life* (London: Faber & Faber, 2008), p. 147 and passim

p. 332 *war and exile*   Nell Dunn, *Grandmothers Talking to Nell Dunn* (London: Chatto & Windus, 1991), pp. 1–4 and passim

p. 333 *before my nose*   Ibid., p. 21

p. 334 *did not stop*   Virginia Woolf, 'A Sketch of the Past', in *Moments of Being*, ed. Jeanne Schulkind (London: Hogarth Press, 1986), p. 69

p. 335 *in their lives*   Anstey Spraggan, 'How to Survive a Stepfamily', *Guardian*, 22 May 2010

p. 336 *leave them*   Adam Phillips, *On Balance*, p. 29

PART SIX: LOVE AND FRIENDSHIP

p. 337 *hoard them*   Emily Dickinson, letter to Samuel Bowles, Aug. 1858(?) in Emily Dickinson, *Emily Dickinson: Selected Letters*, ed. Thomas H. Johnson (Cambridge, Mass.: Belknap Press, 1986), p. 144

p. 340 *individual*   Robert E. Lane, *The Loss of Happiness in Market Democracies* (New Haven: Yale University Press, 2001)

p. 340 *your family*   Matt Lauer, '*Friends* creators share show's beginnings'. The sentence quoted is from the original pitch for a series to be called 'Insomnia Café', which when made was eventually named *Friends*, Dec. 1993. See http://www.msnbc.msn.com/id/4899445/

p. 340 *same to us*   D.W. Winnicott, *Home Is Where We Start From: Essays by a Psychoanalyst*, ed. Claire Winnicott, Ray Shepherd, Madeleine Davis (Harmondsworth: Penguin Books, 1986), p. 117

p. 340 *Emerson*   Frank Waldo Emerson, *Essays and Lectures* (New York: Library of America, 1983), p. 350

p. 341 *characters*   Quoted in John P. Kaminski, *Citizen Jefferson: The Wit and Wisdom of an American Sage* (Madison: Madison House, 1994), p. 40

p. 342 *things about*   Roberts, W. Rhys (trans.), *Rhetorica: The Works of Aristotle*, vol. 11 (Oxford: Clarendon Press, 1924), p. 54

p. 343 *formations*   Stanley Cavell, *Cities of Words: Pedagogical Lectures on a Register of the Moral Life* (Cambridge, Mass. Harvard University Press, 2004), pp. 352–72 and passim

p. 343 *from life*   Cicero, *Laelius de Amicitia* (New York: Loeb Classical Library, 1923), sections 20, 27

p. 346 *continue after him*   Francis Bacon, 'Of Friendship', in *The Essays of Francis Bacon*, http://www.authorama.com/essays-of-francis-bacon-1.html

p. 347 *and world*   See Tom MacFaul, *Male Friendship in Shakespeare and His Contemporaries* (Cambridge: Cambridge University Press, 2007)

p. 349 *he gives*   Alexander Pope, *Essay on Man*, Epistle 3, pp. 311–12 http://www.gutenberg.org/ files/2428/2428-h/2428-h.htm

p. 349 *appearances*   David Hume, *A Treatise of Human Nature*, ed. L.A. Selby-Bigge (Oxford: Clarendon Press, 1978), pp. 604–5

p. 350 *Byron's 'sickly'*   Janet Todd, *Sensibility* (London: Methuen, 1986), p. 7

p. 351 *books and ideas*   Judith N. Shklar, *Redeeming American Political Thought*, ed. Stanley Hoffmann (Chicago: University of Chicago Press, 1998), pp. 22–3

p. 353 *a betrayal*   Luise Eichenbaum and Susie Orbach, *Between Women: Facing Up to Feelings of Love, Envy and Competition in Women's Friendships* (Harmondsworth: Penguin Books, 1989), p. 19

p. 358 *full term*   Helene Deutsch, *Confrontations with Myself* (New York: Norton, 1973) and *The Psychology of Women*, vol. 2 (London: Research Books, 1947), pp. 146–9; see also Lisa Appignanesi and John Forrester, *Freud's Women* (London: Weidenfeld & Nicolson/Orion, Phoenix pbk, 2005), pp. 315–17

p. 358 *abilities*   Barbara M. Newman and Philip R. Newman, *Development through Life: A Psychosocial Approach* (Belmont: Wadsworth Cengage Learning, 2009), p. 2006

p. 358 *helped them*   Marjorie Taylor, *Imaginary Companions and the Children Who Create Them* (Oxford: Oxford University Press, 1999), p. 68 and passim

p. 359 *disappears*   Renata Salecl, *Choice* (London: Profile Books, 2010), pp. 69–72

p. 359 *existing others*   For an interesting discussion of this dynamic, though pre-dating the invention of the virtual, see Michael Balint, 'On Love and Hate', *International Journal of Psychoanalysis* 33 (1952), pp. 355–62

p. 360 *moment in time*   D.W. Winnicott, 'Adolescence: Struggling through the Doldrums', in *The Family and Individual Development* (London: Routledge, 1989), p. 81 and passim

p. 363 *afraid of them*   Margaret Atwood, *Cat's Eye* (London: Virago, 1990), p. 379 and passim

Select Bibliography

Adams, John, and Adams, Abigail, *The Book of Abigail and John: Selected Letters of the Adams Family 1762–1784*, ed. L.H. Butterfield, Marc Friedlaender, Mary-Jo Kline (Cambridge, Mass.: Harvard University Press, 1975)

Aeschylus, *Aeschylus I: Oresteia*, trans. Richmond Lattimore (Chicago: University of Chicago Press, 1953)

Anonymous, *Every Woman's Book of Love and Marriage and Family Life* (Cambridge: Icon Books, 2003)

Ariès, Philippe, *Centuries of Childhood* (Harmondsworth: Penguin Books, 1962)

—— and Béjin, André (eds), *Western Sexuality: Practice and Precept in Past and Present Times*, trans. Anthony Forster (Oxford: Basil Blackwell, 1985)

Arndt, Bettina, *The Sex Diaries: Why Women Go Off Sex and Other Bedroom Battles* (London: Hamlyn, 2009)

Atwood, Margaret, *Cat's Eye* (London: Virago, 1990)

Augustine, *The Confessions*, trans. R.S. Pine-Coffin (London: Penguin Books, 1961)

Austen, Jane, *Pride and Prejudice* (London: Penguin Books, 1985)

Badinter, Élisabeth, *Le Conflit: La Femme et la Mère* (Paris: Flammarion, 2010)

Balint, Michael, 'On Love and Hate,' *International Journal of Psychoanalysis* 33 (1952), pp. 355–62

Balzac, Honoré de, *The Physiology of Marriage* (London: Caxton Publishing Company, 1900)

Baron-Cohen, Simon, *The Essential Difference: Men, Women and the Extreme Male Brain* (London: Allen Lane, 2003)

Barthes, Roland, *A Lover's Discourse*, trans. Richard Howard (London: Vintage, 2002)

Bauman, Zygmunt, *Liquid Love: On the Frailty of Human Bonds* (Cambridge: Polity Press, 2003)

—— *The Art of Life* (Cambridge: Polity Press, 2008)

Beauvoir, Simone de, *The Second Sex*, trans. H.M. Parshley (London: Picador Classics, 1983)

────── *Memoirs of a Dutiful Daughter*, trans. James Kirkup (London: Penguin Books, 1984)

Beck, Ulrich, and Beck-Gernsheim, Elisabeth, *The Normal Chaos of Love*, trans. Mark Ritter and Jane Wiebel (Cambridge: Polity Press, 1995)

Benjamin, Jessica, *The Bonds of Love* (London: Virago, 1990)

Bereczkei, T., Gyuris, P., Koves, P., and Bernath, L., 'Homogamy, Genetic Similarity, and Imprinting: Parental Influence on Mate Choice Preferences', *Personality and Individual Differences* 33.5 (2002), pp. 677–90

Berger, John, *G.* (London: Chatto & Windus, 1985)

Blaufarb, Rafe (ed.), *Napoleon: Symbol for an Age: A Brief History with Documents* (Boston: Bedford/St Martin's, 2008)

Bowie, Malcolm, *Proust among the Stars* (London: HarperCollins, 1998)

Brown, P.G. McC., 'Love and Marriage in Greek New Comedy', *Classical Quarterly* 43 (1993), pp. 189–205

Cavell, Stanley, *Pursuits of Happiness* (Cambridge, Mass.: Harvard University Press, 1981)

────── *Cities of Words: Pedagogical Lectures on a Register of the Moral Life* (Cambridge, Mass.: Harvard University Press, 2004)

Colette, *The Vagabond*, trans. Enid McLeod (London: Penguin Books, 1960)

Cunningham, Hugh, *Children and Childhood in Western Society since 1500* (Harlow: Longman, 2005)

────── *The Invention of Childhood* (London: BBC Books, 2006)

Davis, Madeleine, 'The Writing of D.W. Winnicott', *International Review of Psychoanalysis* 14 (1987), pp. 491–502

d'Emilio, John, and Freedman, Estelle B., *Intimate Matters: A History of Sexuality in America* (New York: Harper & Row, 1988)

Der, Geoff, Batty, G. David, and Deary, Ian J., 'Effect of breast-feeding on intelligence in children: prospective study, sibling pairs analysis, and meta-analysis', *British Medical Journal* 333.7575 (2006), pp. 945–50

Deutsch, Helene, *The Psychology of Women*, 2 vols (London: Research Books, 1946–7)

────── *Confrontations with Myself* (New York: Norton, 1973)

Dickinson, Emily, *Emily Dickinson: Selected Letters*, ed. Thomas H. Johnson (Cambridge, Mass.: Belknap Press, 1986)

Dillner, Luisa, *Love by Numbers: The Hidden Facts behind Everyone's Relationships* (London: Profile Books, 2009)

Drabble, Margaret, *The Millstone* (London: Weidenfeld & Nicolson, 1965)

Dunn, Nell, *Grandmothers Talking to Nell Dunn* (London: Chatto & Windus, 1991)

Eichenbaum, Luise, and Orbach, Susie, *Between Women: Facing up to Feelings of Love, Envy and Competition in Women's Friendships* (Harmondsworth: Penguin Books, 1989)

Ellmann, Richard, *Oscar Wilde* (London: Penguin Books, 1988)

Eshel, Neir, Nelson, Eric E., Blair, James, Pine, Daniel, and Ernst, Monique, 'Neural Substrates of Choice Selection in Adults and Adolescents: Development of the Ventrolateral, prefrontal and Anterior Cingulate Cortices', *Neuropsychologia* 45.6 (2007), pp. 1270–9

Fielding, Helen, *Bridget Jones's Diary* (London: Picador, 2001)

Figes, Kate, *Couples: The Truth* (London: Virago, 2010)

Fine, Cordelia: *Delusions of Gender* (New York: W.W. Norton, 2010)

Fisher, Helen, *Why We Love: The Nature and Chemistry of Romantic Love* (New York: Henry Holt, 2004)

—— *Why Him? Why Her?: Finding Real Love by Understanding Your Personality Type* (Oxford: One World Publications, 2009)

Flaubert, Gustave, *Madame Bovary*, trans. Alan Russell (Harmondsworth: Penguin Books, 1972)

Fonagy, Peter, 'A Genuinely Developmental Theory of Sexual Enjoyment and Its Implications for Psychoanalytic Technique', *Journal of the American Psychoanalytic Association* 56. 1 (2008), pp. 11–36

Freud, Ernst L. (ed.), *Letters of Sigmund Freud 1873–1939*, trans. Tania Stern and James Stern (London: Hogarth, 1970)

Freud, Sigmund, *The Standard Edition of the Complete Psychological Works of Sigmund Freud*, 24 vols, ed. James Strachey in collaboration with Anna Freud, assisted by Alix Strachey and Alan Tyson (London: Hogarth Press and Institute of Psychoanalysis, 1953–74)

—— and Fliess, Wilhelm, *The Complete Letters of Sigmund Freud to Wilhelm Fliess: 1887–1904*, trans. Jeffrey Moussaieff Masson (Cambridge, Mass.: Belknap Press, 1985)

—— and Jung, C.G., *The Freud/Jung Letters: The Correspondence between Sigmund Freud and C.G. Jung*, ed. William McGuire (Princeton: Princeton University Press, 1994)

Fulford, Roger, ed., *Dearest Child: Letters between Queen Victoria and the Princess Royal* (London: Evans Bros, 1974)

Gerhardt, Sue, *Why Love Matters: How Affection Shapes a Baby's Brain* (East Sussex: Brunner-Routledge, 2004)

Giddens, Anthony, *The Transformation of Intimacy: Sexuality, Love and Eroticism in Modern Societies* (Cambridge: Polity Press, 1991)

Gilligan, Carol, *In a Different Voice: Psychological Theory and Women's Development* (Cambridge, Mass.: Harvard University Press, 1982)

Gopnik, Alison, *The Philosophical Baby: What Children's Minds Tell Us about Truth, Love and the Meaning of Life* (London: Bodley Head, 2009)

Gorer, Geoffrey, *Exploring English Character* (London: Cresset Press, 1955)

—— *Sex and Marriage in England Today: A Study of the Views and Experiences of the Under-45s* (London: Thomas Nelson & Sons, 1971)

Gottman, John, *Why Marriages Succeed or Fail* (New York: Simon & Schuster, 1994)

—— and Silver, Nan, *The Seven Principles for Making Marriage Work* (New York: Crown, 1999)

Hume, David, *A Treatise of Human Nature*, ed. L.A. Selby-Bigge (Oxford: Clarendon Press, 1978)

Ignatieff, Michael, *The Needs of Strangers* (London: Chatto & Windus, 1984)

Jacobson, Howard, *The Act of Love* (London: Jonathan Cape, 2008)

Jalland, Patricia, *Women, Marriage and Politics, 1860–1914* (Oxford: Oxford University Press, 2002)

Jeffares, A. Norman, *W.B. Yeats: Man and Poet* (London: Kyle Cathie, 1996)

Jones, Ernest, *The Life and Work of Sigmund Freud*, 3 vols (New York: Basic Books, 1953–7)

Jong, Erica, *Fear of Flying* (St Albans: Panther, 1974)

Kafka, Franz, *The Sons* (New York: Schocken Books, 1989)

Kaminski, John P., *Citizen Jefferson: The Wit and Wisdom of an American Sage* (Madison: Madison House, 1994)

Kipnis, Laura, *Against Love* (New York: Vintage Books, 2004)

Klein, Melanie, *Envy and Gratitude and Other Works* (London: Vintage, 1997)

Kristeva, Julia, *Histoires d'amour* (Paris: Denoël, 1983)

Kureishi, Hanif, *Intimacy* (London: Faber & Faber, 1999)

—— *Midnight All Day* (London: Faber & Faber, 1999)

Lane, Robert E., *The Loss of Happiness in Market Democracies* (New Haven: Yale University Press, 2001)

Langhamer, Claire, 'Adultery in Post-war England', *History Workshop Journal* 62 (2006), pp. 86–115

—— 'Love and Courtship in Mid-twentieth-century England', *Historical Journal* 50.1 (2007), pp. 173–96

Laslett, Peter, Oosterveen, Karla, and Smith, Richard M. (eds), *Bastardy and Its Comparative History. Studies in the History of Illegitimacy and Marital Nonconformism* (Cambridge, Mass.: Harvard University Press, 1980)

Leader, Darian, *Why Do Women Write More Letters Than They Post?* (London: Faber & Faber, 1996)

Lemmings, David, 'Marriage and the Law in the Eighteenth Century: Hardwicke's Marriage Act of 1753', *Historical Journal* 39.2 (1996), pp. 339–60

Levinas, Emmanuel, *Totality and Infinity: An Essay on Exteriority*, trans. A. Lingis (Boston: Martinus Nijhoff Publishers, 1979)

Lichtheim, Miriam, *Ancient Egyptian Literature*, vol. 2: *The New Kingdom* (Berkeley: University of California Press, 1976)

Macaulay, Thomas Babington, *The Letters of Thomas Babington Macaulay*, vol. 2, ed. Thomas Piney (Cambridge: Cambridge University Press, 1974)

McCullers, Carson, *The Ballad of the Sad Café* (Boston: Houghton Mifflin, 1951)

McEwan, Ian, *The Child in Time* (London: Jonathan Cape, 1987)

—— *Saturday* (London: Jonathan Cape, 2005)

—— *On Chesil Beach* (London: Jonathan Cape, 2007)

MacFaul, Tom, *Male Friendship in Shakespeare and His Contemporaries* (Cambridge: Cambridge University Press, 2007)

McMillan, James F., *France and Women 1789–1914: Gender, Society and Politics* (London: Routledge, 2000)

Malin, Suzi, *Love at First Sight* (London: Dorling Kindersley, 2004)

Malinowski, Bronislaw, *The Sexual Life of Savages in North-Western Melanesia* (London: G. Routledge & Sons, 1929)

Millet, Catherine, *The Sexual Life of Catherine Millet*, trans. Adriana Hunter (London: Serpent's Tail, 2002)

—— *Jealousy: The Other Life of Catherine M*, trans. Helen Stevenson (London: Serpent's Tail, 2009)

Montaigne, Michel de, *The Complete Essays*, trans. M.A. Screech (London: Allen Lane, 1991)

Munro, Alice, *Open Secrets* (London: Chatto & Windus, 1994)

Nabokov, Vladimir, *Lolita* (London: Penguin Books, 2000)

Nehring, Cristina, *A Vindication of Love* (New York: Harper, 2009)

Newman, Barbara M., and Newman, Philip R., *Development through Life: A Psychosocial Approach* (Belmont: Wadsworth Cengage Learning, 2009)

Nicholson, Virginia, *Singled Out: How Two Million Women Survived without Men after the First World War* (London: Viking, 2007)

Noddings, Nel, *Caring: A Feminine Approach to Ethics and Moral Education* (Berkeley: University of California Press, 1984)

Nussbaum, Martha, *The Fragility of Goodness: Luck and Ethics in Greek Tragedy and Philosophy* (Cambridge: Cambridge University Press, 1986)

O'Neill, Joseph, *Netherland* (London: Fourth Estate, 2009)

Orbach, Susie, *The Impossibility of Sex* (London: Allen Lane, 1999)

—— *Bodies* (London: Profile Books, 2009)

Perel, Esther, *Mating in Captivity: Sex, Lies and Domestic Bliss* (London: Hodder & Stoughton, 2007)

Person, Ethel Spector, *Love and Fateful Encounters: The Power of Romantic Passion* (London: Bloomsbury, 1990)

Phillips, Adam, *On Kissing, Tickling and Being Bored* (London: Faber & Faber, 1993)

—— *On Flirtation* (London: Faber & Faber, 1994)

—— *Monogamy* (London: Faber & Faber, 1996)

—— *On Balance* (London: Hamish Hamilton, 2010)

—— and Taylor, Barbara, *On Kindness* (London: Penguin Books, 2010)

Pines, Ayala Malach, *Romantic Jealousy: Causes, Symptoms, Cures* (London: Routledge, 1998)

Proust, Marcel, *Remembrance of Things Past*, vols 1–3, trans. C.K. Scott Moncrieff and Terence Kilmartin (London: Penguin Books, 1985–92)

Roiphe, Katie, *Uncommon Arrangements* (London: Virago, 2008)

Romieu, Madame, *La femme au XIXème siècle* (Paris: 1859)

Rougemont, Denis de, *Love in the Western World*, trans. Montgomery Belgion (Princeton: Princeton University Press, 1983)

Salecl, Renata, *Choice* (London: Profile Books, 2010)

Scarfe, Norman, *Innocent Espionage: The La Rochefoucauld Brothers' Tour of England in 1785* (Woodbridge: Boydell, 1995)

Shakespeare, William, *The Complete Works*, ed. G.B. Harrison (New York: Harcourt Brace, 1952)

Shklar, Judith N., *Ordinary Vices* (Cambridge, Mass.: Harvard University Press, 1984)

—— *Redeeming American Political Thought*, ed. Stanley Hoffmann (Chicago: University of Chicago Press, 1998)

Smith, Zadie, *Changing My Mind* (London: Hamish Hamilton, 2009)

Smock, Pamela, 'Cohabitation in the United States', *Annual Review of Sociology*, 26 (2000), pp. 1–20

Stendhal, *Love*, trans. Gilbert and Suzanne Sale (Harmondsworth: Penguin Books, 1975)

—— *The Red and the Black*, trans. Roger Gard (London: Penguin Books, 2002)

Stevenson, Betsey, and Wolfers, Justin, 'Marriage and Divorce: Changes and Their Driving Forces', *Journal of Economic Perspectives* 21.2 (2007), pp. 27–52

Stone, Lawrence, *The Family, Sex and Marriage in England 1500–1800* (London: Penguin Books, 1979)

Surkis, Judith, *Sexing the Citizen: Morality and Masculinity in France, 1870–1920* (Ithaca, NY: Cornell University Press, 2006)

Tanner, Tony, *Adultery and the Novel: Contract and Transgression* (Baltimore: Johns Hopkins University Press, 1979)

Taylor, Marjorie, *Imaginary Companions and the Children Who Create Them* (Oxford: Oxford University Press, 1999)

Thurman, Judith, *Secrets of the Flesh: A Life of Colette* (London: Bloomsbury, 1999)

Todd, Janet, *Sensibility* (London: Methuen, 1986)

Tolstoy, Leo, *Anna Karenina*, trans. Richard Pevear and Larissa Volokhonsky (London: Penguin Books, 2001)

Trumbach, Randolph, *The Rise of the Egalitarian Family: Aristocratic Kinship and Domestic Relations in 18th-century England* (New York: Academic Press, 1978)

Verhaeghe, Paul, *New Studies of Old Villains: A Radical Reconsideration of the Oedipus Complex* (New York: Other Press, 2009)

Walcot, Peter, 'Romantic Love and True Love: Greek Attitudes to Marriage', *Ancient Society* 18 (1987)

Walter, Natasha, *Living Dolls: The Return of Sexism* (London: Virago, 2010)

Warner, Marina, *Alone of All Her Sex* (London: Vintage, 2000)

Wells, H. G., *Experiment in Autobiography* (London: Victor Gollancz and Cresset Press, 1934)

—— *Ann Veronica,* ed. and with notes by Sita Schutt (London: Penguin Books, 2005)

White, Edmund, *A Boy's Own Story* (New York: Vintage, 2000)

—— *My Lives* (London: Bloomsbury, 2005)

Wilson, Frances, *The Ballad of Dorothy Wordsworth: A Life* (London: Faber & Faber, 2008)

Winnicott, D.W., *Collected Papers: Through Pediatrics to Psychoanalysis* (London: Hogarth Press, 1958)

—— *The Child, the Family and the Outside World* (London: Penguin Books, 1964)

—— *Home Is Where We Start From: Essays by a Psychoanalyst,* ed. Claire Winnicott, Ray Shepherd, Madeleine Davis (Harmondsworth: Penguin Books, 1986)

—— *The Family and Individual Development* (Routledge: London, 1989)

Wohl, Robert, *The Generation of 1914* (London: Weidenfeld & Nicolson, 1980)

Woolf, Virginia, *Moments of Being,* ed. Jeanne Schulkind (London: Hogarth Press, 1986)

—— *The Second Common Reader* (London: Hogarth Press, 1986)

Yalom, Marilyn, *A History of the Wife* (London: Pandora, 2001)

Index

Copyright Acknowledgements

Extracts from Miriam Lichtheim, *Ancient Egyptian Literature, Vol. 2: The New Kingdom* (Berkeley: University of California Press, 1976). Reproduced by permission of the University of California Press. Extracts from Sigmund Freud, *The Standard Edition of the Complete Psychological Works of Sigmund Freud*, 24 volumes (London: The Hogarth Press, 1986). Reproduced by arrangement with Paterson Marsh Ltd. Extracts from Stanley Cavell, "Knowledge as Transgression: Mostly a Reading of *It Happened One Night*," *Daedalus*, 109:3 (Spring 1980), pp. 147–76. © 1980 by the American Academy of Arts and Sciences. Extract from "An Arundel Tomb" copyright © the Estate of Philip Larkin, reprinted by permission of Faber & Faber Ltd. Extract from Aeschylus, *The Oresteia* (Chicago: University of Chicago Press, 1989). Reprinted by permission of the University of Chicago Press. Extract from *The Child in Time* by Ian McEwan. Copyright © 1987 by Ian McEwan. Reprinted by permission of Georges Borchardt, Inc., on behalf of the author. Extract from *Saturday* by Ian McEwan reprinted by permission of Random House, Inc.

Epigraph credits: Voltaire, *The Philosophical Dictionary*, 1764. La Rochefoucauld, *Maximes*, 439 (Robert/Laffont, Paris, 1959). Saint Augustine, *Tractates on the Gospel of John*, 40:10. Turgenev, *First Love* (1860; Penguin: London, 1950. Trans. Isiah Berlin). Stanley Cavell, *Pursuits of Happiness* (Cambridge, MA: Harvard University Press, 1981). Goethe, Kanzler Friedrich von Muller, *Unterhaltungen mit Goethe* hsg C.A.H. Burkhardt, Stuttgart 1898. Dr. Johnson, in History of Rasselas, Prince of Abyssinia, *The Complete Works of Samuel Johnson*, vol 3, (London: Longman, 1972). Marcel Proust, *Remembrance of Things Past*, trans. C.K. Scott Moncrieff and Terence Kilmartin (London: Penguin Books, 1981). Honoré de Balzac, *The Physiology of Marriage* (London: Caxton Publishing Company, 1900). Sigmund Freud, *The Life and Work of Sigmund Freud*, 3 vols, Ernest Jones, (New York: Basic Books, 1953–57). Emily Dickinson, *The Letters of Emily Dickinson*, Mabel Loomis Todd (ed.), (Boston: Roberts Brothers, 1894).